1880 Magnolia Dr.

Ph.

$5·35

STATE AND LOCAL

GOVERNMENT

IN AMERICA

DANIEL R. GRANT

Associate Professor of Political Science
Vanderbilt University

H. C. NIXON

Professor Emeritus of Political Science
Vanderbilt University

ALLYN AND BACON, INC.   BOSTON, 1963

STATE AND LOCAL

GOVERNMENT

IN AMERICA

★　★　★

First Printing........April, 1963
Second Printing....August, 1963

★ PREFACE ★

THE TWO AUTHORS of this text have combined their differing talents and experience in an effort to provide a factual and dynamic interpretation of state and local government in our changing American society. The work is primarily concerned with setting in perspective a concept of state and local government as a growing organic process. It is based partly on our experience in teaching, research, and governmental activity, and partly on general observation and reading of new and old works. Attention is given to such masters as Alexis de Tocqueville, James Bryce, and Lincoln Steffens, as well as to the most recent empirical studies of state and local political behavior, including urban, suburban, and metropolitan politics.

We have approached the subject with a recognition that our American society is a compound community of communities of communities, with major and increasing proportions of an urban population, an industrial economy, and national problems in a complex and changing world. We have endeavored to present a general understanding and understandable portrayal of the functioning processes of these community governments below the national level, on all fronts and fields, including the political, legislative, executive, and judicial. We have given attention to our continental geographic base, cultural heritage, and institutional developments as backgrounds for our contemporary multiplicity of governmental units with their unending continuity and continuous change in a highly technological age.

We have sought to offer an accurate view of the relationships among these numerous and varied units of government, both in realistic and hopefully idealistic terms. In this aim we have also given attention to the growing role and relationships

v

of our national government with respect to the governance of states and state subdivisions. State and local government in America today cannot be viewed correctly without an appreciative understanding of the helpful, guiding, and occasionally restraining hand of the national government. In this connection we have also manifested concern for analyzing the relationships between the governing personnel and the governed in the American complex democracy. We have noted the needful role of experts in all units and branches of government in modern America, with appreciation, however, for the proverbial proviso that the expert should be "on tap" rather than "on top."

Special acknowledgment should be made of the assistance received from several sources, first of all to the Vanderbilt University students who obediently "tried out" parts of the manuscript in state and local government classes in 1961 and 1962. Parts have also been tried out on our colleagues, and the process has doubtless tried the patience of these and others, including members of our families and of our publisher's editorial staff. Professor Vincent V. Thursby, of Florida State University, made invaluable contributions in the early stages of the manuscript. Our indebtedness is gratefully acknowledged to Professors Robert J. Harris and John C. Wahlke, of Vanderbilt University, Professor Wilder W. Crane, Jr., of the University of Wisconsin at Milwaukee, and Professor Landon G. Rockwell, of Hamilton College. Mrs. Daniel R. Grant served faithfully above and beyond the call of domestic duty as typist and proofreader. All of these, however, are clearly absolved of any form of contributory guilt.

We hold to a philosophy of the positive and constructive approach to state and local government in the various and complementary aspects. We recognize that in American civilization today the good life is sought in increasing measure through governmental action. While it is not the purpose of this book to insist on any special definition of good government, we do hold that an essential ingredient in the quest for good or effective government is popular understanding of state and local government — what it is and how it works. It is in this spirit we hopefully offer this text to teacher and student.

DANIEL R. GRANT
H. C. NIXON

February, 1963

vi

★ CONTENTS ★

1

2

3

4

5

6

7

8

9

10

11

12

13

14

15

16

17

20

21

22

23

STATE AND LOCAL

GOVERNMENT

IN AMERICA

★ *1* ★

STATE AND LOCAL GOVERNMENT

IN AMERICAN SOCIETY

A STRANGE political paradox pervades the study of contemporary state and local government in the United States. Any realistic analysis of government in the fifty states and the thousands of communities within them is sooner or later complicated by two apparently contradictory facts. First, the power picture of national-state-local relations is characterized by what is variously described as a trend toward "national domination," "centralization," the "eclipse of states' rights," the "decline of local autonomy," and the "movement of power to Washington," to name only a few of the descriptive phrases commonly used. Second, state and local governments are spending more money, employing more people, doing more things of greater impact, and, in short, are more important now than ever before in our history. Few would deny the first statement, but the second may come as a surprise. Is it really true that the national government has won a long series of power struggles with the states and their subdivisions, especially during the past half-century, and yet state and local governments are still more important than ever? The answer to this question is sought in this chapter. Old and new elements are examined, and the added question of "Why?" leads us to consider the revolutionary social and economic changes in the environment of state and local government.

A political paradox

4 THE IMPORTANCE OF STATE AND LOCAL GOVERNMENT: SOMETHING OLD AND SOMETHING NEW

Predictions of state decline

Not many years ago some political scientists were predicting the "withering away" of our states, not in the Marxian sense, but as obsolete appendages which were too small to handle problems of regional or national scope and too large or unnatural in jurisdiction to handle local problems. During the crisis period of the Great Depression of the thirties, one critic went so far as to say, with some logic in the light of the times:

> Is the state the appropriate instrumentality for the discharge of these sovereign functions? The answer is not a matter of conjecture or delicate appraisal. It is a matter of brutal record. The American state is finished. I do not predict that the states will go, but affirm that they have gone.[1]

The political virility of the states was underestimated, however, and new life has grown out of both new and old factors. Any assessment of the significance of state and local government in the 1960's must recognize their vastly increased services and expenditures, the close relationship of their activities to the individual citizen, their roles as proving grounds for national leaders, as experimental laboratories, and as an essential element in federalism, and their continuing importance in the functioning of the American political party system.

Growth of all levels of government

1. *Big Government, even at Lower Levels.* Much of the explanation of the paradox referred to in the preceding paragraphs is found in the simple fact of tremendous growth of government at *all* levels. The growth in power and functions of the national government has added more burdens and responsibilities to the states and their subdivisions than it has taken away from them. The flow of billions of dollars from Washington to state and local agencies and from state to local units calls for more government all along the line. It calls for extensive management of growing intergovernmental relations — for more government of government itself. State and local expenditures have risen phenomenally from one billion dollars in 1902 to over sixty-seven billions in 1961. Although the national government has spent more annually than state and local governments since about 1935, a recent upsurge in state and local spending has narrowed the gap considerably. The

---

[1] Luther Gulick, "Reorganization of the State," *Civil Engineering*, III (August, 1933), pp. 420-421.

ratio now stands at about 60-40 for the $165 billion total for all levels of government. State expenditures more than doubled in the decade from 1950 to 1960, jumping from $15.5 billion in 1951 to $32.8 billion in 1960. City expenditures also more than doubled in this period and the expenditures of all local governments combined were greater than state expenditures.

The steady growth of state and local government is reflected unmistakably in the increase in number of employees, both numerically and proportionately compared with federal employment levels. While federal employment of civilians remained at about the same level (2.4 million) during the decade of 1950 to 1960, state and local employment grew from 4.3 million to 6.4 million in the same period. State and local government domination of the public employment picture may be seen in Figure 1-1. The relative requirements for personnel of the various state and local functions are indicated in Table 1-1. Even if the 2.5 million public education employees should be subtracted, state and local governments employ far more persons than does the federal government. Many of the newer demands made upon state and local governments are among the most expensive to meet, both in personnel costs and equipment or construction costs. Slum clearance, public housing, urban renewal, mental health programs, highway construction and maintenance, and new public works have all been responsible for the growth of state and local

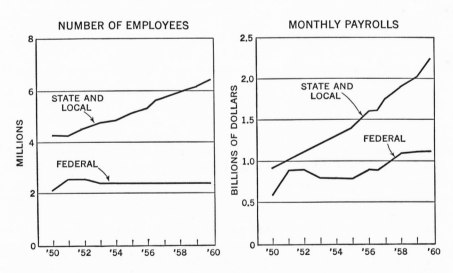

Source: U. S. Bureau of the Census, *State Distribution of Public Employment in 1960* (U. S. Government Printing Office, Washington, 1961), p. 1.

Figure 1-1. State and local share of public employment and payrolls, 1950 to 1960

TABLE 1-1

NUMBER OF STATE AND LOCAL GOVERNMENT EMPLOYEES
IN 1960, CLASSIFIED ACCORDING TO FIELD OF EMPLOYMENT

Field of Employment	Employees (full-time equivalent)	
	Number (in thousands)	Per cent
Education	2,525	45.3
Local schools	2,159	38.8
Institutions of higher education	338	6.1
Other	28	0.5
Hospitals	581	10.4
Highways	499	9.0
General control	338	6.1
Police protection	304	5.5
Local fire protection	145	2.6
Sanitation	139	2.5
Local utilities other than water supply*	130	2.3
Natural resources	121	2.2
Public welfare	114	2.0
Water supply	100	1.8
Health	73	1.3
All other	499	9.0
Total	5,570	100.0

* Electric power, transit, and gas-supply systems.

Source: U. S. Bureau of the Census, State Distribution of Public Employment in 1960 (U. S. Government Printing Office, Washington, 1961), p. 2.

expenditures, taxes, and employment. But public schools remain the largest single item of cost for state and local government, as national defense does for the national government.

2. *Close Relationship to the Individual.* State and local government encompasses a wide range of human relationships. It provides more material for realistic fiction than does the operation of the national government, and has been treated in this century by such writers as Theodore Dreiser, Herbert Quick, Robert Penn Warren, and the American Winston Churchill. The problems it fosters are dealt with in popular detective stories and on radio and television programs, which often refer to the "D. A." or district attorney.

Within their own borders state and local units have the primary responsibility for regulating relations between the sexes, including marriage, divorce, alimony, property rights of wives and widows, and punishment for bigamy, rape, and other types of misbehavior. Most civilian murders are crimes against a state, not the United States, although national statutes may be violated simultaneously: if, for instance, murder were committed in connection with a post office or a national bank robbery. Professional groups, such as lawyers, physicians, accountants, and public school teachers, are licensed under state laws. Making and recording land titles, issuing birth certificates, licensing motor vehicles, requiring dog tags, rendering "shots" compulsory to prevent disease, and administering many kinds of inspection fall within state and local jurisdiction. Every vote in a national election for president must be cast in a political subdivision of a state under the supervision of local officials. States rather than the national government provide for the routine chartering of private corporations, whether corner laundries or billion-dollar giants operating in interstate commerce under national regulation.

Intimate character of state and local functions

3. *Proving Ground for National Leaders.* State and local politics and administration have long been a testing arena for political gladiators en route to national leadership. The state governorship is clearly a key spot for presidential and vice-presidential hopefuls, as shown in Figure 1-2. Some observers go further than simply arguing that the governorship increases the political availability of a presidential candidate; they contend that gubernatorial experience in such large states as New York, California, or Ohio contributes to presidential effectiveness or even greatness. Walter Lippmann has expressed this opinion:

A road to the White House

> It is no accident that since the Nineteenth Century, when the office of President has become so much bigger than it used to be, the successful Presidents have been, with perhaps one exception, men who had learned the art as Governors of states. Whether one likes them or not, the successful Presidents in this century have been Theodore Roosevelt, Woodrow Wilson, Franklin D. Roosevelt, and Harry S. Truman. All but Truman had been Governors. Truman, moreover, was the only President, assuming he was a successful President, who came out of Congress. This is not because Congress is a bad institution but because Congress is very different from that of the Executive. No rule of thumb is absolute. But for my own part there is a reasonable presumption of doubt about the executive competence of any candidate who has never occupied an executive office, as Governor of a state, as Mayor of a big city, or as a Cabinet officer.[2]

---

[2] *New York Herald Tribune*, March 1, 1960, as quoted in Glen E. Brooks, *When Governors Convene* (The Johns Hopkins Press, Baltimore, 1961), p. 229.

IMPORTANCE: OLD   AND   NEW

	REPUBLICAN	DEMOCRAT
1912	William H. Taft	WOODROW WILSON*
	James S. Sherman	THOMAS R. MARSHALL
1916	CHARLES EVANS HUGHES	WOODROW WILSON*
	Charles W. Fairbanks	THOMAS R. MARSHALL
1920	Warren G. Harding*	JAMES M. COX
	CALVIN COOLIDGE	Franklin D. Roosevelt
1924	CALVIN COOLIDGE*	John W. Davis
	Charles G. Dawes	CHARLES W. BRYAN
1928	Herbert Hoover*	ALFRED E. SMITH
	Charles Curtis	JOSEPH T. ROBINSON
1932	Herbert Hoover	FRANKLIN D. ROOSEVELT*
	Charles Curtis	John N. Garner
1936	ALFRED M. LANDON	FRANKLIN D. ROOSEVELT*
	Frank Knox	John N. Garner
1940	Wendell L. Willkie	FRANKLIN D. ROOSEVELT*
	Charles L. McNary	Henry A. Wallace
1944	THOMAS E. DEWEY	FRANKLIN D. ROOSEVELT*
	JOHN W. BRICKER	Harry S. Truman
1948	THOMAS E. DEWEY	Harry S. Truman*
	EARL WARREN	Alben W. Barkley
1952	Dwight D. Eisenhower*	ADLAI E. STEVENSON
	Richard M. Nixon	John J. Sparkman
1956	Dwight D. Eisenhower*	ADLAI E. STEVENSON
	Richard M. Nixon	Estes Kefauver
1960	Richard M. Nixon	John F. Kennedy*
	Henry Cabot Lodge	Lyndon B. Johnson

MAJOR THIRD PARTY CANDIDATES

1912 THEODORE ROOSEVELT (Progressive)
HIRAM JOHNSON

1924 ROBERT M. LA FOLLETTE (Progressive)
Burton Wheeler

1948 J. STROM THURMOND (Dixiecrat)
FIELDING WRIGHT

Source: Adapted from Glen E. Brooks, *When Governors Convene* (The Johns Hopkins Press, Baltimore, 1961), p. 130.

Figure 1-2. Governors who became presidential or vice-presidential nominees, 1912-1960 (governors shown in capital letters; asterisk denotes winner)

Whether such experience is accepted as the *sine qua non* for presidential greatness or not, few would deny that state and local governments make a significant contribution to the training of national leaders, legislative and judicial as well as executive. Many a legislator has reached Congress via his county courthouse or his state capital. John Jay and Justice Holmes can be cited among jurists who have served on both state and federal benches. A reverse movement of office-holders may also occur, with a national position preceding a state office. Ex-congressmen have become governors, and a few, like A. B. Cummins of Iowa and the elder Robert La Follette of Wisconsin, sandwiched tenure as governor between service in the lower and upper houses of Congress. Fiorello La Guardia of New York and Maury Maverick of San Antonio became mayors after service in Congress. Many administrative appointees have switched service from one level of government to another. Political party officials also cross the lines of local, state, and national organizations. This easy mobility from job to job provides a by-product of mutual understanding among numerous parts of the American system.

A road to Capitol Hill

4. *Experimental Laboratories.* One of the classic arguments for continuation of strong state and local governments has been the virtue of having fifty separate "experimental laboratories," each operating under the democratic process to test on a small scale various political innovations. In practice, this function has been performed only to a limited extent. The states are rigidly *non*-experimental in outlook toward certain features of governmental structure and procedure, such as separation of powers, an elective governor, and the bicameral legislative. The one exception which seems to prove the rule is Nebraska's willingness to experiment with a unicameral legislature. In matters of policy and legislation several states have shown greater willingness to break new ground, so that many programs of the national government in such fields as financial reorganization, labor regulation, and welfare legislation had the benefit of prior testing by at least a few states. Fair employment practice legislation might be described as currently in the experimental stage in several states and cities. Other examples can be found in such electoral devices as initiative, referendum, recall, and the presidential primary within certain states.

Experimental and non-experimental states

5. *Essential Element of Federalism, Old and New.* The underlying significance of state government has been, and continues to be, its power position within the working of the federal system. In the formal *constitutional* sense it is quite clear that the state, like the old grey mare, "ain't what she used to be," because of issues settled both recently and as early as the days of Jefferson and Lincoln. Yet in the *political* sense the states still play a prominent part

in shaping the character of national party nominating conventions, determining the make-up of the congress, and influencing the selection of judges.

Persistence of political federalism

Thus, the political facts of life in the United States are frequently "<u>fed-eral facts</u>" — that is, related to the peculiar position of states in our elections, parties, and legislation, rather than "national facts" such as one might expect to find in England, France, and other nations not having a federal form of government. While formal constitutional federalism may seem to be withering badly in the United States, political federalism remains virile principally because of the political virility of the fifty states. States' rights, discussed in detail in the next chapter, are probably much less dependent upon the Supreme Court for their preservation than they are upon the political power and behavior of states *as states*.

THE CHANGING ENVIRONMENT OF STATE AND LOCAL GOVERNMENT

Governmental institutions, like people, are molded in large measure by their environment, and when drastic changes occur in that environment, corresponding governmental changes may be expected sooner or later, in one form or another. The environment of state and local government has been undergoing revolutionary changes in recent years and, while no exhaustive analysis of them is possible here, it is possible to identify briefly some of the main streams of change which have caught up all state and local governments in their current. Among the more important kinds of change are the three "isms" of population movement — <u>urbanism</u>, <u>suburbanism</u>, and <u>metropolitanism.</u> These and other factors such as economic bigness, the impact of depression and of hot and cold war, and the development of a mass culture, help to explain the character of state and local government.

1. *Urbanism and Rural Decline.* The ever-growing tide of urbanism in the United States is demonstrated clearly by a few figures from past census reports on the proportion of U. S. population living in cities of 2,500 or more:

Year	Per Cent Urban	Year	Per Cent Urban
1790	5.1	1880	28.2
1800	6.1	1900	39.7
1820	7.2	1920	51.2
1840	10.8	1940	56.5
1860	19.8	1960	69.9

The change from 5 per cent to nearly 70 per cent of our population living in cities, from one out of 20 to over two out of three, explains many things about our government that are too often not understood. The disappearance of the one-room little red schoolhouse, multiplication of governmental *An urban* functions, transfer of many local functions to the state or national capital, *nation* steadily rising taxes and expenditures, and the feeling that even local government has lost much of the "personal touch" that it had when grandfather was a boy, all may be attributed in large measure to the fact that we are now a heavily urbanized nation. The 1960 census report adds an exclamation mark to the trend which has long been in the making; it shows that only 11 of the 50 states remain with less than 50 per cent of their population classified as urban. As shown in Figure 1-3, no state is less than 35 per cent urban and 18 states are more than 70 per cent urban. Even in Texas, with its boots, saddles, and wide-open spaces, three out of every four persons live in cities. New Jersey is close to 90 per cent urban.

In 1960 the rural decline in the United States was not merely *relative* as in previous census years, that is, representing a decreasing proportion of an increasing total. The decline was *absolute* as the rural population actually decreased in number from almost 54.5 million to just over 54.0 million. The political effect of the rural population's leveling off and declining is not *Persistence of* so important by itself as it is in relation to the urban explosion. The prob- *rural power* lem of legislative apportionment is further aggravated and the rural "rotten boroughs" in legislative representation become even more rancid in the eyes of the badly outvoted, swelling urban populace.[3]

The change to a predominantly urban nation has done far more than complicate the problem of legislative representation, however. A prerequisite to understanding state and local government is appreciating the change that urbanization has wrought in the demands made upon government. *From agri-* Where once the rural character of the population resulted in political *culture to* concern for *agriculture* and the good life on the farm, the urban chorus *"urbiculture"* now cries out through pressure groups, party platforms, and elections for more

---

[3] *See* Chapter 10 for a discussion of the problem of the urban and rural representation.

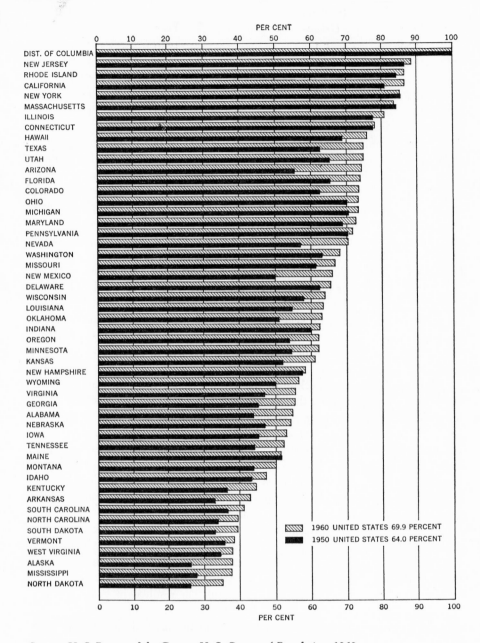

Source: U. S. Bureau of the Census, U. S. Census of Population, 1960.
Figure 1-3. States ranked by per cent of population urban: 1960

and more attention to what has been called urbiculture, and the good life in the city. The focus of politics has been changing faster than we who are in the midst of it realize. Problems on the farm that were the responsibility of the individual such as waste disposal, water supply, fire protection, transportation, recreation, and even health, have become complex and costly group responsibilities in congested cities.

2. *Suburbanism and Central City Decline.* An added dimension to urbanism, vastly accelerated in recent years, has been the flight to suburbia by more than fifty million Americans. There are numerous reasons for this mass movement of population to fringe areas surrounding the major *Flight to* cities — the desire for more room, cleaner air, quietude, social status, *suburbia* lower taxes and many more. But it constitutes a dynamic social revolution on wheels, with its peak still unreached, which is already dealing heavy blows to our traditional patterns of state and local politics. The suburbs of our great metropolitan areas are fast becoming the home of more people than our central cities. The central cities showed a gain in 1960 of 5.6 million, or 7.1 per cent, over 1950. The metropolitan suburbs by 1960 had mushroomed with an increase of 28 million, almost 50 per cent over their 1950 population. The total for the central cities is 58.0 million and the suburban total is a close 54.9 million. Many core cities are already outvoted by their suburbs.

Perhaps even more dramatic than the growth of suburbia is the actual decline in population of many of our largest and oldest cities, the first decline in history for most of them. Of the ten largest cities in 1950 all but one (Los Angeles) were reported in the 1960 census as losing population. *Central city* New York City's suburbs gained by 38.9 per cent but the city decreased *decline* by 1.4 per cent. Chicago lost by 1.9 per cent while its suburbs gained 64.9 per cent. Among the heaviest losers in 1960 were Boston (13.0 per cent), St. Louis (12.5 per cent), Pittsburgh (10.7 per cent), and Detroit (9.7 per cent). In the case of both Pittsburgh and Boston the suburbs contain three times as many people as the area within their city limits. The nation's capital has not been spared; its population declined by 4.8 per cent while its Virginia and Maryland suburbs gained a thumping 87.0 per cent.

These two developments, the rise of suburbia and the decline of the core city, like urbanism and rural decline, have separate but related effects on state and local politics and administration. The centrifugal suburban push is serving as a kind of shock treatment for sleepy, rural-type county *Political* government in the United States. For those counties which can survive *impact* the shock of suddenly being pressured for the full gamut of urban services by hundreds of thousands of demanding citizens no longer served by a core city, a new and vigorous local government may result. For the others a pathetic paralysis of ill-adapted political and administrative structures is inevitable. The core city, too, is undergoing shock treatment. The loss of tax base, growth potential, and, perhaps most serious of all, the loss of the leadership potential of those who lose themselves politically in the isolation of the homogenized suburbs, all contribute to different kinds of blight in the heart of our cities.[4]

    3. *Metropolitanism and Local Government Fragmentation.* Metropolitanism is not a precise technical term, but is a word born out of necessity to describe the advent of a new creature on the political scene — the loose-jointed, often chaotic, yet interrelated mass of people in the larger cities and their suburbs. It is the product of an accelerated urbanism and suburbanism in the frozen context of horse-and-buggy local governments. The growth of metropolitan areas in the United States has compelled the Census Bureau to devise new schemes of reporting population to make it clear that the economic and cultural city of Boston (or Chicago or San Francisco) is a great deal larger than the legal city. It began reporting "metropolitan districts" in 1920 and changed to two terms in 1950, the "urbanized area" and the "standard metropolitan area." The jargon grew further in 1960 with the SMA becoming the "standard metropolitan statistical area." In justice to the Census Bureau it must be said that the metropolis almost defies permanent definition, and setting boundary lines is akin to fencing in a prairie fire.[5]

    The 1960 census makes it clear that the United States is not merely urban; it is distinctly metropolitan and becoming more so each year. The number of metropolitan areas rose from 168 to 212 between 1950 and 1960, and

Metropolitan nation

their population grew from 89 million to 113 million. Thus 62.9 per cent of the people of the United States live within the orbit of the big cities, and about one-half of this metropolitan population live in the fifteen largest areas. These metropolitan areas account for about three-fourths of the nation's economic activity — 79 per cent of all bank deposits, 78 per cent of all manufacturing payrolls, and over 70 per cent of all local tax revenue. To complicate matters further, just when the "metropolitan area" is beginning to make

---

[4] See Robert Wood's *Suburbia: It's People and Their Politics* (Houghton Mifflin Company, Boston, 1959) for an excellent account of the nature of the suburban movement and its political implications. A collection of empirical studies and essays on suburbia may be found in W. A. Dobriner, ed., *The Suburban Community* (G. P. Putnam's Sons, New York, 1958).

[5] The major difference between the "urbanized area" and the "standard metropolitan statistical area" is that the SMSA is based on the whole county or contiguous counties, with a few exceptions, while the urbanized area includes only those reasonably contiguous portions of counties meeting urban criteria. Both must include at least one city of 50,000 inhabitants or more.

some headway toward acceptance in laymen's language, some sociologists and political scientists have begun to talk about the developing "super-metropolitan area" or "megalopolis," formed when two or more metropolitan areas grow together. The most publicized of these is a 600-mile long "Linear City" on the Eastern Seaboard, stretching from lower New Hampshire through Boston, New York, Philadelphia, Baltimore, Washington, and Northern Virginia. The Census Bureau reported that this "great metropolitan complex" reaches into 10 states and 32 major metropolitan areas, and contains 31.5 million persons. A similar linear city on the West Coast is developing from Los Angeles to San Diego, and perhaps eventually up to San Francisco.[6] As pictured in Figure 1-4, many metropolitan areas, even the small and medium-sized ones, have spilled across state boundary lines to become interstate cities. *The super metropolis*

The impact of metropolitanism on state and local government is considered in detail in Chapter 18, but the one outstanding effect is fragmentation of local government. Robert C. Wood describes fragmentation in the extreme in *1400 Governments*, an analysis of the pattern of local government for the New York metropolitan region.[7] The New York region had only 127 governments in 1900. All metropolitan areas are faced with a multiplicity of local governments, on a smaller scale than New York, to be sure, but universally perplexing when it comes to grappling with a variety of area-wide problems. It is out of this context of inadequate local authority or competence that centralization arises, sometimes in the direction of the state capital and sometimes toward Washington. The problems of "metropolitics," metropolitan explosion, urban-suburban rivalries, and related subjects have provided in recent years the stimulus for a whole host of "metro" studies and consolidation movements. With such high stakes as mass transit, tax rates, crime control, public health, local self-government, control of zoning, and metropolitan planning, it is clear that the protagonists of metropolitan reform have "just begun to fight." *Fragmentation of government*

4. *Other Types of Population Migration*. Population changes in the United States have not been limited to urbanism, suburbanism, and metropolitanism, although these are most common to all fifty states. Several states and communities have been affected by special types of mass movements of population with racial, economic, and political overtones. The Western movement of the "Oakies" and "Arkies" during the depression of the 1930's, with its

---

[6] For a definition and classification of "urban regions," see Charlton F. Chute, "Today's Urban Regions," *National Municipal Review*, XLV (June and July, 1956).

[7] Harvard University Press, Cambridge, 1961. See also Raymond Vernon, *Metropolis, 1985* (Harvard University Press, Cambridge, 1960); and Scott Greer, *The Emerging City: Myth and Reality* (Free Press of Glencoe, Inc., New York, 1962).

16

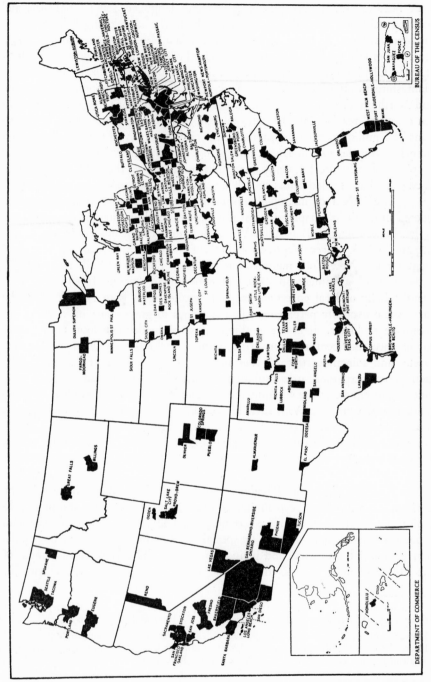

Source: U. S. Bureau of the Census, *U. S. Census of Population, 1960.*

Figure 1-4. *Standard metropolitan statistical areas: 1960*

STATE AND LOCAL GOVERNMENT IN AMERICAN SOCIETY

accompanying welfare problems, is familiar to us all. Negroes have moved in large numbers from Southern farms and towns to cities outside the South, with the total out-migration of nonwhites reaching an all-time high of nearly 1.5 million during the 1950's. The destination states receiving the largest numbers of Negroes by migration were California (345,000), New York (282,000), and Illinois (189,000), with Ohio, Michigan, and New Jersey not far behind. More Negroes — 1.4 million — live in the state of New York than in any other state, southern ones included. Racial tension is not a monopoly of the South. A swelling tide of Puerto Ricans has migrated to New York City in recent years.[8] Still more recently, in the wake of the Cuban crisis, thousands of refugees from that nearby country have flooded the city of Miami and other coastal cities. These and other groups quite naturally tend to live together as sub-communities within the larger cities, complicating the task of political, economic, and cultural assimilation. Their more immediate impact is upon local and state governments, rather than upon the national government.

Racial, economic, and political migrations

5. *Economic Bigness.* If population movements have been the most significant influence in the environment of *local* government, economic changes have undoubtedly been most significant in the changing role of *state* government. The simple term "economic bigness" hardly does justice to the revolutionary impact which this development has had upon state government and the federal system. Nothing even approaching the full extent of the impact of the growth of modern business and labor across state boundary lines was realized until the dark hours and years following the economic crash of 1929. The impact on the states came with devasting suddenness, as described in contemporary accounts by Luther Gulick:

A national economy

> Where were the states when the banks went under? Powerless Maryland, hysterical Michigan, safety-first New York! Where were the states when all the railroads were on the verge of passing into the hands of the bondholders and suspending operation? Where were the states in regulation of power and the control of utilities? Where are the states now in regulating insurance companies, with their fake balance sheets and high salaries? Where were the states in controlling blue sky securities? Where were the states in preventing destructive business competition and in protecting labor and the public? Where were the states in the development of security through social insurance? In none of these fields affecting economic life was it possible for any state to do anything decisive without driving business out of its jurisdiction into areas where there was no regulation and no control.

The same kind of sectional self-interest made it impossible for any state to

---

[8] *See* Oscar Handlin, *The Newcomers: Negroes and Puerto Ricans in a Changing Metropolis* (Harvard University Press, Cambridge, 1959).

go forward boldly with public improvement programs to offset industrial contraction.[9]

The growth and recognition of a tremendous national, and even international, economy, rather than 50 state economies as previously assumed, is a force to which state governments are still reacting and adjusting, sometimes rapidly but more often slowly or almost imperceptibly. Greater emphasis on the "purely local," expansion of grant-in-aid programs, and the birth of "cooperative federalism," rather than "competitive federalism," are all a part of this adjustment. Through it all, the states have continued to grow vigorously.

6. *Social Changes: Rootlessness and Mass Culture.* Some aspects of the dynamic American society have been changing so fast in recent years that sociologists have been kept working overtime in their analytical studies, and political scientists have hardly begun the task of relating these studies to politics and government in a meaningful way. The new-found physical mobility of the population, for example, is producing a variety of social and political changes — some good and some bad as judged by traditional values. Physical mobility provides greater opportunity for people to move away from economic or social "dead-end streets" and provides industry with a more flexible manpower

Effects of physical mobility

situation. Yet this same mobility has produced a rootlessness and a breakdown of "primary controls" with a resulting higher rate of crime, increasing personal insecurity, lack of community identification, low political participation, and other social problems.[10] A more recent stream of analysis of modern society, with Erich Fromm[11] and David Riesman[12] as chief spokesmen, emphasizes the "lonely crowd" aspects of urban living and timid conformity to the expectations of the group. The American culture is said to be a "mass

A mass society?

culture," with entertainment, literature, music, fashions, and comic strips all mass-produced, pre-packaged, and distributed by coast-to-coast communications media.[13] The implications of a mass culture upon the theoretical basis for a federal system to provide for local differences are intriguing, to say the least. It is doubtful, however, that a mass culture has

---

[9] Luther Gulick, *op. cit.,* p. 421.

[10] *See,* for example, R. E. Park and E. W. Burgess, *The City* (University of Chicago Press, Chicago, 1925).

[11] *Escape from Freedom* (Holt, Rinehart & Winston, New York, 1941).

[12] *The Lonely Crowd* (Yale University Press, New Haven, 1950), and *Faces in the Crowd* (Yale University Press, New Haven, 1952).

[13] *See* B. Rosenberg and David M. White, eds., *Mass Culture* (The Free Press, Glencoe, Ill., 1957), William Kornhauser, *The Politics of Mass Society* (Free Press of Glencoe, Inc., New York, 1959); and Maurice R. Stein, *The Eclipse of Community: An Interpretation of American Studies* (Princeton University Press, 1960).

THE CHARACTER OF A STATE AND
ITS COMMUNITIES: FIFTY PATTERNS

In spite of these evidences of a mass culture in certain respects, it must
be recognized that each state still remains different from all others, and that
these differences are important politically. The fifty states collectively provide
an exhibit of national diversity. State histories, for example, read like the
stories of as many different nations. Their historical origins are pictured in
Figure 1-5. Sixteen states are products of the eighteenth century, twenty-nine came
into the Union in the nineteenth century, and three trans-Mississippi
commonwealths and two non-contiguous territories acquired statehood   *Network of*
in the twentieth century. Thirteen former British colonies entered the   *history*
Union as states ratifying the Constitution as provided by the Convention
of 1787. Thirty states moved up to statehood from the status of organized territories. Vermont, Kentucky, Tennessee, and Maine were carved out of original
claims or domains of other states, and West Virginia was admitted as the loyal
part of Virginia during the Civil War. The republic of Texas, which had won
a war of independence from Mexico, was annexed as a state by Congress in
1845. California, part of the Mexican cession of 1848, was the scene of a gold
rush in '49 and became a state the following year without any preliminary territorial step. Eleven southern states were involved in a bloody war of secession,
which, in its failure, stirred up a temporary constitutional question as to
whether these states as state entities had been out of the Union for the war
period or had merely been interfered with by disloyal elements. Oklahoma has
had a unique history, both before and since gaining statehood in 1907 as a
combination of two territories. One of these, the Indian territory, was established
in 1834 for the relocation of five Indian tribes from states east of the Mississippi.
Portions of this territory were thrown open in 1889 to general individual home-
steaders, and thousands rushed in at the scheduled noon hour signal, finding, however, that many had evaded the guards and staked out choice claims ahead of
them. These "sooners" provided a nickname for Oklahomans. The Territory
of Oklahoma was created in 1890 and subsequently combined with the other
territory to give the nation its most Indianized state, socially and politically.
Louisiana is cited as the most distinctive example of a state with a French-
Spanish colonial background and continuing influence of that background on
civil institutions today.

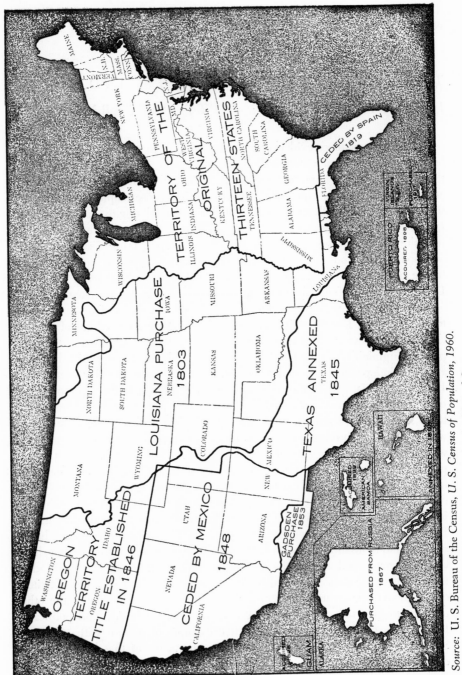

Source: U. S. Bureau of the Census, *U. S. Census of Population*, 1960.

Figure 1-5. Major acquisitions of territory by the United States

STATE AND LOCAL GOVERNMENT IN AMERICAN SOCIETY

The states present a mosaic of inequalities of physical geography, and these inequalities are guaranteed by the Constitution, which protects all the states against compulsory division or combination. Alaska has 475 times Rhode Island's area of 1,214 square miles, and Texas is more than 200 times this smallest state's size. California is nearly as large in area as Oregon and Washington combined, Pennsylvania could cover Delaware nineteen times, North Carolina is three-fifths larger than South Carolina, and Maine dwarfs the other New England states. Table 1-2 indicates the size and ranking of the states as to area.

Lands and people

TABLE 1-2

AREA AND POPULATION OF STATES: 1960

State	Population	Rank in Population	% Increase in Population, 1950-1960	Gross Area [Sq. Miles]	Rank in Area
United States	179,323,175	—	18.5	3,615,211	—
Alabama	3,266,740	19	6.7	51,609	29
Alaska	226,167	50	75.8	586,400	1
Arizona	1,302,161	35	73.7	113,909	6
Arkansas	1,786,272	31	−6.5	53,104	27
California	15,717,204	2	48.5	158,693	3
Colorado	1,753,947	33	32.4	104,247	8
Connecticut	2,535,234	25	26.3	5,009	48
Delaware	446,292	46	40.3	2,057	49
Florida	4,951,560	10	78.7	58,560	22
Georgia	3,943,116	16	14.5	58,876	21
Hawaii	632,772	43	26.6	6,424	47
Idaho	667,191	42	13.3	83,557	13
Illinois	10,081,158	4	15.7	56,400	24
Indiana	4,662,498	11	18.5	36,291	38
Iowa	2,757,537	24	5.2	56,290	25
Kansas	2,178,611	28	14.3	82,264	14
Kentucky	3,038,156	22	3.2	40,395	37
Louisiana	3,257,022	20	21.4	48,523	31
Maine	969,265	36	6.1	33,215	39
Maryland	3,100,689	21	32.3	10,577	42
Massachusetts	5,148,578	9	9.8	8,257	45

Source: U. S. Bureau of the Census, U. S. *Census of Population, 1960.*

TABLE 1-2 (*Continued*)

AREA AND POPULATION OF STATES: 1960

State	Population	Rank in Population	% Increase in Population, 1950-1960	Gross Area [Sq. Miles]	Rank in Area
Michigan	7,823,194	7	22.8	58,216	23
Minnesota	3,413,864	18	14.5	84,068	12
Mississippi	2,178,141	29	0.0	47,716	32
Missouri	4,319,813	13	9.2	69,686	19
Montana	674,767	41	14.2	147,138	4
Nebraska	1,411,330	34	6.5	77,227	15
Nevada	285,278	49	78.2	110,540	7
New Hampshire	606,921	45	13.8	9,304	44
New Jersey	6,066,782	8	25.5	7,836	46
New Mexico	951,023	37	39.6	121,666	5
New York	16,782,304	1	13.2	49,576	30
North Carolina	4,556,155	12	12.2	52,712	28
North Dakota	632,446	44	2.1	70,665	17
Ohio	9,706,397	5	22.1	41,222	35
Oklahoma	2,328,284	27	4.3	69,919	18
Oregon	1,768,687	32	16.3	96,981	10
Pennsylvania	11,319,366	3	7.8	45,333	33
Rhode Island	859,488	39	8.5	1,214	50
South Carolina	2,382,594	26	12.5	31,055	40
South Dakota	680,514	40	4.3	77,047	16
Tennessee	3,567,089	17	8.4	42,244	34
Texas	9,579,677	6	24.2	267,339	2
Utah	890,627	38	29.3	84,916	11
Vermont	389,881	47	3.2	9,609	43
Virginia	3,966,949	14	19.5	40,815	36
Washington	2,853,214	23	19.9	68,192	20
West Virginia	1,860,421	30	—7.2	24,181	41
Wisconsin	3,951,777	15	15.1	56,154	26
Wyoming	330,066	48	13.6	97,914	9

Source: U. S. Bureau of the Census, *U. S. Census of Population, 1960.*

Area is not the only geographic variation. Some states have problems of flood control; others are concerned with irrigation. There are 24 coastal states, a group of Great Lakes states, Mississippi River Valley states, mountain states, and so on. The large state of Texas or an elongated state like Tennessee or California has enough sharp differences in its physical geography to give multiple-state characteristics to its public life.

The distribution of population among and within the states is far from even. Table 1-2 gives significant 1960 population statistics for the states. New York, at the top in 1960, has close to 75 times the population of Alaska, which has displaced Nevada as the least populous state. California ranked second in 1960, but edged out New York in 1963 for first place honors, based on population estimates. Pennsylvania holds third place. The rate of gain for several populous states is considerably above the national average, while a rate much below that average applies to many rural states, and two states, Arkansas and West Virginia, actually lost population. Many states have densely settled metropolitan areas as well as wide-open spaces of few inhabitants. Texas has Houston and Dallas and also its cactus counties. A number of states have a considerable proportion of the total population concentrated in a single city, such as New York, Chicago, Denver, Baltimore, Milwaukee, New Orleans, and Atlanta. A traveller would note differences in the immigrant stocks of the states as he moved from Massachusetts to Virginia, to Louisiana, to Wisconsin, and to states in the Southwest.

Economic activities vary among the states in spite of trends toward national standardization. We single out of the state's economic pattern the activity in which it is preeminent and thereby emphasize the variety of the states — at times almost to the point of caricature. In agriculture there *Economic* are wheat states, cattle states, corn and hog states, cotton states, tobacco *activities* states, and other groupings, although with considerable overlapping. West Virginia is important for coal, Louisiana for oil and natural gas, Florida for winter tourists, Maine for summer tourists, Wisconsin for dairy products, Kentucky for whiskey and horses, and so on through the list. Illinois, thanks to Chicago, says Carl Sandburg, is "hog butcher to the world." New York and New Jersey, between them, have the world's largest water-front business. Pennsylvania leads in the iron and steel industry, Michigan in automobile manufacturing, California in movie productions, and Delaware in charters for corporations with operating establishments flung, empire-like, across the continent. Nevada is the state most conspicuous for legalized gambling.

Aside from differences in types of economic activity, the states show variations in the amount or extent of enterprise within their borders. Banking, for example, is less extensive in Ohio than in New York but greater in the Buckeye state than in Wyoming. Texas grows more cotton than any other cotton state, and Iowa raises more hogs than Virginia in spite of the reputation of Virginia hams.

All these lands, people, and properties make up the states as well as the nation, giving reality and vitality to laws and constitutions. The state governments, along with local units, derive powers, funds, and problems from them, as also does the national government, under the federal equation. The states, through their governments, actually own fractions of these lands and properties, and they employ some of these people in the functions of governance and service for all, with predominant emphasis on private economy, under a living constitutional system.

De Tocqueville, observing and analyzing democracy in America a few years after Jefferson's death, emphasized that the United States had a central government with a network of local administration. According to him,

Diversity and democracy

the diversity of local units and administrative agencies constituted a significant bulwark against the tyranny of a national majority. No particular party, leader, or group could carry or control all of the numerous localities, and at no time would all these numerous localities move with unanimity toward dictatorship or destruction. In other words, the variety of political opinion and administrative practice among the communities and commonwealths would tend to safeguard the democratic nation from the evils of democracy itself.[14]

The general pattern as observed by the astute Frenchman was to prevail for the next hundred and more years after his report on America. His analysis is essentially applicable to government in the United States today,

The pattern today

although many successful and unsuccessful attempts have been undertaken to streamline the system from top to bottom. The nearest approaches to disruption of the pattern of diversity have occurred through solidarity of national action for survival in critical times of war and depression. But, if de Tocqueville could revisit our country today, he might offer the reminder that, thanks to diversity, the United States, with all the defects of federalism and localism, has so far escaped totalitarian government of the right and of the left. He might be disturbed by the tendency toward standardization under the impact of mass communication media, but he could note that we have as yet arrived at no such soulless and traditionless utopia as is set forth in Aldous Huxley's *Brave New World*[15] or George Orwell's *1984*.[16]

The study of state and local government is a close-up study of balancing freedom and power, rights and responsibilities, politics and administration, in a constitutional democracy. It is a study of living institutions shot through

Living problems

with imperfections. Through organic growth and political folklore, these

---

[14] Alexis de Tocqueville, *Democracy in America* (Alfred A. Knopf, Inc., New York, 1945), I, especially Chapters 16-17. De Tocqueville noted other American factors besides local government as safeguards against tyranny by the mass majority. Among these factors were the power and inherent conservatism of the legal profession and the restraining influence exerted by religion which was widely accepted and characterized by democratic diversity.

[15] (Harper & Row, Publishers, New York, 1950).

[16] (Harcourt, Brace & World, Inc., New York, 1949).

institutions are as much a part of American society as freshman and sophomore classes are a part of the traditional society of the campus. If they did not exist, they would, in some form or fashion, have to be created, despite their imperfections and despite their perennial productivity of headaches for central authorities. The significant question for investigation is not whether but how to live with them.

SUPPLEMENTARY READINGS

The American Assembly, *The Forty-eight States: Their Tasks as Policy-Makers and Administrators* (Graduate School of Business, Columbia University, New York, 1955).

————, *Goals for Americans: The Report of the President's Commission on National Goals* (The American Assembly, Columbia University, 1960, reprinted Prentice-Hall, Inc., New York, 1960). *See* especially Chapters 10 and 12.

Benson, G. C. S., *The New Centralization* (Holt, Rinehart & Winston, Inc., New York, 1941).

Brogan, D. W., *The American Character* (Alfred A. Knopf, Inc., New York, 1944).

Gelber, Lionel, *The American Anarchy: Democracy in an Era of Bigness* (Abelard-Schuman Limited, New York, 1953).

Graves, W. Brooke, *American State Government*, Fourth Edition (D. C. Heath and Company, Boston, 1953).

Greer, Scott, *The Emerging City: Myth and Reality* (Free Press of Glencoe, Inc., New York, 1962).

Key, V. O., *American State Politics* (Alfred A. Knopf, Inc., New York, 1956), Chapter 1.

Maass, Arthur, ed., *Area and Power: A Theory of Local Government* (The Free Press, Glencoe, 1959).

Nixon, H. C., *Possum Trot* (University of Oklahoma Press, Norman, 1941).

Rosenberg, Bernard, and David M. White, *Mass Culture* (The Free Press, Glencoe, 1957).

Stein, Maurice R., *Eclipse of Community: An Interpretation of American Studies* (Princeton University Press, 1960).

Wood, Robert C., *Suburbia: Its People and Their Politics* (Houghton Mifflin Company, Boston, 1959).

⋆ *2* ⋆

THE STATES IN THE
FEDERAL SYSTEM

THE AMERICAN form of democratic-republican government is a system of federal relationships of the states and the national government to each other and to the people under the central Constitution. The members of the epochal convention of 1787 at Philadelphia established a national government and turned a "League of States" into a "Commonwealth of commonwealths, a Republic of republics, a State . . . composed of other States. . . ."[1] They provided for a stronger central government than that of the old Confederation, which had lacked direct compulsory power over persons or citizens. But they avoided setting up a unitary government which would have destroyed the states as political entities, leaving them merely geographical divisions of the national government, much like the territorial "departments" of France. They combined a new national government with the state governments, so that each inhabitant of a state would normally have rights, privileges, and responsibilities under two governments without having to go through one to reach the other. This is the essence of federalism, "a device for dividing decisions and functions

Essence of American federalism

---

[1] James Bryce, *The American Commonwealth* (3rd ed.; The Macmillan Company, New York, 1903), I, p. 15.

26

No two federal systems are completely alike. Each is *sui generis* — that is, in some measure, unique. American states differ, in function and power, from the provinces of Canada, the Swiss cantons, or the so-called "republics" of Soviet Russia. If we say that federalism is a division of powers between general and regional governments which are coordinate and independent in their respective spheres, there must be some principle determining the fundamental division. Under the American Constitution, the general government is one of delegated powers, and the states possess "reserved" powers. The provinces of Canada, in contrast, were to possesss specifically delegated powers under the organic act, while the general or Dominion government was to have the residue. Judicial interpretation has tended to limit the powers of the Dominion government strictly, however, and to effect a practical reversal in the power relationship.[3]

Federalism not standardized

It is also true that constitutional changes and other developments have made American federalism quite different today from what it was in the era of Hamilton, Jefferson, and Madison. Both the inner meanings and the descriptive terms or labels have shifted. Partly as recognition of the status of the the states, "union" served to denote the federal system in popular usage up to the end of the Civil War. The framers of the Constitution looked forward in the preamble not to a "nation," but to "a more perfect Union." Daniel Webster, espousing a national view of the Constitution as against the South Carolina doctrine of states' compact, emphasized "Liberty *and* Union, now and forever, one and inseparable!" Andrew Jackson answered the South Carolinians with the toast, "Our Union, it must be preserved!" Abraham Lincoln used political strategy and "Union" troops to save the "Union" or the "Federal Union" from disruption. In his prophetic words at Gettysburg, however, he invoked "a new birth of freedom" for "this nation, under God." Victory and consequent reunion brought forth a wider use of such terms as "nation," "national," and "nationalism" to describe America and American government. "National" was to compete with "federal" as a label for the central government and its many administrative agencies of the twentieth century.[4] "National Guard" became the proper designation of the constitutionally recognized "Militia

A changing pattern

---

[2] Morton Grodzins, "The Federal System," in *Goals for Americans, The Report of the President's Commission on National Goals* (The American Assembly, Columbia University, reprinted Prentice-Hall, Inc., New York, 1960), p. 265.

[3] *See* K. C. Wheare, *Federal Government* (2d ed.; Oxford University Press, London and New York, 1951), on the various applications of federalism.

[4] Regardless of its technical incorrectness, "federal" is accepted usage for designating the central government of the American system. The press says "federal courts," "federal admin-

of the several States," whether serving under orders of the president or of a governor.

STATES' RIGHTS AND STATES' REVOLT

Before the Civil War

Debates over states' rights in the American federal system are as old as the nation and as new as the last political campaign. Different interests and sections have used the doctrine of states' rights in efforts to shape or limit national policy to their liking. Reliance on this doctrine has at different times characterized articulate minorities or groups out of power in national politics. The Jeffersonians used it in criticism of the Alien and Sedition acts of 1798, and then, once in power, incurred the states' rights wrath of New Englanders over the Louisiana Purchase and the War of 1812. South Carolina based its unsuccessful venture into nullification in the Jackson period on strong states' rights views of the Constitution.

The peak in intellectual analysis of this states' rights doctrine was reached in the speeches and writings of John C. Calhoun in behalf of his native South Carolina and South. Expanding on comments of Jefferson and refining the teachings of another Virginian, John Taylor of Caroline, he militantly argued that the Constitution was a compact made by the states in their sovereign capacity, not by the people in any national capacity. The central government, by this theory, was a non-sovereign creature or agent of the states and must not violate the compact under the penalty of justifying state nullification or even secession. The Calhoun thesis was set forth in the Constitution of the Southern Confederacy, which begins with the words, "We, the People of the Confederate States, each State acting in its sovereign and independent character, in order to form a permanent Federal Government. . . ." The late Frank L. Owsley once suggested that a symbolical gravestone of the Confederacy should carry the inscription: "Died of State Rights." He referred to the irony of the South's failure to win its war for states' rights and slavery, the result in large measure of the factional divisions, obstructions, and disunity inherent in states' rights.[5]

---

istration," "federal Congress," etc., even though "federal" technically refers to the relationship between states and nation or to the form of the whole governmental system, rather than to the national government only.

[5] Frank Lawrence Owsley, *State Rights in the Confederacy* (University of Chicago Press, Chicago, 1925).

The Civil War, often called in the South the War Between the States, marked the climax in the conflict over the meaning and application of federalism. It brought about the overthrow of the institution of slavery and added both strength and clarity to the meaning of national power, producing *Climax and* provisions in constitutional amendments to prevent state interference or *after* discrimination in the sphere of human freedoms and civil or political rights. But the war and the constitutional changes left the way open for a continuing recourse to states' rights for purposes short of rebellion.

The Supreme Court might say in 1869 that a state could not secede,[6] but that high tribunal was destined in the next century to put the stamp of unconstitutionality upon a number of regulatory measures of Congress on the ground of encroaching on the reserved powers of the states. It was also to sustain a body of national legislation against such complaints and to find occasion to uphold and disallow sundry state enactments under test by the Fourteenth Amendment. The states' rights argument, in plain terms, was to remain potent, although many of the new champions would be corporation lawyers rather than spokesmen for states or state governments. Democratic leaders made political appeal to states' rights in opposition to the New Nationalism of President Theodore Roosevelt, and Republicans resorted to a similar gospel as they worked their way back to power after the New Deal era of Franklin D. Roosevelt. There is no sign that the states will pass into eclipse for lack of argument or diversity of opinion with respect to their status.

Two of the more recent controversies which have involved the issue of states' rights are the contest over the control of "tidelands oil" and the integration-segregation conflict. Illustrating the stake which the great business corporations have had from time to time in fighting for states' rights, the *States' rights* tidelands issue found oil companies objecting strenuously to national *and tidelands* control of the submerged offshore oil deposits. Professor Robert J. Harris *oil* has described the intermingling of economic interests and political theory in this contest as follows:

> The solicitude of the oil companies for states' rights is hardly based on convictions derived from political theory but rather on fears that Federal ownership may result in the cancellation or modification of state leases favorable to their interests, their knowledge that they can successfully cope with state oil regulatory agencies, and uncertainty concerning their ability to control a Federal agency.[7]

---

[6] *Texas* v. *White*, 7 Wall. 700 (1869).

[7] "States' Rights and Vested Interests," *Journal of Politics*, XV (November, 1954), pp. 457-471.

Contrary to most of the earlier contests, the tidelands controversy ended with a victory by the states' rights advocates. Taking their battle into the election of 1952, the oil interests secured a promise from the Republicans, who were not unmindful of important votes in Texas, Louisiana, and California, to return tideland jurisdiction from the national government to the states. The promise was fulfilled following the Republican victory in 1952.

The controversy over racial desegregation in the South has brought with it a vigorous re-assertion of many of the older states' rights arguments, including the less familiar doctrine of "interposition," a twin brother of the more familiar "nullification." The idea of interposition is that a state can "interpose" its authority between an unconstitutional act and the people of the state. The Supreme Court's desegregation decision in *Brown v. Board of Education*[8] prompted a hundred southern congressmen to draw up the "Southern Manifesto" in March of 1956 with a thundering attack upon the Supreme Court for its "naked judicial power," "clear abuse of judicial power," and "derogation of the authority of Congress," and with strong commendation for the doctrine of interposition and for those states "which have declared the intention to resist forced integration by any lawful means." As a political device to rally massive southern opposition to desegregation, the significance of interposition cannot be ignored. As a constitutional doctrine, however, interposition has been invalid from the start, and is even weaker when it is attempted against Supreme Court decisions than when attempted against acts of Congress, as it was in all previous efforts. If there was any hope for interposition it evaporated in the Little Rock crisis of 1957 and the "Ole Miss" crisis of 1962. Governor Faubus "interposed" Arkansas National Guard units between a federal court desegregation order and Little Rock Central High School, but President Eisenhower removed the "interposers" with units of the United States Army. Subsequent interventions by national authority to insure law enforcement, as in the New Orleans school crisis in 1960 and the Montgomery "Freedom-rider" tensions, made use of U. S. marshals, rather than troops, in an effort to reduce the antagonisms involved. The effort of Governor Ross Barnett to use interposition to block the admission of Negro student James Meredith to the University of Mississippi was countered first by U. S. marshals and finally by U. S. troops.

In the light of current usage it is difficult to avoid the cynical impression that the states' rights argument is merely a political football in the hands of first one and then the other of competing teams as determined by shifting circumstances of the contest. But it should be remembered that the great debate on the issues of federalism has covered close to a century and

*Desegrega-
tion and
"inter-
position"*

*Institutional
significance*

---

[8] 347 U. S. 483 (1954).

three-quarters and it would be difficult to cast the adherents of any given point
point of view exclusively in roles of agents of wisdom and goodness.

The states' rights argument during much of this long history has served, wisely and unwisely, as a conservative support for the unbroken continuity of political institutions. Whatever changes it has sought or accepted have generally been changes of restoration rather than of novel revision. It has pointedly invoked institutional history and prescriptive law rather than philosophical systems or theories of nature. It manifests more concern with rights bequeathed by the past than with responsibilities called forth by the future. The competing argument in the great debate has likewise avowed allegiance to the institutions of federalism, the law of the Constitution, and the teachings of precedent, but has advocated broader highways of interpretation for an expanding traffic of centralized government.

The never-ending debate is a functional organism of our federated democracy. It tends to shape our political institutions to an ever-growing synthesis of the ideas of such men as Hamilton and Jefferson, Webster and Calhoun, Louis D. Brandeis and Robert A. Taft, Wayne Morse and Barry Goldwater. Words balance words and works balance works, again and again, while the states hold their position on a moving landscape of federated powers. In the process, our system of states succumbs neither to prophecies of doom nor to blueprints of national Utopia.

CONSTITUTIONAL RELATIONS
OF STATES AND NATION

The national Constitution contains important provisions concerning state powers, guarantees, and limitations. The Tenth Amendment has figured significantly in Supreme Court cases involving the borderline between state and national powers. It is a single sentence, saying: "The powers not *Reserved powers of the states* delegated to the United States by the Constitution, nor prohibited by it to the States, are reserved to the States respectively, or to the people." Strictly speaking, this is more of a clarification than a grant of powers. In the distribution of powers in the federal system, the national government has only such capacity for action as is delegated expressly or by implication in the Constitution, while the states have unlimited powers except for restrictions or prohibitions provided in the Constitution. The national government must look to the Constitution for powers; the states must look to that document only for limitations. The powers "reserved to the States" are too numerous and flexible

32 to mention and are not classified in the Constitution, although the states limit their own governments through their own constitutions. The principal reserved power is the "police power," which is discussed in Chapter 4, along with major federal limitations placed upon it.

National restrictions on the states, while few, are significant, and carry the strength of the supremacy clause of the Constitution with its binding application upon state courts. Moreover, the Supreme Court of the United States has the final word in reviewing questions of federalism in cases arising under the Constitution. There can be no deadlock between state and national governments in the exercise of American sovereignty.

The Constitution provides a few general guarantees or protections for the states. One of these guarantees to every state is "a republican form of government," although that phrase has never been clearly defined in official terms. The courts have avoided interpreting the point on the ground that it is a "political" matter and is to be determined by the executive and legislative branches of government. In the Dorr rebellion in Rhode Island in the 1840's, the president gave assistance to the claimants whom he deemed the properly constituted authorities, and this action was upheld by the Supreme Court.[9] Congress may pass on the question of what constitutes republican form by denying seats to persons from states concerned, a process applied to southern states pending measures of reconstruction after the Civil War. For the number of states and the length of our constitutional history, the need or demand for invoking this guarantee has been comparatively slight. It has been held by the courts that republican form was not violated by such practices as initiative and referendum elections and the denial of suffrage to women prior to the adoption of the Nineteenth Amendment.[10]

*Guarantees
to the states*

The Constitution provides that the United States shall protect each of the states "against invasion; and on application of the legislature, or of the executive (when the legislature cannot be convened) against domestic violence." This protection has been requested a few times, but in recent years state officers and state troops (National Guardsmen) have been adequate to take care of problems disruptive of order. The national government does not have to wait for a state request to handle violence affecting United States property, business, or laws. President Cleveland ordered troops to Chicago on the occasion of a railway strike in 1894, although Governor John P. Altgeld of Illinois opposed this action, which served the technical purpose of protecting the mail service.

It might be noted that Article V of the Constitution, in providing for

---

[9] *Luther* v. *Borden,* 7 How. 1 (1849).

[10] *Pacific States Tel. and Tel. Co.* v. *Oregon,* 223 U. S. 118 (1912); *Minor* v. *Happersett,* 21 Wall. 162 (1875).

methods of amendment, stipulates "that no State, without its consent, shall be deprived of its equal suffrage in the Senate." This stipulation was in the nature of a proviso limiting the amending power.

Vesting the Supreme Court with original jurisdiction in cases between states indicates respect for state dignity or sovereignty. This respect was further emphasized by the comparatively speedy proposal and ratification of the Eleventh Amendment, which became effective in 1798. This was im- *Eleventh* mediately occasioned by the Court's sustaining a civil suit against the *Amendment* state of Georgia by a citizen of South Carolina.[11] This seemed at the time an undue restriction on state power, although there was clear language in Article III of the Constitution to support the decision. The Eleventh Amendment eliminated the restriction for the states by providing that the "judicial power of the United States shall not be construed to extend to any suit in law or equity, commenced or prosecuted against one of the United States by citizens of another State, or by citizens or subjects of any foreign State." The constitutional change was not necessary to protect the state against suit by its own citizens.

The Eleventh Amendment does not preclude action in lower federal courts by injured persons against state officials for violation or denial of rights provided in the Constitution. Furthermore, states and also the national government may voluntarily provide for claimants of official debts or damage to come into court for settlement.

The national Constitution not only reserves broad powers and sets up important guarantees to the states; it also imposes certain restrictions on state practices. These restrictions are to be found in the original text and in certain amendments adopted after the Civil War. No amendment prior *Prohibitions* to that war reduced the comparative power of the states in the federal *on the states* system. A large number of cases decided by the Supreme Court have hinged on these constitutional restrictions, and so have a few laws of Congress. Detailed discussion of the chief limits on state powers may be found in Chapter 4.

The states are denied certain powers which are delegated to the national government. These concern such subjects as war, standing armies, *Exclusive* foreign relations, foreign and interstate commerce, legal-tender money, *national* patents and copyrights, tariffs, naturalization of aliens, maritime law, *powers* and the government of territories or colonies.

Although the conduct of foreign relations is delegated to the national government and denied to the states, the states do participate, in effect, in American foreign relations in a variety of indirect ways. Action of state legislatures or state officials has on many occasions complicated our relations with other nations, such as the California restriction on landholding by Japanese residents

---

[11] *Chisholm* v. *Georgia,* 2 Dall. 419 (1793).

in President Wilson's administration and the removal of Italian citizens from
jail in New Orleans by a lynching party in 1891. "Red light" bandit
States and Caryl Chessman received an eleventh-hour sixty-day reprieve from the
foreign gas chamber in 1960 when the U. S. State Department relayed to Gover-
relations nor Pat Brown of California an Uruguayan protest against his execution. Uruguayan officials had feared hostile demonstrations at the forthcoming
visit of President Eisenhower to Uruguay. Other State Department efforts to
influence state and local actions have been less successful, such as the insistence
of Mayor Miriani of Detroit on snubbing Soviet deputy premier Koslov when
he visited that city in 1959, even after two appeals from the State Department
for an official welcome.[12]

No state shall "pass any bill of attainder, *ex post facto* law, or law impairing the obligation of contracts, or grant any title of nobility."[13] The Fourteenth
Amendment specifies that citizens of the United States are citizens of the state
where they reside and further states:

> No State shall make or enforce any law which shall abridge the privileges or
> immunities of citizens of the United States; nor shall any State deprive any
> person of life, liberty, or property, without due process of law; nor deny to
> any person within its jurisdiction the equal protection of the laws.

Part of this language is taken from the Fifth Amendment, which restricts the
national government.

Important constitutional provisions equally restrict the state and national
governments. Among these provisions are the amendments prohibiting slavery
and suffrage discrimination.

Congress in admitting a state to the Union may enforce restrictions on
the initial constitution and government as the price of admission. Once in the
Union, however, a new state is on a par with the others in the constitu-
New states on tional system. Most advance pledges have been observed, but there are
equal footing exceptions. Oklahoma disregarded a requirement not to remove the state
capital from Guthrie within five years after admission.[14] Arizona, after
admission, restored a constitutional provision for the recall of judges which had
been deleted as a prerequisite to admission. The equality which the new state

---

[12] For a detailed account of the states' involvement in American foreign relations, *see* Dennis
J. Palumbo's *The States and American Foreign Relations* (Unpublished Ph.D. dissertation,
University of Chicago, 1960).

[13] Article I, section 10.

[14] *See Coyle* v. *Smith*, 221 U. S. 559 (1911), where the Court, sustaining the Oklahoma law
which provided for the removal, established the principle that new states enter the Union
on a footing of constitutional equality with the original states.

enjoys does not render it free to violate contracts or conditions relating to   35
property which have been imposed as requirements for admission. It is a
political equality.[15]

FEDERAL-STATE COOPERATION:
THE "NEW FEDERALISM"

To give only the formal constitutional picture of national-state relations
would be to give an incomplete one, for it is easy to conclude that American
government is a kind of layer cake with its functions and activities care-
fully parceled out either to the states or to the national government, and   *Layer cake or*
with the states parceling out some of its functions to local governments.   *marble cake?*
According to Professor Morton Grodzins:

> A far more accurate image is the rainbow or marble cake, characterized by an
> inseparable mingling of differently colored ingredients, the colors appearing
> in vertical and diagonal strands and unexpected whirls. As colors are mixed
> in the marble cake, so functions are mixed in the American federal system.[16]

Irrespective of whether the layer-cake analogy for American government
actually was at one time a true picture (Grodzins thinks it *never* was), few
would deny that today federal-state relationships are characterized far
more by cooperation, coordination, and the sharing of power, than by   *Cooperative*
separation and competition. State government, national government, and   *federalism*
local government may get together in joint action on a highway project,
in fighting an epidemic, or in running down a "public enemy number one"
wanted for trial in their several courts. All three may act jointly in serving
farmers through a county agent, in assisting welfare clients, in providing lunches
for needy school children, in utilizing hydroelectric power, and in numerous
other ways. The state may receive money from the national treasury and use
it for direct benefits to citizens or through the agency of local governments,
according to legal provisions at Washington and the state capital. The citizen

---

[15] See *Stearns* v. *Minnesota,* 179 U. S. 223 (1900), and *Ervien* v. *United States,* 251 U. S.
41 (1919), cases in which such non-political, or business, conditions were enforced.

[16] Grodzins, *op. cit.,* p. 265. See also Daniel J. Elazar, *The American Partnership. Intergovernmental Co-operation in the Nineteenth-Century United States* (University of Chicago
Press, Chicago, 1962).

36   as taxpayer may know which government is taking his money, but the citizen as recipient does not always know which government or governments should be credited for the services. Taxes go increasingly to the central government, whether state or national, and expenditures flow increasingly from the center. The criteria for taxing and for spending reflect the disparate resources of the different levels of government and the need to equalize governmental services in rich and poor jurisdictions.

The interplay of federal, state, county, and city responsibilities in most contemporary governmental activity may be illustrated by the following descrip-

The case of the inter-related sanitarian

tion of the work of the health officer, known as "sanitarian," in a rural county in a border state:

> The sanitarian is appointed by the state under merit standards established by the federal government. His base salary comes jointly from state and federal funds, the county provides him with an office and office amenities and pays a portion of his expenses, and the largest city in the county also contributes to his salary and office by virtue of his appointment as a city plumbing inspector. It is impossible from moment to moment to tell under which governmental hat the sanitarian operates. His work of inspecting the purity of food is carried out under federal standards; but he is enforcing state laws when inspecting commodities that have not been in interstate commerce; and somewhat perversely he also acts under state authority when inspecting milk coming into the county from producing areas across the state border. He is a federal officer when impounding impure drugs shipped from a neighboring state; a federal-state officer when distributing typhoid immunization serum; a state officer when enforcing standards of industrial hygiene; a state-local officer when inspecting the city's water supply; and (to complete the circle) a local officer when insisting that the city butchers adopt more hygienic methods of handling their garbage. But he cannot and does not think of himself as acting in these separate capacities. All business in the county that concerns public health and sanitation he considers his business. Paid largely from federal funds, he does not find it strange to attend meetings of the city council to give expert advise on matters ranging from rotton apples to rabies control. He is even deputized as a member of both the city and county police forces.[17]

Intergovernmental relations are more prevalent in disbursing than in collecting public funds. The pattern in government as in business points toward centralization and standardization of financial management for reasons of

Centralized taxing with decentralized spending

economy, efficiency, and accountability. The closer government is to the people, the harder it finds the task of extracting revenue from the people but the easier or less restrictive it finds the role of spending avail-

----

[17] *Ibid.*, pp. 265-266.

able funds. The one national government surpasses most of the fifty state governments in the effectiveness and efficiency of revenue policies, including taxation and borrowing. The fifty state governments likewise surpass most of the thousands of local jurisdictions in revenue management, although many of the local jurisdictions surpass their state governments in this respect. Moreover, centralized taxes on incomes, business, and business transactions of a burdensome nature are less disruptive of the private economic system than would be equivalent exaction through a variety of taxes imposed by the many local units of government. Hence the national and state governments collect billions in revenue to be expended through decentralized local channels with accountability to central authorities. Such a pattern of government seems to fit into a pattern of human behavior. Many a respectable citizen complains bitterly because he pays heavy taxes to the national government but at the same time he praises his governor or local official for achieving progress based partly on federal funds made possible by the taxes he objects to. To spend is more politic than to tax, and intergovernmental relations seeem to thrive on joint sponsorship of popular projects and services.

Much of the expansion of government has been brought about by federal aid to the states. Federal aid is not new, although it has taken on new scope and variety since 1900. It is as old as the Constitution. In planning for territories beyond the Alleghenies before Washington became president, *The beginnings of federal aid* Congress provided for land grants to support public education in the future states. This policy was followed for other territories and states carved out of the national domain. The "land grant" colleges, which were launched under legislation enacted during the Civil War to meet vocational needs, exemplify federal and state cooperation in sponsoring higher education. The older states containing no United States lands were given titles to lands in other states which were to be sold and the proceeds used to help underwrite the costs of such colleges. Congress subsequently adopted plans for cash support for experiment stations and extension services at these colleges. The Smith-Lever Act of 1914 inaugurated further aid for agricultural education in the form of federal-state support of farm demonstration agents in the hundreds of rural counties on a fifty-fifty basis. Early federal aid for internal improvements and the later land grants for railroads in the states and territories foreshadowed the federal-state highway program of the twentieth century.

The Federal Aid Road Act of 1916 anticipated the large-scale policy of federal aid to the states as known today. The coming of the automobile stimulated an existing demand for improvement of public roads, a legitimate government enterprise. County and private maintenance could no longer *The "good roads" movement* meet the needs of modern America. Organizations and individuals got behind a "good roads" movement, on which many state leaders and

FEDERAL-STATE COOPERATION

national legislators founded political careers. To accommodate interstate and local traffic and to offset the financial inadequacies of many states, the federal government was brought into the picture. There was no hesitancy on scores of "bureaucracy," "creeping socialism," or "violation of states' rights." Government and people, as on other occasions, were meeting a condition, not following a theory. It was understood that both the state and national governments possessed the constitutional power to develop public highways. Congress has the expressed authority to "establish post offices and post roads" as well as the implied power to provide transportation facilities for defense and possibly for other purposes. The "post roads" power was not a mere pretext for granting federal aid, as the new system of rural free delivery of mail was rapidly spreading over all important roads.

Congress and the state legislatures coordinated efforts in expanding the matching pattern, which was to become a permanent practice for highway construction as well as for other purposes. Under this policy Congress grants money to the states for specified purposes, provided the states match the funds or meet a specified ratio and also comply with certain other requirements as to standards of work. Every offer is an inducement, not a club, and state acceptance is virtually the universal rule. By 1960 the national government was annually advancing more than three billion dollars to the states for the aid of primary highways, secondary or feeder roads, urban connections, and the new interstate highways. This aid has combined with state gasoline taxes in providing the chief means for establishing the most extensive highway system in the world.

The federal highway legislation of 1916 set up standards of cooperation for the state and national governments in the administration of joint projects, with the states exercising the initiative within defined limits and the

Joint administration government at Washington acting in an advisory, supervisory, and auditing capacity. The states were required to have or to establish central highway departments or agencies to execute their part of the undertakings. A national agency eventually known as the Bureau of Public Roads was set up to manage the national phases of the work. It was first in the Department of Agriculture, then in the Federal Works Agency, and finally, in 1949, in the Department of Commerce. Much of the local government responsibility for road construction and maintenance thus passed to the joint central management of state and national authorities.

Highways are not the only purposes served by federal grants-in-aid. As already indicated, agriculture and education receive assistance, and the great depression of the 1930's brought vast sums of federal money to the states

Other uses of grants-in-aid for relief and welfare activities, much of it on a non-matching basis. Local units of government also shared in various ways in federal grants in those days of need, and this sharing was to continue after the back of the depression was broken. Not only city streets but also city building and sewage projects were made legitimate purposes for federal aid. The problem of planning for civilian defense in the event of atomic warfare has opened up a broad new field of federal aid to the states and their urban communities.

A vast amount of federal financing in cooperation with the states is involved in the system of Social Security, which was started by congressional legislation in 1935, amended in 1939, and widely expanded after World War II. Besides receiving grants-in-aid for important welfare purposes, *Social* all the states are eligible for funds for insuring workers against unem- *security* ployment. The funds are derived from taxes on payrolls of employers of eight or more workers in business and industry. The national tax for the purpose is compulsory, but a 90 per cent credit or offset is allowed for state collections from the taxpayper for unemployment insurance. There is also provision for financial assistance to the state "for the proper and efficient administration of its unemployment compensation law and of its public employment offices" out of the remaining federal 10 per cent. Wisconsin already had a plan of unemployment insurance, and all the other states fell in line with plans and funds after the action by Congress in 1935. Subsequent discussion will show wide variations among the states in the scope and methods of unemployment insurance. But all of them have met national standards through legislative and administrative action, including the establishment of personnel merit systems extending down to county administrative employees.

Federal aid, particularly for welfare purposes, has not escaped challenge in the courts. Two Massachusetts suits claiming unconstitutionality of the Federal Child Hygiene Act reached the Supreme Court for decision in 1923. The Court, rejecting the argument that the law, through federal *Federal aid* aid, was effectively inducing the states to yield a portion of their sovereign *before the* rights, dismissed the cases as not having a jurisdictional basis under the *courts* constitutional tax clauses.[18]

A somewhat similar case against the unemployment insurance features of the Social Security program brought forth a sweeping majority opinion by Justice Cardozo. This opinion denied the employer's claims of unconstitutionality, unfairness, and abuse of the federal tax power, holding that the congressional provisions were not coercive but were designed to facilitate voluntary joint action by the national and state governments in meeting welfare problems of vital concern to both. The Court observed that "the relief of unemployment" was a task on which "nation and state may lawfully cooperate."[19] That lawful cooperation was to expand without effective constitutional challenge.

---

[18] *Massachusetts* v. *Mellon* and *Frothingham* v. *Mellon,* 262 U. S. 447 (1923).
[19] *Steward Machine Co.* v. *Davis,* 301 U. S. 548 (1937).

40

*Appraisal of
federal aid*

The Federal aid technique enables the national government to walk the tight-rope of avoiding legal encroachment upon reserved powers of the states by entering into partnership with state governments. The United States government in this manner seeks to maintain national standards in public service by providing aid at the weakest spots. Federal aid to state education may bring funds from the wealthier sections to poorer sections for children who are likely in time to seek opportunity in the wealthier sections. The grant-in-aid policy serves partly to balance or distribute the financial burden of government in the federal system. It tends to synchronize continent-wide spending with decentralized needs and with the centralized taxing power, borrowing power, and monetary power of the United States government.

Federal aid is sometimes criticized as a form of bribery to the states to waive their constitutional rights, as centralized extravagance in government, and as an unfair method of taking from the more provident states which have made a real tax effort and giving to the less responsible states which have been willing to impose only light taxes upon their citizens. It is further criticized as a distorting influence upon state governments to slight important needs outside the scope of federal aid in favor of too much attention to fields in which there is national help. Opposition is strongest in realms where public and private enterprise are both involved, as in housing and education. In public education additional issues arise over the separation of church and state, in connection with the question of aid to parochial schools, as well as over racial segregation.

However, with allowance for criticisms and exceptions, it may be said that the general trend is toward an increasing reliance by the states and their local units upon federal grants-in-aid. It may be expected that such funds will continue to constitute important items in national and state budgets.

*Other forms
of coop-
eration*

There are other ways, outside the scope of grants-in-aid, by which the national and state governments work together, formally and informally. Congressional legislation frequently dovetails with state laws. An example has been the regulation of the liquor traffic so as not to permit interstate shipment into dry states. Another is the provision against the interstate shipment of prison-made products into states where the sale of such merchandise is illegal. In support of petroleum conservation, the Connally Act of 1935 banned interstate shipment of "hot oil" produced or supplied in violation of state law.

A high degree of uniformity in state inheritance levies resulted from the national policy, started in 1926, of allowing persons liable for federal inheritance taxes a credit or offset up to 80 per cent of the national obligation for payment of state inheritance taxes. This provision was unsuccessfully challenged by the government of Florida, which had been attracting aged rich from other states by its lack of inheritance levies. But the arrangement was satisfactory to the states having such a tax, and Florida within a few years moved into line to get funds which otherwise would fall to the United States government. Only Nevada is now without this tax.

Officials of the federal and state governments cooperate in many kinds of activities, both informally and through legal arrangements. The Federal Bureau of Investigation gives technical instruction and assistance to state law enforcement officers and aids in running down particular criminals. Federal and state health authorities work together, as do their colleagues in the agricultural agencies. The Tennessee Valley Authority cooperates with state agencies and institutions in numerous activities. Important state and private libraries serve as depositories for United States government documents as a service to the public. Many other cooperative activities might be cited such as President Theodore Roosevelt's initiation of the annual state governors' conference to explore problems common to the states and the nation, at the time notably that of conservation. Experience during World War II revealed that federal-state cooperation could take place with surprising speed when the circumstances required it. Barely a week after the attack on Pearl Harbor, the Office of Price Administration asked the governors to set up cooperative machinery in the states for the rationing of scarce commodities. The result was one of our more remarkable administrative feats, a nationwide rationing program beginning with tires, automobiles, and sugar, put into action in the space of three weeks. It was a committee of federal and state officials which made plans for the nation-wide 35 mph speed limit enforced during World War II by all states for the conservation of tires and gasoline.[20]

Executive and administrative cooperation

EFFORTS TO REVERSE THE NEW FEDERALISM: A CASE SUMMARY

Within the past decade or two there have been several serious and well-organized efforts not only to *halt* the trend toward increased federal responsibilities, expenditures, and grants-in-aid, but also to *reverse* the trend by returning to the states as many functions as possible. The first and second Hoover Commissions on Executive Organization (1947-49 and 1953-55), the Kestnbaum Commission on Intergovermental Relations (1953-55), and the Joint Federal-State Action Committee (1957-59), were all con-

Four special study commissions

---

[20] For details of these and other examples of federal-state cooperation, *see* Glenn E. Brooks, *When Governors Convene* (The Johns Hopkins Press, Baltimore, 1961).

42 cerned in varying degrees with minimizing federal activities. The almost monotonous failure of each group to accomplish this purpose should not have been surprising to anyone who has followed the history of the development of increased federal responsibilities, and who has observed with some degree of realism the interplay of forces which produced and sustain the new, "cooperative federalism." It was certainly ironic that one of the few tangible results of the Kestnbaum Commission's recommendation was legislation *increasing* federal responsibility in the field of civil defense.

Why have such efforts to reverse the centralization trends been so unsuccessful? A brief account of the work of the Joint Federal-State Action Committee should be helpful in answering this question.[21] The JFSAC came

The Joint Federal- State Action Committee

into existence as a result of an address by President Eisenhower to the Governors' Conference in 1957 calling for a committee to move from the study phase to the action phase in the matter of reallocating responsibilities and taxes in the federal system. The President suggested the following tasks for the commitee:

1. To designate functions which the states are ready and willing to assume and finance that are now performed or financed wholly or in part by the federal government;

2. To recommend the federal and state revenue adjustments required to enable the states to assume such functions; and

3. To identify functions and responsibilities likely to require state or federal attention in the future and to recommend the level of state effort, or federal effort, or both, that will be needed to assure effective action. In designating the functions to be reassumed by the states, the committee should also specify when those functions should be assumed — the amounts by which federal taxes should be reduced — and increases in state revenues needed to support the transferred functions.[22]

The governors responded quickly and the committee which was subsequently established seemed, on the surface at least, to have every prospect of success in its task. The President's appointees were distinguished and

An auspicious beginning

able men, including three leading members of the President's cabinet and the director of the Bureau of the Budget. Ten governors represented the Governors' Conference on the committee, and the chairmanship was shared by a governor and a national official. No representatives of Congress or of local government served on the committee, however. Its members received strong support from the President and worked hard and seriously at the job,

---

[21] This account relies heavily on the description by Glenn E. Brooks, *op. cit.*, pp. 100-105.

[22] *Proceedings of the Governors' Conference*, 1957, p. 99, as quoted in Brooks, *op. cit.*, p. 101.

with excellent staff studies being supplied by the Budget Bureau, the White
House, the Treasury Department, and the Council of State Governments. In
addition they had the benefit of sixteen volumes recently completed for the
Kestnbaum Commission. Morton Grodzins has summarized the initial favorable
prospects of the committee as follows:

> There existed no disagreements on party lines within the committee and, of
> course, no constitutional impediments to its mission. The President, his cabi-
> net members, and all the governors (with one possible exception) on the com-
> mittee completely agreed on the desirability of decentralization-via-separation-
> of-functions-and-taxes. They were unanimous in wanting to justify the
> committee's name and to produce action, not just another report.[23]

The committee worked for more than two years before abandoning its
efforts. At the outset it began with caution, avoiding such tough problems as
employment security, public assistance, and highway construction, and easing
into the less controversial matters, such as migratory labor, flood insurance, federal lands, estate taxes, state taxation of interstate business, vocational education,
and municipal waste treatment plant construction. Only in the case of the last
two programs did the committee recommend transfer from federal to state
hands. These two programs, which concerned vocational education and municipal waste treatment plants, accounted for about two per cent of all federal grants
to the states in 1957, or less than 80 million dollars. Effectuation of even these
modest proposals bogged down in the difficulties of finding an acceptable financial arrangement for the transfer to the states. The committee first recommended
that the states be credited with 40 per cent of the federal local telephone
service tax, but a number of governors protested that a change to local collections of such a tax would favor the more populous states. The committee then
reworked its proposals to provide for complicated equalizing arrangements and
for gradual federal disengagement rather than immediate withdrawal.

Glen Brooks reports that the Governors' Conference "responded warily
to the work of the committee." The first co-chairman of the committee, Governor
Lane Dwinell of New Hampshire, made the following comment in 1958
on the difficulties of getting down to specific cases:

*Resistance
to change*

> Nothing is easier . . . than to speculate *philosophically* on the respective roles
> of the various levels of government. On the other hand . . . nothing is more
> difficult than to attempt to spell out recommendations for the assignment or
> reassignment in specific areas. As is ever the case, interested groups are willing
> to modify or alter relationships in other fields than their own; but when it

[23] Grodzins, *op. cit.*, p. 268.

concerns a subject matter close to their own hearts, not even divine intervention is permissible without much and heavy protest.[24]

Some of the governors' comments were openly critical of the recommendations of the joint action committee, such as this statement by Governor
Orville L. Freeman of Minnesota:

> These recommendations have failed to generate any enthusiasm among the
> Governors or, for that matter, anyone else — the White House, Congress, state
> legislators or public groups. In fact, the most notable aspect of the report is
> the heavy silence that has followed its release. The cool response is due, sim-
> ply, to the fact that the recommendations are all politically and financially
> unrealistic. Many Governors shudder at the prospect — remote as it is — that
> one or more of them might in time be adopted.[25]

President Eisenhower included in his legislative recommendations to
Congress the withdrawal of the national government from vocational education
and waste treatment programs, with corresponding credits on the federal local
telephone tax. Any chances of adopting his plan were destroyed when Congress
repealed the local telephone service tax in its entirety. The governors showed
no enthusiasm for taking over two federal programs if it required re-enacting
locally a tax just repealed nationally by Congress. Columnist Roscoe Drummond
expressed the belief that the states had no desire to take back any
functions. Concerning the work of JFSAC he concluded that nothing
was accomplished. "No State has acted to take back a single function."
Three reasons stood out, in his view, for the failure: (1) governors of
the wealthy states did not fear national encroachments; (2) those governors who
genuinely wanted to take over certain federal programs were unwilling to pay
the political price involved in raising the necessary taxes, even if the way were
paved by federal abandonment of the same taxes; and (3) some governors "would
rather have the states' rights issue to talk about than to solve." The latter governors, according to Drummond, are really opposed to the performance of
certain services by *any* level of government, national or state, and the claim
that the service should be performed by the states rather than the national
government is merely a smoke screen for their opposition to the activity itself.[26]

Reasons for failure

The "post-script" to this case summary of fruitless efforts to reverse the
"new federalism" may seem strange, indeed, but a new (permanent) Advisory

---

[24] *Proceedings of the Governors' Conference*, 1958, pp. 11-12, as quoted in Brooks, *op. cit.*,
p. 103.

[25] *Ibid.*, p. 29, as quoted in Brooks, *op. cit.*, p. 103.

[26] *New York Herald Tribune*, August 5, 1959, as summarized in Brooks, *op. cit.*, pp. 104-
105.

Commission on Intergovernmental Relations was created by act of Congress 45
in 1959. After this enactment the JFSAC, which had no statutory
basis discontinued operations and gave its records to the new commission. Membership on the advisory commission was made sufficiently
different from that of the JFSAC that one former governor expressed
the fear that there was an attempt to "outflank the governors" with
local government officials and state legislators.[27]. Only four governors were
appointed to the twenty-six member commission, along with four mayors and
three county officials. The insignia appearing on the commission's reports,
shown in Figure 2-1, contain the slogan: "FOR A MORE PERFECT UNION — FED-
ERAL, STATE, LOCAL," possibly symbolizing a new status for *local* governments in
a three-way partnership. The advisory commission's functions coincide in many
respects with previous commissions, but its early work indicates at least two
principal differences: (1) a greater concern for urban and metropolitan
aspects of intergovernmental relations; and (2) more emphasis upon coordinating federal-state-local relationships than upon finding ways of separating
specific functions on the basis of levels of government.[28]

*Advisory
Commission
on Inter-
governmental
Relations*

Figure 2-1. Insignia of U. S. Advisory Commission on Intergovernmental Relations

---

[27] Brooks, *op. cit.*, p. 107.

[28] *See*, for example, their action-oriented study of *Factors Affecting Voter Reactions to
Governmental Reorganization in Metropolitan Areas* (Advisory Commission on Intergovernmental Relations, Washington, May, 1962), and an earlier report by this commission on
*Intergovernmental Responsibilities for Mass Transportation Facilities and Services in Metro-
politan Areas* (April, 1961).

EFFORTS TO REVERSE THE NEW FEDERALISM

Intergovernmental relations for the states are not all vertical (between a state and the national government); there are also horizontal relationships among states. These were given some attention by the Founding Fathers, though not very much, but in recent years the area of interstate cooperation has grown steadily. The Constitution requires that "Full faith and credit shall be given in each State to the public acts, records, and judicial proceedings of every other State." This enjoinder applies only to civil matters, for no state is expected to enforce the criminal laws of another. A deed, mortgage, contract, will, property judgment, or other civil instrument executed and recorded according to law in one state is recognized and accepted in every other state concerned. A marriage in one state is recognized in another, although the marriage laws of the two states may differ. "Full faith and credit" usually applies to divorces in the case of removal of divorcees from state to state. The United States Supreme Court has held, however, that North Carolina need not recognize a migratory divorce secured in Nevada by actual inhabitants of North Carolina, who, according to proof, had never become bona fide residents of Nevada.[29] Subsequently the Court held that where both parties participate in the proceedings and have opportunity to contest the jurisdictional issues, the decree may not be subjected to attack in the courts of another state on the ground of jurisdiction. Full faith and credit must be accorded to the decree.[30]

State-to-state obligations "full faith and credit"

Another state-to-state obligation concerns the rendition of fugitives accused or convicted of crime. The Constitution states:

Rendition of fugitive criminals

> A person charged in any State with treason, felony, or other crime, who shall flee from justice, and be found in another State, shall on demand of the executive authority of the State from which he fled, be delivered up, to be removed to the State having jurisdiction of the crime.

Under this provision as supplemented by national legislation, a fugitive, to be extradited, must be officially accused of committing crime within the borders of the state seeking his return. If a person, for example, commits murder in Louisiana and is arrested as a fugitive in California, the governor of Louisiana sends a signed requisition, with a copy of the indictment, for return of the fugitive. Normally the governor of California honors the requisition, and the

---

[29] *Williams v. North Carolina,* 325 U. S. 226 (1945).

[30] *See Sherrer v. Sherrer,* 334 U. S. 343 (1948), and *Coe v. Coe,* 334 U. S. 378 (1948).

prisoner is brought back by a Louisiana officer to be tried in a court of the latter state. However, there are occasional exceptions to the policy of returning fugitives, with no provision for overriding the will of a governor refusing to honor a requisition. The Supreme Court has declined to intervene. A conspicuous case some years ago was that in which the governor of New Jersey deciding disputes and adjusting problems between states. Article III extends story in *I Am A Fugitive From A Georgia Chain Gang!*[31]

The framers of the Constitution authorized two important methods for deciding disputes and adjusting problems between states. Article III extends the judicial power of the United States to controversies between two or more states, with the Supreme Court having original jurisdiction in such cases. Many disputes have been settled in this manner. Article I, section 10, permits a state, with the consent of Congress, to enter into an "agreement or compact with another State." Congress and groups of states have utilized this permission, expressed or implied, for more than a hundred interstate compacts. Most of the earlier compacts were merely agreements on boundary lines, but more recent compacts have ventured into areas of economic and social regulation where two or more states share the same problem. *Disputes and agreements between states*

One of the better known compacts established the Port of New York Authority in 1921, with New York and New Jersey jointly tackling the construction and management of port facilities, interstate bridges, tunnels, bus and truck terminals, and airports. Several interstate compacts deal with the conservation of natural resources, such as the Columbia River salmon runs and the migratory fisheries of the Atlantic states, where action by one one state would be futile. *Interstate compacts*

The future growth and effectiveness of interstate compacts is by no means clear. As states move more and more into regulatory and service fields, they run into increasing difficulties of interstate negotiation and congressional approval. States have urged Congress to adopt consent-in-advance legislation in certain fields as a means of encouraging intergovernmental cooperation, but advance consent has only rarely been given. A variety of political cross-currents, including opposition pressures from federal agencies, constitute obstacles to many proposed interstate compacts. The "consent-of-Congress" requirement has been held by the Supreme Court to apply only if they tend "to increase the political power in the states, which may encroach upon or interfere with the just supremacy of the United States."[32] After efforts of the Conference of Southern Governors to obtain congressional consent *Requirement of congressional consent*

---

[31] Vanguard Press, New York, 1932.

[32] *Virginia* v. *Tennessee,* 148 U. S. 503.

to a regional education compact were rebuffed, the Conference in 1948 decided that consent was not required after all and proceeded to put the plan into operation. The plan involved joint state tax support for professional and higher education for both whites and Negroes in the southern states, but because it was looked upon by many as a device to preserve segregated education, the Senate sent it back to the judiciary committee by a vote of 38 to 37. The southern argument that, since education is one of the states' reserved powers, the compact did not require congressional approval, seems to have prevailed. As a device to preserve racial segregation, however, the contracting states could hardly expect it to obtain court approval.[33]

The Interstate compact is by no means the only method of interstate cooperation. Through the years various interstate organizations have arisen to work in a multitude of ways for cooperation among the states. The

Other forms of coop- eration

oldest is the National Conference of Commissioners on Uniform State Laws, organized in 1892. Its purpose has been to simplify transactions across state lines, and more than 100 "model laws" have been drafted and recommended to state legislatures. All states have adopted the model laws on negotiable instruments, warehouse receipts, and stock transfer. Progress in adopting the others has been less successful, with only nine model laws being accepted by as many as 40 states. Several organizations of state officials have been established on a national basis, including the governors, attorneys general, budget officers, and chief justices.

The Council of State Governments, established in 1925, has been called the "holding corporation" or "clearinghouse" for interstate cooperation. Serving as an overall umbrella for interstate exchange of information, conferences, and research projects, "Cosgo" acts as secretariat for several of the organizations of state officials and publishes *The Book of the States* (a biennial reference book on state government), *State Government* (a monthly journal), and special reports from time to time. It has been an active participant in the recent national studies of intergovernmental relations.

---

[33] For details of the political and constitutional issues involved in the Southern Regional Education Compact, see Vincent V. Thursby's *Interstate Cooperation* (Public Affairs Press, Washington, 1953). On interstate compacts generally, see Richard H. Leach and R. S. Sugg, *The Administration of Interstate Compacts* (Louisiana State University Press, Baton Rouge, 1959) and Frederick L. Zimmermann and Mitchell Wendell, *The Interstate Compact Since 1925* (Council of State Governments, Chicago, 1951).

Anderson, William, *The Nation and the States: Rivals or Partners?* (University of Minnesota Press, Minneapolis, 1955).

Clark, Jane, *The Rise of a New Federalism* (Columbia University Press, New York, 1938).

The Federalist, ed., H. C. Lodge (New York, 1888), Numbers 8, 44-46.

Grodzins, Morton, "The Federal System," in *Goals for Americans, The Report of the President's Commission on National Goals* (The American Assembly, Columbia University, 1960).

Leach, Richard H., and R. S. Sugg, Jr., *The Administration of Interstate Compacts* (Louisiana State University Press, Baton Rouge, 1959).

Maass, Arthur, ed., *Area and Power: A Theory of Local Government* (The Free Press, Glencoe, 1959).

Macmahon, A. W., ed., *Federalism Mature and Emergent* (Doubleday & Company, Inc., Garden City, N. Y., 1955).

Mansfield, Harvey C., "The States in the American System," in *The Forty-eight States: Their Tasks as Policy Makers* (School of Business, Columbia University, New York, 1955).

Nixon, H. C., *American Federal Government* (Charles Scribner's Sons, New York, 1952), Chapters 5 and 31.

Swisher, C. B., *Theory and Practice of American National Government* (Houghton Mifflin Company, Boston, 1951), Part 8.

Thursby, Vincent V., *Interstate Cooperation: A Study of the Interstate Compact* (Public Affairs Press, Washington, 1953).

U. S. Commission on Intergovernmental Relations, *A Report to the President for Transmittal to the Congress* (Government Printing Office, Washington, 1955).

Vile, M. J. C., *The Structure of American Federalism* (Oxford University Press, Inc., New York, 1961).

White, Leonard D., *The States and the Nation* (Louisiana State University Press, Baton Rouge, 1953).

★ 3 ★

CITIES IN THE FEDERAL SYSTEM

A<small>LTHOUGH IT</small> is essential to view the federal system through the eyes of the states, as we did in the preceding chapter, this view by itself is not enough. It is becoming increasingly important to look at the federal system through the eyes of cities. The former view is traditional and time-honored, whether in classroom courses in American government and history, or in U. S. Senate orations on the illustrious origins of states' rights. But the rising tide of urbanism, suburbanism, and metropolitanism in the United States has thrust a third force into the workings of federalism, and its magnitude is too great to ignore or to accommodate with a few minor adjustments in the system.

The urban view of federalism

The rural and agricultural America described by Katherine Lee Bates in "America the Beautiful," with her "spacious skies," "amber waves of grain," "purple mountain majesties," and "fruited plain," is an America seen by most urbanized Americans only in their memory or on vacation trips. In the fourth stanza Miss Bates seems to have prophesied present reality with her reference to "alabaster cities" seen only in patriots' dreams. A few of the implications of the shift from a nation only 5 per cent urban in 1790 to a nation 70 per cent urban in 1960 were touched upon in Chapter 1, but it is the purpose of this chapter to consider more fully the relationship of cities and the federal system.

50

This involves more than the impact of cities on the federal system; it includes the oft-ignored other side of the coin — the impact of the federal system on cities and, perhaps more important, on metropolitan areas.

THE CONSTITUTIONAL STATUS OF CITIES

It is no accident that American history is filled with accounts of men's political, economic, and even military activity revolving around the doctrine of states' rights, with almost no corresponding activity involving a doctrine of "cities' rights." Under the federal Constitution, cities simply have no rights as cities. The city is completely ignored by the Constitution and its language is not the place to look if one is studying the legal status of cities. So far as the federal Constitution is concerned, the only existing sub-national level of government is the state. Cities, not being mentioned, are thus nonexistent in the formal sense.

Constitutional silence on cities

In sharp contrast to this rather amazing constitutional picture of urban nonexistence is the actual picture of federal awareness of cities. In their study of *The Federal Government and Metropolitan Areas*,[1] Connery and Leach describe the staggering scale of some of the federal operations within the New York metropolitan area alone: 52 slum clearance and urban renewal projects involving federal grants of $120 million; commitments for 90,000 low-rent government housing units to the extent of $30 million per year for 40 years; $10 million to help construct 10 airports between 1947 and 1957, with $6 million pledged for additional work; $129 million for highway and bridge construction between 1953 and 1957, not counting any funds for the new interstate expressway system; 16,000 home mortgages insured by FHA in 1955 alone, totaling $170 million, with an even larger number guaranteed by the Veterans Administration in the same year; Veterans Administration hospital construction exceeding $54 million during 1957, with additional grants of $10 million and $3 million for hospitals by the Public Health Service and Defense Department; and 30 projects for port improvement in the New York area by the Army Corps of Engineers, totaling well over $100 million, and involving commitment by the Corps to maintain them at federal expense when completed. This picture of federal involvement can be found, in lesser proportions, in each metropolitan area in the United States.

Federal operations in cities

---

[1] Robert H. Connery and Richard H. Leach, *The Federal Government and Metropolitan Areas* (Harvard University Press, Cambridge, 1960), pp. 7-8.

52

It is important to realize, therefore, that federal-city relations are characterized by a constitutional and political paradox. In spite of a growing network of direct and indirect communication lines between city governments and federal agencies, the city continues to be solely a creature of one of the fifty states, subject to such obligations, privileges, powers, and restrictions as the state sees fit to prescribe. The state may create or destroy cities, which are simply "municipal corporations." With respect to *all* units of local government, including cities, "the state giveth and the state taketh away." To the extent that cities exercise power to collect taxes, regulate traffic, or enact city zoning ordinances, they are actually exercising the *state's* powers, reserved under the Tenth Amendment of the federal Constitution and duly delegated to the cities by state constitutional or statutory provision. An early effort in a few state courts to establish a doctrine of the inherent right of local self-government, such as Judge Cooley's famous Michigan decision in 1871,[2] was never able to dislodge the state supremacy doctrine. The larger cities have increasingly complained of state restrictions and especially of state legislative apportionment schemes heavily favoring rural areas as illustrated in Figure 3-1. This representation controversy is discussed in detail in Chapter 10.

The picture of the constitutional status of cities is not complete without a consideration of the application to cities of federal restrictions on states. While states may be supreme over cities, the federal government is supreme over states in many areas and these limitations apply with equal strength to cities. There are many such limitations but four will serve to illustrate. (1) The "obligation of contracts" clause in the Constitution forbids any state to pass a law impairing the obligation of contracts, and this has come to mean that a municipal corporation cannot normally withdraw from an agreement, whether that agreement is a franchise permitting a transportation company to have a 30-year monopoly on mass transportation service, or a simple contract to borrow money. On occasion, however, the state's police power takes precedence over the obligation of contracts, as discussed in Chapter 4. (2) The "tax immunity" decisions of the Supreme Court have come to mean that post offices, arsenals, navy yards, and other federal property cannot be taxed by a city except where Congress has given its consent. (3) The "equal protection of the laws" clause applies to the action of city officials and has come increasingly into the spotlight in civil rights cases where racial discrimination is charged against city schools, parks, buses, libraries, and similar services. It is this restriction which makes racial segregation of residential areas by city zoning regulations unconstitutional. (4) The "due process of law" clause becomes a federal limitation

---

[2] *People v. Hulburt*, 24 Mich. 44 (1871). See Chapter 17 for a discussion of the municipal charter and home rule.

'If You Don't Like This Situation You Can Cast Your Twentieth of a Vote Against It'

—Herblock in Washington Post

Figure 3-1. Herblock in the Washington Post

THE CONSTITUTIONAL STATUS OF CITIES

upon cities when an attempt is made to take the "life, liberty, or property" of a person (his freedom of speech, for example) in a manner the courts have come to consider arbitrary, unreasonable, or unfair.

EARLY FEDERAL-CITY RELATIONS

How can we explain the apparent discrepancy between the completely negative constitutional view of federal-city relations and the drastically revised picture one gets from looking at the realities of extensive present-day federal involvement in urban affairs? The explanation is found primarily in the use which the federal government has made of its own powers — especially the war powers, commerce powers, and spending powers, and the inevitable impact of such action on the growing urban sector of the nation. As a result of exercising its delegated and implied powers the federal government began to have direct and indirect contacts with cities, although prior to 1933 most of them were of a peripheral nature and more or less accidental.

The turning point in federal-city relationships was probably in 1932, even before the Roosevelt administration came to power. It was in that year that Congress first mentioned the word "municipalities" in a federal statute and authorized the Reconstruction Finance Corporation to make loans to states and cities in economic distress because of the depression.

Depression assistance

Although a self-liquidation restriction stymied the early operation of much of this program, it was a forerunner for a great deal more federal acceptance of direct responsibility for problems in urban centers previously thought to be purely a local responsibility. In 1933 and the years immediately following, the New Deal poured forth an avalanche of anti-depression programs through newly created "alphabetical" agencies — FERA, CWA, WPA, PWA, NRA, and many others. Many of these agencies were authorized to deal directly with the cities as well as with states, and the city-federal contract mushroomed into a very common instrument in intergovernmental relations.

Between 1933 and 1939 the Public Works Administration made grants to states, cities, and other public bodies for approved public works projects, with up to 30 per cent of the cost being paid outright and the remaining 70 per cent being financed through federal loans. Cities applied for such assistance directly to the PWA, were required to observe federally prescribed standards, and were subject to PWA inspection and audit. A different agency, the Works Progress Administration, was more exclusively an emergency work relief program aimed at immediate reduction of unemployment. Local

PWA and WPA

units of government made application to the WPA and agreed to provide most of the material and equipment, while the federal government furnished the labor and much of the administration for the projects. WPA was made the butt of many anti-administration jokes, including the label "we piddle around," but its efforts to cushion the effects of the depression resulted in the construction of thousands of miles of city streets and sewer lines, thousands of school buildings, as well as hundreds of hospitals and airports. The states were by-passed by most of these and other federal-city relationships and tended to lose face in the process, while most cities were highly satisfied with this newly acquired recognition which had previously been denied them.

Direct federal-city relationships were continued and expanded during World War II, particularly in the fields of emergency defense housing and airport construction. Even the local jails came into direct relationships with the federal government, growing out of the overcrowded conditions of *War programs* federal prisons and their need to farm out some of their prisoners. Local jails were eligible for this "extra business" only if they complied with rather rigid federal standards for facilities and operation.

RECENT FEDERAL-CITY RELATIONS

As the relationships between cities and the federal government have become more complex in the years since World War II, it has become clear that these can no longer be considered merely "emergency programs" with the obvious flavoring of depression or war. In an increasing number of federal aid programs there is an open avowal of federal responsibility to assist in meeting certain urban problems, such as for mass transportation, urban renewals, and the preservation of open space, to mention a few recent examples. Congress has responded to the growing tendency of pressure groups and *Urban* study groups interested in particular urban problems to speak of urban *problems as* problems as *national* problems and to organize themselves on a *national* *national* scale. Recent examples would include the *National* Committee on Urban *problems* Transportation, the *National* Committee on Uniform Traffic Control Devices, the *National* Outdoor Recreation Resources Review Commission, and a *national* Municipal Manpower Commission, to name only a few. Even the President's Commission on *National* Goals included as part of the "goals at home" the necessity of reversing the "process of decay in the larger cities," and for improving living conditions both in central cities and suburbs.[3]

---

[3] The italics in this paragraph have been inserted by the authors.

56

City officials have long contended, and with considerable justification, that they have been forced to go to Washington with hat in hand simply as a last resort after exhausting all efforts to secure help from the rural-dominated state government, in attacking the new problems on the urban scene. The cities have become increasingly convinced that their plea for help receives a more sympathetic ear in Washington than at their state capital; that their political leverage is weak at the state capital and strong in Washington. "Rural domination" through malapportioned state legislatures has given cities a made-to-order argument for bypassing the states and going directly to Congress with requests for financial assistance. It is not by chance that four of the more important national associations of local officials — the American Municipal Association, the United States Conference of Mayors, the National Association of County Officials, and the International Association of Chiefs of Police — have established their main offices in Washington, D. C. Some of the more recent areas of federal-city relationships are considered briefly in the discussion which follows.

Present federal activities in the field of housing reflect a historical background of wide diversity in origin and purpose. Beginning with the construction of some 16,000 units for shipyard workers during World War I, the federal government moved into additional housing programs in the depression of the thirties, during World War II, and in the post-war period. These programs were aimed at alleviating threats of wide-spread mortgage foreclosures on homes, providing more capital for private home construction by guaranteeing new mortgages, insuring small loans for home modernization and repair, providing low-rent public housing through hundreds of local housing authorities, and providing liberal housing credit for veterans under the so-called "G. I Loan Program." The total impact of these programs during the past thirty years has been to influence greatly the character of land use and the developmental pattern of virtually every city in the United States. In spite of their coercive effects on the shape of the urban community, the focus and justification of the various housing programs have been in assorted directions other than over-all community development. Symbolic of this fragmentation of purpose is a listing of some of the principal federal agencies involved in some aspect of housing: the Housing and Home Finance Agency with its several subdivisions, TVA, the Veterans Administration, the Atomic Energy Commission, and the departments of Defense, Commerce, Agriculture, and Health, Education and Welfare.

In recent years an increasing crescendo of criticism of federal housing programs has arisen, including charges that they are an "unrelated hodgepodge," have caused the rapid construction of "cracker-box suburbs," have shown little imagination in their design of low-rent public housing as barracks-like block-

houses, have been guilty of a bias against apartment houses, have not been adequately linked to other federal aid programs such as those for express
highways, and have shown a concern "too little and too late" for relating
housing programs and policies to over-all urban planning. Some of this
criticism and changing philosophy has come from the housing officials
themselves, as illustrated in a 1957 speech by Housing Administrator Albert
M. Cole:

The changing housing philosophy

> Twenty years ago we thought in terms of individuals, of houses to shelter
> them, of special aids administered through special and separate governmental
> units. Then we recognized that this was too limited, too piecemeal. We began
> to think in terms of local areas and neighborhoods and we tried to bring
> some units into government aids through a loose coordination in a single
> overall agency.
>
> In the Housing Act of 1954 we moved another long step forward. We dealt
> with the community as a whole and with housing in relation to other aspects
> of the community. In the urban renewal program, we established an approach
> that was based on overall planned action for the whole community and on
> closely integrated administration of government aids.
>
> But as we top one hill and look ahead, we find an even wider horizon ahead
> of us — another hill to climb if we are to continue to progress. In these few
> years I have discovered that even the community is not the final entity that
> we must consider — that it is part of a growing and expanding urban economy
> which moved with giant strides not only into the suburbs but into the inter-
> urban stretches that no longer define the country and the town. Today it is
> in these broader terms that we must think and plan — the community as part
> of the region, the neighborhood as part of the community, the individual home
> as part of the neighborhood. This is a far cry from the hope of twenty years
> ago that we could solve our city's problems of slums and bad housing simply
> by providing good homes for low-income families and tearing down the city's
> slums one by one, as we went along.[4]

The Housing Act of 1949 provided assistance for slum clearance and
urban redevelopment, and was broadened by the Housing Act of 1954 to introduce the concept of "urban renewal." This act authorized federal assistance to local communities not only for clearing and redeveloping slum
areas as originally provided but also for preventing the spread of slums and
urban blight by rehabilitation and conservation measures in deteriorating
areas. The federal assistance includes survey and planning advances,
loans, and capital grants of up to two-thirds of the net project cost. Subsequent
legislation has liberalized the matching provisions for localities which bear

Slum clearance and urban renewal

---

[4] Address before the National Housing Conference, Washington, D. C., June 17, 1957, as
quoted by Connery and Leach, *op. cit.*, pp. 11-12.

58   their own planning and administrative expense, and for counting approved private renewal expenditures as part of the localities' matching obligation. Under urban redevelopment a slum area is acquired through the power of eminent domain, the slum structures are cleared, the area is planned for re-use, and the cleared area is sold to private (or public) developers who are committed to develop it in compliance with the community plan. It is clear that the concepts of urban redevelopment and urban renewal involve far more than the subject of housing, but the programs are still organizationally located in housing agencies, both federal and local.

Another program of federal assistance to cities growing out of housing legislation is the program of assistance for urban planning. The Housing Act of 1954 and later amendments not only authorized grants to state planning agencies for planning assistance to cities of less than 25,000 population; grants have also been authorized to state, metropolitan, or regional agencies for planning on a metropolitan basis. By 1960 close to 100 metropolitan areas, urban regions, and special areas had received federal approval for planning projects. Federal grants are thus encouraging community-wide planning which is not limited to the boundary lines of the patchwork quilt of local governments.

Urban planning assistance

A new program to assist state and local public bodies in open-space land preservation was created by Congress in the Housing Act of 1961. It provides for federal grants of up to 20 per cent of the cost of acquiring land to be used as permanent open space, and up to 30 per cent if it involves a substantial portion of a metropolitan area or urban region. Approved uses of the open space are for parks and recreation, conservation of land or other natural resource, and for scenic or historic purposes. Its basic objectives are to help localities curb urban sprawl, blight, and deterioration, and to encourage a more desirable pattern of urban development than the asphalt landscape illustrated in Figure 3-2. Although the federal government has long been involved in recreation through its national parks, national forests, and reclamation projects, it has only recently begun to recognize that recreation is primarily an urban and metropolitan problem. The congestion of urban living, coupled with the steady increase in automation-produced leisure time, has meant that recreational pressure groups have become metropolitan pressure groups in large measure. If state governments do not move quickly to meet these new metropolitan needs, the cities can be expected to take their case to Washington.

Open-space preservation

Recreation for the metropolis

The federal government has recently taken official notice for the first time, in any specific way, of the urban problem long considered to be the most frustrating and perhaps even the most hopeless — mass transportation. Congress responded in 1961 to pleas of help for these floundering enterprises in American

'Just think, son, I remember when all this pleasing asphalt area was nothing but bushes, trees and brooks.'

Figure 3-2. Bissell in the Nashville Tennessean

cities by authorizing two programs of modest assistance. One is a mass transportation demonstration program involving grants from the Housing and Home Finance Agency to public agencies for the demonstration of new urban transportation methods, techniques, and systems designed to carry out urban transportation plans and research. Up to two-thirds *Urban mass transportation* of the cost of such "pilot projects" will be paid by the federal government, but it is required that the project be applicable or relevant to the urban transportation needs of *other* areas. In the same act Congress authorized low-interest loans, when unobtainable from private sources, for the acquisition, construction, or reconstruction and improvement of mass transportation systems in urban areas. The future role of the federal government in the field of urban mass transit is discussed at a later point in this chapter.

The federal aid program for urban streets and expressways involves important informal federal-city relations, but the states have insisted on keeping the formal relationships "very proper" in the constitutional sense, with the federal-state contacts being the primary ones. Cities have chaffed *Urban highways* under the arrangements, feeling that the result was the dominance of a *rural* roads program. The federal Bureau of Public Roads even started as an agency of the rural-oriented Department of Agriculture, where it re-

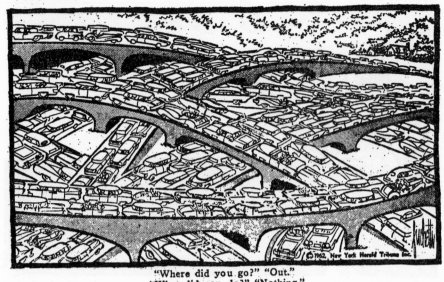

"Where did you go?" "Out."
"What did you do?" "Nothing."

Figure 3-3. Fischetti in the New York Herald Tribune

mained until 1939 when it was moved to the Federal Works Agency. It was moved to the Department of Commerce in 1949 and more recently was given an Urban Division. In recent years urban political strength in Washington has been apparent in the increased share of federal highway aid earmarked for use in cities and in federal officials' encouragement of state highway officials to work more closely with cities. For example, state highway departments are required to hold public hearings on all proposed highway construction giving all affected cities an opportunity to state their views. Subsequent project requests from the state to the federal Bureau of Public Roads will be rejected unless accompanying transcripts of public hearing indicate the affected cities have been consulted. Even the vast new program for the Interstate and Defense Highway System is essentially an urban highway program. As originally proposed it was a highway network linking the great cities of the nation, but Congress gave it the "interstate" label in apparent deference to the sanctity of federal-state relations. Even so, as Connery and Leach suggest, "it might more correctly be called the Intercity Highway System, because people want to go in and out of cities, not in and out of states."[5] The roads will carry not only

---

[5] Connery and Leach, *op. cit.,* p. 48.

long-distance traffic between 90 per cent of the nation's cities, but will carry a heavy load of urban and suburban commuter traffic.

In contrast to the pattern of highway assistance, federal-local relationships in airport construction have been direct, by-passing the states from the beginning. Prior to World War II a considerable amount of federal money was spent for constructing city airports, but it was a by-product of the depres- *Airports* sion public works programs rather than a result of a specific national airport program. Approximately 550 airports were constructed during World War II with emergency military considerations being dominant. The basic question of which level or levels of government should be responsible for airport planning, construction, and operation, was finally determined in the Federal Airport Act of 1946, which provided for essentially a direct federal-local pattern. States can be by-passed by local governments applying for federal assistance unless specifically prohibited by state law. The federal government is responsible for preparing and revising annually a national airport plan, and any "public agency" may seek assistance for projects consistent with the federal plan.

One of the strongest influences which the federal government has on cities today comes not from a consciously designed urban program but as a by-product of its most expensive activity — national defense. Citizens of Norfolk, San Diego, Corpus Christi, or Detroit do not need to be told how much *Military* military installations or defense industries can shape the physical, eco- *installations* nomic, and social development of an urban area. City chamber of com- *and defense* merce representatives vie with each other for each new prospective defense *industries* establishment, confident that it is synonymous with prosperity, but city planners, traffic officials, and budget directors know that there is another side to the picture. The necessity for large undeveloped tracts of land usually results in a location far beyond the boundaries of the city, leaving such vital matters as street design, traffic control, and land-use planning and control in the hands of ill-prepared township or county officials. By the time adequate controls have come into existence, the ribbon-like developments around the project have frequently become eyesores as well as serious problems of public health, education, law enforcement, and the like. This is a very complex and relatively unexplored problem of federal-local relations, particularly with respect to governmental obligations and opportunities for making cities liveable communities.

The impact of civil defense policies and programs on the shape of cities is *potentially* greater even than that of military programs and installations. Any really serious effort to prepare the nation for atomic attack would involve an industrial dispersion program of such magnitude as to make con- *Civil* temporary suburban sprawl seem mild by comparison. It is clear that *defense* the problem of civil defense is first of all a problem of the metropolitan areas, both because of the greater vulnerability which their congestion brings, and because they contain a majority of our human and industrial resources. Yet civil defense programs thus far have been distinguished by their failure to make any appreciable impact on cities and, in the absence of greatly heightened Cold War tensions, there seems to be little prospect for such impact. A program of federal grants-in-aid to states on a 50-50 matching basis is designed to help states and the local governments acquire civil-defense equipment and train civil-defense workers. Federal-local relationships are normally routed through the states, but can be direct under certain circumstances.

Water resources

Although the federal government has long been involved in the development and use of water resources — Congress authorized the first river improvements in 1924 — it has been only recently that cities as such have fought their way into the policy-making process for water. The federal government's relation to water resources has become unbelievably complex, involving the very old programs of improving navigation in rivers and harbors, the later programs of flood control, irrigation, and power development, and the more recent activities for water pollution control, and meeting the growing problem of water for human and industrial consumption. Irrigation policies have come increasingly under fire from cities seeking to satisfy their swelling population's seemingly unquenchable thirst. Water used for irrigation is lost for downstream urban use, and the federal government must ultimately decide whose priorities are higher. Urban involvement in stream pollution, sometimes as the offender and sometimes as the plaintiff, has also increased in recent years. A federal grant program which began in 1950 by providing assistance for studies of the problem was later expanded to include matching grants for actual construction of sewage treatment plants.

EMERGING PROBLEMS IN FEDERAL-CITY RELATIONS

The foregoing summary of federal programs affecting cities in fairly direct ways has not described in any detail the content of such programs; more detailed treatment of the specific program content may be found in later chapters. The purpose of such a quick panorama has been to focus attention on what seem to be steady and perhaps even inevitable trends toward closer federal-city ties. Out of these trends and new relationships several basic problems or questions emerge, however.

1. *Federal Relationships with Fragmented Metropolitan Areas.* Most federal aid programs, whether for urban expressways, urban renewal, or civil

defense, are strongly influenced at the performance level by the fragmentation
of "natural metropolitan communities" into small bits and pieces of governmental
units. With a few rare exceptions, federal agencies have felt compelled
to deal with these separate governmental fragments rather than with
the metropolitan area as a single entity, for the simple reason that virtually no metropolitan area is a single political entity. Some of the
federal programs require all approved projects to comply with a "regional
plan," but this is difficult to enforce meaningfully when so many metropolitan
areas have no regional planning. Congress has not seen fit to use the federal
spending power to coerce fragmented local governments into some degree of
metropolitan coordination, but by its silence Congress has undoubtedly strengthened the independent status of the small cities and special districts which make
metropolitan and regional planning and development so difficult. The result
is frequently a case of federal failure to see the metropolitan forest because of
focusing attention on the separate city trees.

City trees and metropolitan forests

2. *City Relationships with a Fragmented Federal Government.* Strangely
enough, a situation somewhat analogous to metropolitan fragmentation can be
found at the federal level. The federal fragmentation is functional rather than
geographic, however. There has never been a federal *urban* program
presented in a package to Congress in the same way that a *farm* program
is packaged for legislative purposes. Connery and Leach point out that
urban programs "are created as isolated units and are administered in
isolation from one another," and contend that the result is "a jungle of discon-
nected programs and projects, strewn among a variety of administrative agencies."[6]

Uncoordinated federal programs

The federal highway program is probably most often cited as an example
of isolation from other programs. Urban highways are only one part of the
urban transportation problem which includes the traffic and parking problems,
and bus, railroad, and air facilities and policies. To take it a step or two further,
the whole transportation problem is only one part of the problem of land-use
planning which, in turn, is only one part of over-all metropolitan planning.
Such coordination of the interstate highway program with public housing and
urban renewal programs as has actually occurred has tended to be too limited
and too late, and it has taken place in spite of the organizational isolation of
the federal programs. Similarly, the airport planning responsibility of the federal
government has not been geared in with an integrated view of the various urban
problems related to federal programs. Even with respect to the single function
of aviation, conflicts are not uncommon between the civilian and military programs in their impact on cities. Within the past few years the city of San Diego

---

[6] *Ibid.*, p. 98.

had the unusual experience of having one agency of the federal government declare its airport obsolete and approve the city's proposed new site after a long search, only to have another federal agency object to the location on grounds of interference with the near-by Naval Air Station. As the federal government moves into more and more areas — recreation, open space preservation, water supply, water pollution control, mass transportation, and others closely related to the life of cities, this problem of coordination at the federal level will become increasingly important.

3. *The Dilemmas of a Federal Department of Urban Affairs.* For many years a variety of proposals have been advanced for a new agency at the federal level devoted entirely to urban affairs. They have varied from a simple *A Depart-* inter-agency committee, which is generally recognized as a rather feeble *ment of* administrative device, to a proposal for a cabinet-level Department of *"Urbi-* Urban Affairs. The latter proposal, blessed with increasing political *culture?"* support in recent years, is not a new idea by any means. A Department of Municipalities was suggested as early as 1912 and in more recent years it has not been uncommon to have speeches in Congress on behalf of a Department of "Urbiculture" to counterbalance the rural-minded Department of Agricul- *Arguments* ture. The arguments for such a department have centered around the grow- *pro* ing need for an effective spokesman for urban interests in national policy- making at the Cabinet level. It is pointed out that 80 per cent of our population lived on farms or in rural areas in 1862 when the Office of Agricul- ture was established, but with urban population pushing toward that same percentage today, special recognition of the urban dweller's needs is now called for. It is argued that existing urban programs at the federal level, without the ad- dition of any new ones, are already of sufficient size to warrant departmental status and that the correction of the "step-child status" of several of the urban programs is long overdue. There are persuasive administrative arguments given in favor of a national Department of Urban Affairs. These arguments center upon the failure of fragmented federal agencies with isolated urban programs to treat "the whole city" in coordinated fashion, rather than in often unrelated segments. Another administrative argument pertains to the convenience of establishing a central contact point in Washington for all federal relationships with cities, rather than requiring city officials to go back and forth among several agencies in handling their business with Uncle Sam. Finally, it is contended that creating a single cabinet-level department would be the quickest and most effective way to accelerate much-needed research on a variety of urban problems, providing a unified information center for and about cities.

The idea of such a department is not without its critics, however, and not all of them are persons unfriendly to urban interests. The principal arguments against a Department of Urban Affairs, according to Connery and Leach, are that it would be "politically unwise, administratively unsound, and functionally unnecessary."[7] Politically, it is difficult to avoid the "big-city" *Arguments con* brand on the department with the word "urban" tending to alienate not only certain rural interests but also some suburban interests, which are often as opposed to the big city as their rural neighbors. Administratively, there are serious questions about the feasibility of extracting the "urban aspects" of all or parts of the federal programs and placing them in a single department. It would be the only department based on a geographical concept, as distinguished from the normal functional concept, causing some to term it an "organizational misfit" likely to create more problems than it would solve. Related to this is the argument that the real need is not for a single department dealing with cities but for a greater urban consciousness to permeate *all* federal agencies in their urban activities. In keeping with this view, some have recommended creation of a Council of Urban Affairs as a staff agency of the President, *A Council of Urban Affairs?* similar to his Council of Economic Advisors. It would be primarily an *emphasis* agency engaging in urban research and assistance to the President, who would have the job of coordinating the urban programs of the various federal agencies.

4. *Are the Cities Outgrowing the States?* The question of whether the cities are outgrowing the states is hardly a *recently* emerging problem, for it has been asked by many students of government for many years. In the 1920's Professor Charles E. Merriam repeatedly affirmed his belief that "the nation and the cities are vigorous organs," but that states are stumbling blocks which neither govern the cities nor permit the cities to govern themselves.[8] Merriam's contention that the states are going downhill has hardly been borne out in recent history, as indicated in Chapter 1, but the question continues to crop up in various contexts. The burgeoning growth of metropolitan areas across state boundary lines makes one wonder whether interstate cities, like interstate commerce, must inevitably come under federal regulation. The 1960 census revealed that one out of five citizens live in the 26 interstate metropolitan *The interstate metropolis* areas, adding up to more than 38 million persons. (*See* Table 3-1). Millions more live in metropolitan areas which border but do not yet cross state lines, making it conceivable that the time may come within the next generation or so that more people live in interstate cities than in intrastate cities.

---

[7] *Ibid.*, p. 182.

[8] *See* W. Brooke Graves, *American State Government* (3d ed.; D. C. Heath and Company, Boston, 1946), p. 943.

TABLE 3-1

INTERSTATE METROPOLITAN AREAS

Metropolitan Area	States with Part of Territory	Number of County Areas	1960 Population
New York-Northeastern New Jersey	N.Y.-N.J.	13	14,759,429
Chicago-Northwestern Indiana	Ill.-Ind.	8	6,794,461
Philadelphia	Pa.-N.J.	8	4,342,897
St. Louis	Mo.-Ill.	6	2,060,103
Washington	D.C.-Md.-Va.	7	2,001,897
Cincinnati	Ohio-Ky.	3	1,071,624
Kansas City	Mo.-Kans.	4	1,039,493
Portland	Ore.-Wash.	4	821,897
Providence-Pawtucket	R.I.-Mass.	8	816,148
Louisville	Ky.-Ind.	3	725,139
Allentown-Bethlehem-Easton	Pa.-N.J.	3	492,168
Omaha	Neb.-Iowa	3	457,873
Wilmington	Del.-N.J.	2	366,157
Chattanooga	Tenn.-Ga.	2	283,169
Duluth-Superior	Minn.-Wisc.	2	276,596
Davenport-Rock Island-Moline	Iowa-Ill.	2	270,058
Huntington-Ashland	W.Va.-Ky.-Ohio	4	254,780
Columbus	Ga.-Ala.	3	217,985
Augusta	Ga.-S.C.	2	216,639
Evansville	Ind.-Ky.	2	199,313
Wheeling	W.Va.-Ohio	3	190,342
Lawrence-Haverhill	Mass.-N.H.	2	187,601
Steubenville-Weirton	Ohio-W.V.	3	167,756
Fall River	Mass.-R.I.	2	138,156
Fargo-Moorhead	N.D.-Minn.	2	106,027
Texarkana	Tex.-Ark.	2	91,657

Source: Adapted from U. S. Advisory Commission on Intergovernmental Relations, *Intergovernmental Responsibilities for Mass Transportation Facilities and Services in Metropolitan Areas* (Washington, 1961), p. 12.

Whose responsibility is it, ultimately, to govern the giant cities in such a way
as to solve or alleviate the frustrations of blight, congestion, slum housing,
open-space disappearance, and unplanned sprawl? Is the answer to be   *Who is*
sought in increased federal-city relationships? Some observers, such as   *responsible?*
Connery and Leach, conclude that "federal involvement in metropolitan
areas is no longer a matter of conjecture," and that the federal government
inevitably will move in the direction of further commitment.[9] Urban interest
groups argue for greater federal leadership and assistance by pointing out that
while slum dwellers now outnumber farm dwellers by one million, annual federal
expenditures amount to $3,000 per farm family and only $84 per slum family.

Still others, such as the Kestnbaum Commission, do not consider increased federal involvement inevitable, but their message is principally one of
warning to the states:

> If States do not give cities their rightful allocation of seats in the legislature,
> the tendency will be toward direct Federal-municipal dealings. These
> began in earnest in the early days of the depression. There is only one   *A warning*
> way to avoid this in the future. It is for the States to take an interest in   *to states*
> urban problems, in metropolitan government, in city needs. If they do
> not do this, the cities will find a path to Washington as they did before, and
> this time it may be permanent. . . .[10]

The most vigorous opponents of federal action in urban affairs have been
taxpayers' groups fearful of the impact of such programs on their tax bill. Their
arguments are strong in reliance on states' rights and on such suggestive
questions as that expressed in the title of an article in a business news   *Opposition*
magazine,[11] "Should Uncle Sam Be Your Mayor?" Governor Smylie of   *to federal*
Idaho, in dissenting from a recommendation of the Advisory Commission   *intervention*
on Intergovernmental Relations for federal financial assistance to metropolitan
area planning agencies, stated:

> I can see little justification in the assumption of a permanent financial re-
> sponsibility by the National Government for a function which in a great many
> of our metropolitan areas is and will continue to be an intrastate affair. Our
> Federal system of Government under the Constitution is already characterized

---

[9] Connery and Leach, *op. cit.*, p. 8.

[10] U. S. Commission on Intergovernmental Relations, *A Report to the President for Transmittal to the Congress* (U. S. Government Printing Office, Washington, D. C., 1955), pp.
39-40.

[11] *Nation's Business*, XLIX (January, 1961), p. 14.

68

by a large number of grants-in-aid which began as stimulative devices but evolved quickly to the status of permanent subsidies.[12]

Ultimately, the determination of responsibility for containing and regulating the "urban revolution" is a *political* question whose answer will come only in part through rational arguments concerning the constitutional rights of states to be the ruler of their urban household. The coercive effects of geographic, economic, and technological developments will also help to shape the answer.

A multi-factoral answer

Probably more than any other single factor, the U. S. Supreme Court's 1962 decision in the Tennessee reapportionment case, and the quick chain reaction of companion suits by cities in many other states, hold the key to the future in federal-state-local relationships. In reversing its long-standing policy of refusing to become involved in reapportionment disputes, the Supreme Court gave very few answers in the Baker v. Carr decision[13] except to say that federal courts can entertain such cases. The months immediately following this ruling saw a veritable floodtide of cases brought to state and federal courts in a massive attack on the rural domination of state legislatures.

The impact of Baker v. Carr

Two seemingly contradictory conclusions may be drawn concerning the significance of *Baker* v. *Carr,* one relatively disturbing to "states' righters," and the other more comforting to them. As a symbol of Supreme Court interference in the "private affairs" of the states, this case will undoubtedly be placed alongside several others which are currently anathema to states' rights advocates. Yet it is entirely possible that this particular "interference" by the Supreme Court may have released the log jam which has long blocked states from responding to urban pressures for assistance. It is possible that the urban path to Washington is already too well travelled for any significan turning back, but if the states should put their legislative houses in order by giving equitable representation to urban citizens, one of the strong arguments for federal aid to cities would be blunted.

---

[12] U. S. Advisory Commission on Intergovernmental Relations, *Governmental Structure, Organization, and Planning in Metropolitan Areas* (U. S. Government Printing Office, Washington, D. C., 1961), p. 44.

[13] 369 U. S. 186 (1962). *See* Chapter 10 for further discussion of the impact of *Baker* v. *Carr* on legislative apportionment.

Advisory Commission on Intergovernmental Relations, *Governmental Structure, Organization, and Planning in Metropolitan Areas* (U. S. Government Printing Office, Washington, D. C., 1961).

Alderfer, Harold F., *American Local Government and Administration* (The Macmillan Company, New York, 1956), Chapter 5.

Baker, Gordon E., *Rural Versus Urban Political Power* (Doubleday & Company, Inc., Garden City, N. J., 1955).

Betters, Paul V., *Recent Federal-City Relations* (United States Conference of Mayors, Washington, D. C., 1936).

Commission on Intergovernmental Relations, *The Impact of Federal Grants-in-Aid on Structure and Functions of State and Local Governments* (U. S. Government Printing Office, Washington, D. C., 1955).

Connery, Robert H., and Richard H. Leach, *The Federal Government and Metropolitan Areas* (Harvard University Press, Cambridge, 1960).

Grant, Daniel R., "Federal-Municipal Relationships and Metropolitan Integration," *Public Administration Review,* XIV (Autumn, 1954), pp. 259-268.

Ludwig, C. C., "Cities and the National Government Under the New Deal," *American Political Science Review,* XXIX (August, 1935), pp. 640-648.

Martin, Roscoe C., *Grass Roots* (University of Alabama Press, University, Alabama, 1957).

National Resources Committee, *Our Cities: Their Role in the National Economy* (U. S. Government Printing Office, Washington, D. C., 1937).

Vernon, Raymond, *Metropolis: 1985* (Harvard University Press, Cambridge, 1960).

Walker, Harvey, *Federal Limitations Upon Municipal Ordinance Making Power* (Columbus, Ohio, 1929).

(*See also* readings listed for Chapters 2 and 18.)

EMERGING PROBLEMS IN FEDERAL-CITY RELATIONS

★ *4* ★

LIBERTY UNDER LAW:

THE POLICE POWER

THE WEB of government as developed by our states and localities has two significant threads of thought and practice, intertwined in an ever-lengthening development. One perpetuates the idea of liberty for the individual with *Two threads* respect to his person, opinion, and property. It embraces substantive and procedural guarantees traceable to origins in the Magna Carta, British common law and statutes of rights, doctrines of natural rights, and American pre-national experience. The other thread, also a heritage from olden times, is the concern for community interests and the recognition of citizens' responsibility for serving or respecting these essential public interests. The twin threads of the individual's right and the public's power are roughly defined by the phrase "Liberty under Law." The public power is manifest in various forms, fundamental among them being the power to tax, the power of eminent domain — that is, the power to take private property for public use — and the police power. It is the reconciliation of liberty with authority in the form of the police power which is the concern of this chapter.

The American states historically have led the nation in emphasizing bills of rights and in the broad exercise of police power. They have followed, with degrees of imperfection, the teaching that there must be liberty but not the liberty to injure others. When states have been thought to be remiss in providing such protections, the national government, through constitutional change or judicial interpretation, has buttressed or modified state protections and powers against discriminatory practices. It has not reduced the length or strength of the great threads in the web of state government. The purpose or ultimate effect of the Civil War amendments, for example, was to place all persons, regardless of color, on the same basis with respect to rights and powers. In one application of those amendments the "white primary" was held unconstitutional as a denial on racial grounds of the rights to participate in the choice of elected officials.[1]

Police power should not be thought of as simply the authority of a uniformed officer with a badge on his breast and a pistol on his belt, although it is basic to that authority. It is the general power, whether expressed, implied, or inherent, to establish and apply laws or regulations for the *Scope of police power* maintenance or advancement of public safety, health, welfare, and morals. Miscellaneous and unrelated examples of its use are provisions for milk inspection, preventing fire hazards in city or forest, smoke control or abatement, fixing maximum interest rates, compulsory vaccination, compulsory school attendance, limiting child labor, enforcing standards of weights and measures, zoning to exclude shops and factories from residential areas, prohibiting or regulating the sale of liquor, and banning the sale or display of obscene pictures and publications. The old "blue laws" providing rules for Sabbath observance and the modern speed laws providing rules of the road are also manifestations of police power. So is the Tennessee statute designed to prevent the public use of rattlesnakes in worship. Police power is just about as broad in meaning as government itself. It is not a specific derivative from a constitutional clause or provision. It is inherent in the very concept of government. Its limits are to be found primarily through the interpretation of other constitutional or governmental features to which it must be adjusted.

The application of police power varies according to change in the needs and circumstances of different regions and different eras. There may be differences in water regulations between desert areas and areas of heavy flood. Compulsory insurance of workers against occupational accident was brought on by the industrial revolution, and many types of health regulation had to await the scientific findings of Pasteur and others. The atomic future may expand the use of this power in ways not now foreseen.

In the American federal system the police power belongs to the states with the exception of such power as may be delegated by the Constitution,

---

[1] *Smith* v. *Allwright*, 321 U. S. 649 (1944), overruling *Grovey* v. *Townsend*, 295 U. S. 45 (1935).

expressly or by implication, to the national government or forbidden to the states.
Thus it is necessary to look at police power in terms of federalism. The po-

State police power in the federal system   lice role of the national government within the states is distinctly limited, but nevertheless effective and significant in modern times, as will be subsequently explained. It may duplicate, reinforce, or complement the role of the states, as in prohibiting the shipment of liquor into a state for delivery and consumption contrary to state law. But the average American has more day-to-day contact with state police power, has more opportunities to obey or violate state or local laws and ordinances than to make contact with national powers.

STATE POLICE POWER AND THE FEDERAL JUDICIARY

The use of police power by one state or another has been challenged from time to time as unconstitutional in cases reaching the Supreme Court. The

Challenged under the "obligation of contract" clause   states can be point to both victories and defeats for police power in these cases. From the record of such victories and defeats the scope of the state police power in the American constitutional system gradually unfolds.

An important basis for challenge has been the provision in Section 10 of Article I of the Constitution that no state shall "pass any . . . law impairing the obligation of contracts." This prohibition was invoked in the famous Dartmouth College case, decided in 1819 by the United States Supreme Court in an opinion written by Chief Justice John Marshall.[2] The legislature of New Hampshire had modified the Dartmouth charter, presumably making valid use of its police power, partly shifting the institution from private to public control without the trustees' consent. Daniel Webster, a Dartmouth graduate, argued the case for his alma mater. The Marshall opinion, conforming to the Webster argument, pronounced the corporate charter a contract and held the statute of modification unconstitutional as an impairment of that contract. The state was not privileged to use its police power so as to impair the obligation of a contract.

Webster and legal colleagues, however, were to meet different luck in arguing the same constitutional point in the Charles River Bridge case[3] when Roger B. Taney was Chief Justice. The Massachusetts legislature, after charter-

---

[2] *Dartmouth College v. Woodward*, 4 Wheaton 518 (1819).

[3] *Charles River Bridge v. Warren Bridge*, 11 Peters 420 (1837).

ing the Charles River Bridge corporation to build a bridge and operate it for tolls, chartered another company to build and operate a bridge nearby in effective competition with the earlier company. The Charles River Bridge group claimed that this unexpected competition was an impairment of business and of contract. Taney, writing the majority opinion, rejected the claim that monopolistic privileges were implied in the original charter, insisting that any doubt or ambiguity should be resolved in favor of the public or the community. In upholding the constitutionality of the challenged statute, he cited precedents in British law and interpretation and laid down the proposition that "While the rights of private property are sacredly guarded, we must not forget that the community also have rights, and that the happiness and well-being of every citizen depends on their faithful preservation." This Taney doctrine emphasized the power and the responsibility of the state both as grantor of privileges to vested interests and as continuous guardian of the public interest involved in the grants. It foreshadowed the coming of a wider usage of police power by state and municipal governments, particularly in connection with utility franchises.

Almost a century after the Charles River Bridge decision, Chief Justice Charles Evans Hughes further strengthened the police power in an opinion upholding a Minnesota mortgage moratorium law.[4] This law had been passed for the relief of debtors during the great depression of the 1930's. The act, providing for the postponement of foreclosures, was challenged by creditors as impairing the obligation of contract. To the layman it would seem that this was a case in which the Supreme Court had no choice but to declare that Minnesota had used its police power improperly to change the terms of legally binding contracts, in violation of the federal constitution. But the Court ruled to the contrary, and it might be observed that this decision was not by a "New Deal Court," occurring, as it did, three years before Franklin D. Roosevelt named a justice to the bench. In denying the claim of unconstitutionality as spokesman for the Court, Hughes noted the increase of social and economic complexities with the passing of frontier conditions:

> Where, in earlier days, it was thought that only the concerns of individuals or of classes were involved, and that those of the State itself were touched only remotely, it has later been found that the fundamental interests of the State are directly affected; and that the question is no longer merely that of one party to a contract as against another, but of the use of reasonable means to safeguard the economic structure upon which the good of all depends.

---

[4] *Home Building and Loan Association* v. *Blaisdell*, 290 U. S. 398 (1934).

74 The literal restraint of the Constitution is not to stand in the way of the state's use of police power within the scope of "reasonable means" for economic survival in a crisis. The police power of the state may not be contracted out of existence.

The police power of the state is restricted in important ways by the power of Congress to "regulate commerce with foreign nations, and among the several States, and with the Indian tribes." The overlapping of the state police

Factor of interstate commerce

power and the federal commerce power has provided material for discourse and decision by the Supreme Court in numerous cases since Marshall made their relationship important in *Gibbons v. Ogden* in 1824.[5] The broad opinion in this case interpreted "commerce" as including "navigation" and invalidated a New York state law which granted a monopolistic shipping license in New York waters to a group of steamboat operators, and which consequently penalized a rival operating between New York and New Jersey under a license from the national government. The state could not use its police power so as to interfere directly with navigation in interstate commerce as provided for by legislation of Congress.

In a case decided in 1852, the Supreme Court held that Pennsylvania might regulate pilotage in interstate commerce, since Congress had not regulated it, and the state regulation had only local and indirect effect on interstate commerce.[6] This by no means reversed the Marshall ruling of 1824, the doctrine remaining that the states could not place an unreasonable or direct burden on interstate commerce and could not interfere with the valid use of the commerce power by Congress. The Supreme Court in 1886 put the stamp of unconstitutionality upon statutory provisions of Illinois prohibiting certain specified rate practices by railroads moving interstate freight originating in that state.[7] Absence at the time of congressional legislation on the subject was held to be no justification for state action, since the shipping process involved was clearly national in scope and affected persons far beyond the bounds of Illinois. After Congress created the Interstate Commerce Commission and endowed it with authority over rate-making, the Supreme Court sustained that agency's steps to bring Texas' intrastate rates into relation with interstate rates. The national action was designed to prevent freight-rate injury to Shreveport, Louisiana, near the eastern border of Texas, and overrode and curtailed the authority of the Texas railroad commission.[8]

A still different use of the national commerce power to check the police power of the state is illustrated by the 1946 decision of the Supreme Court in-

---

[5] 9 Wheaton 1 (1824).

[6] *Cooley v. Board of Wardens of Port of Philadelphia*, 12 Howard 299 (1852).

[7] *Wabash, St. L. and P. Ry. Co. v. Illinois*, 118 U. S. 557 (1886).

[8] *Houston, East and West Texas Ry. Co. v. United States*, 234 U. S. 342 (1913).

validating a Virginia requirement for racial separation of bus passengers insofar as applicable to persons travelling in interstate commerce.[9] The opinion classed segregation by state action as an undue burden on national commerce. The national government's power under the commerce clause does not prevent state regulation under the police power, however. In the absence of conflicting federal legislation, Florida, for example, may enact a quarantine against the entry of citrus fruit into the state to protect her citrus orchards from the Mediterranean fruit fly. Similarly, interstate trucks may be required by a state to comply with a variety of specifications as to weight, height, width, and lighting, in the interest of highway safety. But the Court has ruled that Arizona cannot limit the length of interstate trains, and that California cannot keep indigent persons from moving into the state. Many other examples might be cited of the border problems arising between the national commerce power and state police power. That border is not definitely fixed in law or fact. It requires continuous reinterpretation and readjustment in the light of changing conditions.

The Fourteenth Amendment, since its adoption in 1868, has provided the basis for hundreds of cases as well as extensive national legislation and investigation bearing on the scope of state police power. Its first section, after defining citizenship and determining that American citizens are citizens "of the State wherein they reside," imposes three overlapping restrictions on the states. The first is that no state "shall make or enforce any law which shall abridge the privileges or immunities of citizens of the United States." The second restriction is that no state shall "deprive any person of life, liberty, or property, without due process of law." The third is that no state shall "deny to any person within its jurisdiction the equal protection of the laws." It should be noted that the shift from the term "citizen" to "person" expanded the coverage of the restrictions for the purposes of law and jurisprudence. A corporation is a legal person for many purposes, although it is not an individual citizen, and aliens, of course, are persons but not citizens. *Fourteenth Amendment; three points*

The Fourteenth Amendment, although an outgrowth of the Civil War and the emancipation of the slaves, was to be used far more extensively by private corporations than by Negroes during the first sixty years of its existence as part of "the supreme law of the land."[10] Business interests failed conspicuously, however, in some of their early attempts to side-track state regulatory legislation by invoking this portion of the Constitution. In deciding the *Slaughterhouse Cases*[11] in 1873, the Supreme Court, with *Use by private corporations*

---

[9] *Morgan v. Virginia,* 328 U. S. 373 (1946).
[10] *See* C. W. Collins, *The Fourteenth Amendment and the States* (Little, Brown & Co., Boston, 1912).
[11] 16 Wall. 36 (1873).

four dissents, upheld a Louisiana statute which provided for monopolistic private control of premises in New Orleans for slaughtering meat under public inspection and required all local butchers to use these facilities. The butchers complained that they were victims of abridgement of "privileges or immunities," of deprivation of "due process," and of denial of "the equal protection of the laws." The opinion of the Court emphasized the enduring regulatory power of the states in our federal sytem and stressed the close but not exclusive connection of the Fourteenth Amendment with the rights of ex-slaves.

In the post-Civil War period rapid expansion of railroads into the sparsely settled areas of the West led to transportation conditions which the western farmers thought intolerable. The farmers banded together in the Granger movement to secure legislative regulation of the railroads in the interest of adequate service at reasonable rates. The farmers also sought regulation of auxiliary services essential to movement of their produce to market. The states' regulatory power was soon challenged under the Fourteenth Amendment. In *Munn v. Illinois*,[12] the first of the Granger cases, the Supreme Court upheld an Illinois statute fixing maximum charges for storing grain in warehouses in large cities. Chief Justice Morrison R. Waite, in delivering the opinion, cited Taney and British authorities on police power and observed that the Illinois law was not violative of the "due process" clause of the Fourteenth Amendment, since it applied controls to private property "affected with a public interest." Such controls, the Chief Justice said, were amply justified by precedents in English common law "from whence came the right which the Constitution respects." But just what is a business affected with a public interest? The Court subsequently stated that in the Munn case it had conceived the term "affected with a public interest" as the equivalent of "subject to the exercise of the police power."[13] This somewhat circular definition simply means that the scope of the state police power in this field is determined by the slow process of judicial inclusion and exclusion, case by case.

Regulating businesses "affected with a public interest"

Subsequent opinions of the Court were to show a cyclic trend toward viewing the fourteenth amendment of the Constitution as a businessmen's amendment, in a fashion highly disturbing to proponents of the police power. Broad clearance was set up in 1886 by the Supreme Court in a categorical statement that corporations were persons entitled to "equal protection of the laws."[14]

In 1905 the high tribunal set aside a New York statute fixing maximum hours for employees of bakeries, holding it an unreasonable use of police power in violation of the "due process" protection of the liberty of contract to sell and

---

[12] 94 U. S. 113 (1876).

[13] *Nebbia v. New York*, 291 U. S. 502 (1934).

[14] *Santa Clara County v. Southern Pacific Railroad Company*, 118 U. S. 394 (1886).

purchase labor.[15] This laid down a pattern for later decisions, provoking Justice Holmes, in dissent, to object to deciding cases on economic theory and to observe that the "Fourteenth Amendment does not enact Mr. Herbert Spencer's Social Statics." This dissenting opinion foreshadowed the majority slant of later years. In 1937 the Court frankly reversed itself with respect to state power to regulate labor conditions, Chief Justice Hughes noting in the opinion that "the liberty safeguarded is liberty in a social organization."[16]

Support for narrowing the Fourteenth Amendment's protection for corporations came from such Justices as Louis Brandeis, Hugo Black, William Douglas, and others. The constitutional history of the shift is one which would fill many pages. Suffice it to say with the Court in the Nebbia case,[17] where it sustained New York's regulation of the price of milk:

> So far as the requirement of due process is concerned, and in the absence of other constitutional restriction, a state is free to adopt whatever economic policy may reasonably be deemed to promote public welfare. . . .
>
> . . . The Constitution does not secure to anyone liberty to conduct his business in such fashion as to inflict injury upon the public at large, or upon any substantial group of the people. Price control, like any other form of regulation, is unconstitutional only if arbitrary, discriminatory, or demonstrably irrelevant to the policy the legislature is free to adopt, and hence an unnecessary and unwarranted interference with individual liberty.

We had come a long way by the middle 1930's from the doctrine that the state's police power applied only to businesses rather narrowly conceived as "affected with a public interest."

The Fourteenth Amendment has afforded the Supreme Court a new role as defender of humane democracy.[18] The use of the amendment for protection of human rights, at ebb tide around the turn of the century, registered a genuine revival between 1930 and 1960 when corporations were finding it a less useful weapon against state police power. The story of the Fourteenth Amendment as a shield for human rights is too long to be given here except in summary of significant points. It is correlative with the advancement of Negroes, although by no means limited in application to racial relations. It involves the relationship of state and local police power to the freedoms of labor, speech, press, worship, and assembly, as well as to equality of oppor-

Shield for human rights

---

[15] *Lochner* v. *New York,* 198 U. S. 45 (1905).

[16] *West Coast Hotel Company* v. *Parrish,* 300 U. S. 379 (1937).

[17] *Nebbia* v. *New York, loc. cit.*

[18] *See* Robert G. McCloskey, "The Supreme Court Finds a Role: Civil Liberties in the 1955 Term," *Virginia Law Review,* XLII (October, 1956), pp. 735-760.

78   tunity in public education and recreation. It is the story of evolution in both
procedural and substantive rights, with an increasing sensitivity of the Supreme
Court to the rights of human beings.

The "due process" clause has served more and more in recent decades to
require state courts to exercise fair and proper procedure in criminal cases. The
Supreme Court, for example, in 1923 sent a case back to an Arkansas

Right to a
fair trial
court for retrial on the ground that the jury had brought in a hasty
verdict under the influence of a mob.[19] Some years later the Court
similarly interfered with the trial of a group of Negroes at Scottsboro,
Alabama, because the accused transients were shunted through proceedings
to conviction without any advance provision for counsel.[20] A sequel to this
case met similar treatment because Negroes had been systematically and traditionally excluded from jury service in that Alabama jurisdiction.[21] Convictions
in state courts have been set aside because they were based on forced con-
fession of guilt. Such methods of securing conviction, in the words of Justice
Black, constitute "a denial of due process of law as guaranteed in the Fourteenth Amendment."[22] Unnecessary brutality to prisoners under arrest or in
custody has subjected state or local officers to prosecution in federal court under
civil rights legislation passed by Congress in conformity with the Fourteenth
Amendment.[23] The Supreme Court has not brought the states under the same
procedural limitations as the national government, however. Such national
requirements in the Bill of Rights as the right to jury trial, grand jury indictment,
privilege against self incrimination, and protection against double jeopardy, have
all been held as not binding on the states unless they so desire.[24]

The Supreme Court in the second quarter of the twentieth century
strengthened the Fouteenth Amendment as a protection of our basic freedoms
against unreasonable interference from state police power. The Court

Freedom of
speech and
press
gradually absorbed the specific restraints imposed by the First Amendment upon the national government into the "liberty" protected under
the Fourteenth Amendment against infringement by the states. In effect,
under the rulings of the Court, the states must observe the restrictions of the
First Amendment in respect to speech, press, assembly, and religion. Municipal
regulations have been voided by the Supreme Court for interfering unduly

---

[19] *Moore* v. *Dempsey,* 261 U. S. 86 (1923).

[20] *Powell* v. *Alabama,* 287 U. S. 45 (1932).

[21] *Norris* v. *Alabama,* 294 U. S. 587 (1935).

[22] *Chambers* v. *Florida,* 309 U. S. 227 (1940).

[23] 18 U. S. *Code Annotated* §242; *see Screws* v. *United States,* 325 U. S. 91 (1945), and
United States v. *Sutherland,* 37 F. Supp. 344 (1940).

[24] *Walker* v. *Sauvinet,* 92 U. S. 90 (1876); *Hurtado* v. *California,* 110 U. S. 516 (1884);
Twining v. *New Jersey,* 211 U. S. 78 (1908); *Palko* v. *Connecticut,* 302 U. S. 319 (1937).

with the liberties of religious, labor, and other groups wishing "to speak, write, print or distribute information or opinion." This was made clear by Justice Owen J. Roberts in a Court opinion in 1939 with numerous citations from other cases.[25] The 1949 decision in the *Terminiello* case sustained freedom of speech in a fashion that has been criticized as too restrictive of the use of police power for the local preservation of order in inflammatory circumstances.[26] It has also been decided that publication of a newspaper or periodical may not be suppressed or enjoined by state action for obnoxious and derogatory remarks concerning public officers,[27] and protection through the Fourteenth Amendment has invalidated the banning of movies under claims of their being sacrilegious or suggestive of crime and immorality.[28] But the Supreme Court has ruled that it is not violative of free speech, as thus protected, for a state to bar persons holding subversive doctrines or membership in subversive organizations from employment in public schools. The right of such persons to "assemble, speak, think and believe as they will" is not the "right to work for the State in the school system on their own terms."[29]

The Fourteenth Amendment has protected freedom of worship in ways other than by safeguarding religious speech from interference by local authorities. The Supreme Court has insisted rather strictly upon the separation of church and state in public education. Its insistence has extended to outlawing the release of time for religious activity or instruction on school premises even where such instruction was at the request of parents.[30] *Religious freedom* The school action was held to be contrary to the religious "establishment" clause of the First Amendment and, therefore, violative of the Fourteenth Amendment. Four years later, in the *Zorach* case, the Court reconsidered the problem of "released time" and approved the New York system of permitting students to go to religious centers not on public school property for instruction during the school day.[31] Reversing a former decision, the Court in 1943 overruled the action of a school board expelling Jehovah's Witness children for refusing to salute the

---

[25] *Schneider* v. *State (Town of Irvington)*, 308 U. S. 147 (1939).

[26] *Terminiello* v. *City of Chicago*, 337 U. S. 1 (1949).

[27] *Near* v. *Minnesota*, 283 U. S. 697 (1931).

[28] *Joseph Burstyn, Inc.* v. *Wilson*, 343 U. S. 495 (1952).

[29] *Adler et al.* v. *Board of Education of the City of New York*, 342 U. S. 485 (1952). A subsequent decision indicated, however, that a state violates due process of law when it discharges an employee on the sole ground that he has invoked the Fifth Amendment's safeguard against self-incrimination before a committee of the U. S. Senate. *Slochower* v. *Board of Higher Education of City of N. Y.*, 350 U. S. 551 (1956).

[30] *Illinois ex rel. McCollum* v. *Board of Education*, 333 U. S. 203 (1948).

[31] *Zorach* v. *Clauson*, 343 U. S. 306 (1952).

national flag in school exercises because of religious scruples.[32] But the practice of transporting school children in public buses to parochial schools has been upheld.[33]

The relationship of local police power to religion and religious freedom is somewhat flexible and not easy to define at any one time. Through the years all levels of government have offered special concessions to churches **Borderline** including tax exemption of church property and income, recognition of **church-state** Sunday as a legal day of rest in every state, Sunday "blue laws," require- **relations** ment of daily reading of the Bible in many public schools, and legal observance of such Christian holidays as Christmas and Easter. What happens when one's religious freedom conflicts with a state or local government regulation for public health or welfare? In recent years courts have supported the police power in three unusual cases: in spite of religious objections of parents who were Jehovah's Witnesses, a court ordered that an Rh baby be given a blood transfusion; a compulsory chest X-ray requirement at the University of Washington was held to apply to all students, including a Christian Scientist with religious objections; and a nine-year-old girl helping her guardian aunt to sell publications of Jehovah's Witnesses was held subject to the child labor law in Massachusetts.[34]

The perplexing relationship between the requirement of religious freedom and the state's police power as manifested in Sunday laws, was considered by the Supreme Court in four cases in 1961. These cases challenged the **Sunday** constitutionality of laws in Pennsylvania, Massachusetts, and Maryland, **"blue laws"** on the ground that they impose a "Christian Sabbath" on non-Christians. Orthodox Jewish merchants who close their stores on Friday evening and Saturday are then prevented by law from being open on Sunday. The Court upheld the Sunday closing laws, saying that such laws are legal if designed to promote a day of rest and recreation. The Court served notice, however, that such laws would be declared unconstitutional if they are found, on their face or by examining their legislative history, to be primarily designed to promote religious observance and church attendance.[35] The Court rejected at the same time an appeal to review South Carolina's law against commercial movies on

---

[32] *West Virginia State Board of Education* v. *Barnette*, 319 U. S. 624 (1943), reversing *Minersville School District* v. *Gobitis*, 310 U. S. 586 (1940).

[33] *Everson* v. *Board of Education*, 330 U. S. 1 (1947).

[34] See Robert E. Cushman, *Civil Liberties in the United States* (Cornell University Press, Ithaca, 1956), Part III, "Freedom of Religion: Separation of Church and State." For the most complete history of church-state relations, see Anson Phelps Stokes, *Church and State in the United States* (3 vols., Harper & Row, Publishers, New York, 1950).

[35] *McGowan* v. *Maryland*, 366 U. S. 420 (1961); *Two Guys* v. *McGinley*, 366 U. S. 582 (1961); *Braunfeld* v. *Brown* 366 U. S. 599 (1961); and *Gallagher* v. *Crown Kosher Market* 366 U. S. 617 (1961).

Sunday. The law, enacted long before the days of movies, prohibits commercial entertainments on Sunday and has been interpreted as including movies. The state court decision, from which the appeal was made, upheld the state's power to enact such a law and concluded that if it was "out of step with the times" as alleged, it was the job of the legislature, not the courts, to change it.

On the same day, the Supreme Court rejected an opportunity to rule on the constitutionality of Connecticut's eighty-two-year-old law prohibiting the sale or use of contraceptives or giving medical advice on birth control. A sharply divided court said in its majority opinion that Connecticut had, *Legislation* in effect, nullified its own law since no prosecution has ever occurred *restricting* *birth control* except for a 1940 test case thrown out on a technicality.[36] A new test case was instituted in late 1961 following the closing by police of the Planned Parenthood Center of New Haven, Connecticut. In still another 1961 decision in the church-state area of the law, the Supreme Court struck down a Maryland requirement that each state officeholder must make a sworn statement of his belief in a Supreme Being. In a unanimous opinion the court held *Religious* that no religious test whatsoever may be applied by either federal or *tests for* *officeholding* state governments to disqualify a person from holding public office, and that atheists have as much right to disbelieve as other citizens have to believe.[37] The 1962 decision invalidating an "official prayer" to be used in New York public schools (*Engel* v. *Vitale, 370 U. S. 421*) is discussed in Chapter 22 in connection with the education function of state and local government.

The Fourteenth Amendment's provision for "equal protection of the laws" has come to mean much more than the guarantee of fundamental freedoms against the unreasonable application of state or local police power. According to the highest judicial interpretation, it also means equality *Equal oppor-* of opportunity in state-supported institutions of learning. With that *tunity in* *public* principle assumed, compulsory segregation of races in the public assem- *education* blages and facilities of one-third of the states was to burden the courts with a weighty problem of interpretation in terms of sociological jurisprudence. In this American dilemma, was segregation in itself a denial of equal protection to the minority race? And, if not, what was essential to equal protection within the pattern of segregation?

Doctrinal guidance for half a century was set forth in 1896 by the Supreme Court in *Plessy v. Ferguson*,[38] a case concerning racial separation in railway travel in Louisiana. The Court held that the state requirement of separation was not contrary to the "equal protection" clause but was a reasonable use

---

[36] *Poe* v. *Ullman* 367 U. S. 497 (1961).

[37] *Torcaso* v. *Watkins* 367 U. S. 339 (1961).

[38] 163 U. S. 537 (1896).

of police power in accordance with established "usages, customs, and traditions." Separate but equal accommodations would meet the constitutional test. In support, the opinion pointed to legislation by Congress for segregation in the public schools in the District of Columbia. A vigorous dissent by Justice John M. Harlan, a Kentuckian, posed a point for the future with the observation that the "Constitution is color blind." After forty years the Supreme Court began to weigh the facts of institutional segregation, although without departing from the constitutional formula of the Plessy case. In 1938 it held that a Negro citizen of Missouri, with proper academic qualifications, was "entitled to be admitted to the law school of the State University in the absence of other and proper provision for his legal training within the State."[39] State provision for his training in another state fell short of "equality of legal right." This case was followed by similar suits which gained admission of Negroes to several southern state universities for the study of law or other advanced subjects.

In 1950 the Supreme Court took further steps. It decided that the refusal to admit a Negro to the law school of the University of Texas was denial of equal protection, although he was offered training at a law school for Negroes in the state.[40] The opinion pointed out that the latter school was not equal to that for whites in faculty, facilities, recognition, and opportunity for contacts. In the same session the Supreme Court decided that Oklahoma, after admitting a Negro to the graduate school of the state university, was denying him equal protection by segregating him in classrooms, library, and cafeteria. The opinion branded unconstitutional the state statutory provision for admitting Negroes under special circumstances to the University of Oklahoma "upon a segregation basis."[41]

The Court next considered the constitutional validity of segregated public schools. The issue was no longer the equality of segregated facilities, upon which most of the earlier gains had been scored for Negroes in cases before the Court. Instead, segregation itself was challenged in the light of its sociological and psychological implications. The Court gave consideration to a group of cases on this issue for a period of more than a year, extending into 1954. The cases came up from South Carolina, Virginia, and Kansas, along with one from the District of Columbia not involving the Fourteenth Amendment. The Department of Justice entered the contest against segregation. The battle of briefs in these cases provided the sharpest collision yet between the protagonists of integration and segregation. In May, 1954, Chief Justice Warren in a unanimous opinion of the Court in Brown v. Board of Education[42] observed

---

[39] *Missouri ex rel. Gaines* v. *Canada*, 305 U. S. 337 (1938).

[40] *Sweatt* v. *Painter*, 339 U. S. 629 (1950).

[41] *McLaurin* v. *Oklahoma State Regents for Higher Education*, 339 U. S. 637 (1950).

[42] 347 U. S. 483 (1954).

categorically that in public education "the doctrine of 'separate but equal' has no place." "Separate educational facilities are inherently unequal." In terms of psychological jurisprudence, he wrote that the segregation of Negro children "may affect their hearts and minds in a way unlikely ever to be undone." Methods of implementing the reversal of policy were left to future argument and decision, and in an opinion one year later the Supreme Court cleared the way for enforcement through the federal district courts of the states concerned. Desegregation in the South, like the building of Rome, was not to be achieved in a day. It soon became apparent that the court requirements for "all deliberate speed" would be met with more deliberation than speed.

Segregation by law first disappeared in the District of Columbia, with slower and more gradual desegregation beginning in the border states of Delaware, Kentucky, Maryland, Missouri, Oklahoma, and West Virginia. Token integration took place in parts of Arkansas, North Carolina, Tennessee, Virginia, and Texas, with some sections following the moderate patterns of the border and others following the Deep South pattern of hard core resistance. Efforts of the Deep South to maintain segregated education have been described by Professor Robert J. Harris as follows:

> Many of the states in the South, in addition to noncompliance with the Court's decision, pursued policies of aggressive defiance. Official resistance took such forms as public school closing and leasing laws, pupil placement laws, interposition resolutions, closing of schools by executive proclamation, and executive maintenance of segregated education by force in the name of law and order, as exemplified by the employment of state police by Governor Allan Shivers to maintain segregated education in Mansfield, Texas, and employment of the National Guard by Governor Orval Faubus in Little Rock to prevent nine children from entering Central High School. Semiofficial and unofficial defiance has also been common in the states of the former Confederacy. Leaders of thought and opinion in politics and journalism employed the ancient shibboleth, "a government of laws and not of men," to encourage lawlessness under labels like "massive resistance," as proposed by Senator Harry Byrd, and resistance by all legal means, as advocated by one hundred southern congressmen who signed the so-called Southern Manifesto. Most . . . did not overtly advocate violence, but their intemperate language and distortion of the law created an atmosphere conducive to disorder generally and encouraged such sporadic outbreaks of violence which resulted in mob action at Little Rock, Mansfield, and Clinton, Tennessee, and in bombings of schools, synagogues, or churches in Nashville, Clinton, Atlanta, Birmingham, and Jacksonville.[43]

---

[43] Robert J. Harris, *The Quest for Equality* (Louisiana State University Press, Baton Rouge, 1960), pp. 154-155. For a more detailed account of state resistance measures see "Race Relations Law Survey, May, 1954 – May, 1957," *Race Relations Law Reporter*, II (1957), p. 881.

Cracks in the segregationist armor of the Deep South appeared in 1960 and 1961 when token integration was carried out under court orders in the New Orleans public school system and at the University of Georgia. Early in 1961 the Georgia legislature abandoned its rigid segregation laws and replaced them with four measures proposed by Governor Ernest Vandiver as the "most feasible method of holding integration to a minimum." The new methods emphasize local option referenda on closing and opening schools which have been integrated, tuition grants for pupils who prefer private schools to integrated public schools, and a constitutional declaration that no child can be forced to attend integrated schools against his will. Opposition to the bills in the legislature was light, but one spokesman for total segregation said, "The white flag will be the symbol of this legislature. Isn't it ironic in this, the centennial year of the Civil War, that Georgia surrenders again."[44]

Because neither the President nor Congress, as Professor Harris points out, has developed a policy or plan for meeting the constitutional crisis in race relations,

> . . . the burden of implementing the Supreme Court decision has fallen almost exclusively on the federal judiciary, and primarily on the United States district courts. Accordingly, one of the most important policies of social change in the twentieth century was committed to the tedious and fortuitous process of private litigation, with the final judgment affecting only the parties in controversy. The relative inadequacy of judicial precedents as vehicles for social change, in contrast to the efficiency of legislation and administration to effectuate change rapidly, has long been a theme of text writers in jurisprudence, who are amply corroborated by . . . the events that have occurred in the area of race relations since May, 1954.
>
> The decisions of the Court aimed at the attainment of equality before the law, inadequate as they are when standing alone, are, nevertheless, in accord with the trend of history noted by de Tocqueville in 1835, when he wrote that there was scarcely a single event of the preceding seven hundred years that did not promote equality of condition, and then declared: "The gradual development of the principle of equality is, therefore, a providential fact . . . it is universal, . . . it constantly eludes all interference, and all events as well as all men contribute to its progress."[45]

The logical extension of the decision in the Brown case to other areas of public activity has been taking place slowly but steadily since 1954. Federal courts have invalidated segregation by law in publicly supported parks, golf

---

[44] Associated Press report in the Nashville *Tennessean*, January 25, 1961.

[45] Harris, *op. cit.*, p. 157; and Alexis de Tocqueville, *Democracy in America* (Alfred A. Knopf, Inc., New York, 1945), Vol. I, pp. 5-6.

courses, swimming pools, and other recreation facilities, publicly operated eating places, public transit facilities, public libraries, and other state and local activities involving service to Negroes and whites. Tests of segregation in many other areas of southern life continue, with "sit-in demonstrations" relying more on the power of economic boycott than upon legal action to desegregate lunch counters, and "freedom-rides" focusing attention on bus terminal segregation.

LOCAL ASPECTS OF NATIONAL "QUASI-POLICE" POWERS

The Constitution of the United States does not confer a "police power" as such upon the federal government. But several of the powers which it does confer afford Congress authority to exercise something very much akin to the power to regulate in the interest of the public safety, health, welfare, and morals — a kind of "quasi-police" power. Congress uses its delegated powers in various ways to supplement or even supersede the local workings of state police power. *Policing interstate commerce* This is notably true in the regulation of interstate commerce, and it is by no means limited to strategic attention to intrastate freight rates. Regulation of interstate trade in foods requires inspection, not at the state lines, but at places of processing, and this relieves the states of large regulatory burdens. The regulation of wages, hours, and bargaining conditions of labor in business affecting interstate commerce often brings federal "police power" to the local scene. The Interstate Commerce Commission in 1955 ordered an end of segregation of interstate passengers in southern stations. The interstate commerce power is used to prohibit the shipment of prison products into states where the sale of such products is contrary to state law. There can be no practical differentiation at the state line for the regulation of aviation, radio, and TV, and consequently national supervision of these activities applies to both interstate and intrastate operations. National legislation against interstate kidnapping, "white slave" traffic, and auto theft duplicates state jurisdiction and aids the states in punishing violators. State regulation of the issuance and marketing of securities, as in the case of railroad regulation, proved inadequate, and, to close the gap, the national government entered the field through the commerce power.

Congress finds constitutional powers for local regulation outside the commerce clause. Use of the mails for fraudulent purposes is punishable by legislation based on the postal power, regardless of whether or not it is interstate. Local narcotics peddling is violative of a federal tax law, as is "wildcat" distilling of liquor. In the exercise of its spending power, the national government stipulates the conditions of labor working for contractors with government

Other national uses of police power contracts, not a small item in the nation's economy. The war or military powers are used to regulate civilian activities around centers where armed forces are located, and certain practices are prohibited in the interest of military morals and morale. The national government protects its own property wherever that property is located.

Hunting migratory birds is regulated under legislation which implements a treaty which provided for the protection of migratory birds by Canada to regulate the hunting of migratory birds in 1913, but the law was de-

States, Congress, and the treaty power clared unconstitutional in the lower federal courts.[46] Power to regulate the hunting of migratory birds was not one of the powers delegated to the national government. The United States subsequently entered into a treaty which provided for the protection of migratory birds by Canada and the United States. In implementation of the treaty Congress passed a new migratory bird act, and on test in the Court the constitutionality of the act was sustained.[47] Congress is empowered by the Constitution to "make all laws which shall be necessary and proper for carrying into execution the foregoing [listed] powers, and all other powers vested by this Constitution in the government of the United States, or in any department or officer thereof." The power to make treaties is one of the other powers. The decision in *Missouri* v. *Holland* indicates that Congress may do something in implementation of a treaty which it could not do under the Constitution prior to the treaty's existence, that is, regulate the hunting of migratory birds. The implications for the federal system are far-reaching, indeed, and considerable controversy has ensued as to the proper scope of the treaty-making and treaty-implementing authority. The "Bricker" amendment proposed in the United States Senate early in 1953 provided in part that a treaty provision in conflict with the Constitution "shall not be of any force or effect" and that a treaty "shall become effective as internal law in the United States only through legislation which would be valid in the absence of treaty." The amendment failed to pass in the Senate in 1954 by only one vote, but the issue is likely to recur.

Americans of this century have utilized national processes increasingly for important applications of police power as well as for many important de-

Centralized and decentralized processes terminations of civil rights. They have come to rely increasingly upon the functioning of national and state governments, in coordination or in counterbalance, for the effective exercise of power and for the effective preservation of liberty. Thus do they recognize, in terms of a

---

[46] *United States* v. *Shauver,* 214 Fed. 154 (1914); *United States* v. *McCullagh,* 221 Fed. 288 (1915).

[47] *Missouri* v. *Holland,* 252 U. S. 416 (1920).

SUPPLEMENTARY READINGS

American Civil Liberties Union, reports and pamphlets (American Civil Liberties
    Union, New York).

Bachrach, Peter, *Problems in Freedom* (The Stackpole Co., Harrisburg, Pa., 1954).

Chafee, Zechariah, *Free Speech in the United States* (Harvard University Press,
    Cambridge, 1946).

Corwin, Edward S., *Liberty Against Government* (Louisiana State University Press,
    Baton Rouge, 1948).

Cushman, Robert E., *Leading Constitutional Decisions* (10th ed.; Appleton-Century-
    Crofts, New York, 1955).

Emerson, T. I. and David Haber, *Political and Civil Rights in the United States*
    (Dennis & Co., Buffalo, 1952).

Frankfurter, Felix, *The Public and Its Government* (Yale University Press, New
    Haven, 1930).

Hamilton, W. H. and C. C. Rodee, "Police Power," *Encyclopaedia of the Social
    Sciences* (The Macmillan Company, New York, 1951) XII, pp. 190-193.

Harris, Robert J., *The Quest for Equality* (Louisiana State University Press, Baton
    Rouge, 1960).

Konvitz, Milton R., *Bill of Rights Reader; Leading Constitutional Cases* (Cornell Uni-
    versity Press, Ithaca, 1954).

President's Committee on Civil Rights, *To Secure These Rights* (United States Gov-
    ernment Printing Office, Washington, 1947).

Tussman, Joseph, ed., *The Supreme Court on Church and State* (Oxford University
    Press, New York, 1962).

Weintraub, Ruth G., *How Secure These Rights* (Doubleday and Company, New York,
    1949).

White, Walter, *A Man Called White* (The Viking Press, Inc., New York, 1948).

★ *5* ★

STATE CONSTITUTIONS

THE UNITED STATES is a land of constitutions, constitutional law, and constitutional interpretation. Americans have an abiding faith in the doctrine and workings of judicial review for defining or checking a multiplicity of statutes, and they place great reliance upon basic documents like written constitutions, fundamental charters, and organic acts for guidance in carrying on public affairs. As early as 1620 a small group of "Americans" aboard an anchored ship off Plymouth Rock signed a compact pledging:

Land of constitutions

> We . . . doe by these presents solemly and mutually in the presence of God, and one another, covenant and combine our selves togeather into a civill body politick . . . and by vertue hearof to enacte, constitute and frame such just and equall lawes, ordinances, acts, constitutions, and offices, as shall be thought most meete and convenient for the generall good of the colonie. . . .

Although it is evident from British experience that constitutions need not be written to be effective, Americans, from the Mayflower Compact to the most recent constitutional referendum, have insisted on prescribing and circumscribing the powers of government in textual terms. Every state inevitably has a formal constitution to say what its officers and subdivisions may and may not do and to say how the functions of government are to be performed. A

88

constitution is necessary to chart the course of government within the broad field of powers reserved to the states by the Tenth Amendment of the federal Constitution.

Venerated though they may be, state constitutions should be recognized at the outset as *political* documents. If politics "is the study of influence and the influential," as Harold Lasswell has said, and the "influential are those who get the most of what there is to get,"[1] it is not too difficult to identify the "influential" within a state by the privileges and protections they have secured in their state constitution. Taxpapers' groups and property interests have been able to secure strict and detailed limits on state legislatures' taxing, borrowing, and spending powers. The strength of veterans' groups and their lobbyists is revealed in constitutional guarantees of veterans' preference in public employment and even constitutional provisions for bonuses, pensions, tax exemptions, and other privileges. The influence of church groups, sometimes as opposed to other church groups, may be measured in constitutional contests. A case in point is the conflict over outlawing bingo as a form of gambling, as Protestant groups have urged, or making it legal, as urged by Catholic groups. The influence of farm interests is reflected in a variety of special privileges, but the chief constitutional stronghold of farmers is the "rigged formula" for over-representation of rural areas in the state legislature. Labor union influence, conversely, is reflected at a low level in most state constitutions. Only four states — New York, New Jersey, Missouri, and Hawaii — specifically guarantee the right to join unions and to bargain collectively. More states have passed so-called "right to work" amendments to their constitutions, actions usually regarded by organized labor as anti-labor victories for coalitions of business and farm groups. State constitutions reflect the political status of racial or ethnic groups, especially if the dominant group feels insecure in its position, but state influence may be counterbalanced by national influence, not only with respect to racial provisions but to all of the foregoing examples of constitutional politics, and many others which might be cited.

Constitutions as political documents

State constitutions are subordinate to "the supreme law of the land," as defined in Article VI of the United States Constitution. In other words, state governments are not to have powers in conflict with federal constitutional provisions, with congressional legislation that is constitutional, or with treaties properly made "under the authority of the United States." But these national restrictions, which are exceedingly important, are really few

State constitutions and "the supreme law of the land"

---

[1] *Politics: Who Gets What, When, How,* quoted in *The Political Writings of Harold D. Lasswell* (The Free Press, Glencoe, 1951), p. 295. This emphasis on constitutional politics follows closely Robert B. Dishman's *State Constitutions: The Shape of the Document* (National Municipal League, New York, 1960), pp. 7-8.

in number in comparison with the wide range of activities they leave open to the states. The United States Constitution leaves a great vacant space in the field of government, and each state undertakes to fill this space with a constitutional structure, using its own methods for establishing and changing this structure. A state's constitution is the supreme law of the state for all matters which fall outside the national jurisdiction or which are not forbidden to the states. It also may duplicate the national jurisdiction in significant areas over which states and the nation have concurrent powers, as in taxation or liquor regulation. In the end, the citizen may meet more overlappings than gaps of government in this constitutional duality.

The state constitutions offer a wide variety of subject matter and arrangement, along with an approximate similarity in the statement of fundamental rights and powers. They are longer than their forerunners of the *Variety of* Revolutionary period, when Virginia based its government on a constitu-
lengths tional document of fifteen hundred words. Professor Alfred de Grazia has graphed the trend towards longer state constitutions in American history, demonstrating a marked increase in length for the period from 1776 to 1910. The pattern is not clear for the constitutions adopted thereafter, although the longest for the entire span from 1776 to the middle of the twentieth century was adopted in 1921.[2] The constitutions vary in length from an estimated 6,650 words for Rhode Island to an estimated 350,000 words for Louisiana. Notable for length in addition to Louisiana's are those of California, Texas, Alabama, and Oklahoma. Alaska and Hawaii each came into the Union with relatively brief constitutions of approximately 12,000 words. Constitutions which originated in the Victorian period "are much like the mansions of the time — massive, rambling and adorned with gingerbread."[3]

The longer the constitution, the more likely it is that it contains legislative minutiae or deals with transitory matters. The long constitutions mentioned as well as many others are not limited in coverage to fundamental prin-
Concern for ciples but are used for purposes of authorizing or preventing all sorts of
minutiae practices which in early days were unheard of or were left to the discretion of legislators. The Louisiana document, for example, regulates miscellaneous minor matters concerning local government and public administration, devoting 4,032 words just to delineation of the powers, duties, mode of selection and other matters pertaining to the Board of Commissioners of the Port of New Orleans, with special attention to the subject of bond issues. In addition, the Louisiana constitution names two Mississippi River bridges for the

---

[2] Alfred de Grazia, "State Constitutions — Are They Growing Longer?" *State Government,* XXVII (April, 1954), pp. 82-83.

[3] Dishman, *op. cit.,* p. 1.

late Huey P. Long, and proclaims his birthday a legal holiday forever. The Alabama constitution puts rigid limitations on local tax rates, and, in consequence, has been amended frequently to provide needed taxing power for local jurisdictions. Distrust of legislatures is manifest in many constitutional details of prohibition and procedure. And court action or decision may be overruled by the constitutional process, as when a California amendment validated a primary election plan which the judiciary had rejected.

The natural growth of government and the problems of government partly account for the expansion of the contents of constitutional texts. But straight-jacket provisions sometimes get into these basic documents in response to the whims or pressure of groups, organizations, and sections. Examples are Oklahoma's constitutional requirement that all public schools must teach the "elements of agriculture, horticulture, stock-feeding, and domestic science," the Florida ban on taxation of incomes, the New York requirement that the state's forest preserve be "forever kept as wild forest lands," and guarantees in many states against loss of legislative representation by rural units regardless of population status.

FEATURES AND CONTENTS OF
STATE CONSTITUTIONS

American state constitutional systems have much in common, and their fundamental documents reflect common features in essential matters despite a wide diversity of detail and language. Most constitutional texts start with a preamble, stating broad purposes and in many cases invoking divine guidance: "We the people of Alaska, grateful to God. . . ." As in the national Constitution, the preamble is the introduction to provisions of rights and powers, usually a collection of glittering generalities, rather than an actual statement of rights and powers.

Common features: a preamble

More common than the preamble is a statement, bill, or declaration of rights, partly duplicating the provisions of the first ten amendments of the national Constitution. This feature of state constitutions, however, takes first place in historical importance and is incorporated in the main texts instead of being attached in the form of amendments. It sometimes comes next after the preamble. Its provisions are designed, in part, to prevent state and local authorities from interfering with the individual freedoms of worship, speech, press, assembly, and petition; to safeguard private property

Bill of rights

92 rights; and to insure fair or proper trial and treatment of accused persons. Some old-fashioned bills of rights, as in the constitutions of Kentucky and Tennessee, provide superfluous sermons on popular sovereignty and natural rights, even asserting or implying a doctrine of revolt against abusive and arbitrary exercise of governmental power. There are also examples of modern additions to bills of rights, as in the Montana provision that "laws for the punishment of crime shall be founded on the principles of reformation and prevention." The essential points of the state bills of rights are embodied in vital traditions. Those vital traditions afford the best possible guarantee that the governments will abide by the constitutional rules. Furthermore, the Fourteenth Amendment of the national document requires that every state respect certain fundamental rights and freedoms regardless of its own written constitution.

Every state constitution provides for a structure or framework of government. In general or specific terms, it outlines three branches of government, legislative, executive, and judicial. It sets forth powers, functions, and limitations for these branches and authorizes ways or means for putting men

Framework of and money to work in carrying on their functions. It provides for
government separation of powers combined with a system of inter-branch checks.

It has clauses or sections on such subjects as taxation and finance, administrative agencies and departments, suffrage and elections, county and city government, public education and state institutions, state lands and property, conservation, privileges and responsibilities of corporate enterprise, law enforcement, the state militia, etc. Provision of a process for amendment or revision is a usual constitutional feature. It is also common among many states, as already indicated, to have a body of miscellaneous provisions and amendments embedded in the constitution, thus making the fundamental document read more like a code of legislative statutes than a statement of the organic basis of law and government.

A composite "average" constitution would contain seventeen or eighteen articles, which are set off on the facing page opposite the contents of the Model State Constitution.

The *Model State Constitution* of the National Municipal League has influenced the development of state constitutional revision since the publication of the first edition of that work in 1921. The fifth edition, with explana-

Model State tory articles, appeared in 1948 and the sixth edition in 1963. This latest
Constitution "model" fills only a few pages and contains nine articles of subject matter, with a final tenth article providing a "schedule" of transition from the old to the new constitutional order. This document reflects the work and

Article	*Article*
I. Bill of Rights	I. Bill of Rights
II. Distribution of Powers	II. Suffrage and Elections
III. Legislative	III. Legislature
IV. Executive	IV. Executive
V. Judicial	V. Judiciary
VI. Suffrage and Elections	VI. Finance
VII. Taxation and Finance	VII. Local Government
VIII. Local Government	VIII. Miscellaneous Provisions; Public Welfare; Public Education; Civil Service; Intergovernmental Relations; Oath of Office.
IX. Corporations	IX. Constitutional Revision
X. Education	X. Schedule
	Appendix: Initiative and Referendum
XI. Militia	
XII. Amendment	
XIII. Miscellaneous	

A Schedule article or unnumbered schedule provision will also be included, and four or five additional articles most commonly will be drawn from the following:

Impeachments and Removals
Oath of Office
State and School Lands
Water Rights
Labor
State Indebtedness
Officers
Boundaries
Apportionment
Homestead and Exemptions
Public Institutions

---

[4] Adapted from Florida Constitution Advisory Commission, *Subject Matter of Articles in State and Territorial Constitutions,* Research Report No. 2, mimeographed, 1956.

{thinking of political scientists and administrators as well as of lawyers and laymen. As the preface to the model constitution points out, "Strictly speaking there can be no such thing as a 'Model State Constitution,' because there is no model state." Obviously it is a suggested model which would require adaptation to fit the conditions of any one of the fifty states. For a closer acquaintance with the documentary basis of constitutional government in actual operation, the student should take the time to examine the constitution of his own state.

STATE CONSTITUTIONS UNDER ATTACK

Students of contemporary state government approach unanimity in their attacks on the obsolescence of state constitutions and their support for thorough-going revision. After a committee of distinguished legal scholars study-

Widespread criticism

ing the New York Constitution reported that it was "literally amazed by the extent to which . . . [it] contains hollow phrases, defective provisions, and creakingly antiquated policies,"[5] the *New York Times* reinforced the report with the editorial statement that the state constitution was characterized by "haphazard arrangement, slipshod and confusing phraseology, relics of long-gone fears, verbosity, frustrated efforts to fit law to new circumstances, a testimonial to the force of inertia."[6] The late Professor Kimbrough Owen wrote of the long-winded Louisiana constitution:

> A layman who starts out to study the Louisiana Constitution . . . is confronted with a Herculean task. . . . The document will trip, entangle, infuriate and then exhaust him. The difficulties presented to the inquiring citizen include the vast detail, the dispersion of subject matter, confusing terminology, inconsistencies, errors, references to other legal documents, informal amending procedures, duplication of material, contradictions and omissions.[7]

A critique of the Florida Constitution by Professors Dauer and Havard found both its draftsmanship and its provisions for Florida government to be

---

[5] Inter-Law School Committee, *Report on the Problem of Simplification of the Constitution to the New York Special Legislative Committee on the Revision and Simplification of the Constitution*, Staff Report No. 1 (April, 1958), p. 330, as quoted in David Fellman's "What Should a State Constitution Contain?" in *Major Problems in State Constitutional Revision*, ed. W. Brooke Graves (Public Administration Service, Chicago, 1960), p. 140.

[6] *New York Times*, June 2, 1958.

[7] "The Need for Constitutional Revision in Louisiana," *Louisiana Law Review*, VIII (November, 1947), pp. 1-104, as quoted by Fellman, *op. cit.*, pp. 140-141.

sadly defective. The discovery of more than 200 errors of spelling and grammar by a casual count in the Florida Constitution, while of no great import in itself, was said to be indicative of many more serious deficiencies.[8] Many other individual state examples could be cited, but the final report of the (Kestnbaum) Commission on Intergovernmental Relations made a general indictment of state constitutions, concluding that ". . . many State constitutions restrict the scope, effectiveness and adaptability of State and local action. These self-imposed constitutional limitations . . . have frequently been the underlying cause of State and municipal pleas for Federal assistance."[9]

Probably the most common criticism of state constitutions is failure to adhere to the axiom that constitutions should be confined to fundamentals. Defining fundamentals should involve some latitude, to be sure, but few would accept as really fundamental the South Dakota constitution's authorization for a twine and cordage plant at the state penitentiary, the South Carolina clause defining what constitutes a "durable hard surface" street in the city of Greenville, or the Texas constitutional provision for the popular election of the inspector of hides and animals. The tendency to legislate details into the constitution seems to result from an unwillingness to trust future legislatures to make even little decisions concerning their government. A member of the Illinois Constitutional Convention of 1870 chided his colleagues on this point:

Details rather than fundamentals

> It is assumed that when we depart from this hall all the virtue and all the wisdom of the state will have departed with us. We have assumed that we alone are honest and wise enough to determine for the people the ordinary, and in many instances even the most trivial, questions affecting the public welfare; as if the mass of people of the state of Illinois were not as competent hereafter to select others that are honest and capable as they were to select us.[10]

What are the effects of this common state practice of incorporating statutory details into the "fundamental law"? Professor David Fellman does not hesitate to judge the results as bad, and summarizes his arguments as follows:

Effects of excessive detail

> Excessive constitutional detail is bad for many reasons. It solidifies the entrenchment of vested interests. It makes temporary matters permanent.

---

[8] Manning J. Dauer and William C. Havard, "The Florida Constitution of 1885 — A Critique," *University of Florida Law Review*, VIII (Spring, 1955), p. 12.

[9] Commission on Intergovernmental Relations, *A Report to the President for Transmittal to the Congress* (Government Printing Office, Washington, 1955), pp. 37-38.

[10] Quoted by Walter F. Dodd, *State Government*, 2d ed. (Appleton-Century-Crofts, New York, 1928), p. 96.

It deprives state legislatures and local governments of desirable flexibility and diminishes their sense of responsibility. It encourages the search for methods of evading constitutional provisions and thus tends to debase our sense of constitutional morality. It makes frequent recourse to the amending processes inevitable. It hinders action in time of special stress or emergency. It stands in the way of healthy progress. It blurs the distinction between constitutional and statute law, to the detriment of both. It creates badly written instruments full of obsolete, repetitious, misleading provisions. Above all, it confuses the public, and in fact makes it certain that few will ever bother to read the state constitution. This is extremely unfortunate, since one of the main purposes of a constitution is to educate the public in first principles. How can the people be expected to respect a constitution they never read, and which may in fact be altogether unreadable. . . .[11]

The previously mentioned "forever wild" provision in New York's constitution prohibiting the removal of any trees from the state's forest preserve led to two separate constitutional crises before ski trails could be constructed in the area. Two amendments were necessary — once in 1941 permitting "not more than twenty miles of ski trails 30 to 88 feet wide on the north, east and northeast slopes of Whiteface Mountain" and the second in 1947 to provide for skiing on Peter Gay Mountain. Loss of flexibility to meet new problems was emphasized by Governor Driscoll in addressing the New Jersey Constitutional Convention of 1947. He warned:

> When legislation is permitted to infiltrate a constitution, it shackles the hands of the men and women elected by the people to exercise public authority. The longer a constitution, the more quickly it fails to meet the requirements of a society that is never static.[12]

Obsolescence: language and provisions

Criticisms of obsolescence extend not only to obsolete *language* (such as continued use of "doth," "hath," and "dwelleth" in the New Hampshire Constitution, and reference to citizens as "subjects"), but also to obsolete *provisions*. Archaic offices of county and township, such as justice of the peace and constable, are perpetuated in the constitutional granite of many states. Salary limits placed in many constitutions are completely obsolete today. Constitutions are cluttered with dead-wood clauses related to street railway construction, dueling, Civil War disabilities, slavery, hereditary privileges, and the powers of San Francisco in connection with the 1915 World Fair, to name only a few.

---

[11] Fellman, *op. cit.*, p. 146.

[12] *Record of the New Jersey Constitutional Convention of 1947* (Trenton, 1947), Vol. I, p. 7.

As colorful as lists of outmoded constitutional clauses are, the more far-reaching criticisms of state constitutions are those which cite their failure to deal with many contemporary problems of government. Tremendous population growth and mobility, and the sudden arrival on the scene of sprawling metropolitan areas, have complicated the tasks of state and local government in ways hardly imagined by the rural framers of most state constitutions. The radical nature of the change is illustrated by former governor LeRoy Collins' statement, " Florida's population in my lifetime will have shifted from eight out of ten in rural to eight out of ten in urban areas."[13] The executive article comes in for special criticism for its failure to deal with the growth of public administration and modern managerial demands on state and local chief executives. Urbanization is a development that many state constitutions simply made no provision for in the representative structure of the legislature. Constitutional provisions for local government structure and boundary lines fail to deal with the current problem of a rootless and mobile population. Who could have envisioned the need for states to go into the metropolitan water supply business? And, perhaps most serious of all, nineteenth-century constitutional articles on taxation and finance fail to deal with the demands of twentieth-century public finance.

Failure to deal with contemporary problems

Related to all of these criticisms is the charge that the amending procedure is unreasonable in many states — either much too easy or much too difficult. This is a question which can best be discussed in connection with constitution-making and re-making, a subject to which we now turn.

Amendments: too easy or too difficult

CONSTITUTION-MAKING AND RE-MAKING

As stated previously, our constitutions are political documents; it follows inevitably that constitution-making is a highly political enterprise. The mythological image of high-principled men, an assembly of demi-gods, engaged in a selfless operation of translating abstract precepts into constitutional articles, is no more appropriate for describing a constitutional convention than it is for describing a state legislature or a city council. Constitutions help lay the ground rules for politics and it is only natural that they

The politics of constitution-making

---

[13] *Fortune,* XV (March, 1958), p. 30.

should become a prize to be competed for by the various interests making up society. The strong desire of particular groups to write into a constitution their own point of view or policy may be good or bad, depending on the student's own values. But it is important here as an essential factor in understanding constitutions. The predominant political interest of one group of constitution makers is revealed in the story told about a prominent rural member of the Tennessee Constitutional Convention of 1870. He stopped at a country store to buy cheese and crackers for the road.

> "Well, John, whar you been?"
> "Oh, I've been to Nashville — writing the new state constitution."
> "Well, what does it do?"
> "Derned if I know — but it shore gives the damn Yankees a fit."[14]

The American commonwealths virtually possess the constitutent power under the federal system of independent unitary states; they are free within the framework of republican institutions to go their own way in making and modifying their constitutions. Collectively the states exhibit evolution and diversity in the exercise of this constituent power. The state constitutions adopted during the war for independence were chiefly the work of legislatures or other revolutionary assemblies. Connecticut and Rhode Island adapted their colonial charters to constitutional purposes with few changes. Massachusetts started with a provisional arrangement, but in 1780 became the first state in the Union to establish a constitution through the combination of adoption by an elected convention and ratification by popular vote. Massachusetts' example was followed in launching the national Constitution. The method had the blessings of Jefferson and became the prevailing practice among the states. Old states have used it for acquiring new constitutions, and states in the making have used it to meet congressional requirements for admission to the Union. This method is one of the ways for revising or amending constitutions. There are various ways of putting conventions into operation and making their work effective. A few conventions since the Civil War have been clothed with the power to promulgate constitutional provisions without voter ratification. The present Louisiana constitution was thus established in 1921.

Evolution and diversity

The usual method of bringing a constitutional convention into existence is for the state legislature to provide for submitting the question to the voters in an election. This step is mandatory at specified intervals of years in New Hampshire, New York, Ohio, Iowa, and a few other states. Most of the states

---

[14] Joe Hatcher, "Politics," The Nashville *Tennessean*, April 23, 1961.

have constitutional provisions for legislative action to secure an election on calling a convention. Such provisions are absent from a few state constitutions, but legislatures nevertheless have exercised a sort of inherent authority to provide for election of a constitutional convention and have been sustained therein by the state supreme court. Some constitutions restrict the legislatures as to when and how to call a convention election, such as requiring a two-thirds affirmative vote or passage at two successive sessions, or limiting the frequency of such action.

Calling a constitutional convention

The question of calling a convention may also be put to the voters in certain states by an initiative petition. This device permits a certain number or percentage of the voters to propose an amendment or constitutional convention and requires action by the electorate to be rejected.

If, by one of these methods, a constitutional convention is called for, members of the convention are then elected, generally from legislative districts, but sometimes with the addition of a limited number from the state at large. Frequently, able men are more willing to serve in a constitutional convention than in a legislature, the thought being that they can contribute to the formulation of the basic laws and yet not sacrifice the amount of time which legislative service would entail. While efforts are usually made to minimize the role of party politics in constitutional conventions, this may result not so much in non-partisanship as in a kind of "honor system" of bi-partisan equality, as in Missouri in 1943 and New Jersey in 1947. The Missouri constitution specifies that one Republican and one Democrat shall be chosen from each of the senatorial districts and fifteen at-large delegates agreed upon by the state party committees. Of the fifteen at-large delegates, seven were Democrats, seven were Republicans, and one was a self-styled "anti-New Deal Democrat" who, significantly, was selected to be president of the convention. New Jersey's efforts for party equality came through informal party agreement rather than by constitutional directive.

Convention personnel

Party politics

Conventions are customarily unicameral and thus avoid the problems and delays of two-house deadlocks. They are also free from the check of executive vetoes. A convention may meet in a legislative chamber of the state capitol at a time when the legislature is not in session, and may split its session into two periods with a recess to provide time for study and consultation. The tradition of holding the convention in the state capital was broken by New Jersey in 1947 when the constitutional convention met on the campus of Rutgers University in New Brunswick. Delegates were said to enjoy greater insulation from the "statehouse politics" of Trenton because of their retreat behind the ivy-covered walls. Alaska followed this example and convened its constitutional delegates on the campus of the University of Alaska, five frozen miles from Fairbanks, and some 500 miles from the capital city of

Physical setting

100 Juneau. The unusual protections of mid-Alaska in mid-winter could hardly be duplicated, however, in the constitutional deliberations of other American states.[15]

A constitutional convention is essentially similar to a regular lawmaking body in methods of organization and procedure, with important committees performing much of the actual work. Convention deliberations normally *Procedure* stimulate less parliamentary maneuvering and obstructive tactics than one sometimes observes in a legislature, although these deliberations are nonetheless subject to the pressure of groups, parties, and sectional interests from within and without. The delegates to a convention are not likely to be swamped with details and local matters, which too often plague the members of legislative assemblies.

The work of a convention, as a rule, is cut out for it in the official call. The call may provide for consideration of only a certain number of specified subjects, for unlimited power to write a new constitution, or for general power to revise or rewrite a constitution subject to specific reservations. Attempts to set limits to its activity in this manner may be ignored by the convention itself. Still, except in the case of a territory achieving statehood, every constitutional convention is primarily concerned with revision and modernization rather than with sweeping changes in the fundamentals of government. Any drastic break with constitutional traditions would only invite rejection of the proposals by the voters at the election on ratification. Conventions not infrequently receive criticism for doing too little rather than too much; i.e., for omitting meritorious proposals lacking appeal to voters.

Constitutional conventions of modern days have come increasingly to recognize their need of research and reference staffs. It has seemed advisable in a number of cases to have a commission set up in advance of the *Preconven-* convention to explore the whole subject of state constitutions and *tion com-* constitution-making in order to supply the convention delegates with *missions* useful information and even recommendations for their guidance. The commission may make use of research experts in the fields of law, political science, local government, and public administration. Among the states which have emphasized the work of commissions in this way are Alaska, Illinois, New York, Massachusetts, Missouri, and Tennessee. The Alaska Statehood Committee served as the preparatory commission for that state and farmed out the research job to the Public Administration Service, a private consulting group. A New York commission in 1956 hired its own staff of researchers and con-

---

[15] John P. Wheeler, Jr., *The Constitutional Convention: A Manual on Its Planning, Organization and Operation* (National Municipal League, New York, 1961), and John E. Bebout and Emil J. Sady, "Staging a State Constitutional Convention," in Graves, *State Constitutional Revision, op. cit.*, pp. 67-85.

sultants. The published findings of these bodies not only provide valuable service for convention members and committees but also prove beneficial in stimulating an informed public interest in constitutional problems.

Several states have undertaken important constitutional revision by creating commissions to function in lieu of conventions, seeking thereby the advantages of the convention method without the trouble and expense of assembling such a large body. This method permits compactness and expertness of study and deliberation. It attracts less press and radio coverage while the work is in progress, although the final offerings come under public gaze when submitted for ratification. Use of the commission has come into prominence in recent years, partly because of successful experiments in Georgia and New Jersey.[16] The New Jersey legislature in 1941 created a Constitutional Revision Commission to prepare a new draft for a century-old document which had been changed by only four amendments since 1875. The resulting draft, as modified by the legislature, incurred the opposition of Mayor Frank Hague's political machine of Jersey City and failed of ratification at the polls. But the movement for revision continued, and a constitutional convention met in 1947 under the joint encouragement of Republican Governor Alfred E. Driscoll and the Democratic leader, Mayor Hague. The convention proposal was overwhelmingly approved by the voters and took effect on the first day of 1948. In Georgia the legislature in 1943 created a commission, headed by Governor Ellis Arnall, to formulate a draft to replace a constitution cluttered up with more than three hundred amendments. The commission's proposal was modified by the legislature in 1945 and ratified the same year by a vote of two to one. The revision, like the work of a typical convention, fell short of the wishes of reformers, although it improved the basis of local government, abolished the poll-tax requirement for voting, and reduced the voting age to eighteen.

Constitutional commissions

The method of initiating proposals for constitutional change by petition is similar to the method of initiating legislation by petition, which it has paralleled as a twentieth-century development, notably in the West. Oregon adopted it in 1902, and since then it has spread to about a dozen other states. To put a proposed amendment before the electorate in this manner, a petition for such action must bear the signatures of a specified proportion or number of voters. Such a requirement might be 10 per cent of the votes as in the last election for a justice of the supreme court in Oregon, a flat minimum of 20,000 signatures as in North Dakota, or 3 per cent of the vote cast for governor in the preceding biennial election as in Massachusetts.

Amendments proposed by initiative petition

---

[16] *See* B. M. Rich, "Convention or Commission," *National Municipal Review,* XXXVII (March, 1948), pp. 133-139.

102   Most of the hundreds of amendments of state constitutions in force today
originated through legislative proposal. This method has proved the most
convenient and workable for making minor changes or adding one or

Amendments proposed by legislative action   two amendments at a time, while conventions have seemed more suitable for overhauling constitutions. Many western states have not adopted
new constitutions since becoming states but have added many scores of
amendments through legislative proposal as well as a few through initiative petition. All but one of the states have constitutional arrangements for
legislative proposal of amendments to the voters. New Hampshire stands alone
in restricting proposals to the convention process, and, at the other extreme,
Delaware permits passage by two successive legislatures with a two-thirds majority
to put amendments into effect without further action. Among the other forty-
eight states the constitutional requirements vary widely as to procedure and
house majorities necessary to submit amendments to the electorate.[17] About
one-third of these states require passage of a proposal at two successive regular
sessions, one state insisting upon a two-thirds majority each time. The others
permit submission of proposals by action at a single session, more than half
of them requiring a two-thirds or three-fifths majority of both houses. There are
other restrictions, such as limiting the frequency of proposals or the number
per session. Louisiana requires that proposals be introduced within the first
twenty-one days of a session, except in case of an emergency and then only
by a vote of two-thirds of the elected members. Custom and tradition also
affect the feasibility of legislative preoccupation with constitutional change.

Ratification by the electorate is normally the final step in putting constitutional amendments or revisions into effect, with most states requiring ratification of amendments proposed by legislative action or initiative petition.

Ratification   Many states also have constitutional provisions prescribing the popular
ratification of convention offerings, and the others customarily accept
ratification of convention drafts as necessary and proper practice. South Carolina
and Mississippi further require that popular ratification of legislative proposals
be reinforced with subsequent passage by the legislature to make constitutional
changes effective.

Ratification elections are sometimes crucial, and the constitutional work
of a legislature or convention may come to nought unless a statewide campaign
is launched to explain the issues to the voters. New York and other states have
experienced rejection of revision proposals at the polls. The recent trend is
toward the utilization of citizen organizations, leaders, and experts to secure
ratification. Such groups actively supported ratification of the Missouri consti-

---

[17] For amendment procedure and other constitutional information in the various states, *see*
The Book of the States, 1962-63, pp. 5-11.

tution in 1945 and the New Jersey constitution in 1947. The spade work of such groups is no less significant than the spade work performed in advance of the drafting of the proposals.

The final draft of a constitutional convention is usually submitted for acceptance or rejection as a whole at the polls. Through technical requirement or convention decision, however, proposals may be passed upon separately, as is normally the case with amendments presented by the legislative or petition process. Of a group of amendments offered separately, one may pass, while another may fail. A simple majority is adequate for popular ratification or constitutional changes in most states. But there are a few exceptions, as in Minnesota, where the majority for ratification of an amendment must be a majority of those voting in the election; in Illinois, where a proposed amendment is adopted if approved either by a majority of the electors voting in the election or by two-thirds of the electors voting on the amendment; and in Tennessee, where a legislative proposal must be ratified by a majority equal to the majority cast for governor. Such a requirement is an arithmetical handicap for the amendment, since voters are normally more attracted to names of persons of prominence on the ballot than to impersonal propositions. Much more than a simple majority, under such conditions, must be cast for a constitutional proposal in order to put it over. Attesting to the effectiveness of such an arithmetical handicap, Tennesseans until 1953 were able to claim the dubious honor of having the "oldest unamended constitution in the world." [18]

Proliferation of constitutional detail through a floodtide of amendments goes on unabated in some states. Since the adoption of the Louisiana constitution in 1921, that state adopted 407 amendments in the 20 years which followed. This total was 79 per cent of the 518 proposed amendments placed before the voters. In 1962 a bumper crop of 32 amendments out of 48 proposed was adopted by Louisiana voters in a single election. In the same year Georgians voted on 137 proposed amendments, 121 being of local application only, and adopted 107. One of the arguments for adoption of a new Georgia constitution in 1945 was the fact that the old 1877 constitution had been amended 301 times in 68 years. Yet in just 17 years Georgia's 1945 constitution had already been amended 273 times. [19]

Constitutions grow in ways other than through formal amendment. Every state constitution is subject, more or less, to modification and development through judicial interpretation, statutory amplification, and official custom or usage. And state constitutions, like state statutes, may become invalid

Other modes of growth

---

[18] See *William H. Combs*, "An Unamended State Constitution: the Tennessee Constitution of 1870," *American Political Science Review*, XXXII (June, 1938), pp. 514-524.
[19] See *National Civic Review*, LII (January, 1963), pp. 23-24.

through national action, as has happened with respect to questions of suffrage and issues of racial discrimination.

A constitutional provision can be and sometimes is judicially interpreted to permit governmental action which according to an earlier judicial interpretation it prohibited, and for all practical purposes the constitution means what the judges say it means. More often, however, is the scope of a provision extended by gradual interpretation to accord with the governmental needs of a developing community. The courts of our states and of the United States in dealing with matters fundamental to our governmental system constitute, in effect, continuing constitutional conventions.

Insofar as a constitution deals with matters which are bound to be rendered obsolete by rapidly changing conditions, an easy mode of change becomes essential to the functioning of government. One such method is through ordinary legislation designed to supplement or even to circumvent the intent of the framers. Oregon in 1956 submitted to the voters an amendment designed to alter the constitutional prescription of a $1,500 annual salary for its chief executive. The salary appropriated for the governor for 1955 was just ten times the constitutional limit, indicating legislative recognition that the salary set by the constitution was obviously out of keeping with current economic conditions. If, on the other hand, the constitution sets up a skeletal framework, allowing legislative discretion in the prescription of details and in the adaptation to changing conditions, the role of the legislature is no less important. The 1947 constitution of New Jersey, for example, vests the judicial power in a "Supreme Court, a Superior Court, County Courts and inferior courts of limited jurisdiction." Then it provides that the "inferior courts and their jurisdiction may from time to time be established, altered or abolished by law." Perusal of the 1956 study of State Intermediate Appellate Courts published by the Institute of Judicial Administration demonstrates in this one area of government the degree to which legislative enactments augment constitutional provisions, even determining such fundamental matters as jurisdiction. Footnotes to the study include more references to statutes than to constitutions.

Usage also has its impact upon the constitution, modifying its provisions or determining the way in which provisions will be applied or even judicially construed. An example of commingling forces for constitutional change is afforded by Schardein v. Harrison et al.[20] In that case Kentucky's Court of Appeals, applying the principle that "legislative or executive construction of constitutional provisions adopted and acted upon with acquiescence of the people for many years is entitled to great weight with the courts," permitted an incumbent to succeed himself despite constitutional ambiguity as to whether he was

---

[20] 18 S. W. (2d) 316 (1920).

eligible to do so. Party practices obviously determine the way in which the government operates in many instances without being covered wholly in constitution or law. A broad view of the constitution, which would hold that the constitution consists of everything determinative of the structure and functioning of the government, would take into account changes wrought in the fundamental law by practice. Many analysts believe modification of a constitution by means other than formal amendment is at least as important as modification by formal amendment.

Reading over a state constitution, then, will provide one with only a limited understanding of its meaning. As with the United States Constitution, it is necessary to have an acquaintance with a number of significant statutes, court opinions, and practices of executive officials in order to know what the constitution means today. In other words, we must look at the state government both as a whole and in terms of its operating parts to get a valid view of its constitutional features. The foundation takes on meaning according to *Understanding state constitutions* the superstructure which it sustains, and it must not be pictured in isolation or detachment. Hence, all the chapters of this text throw light on the meaning of the living state constitutions, and the student should take care to treat this chapter more as an introduction than as a full explanation of the state constitutional system.

Constitution-making in the state and the nation is much like the proverbial woman's work which is never done. It is always in dynamic process with a miscellany of shifts and trends. The trend in the states toward enlarging the textual contents with the inclusion of virtual codes of rules and laws *Trends* has brought about a counter trend to return constitutions to the exclusive domain of fundamentals. New Jersey, Alaska, and Hawaii have all moved in this direction. Closely related to this counter trend is the movement in many commonwealths for the expert study of constitutional needs and features as preparatory planning for constitutional revision. The constitutional commissions, already mentioned, have made use of scholarly studies and monographs. Governmental research bureaus and university groups have aided in exploring the field in many states. By these methods the gains and experience of one state become useful in another.

Bebout, John E., "Recent Constitution Writing," *Texas Law Review,* XXXV (October, 1957), pp. 1071-1089.

"Constitutions and Elections," continuing article in *The Book of the States* (Council of State Governments, Chicago).

Dauer, Manning J., and William C. Havard, "The Florida Constitution of 1885 — A Critique," *University of Florida Law Review,* VIII (Spring, 1955), pp. 1-92.

Graves, W. Brooke, ed., *State Constitutional Revision* (Public Administration Service, Chicago, 1960).

Hobbs, Edward H., ed., *Yesterday's Constitution Today: An Analysis of the Mississippi Constitution of 1890* (Bureau of Public Administration, University of Mississippi, 1960).

Keith, John P., *Methods of Constitutional Revision* (Institute of Public Affairs, University of Texas, Austin, 1949).

National Municipal League, State Constitutional Studies Project (a series of background studies published in 1960 and 1961):

    Robert B. Dishman, *State Constitutions: The Shape of the Document*
    Gordon E. Baker, *State Constitutions: Reapportionment*
    Bennett M. Rich, *State Constitutions: The Governor*
    Ferrel Heady, *State Constitutions: The Structure of Administration*
    Robert S. Rankin, *State Constitutions: The Bill of Rights*

    A corollary series on state constitutions includes:

    The Future Role of the States; How to Study a State Constitution; A Manual for State Constitutional Conventions (by John P. Wheeler, Jr.); and *How to Study a State Constitution.*

New York Constitutional Convention Committee, *Reports* (12 vols.; New York, 1938).

O'Rourke, V. A. and D. W. Campbell, *Constitution-Making in a Democracy* (Johns Hopkins Press, Baltimore, 1943).

Sturm, A. L., *Methods of State Constitutional Reform* (University of Michigan Press, Ann Arbor, 1954).

Swisher, C. B., *The Growth of Constitutional Power in the United States* (University of Chicago Press, Chicago, 1946).

Temporary Commission on the Revision and Simplification of the Constitution of New York State, *First Steps Toward a Modern Constitution,* New York State Legislative Document No. 58 (1959).

Uhl, Raymond, and others, *Constitutional Conventions: Organization, Powers, Functions and Procedures* (Bureau of Public Administration, University of South Carolina, Columbia, 1960).

* 6 *

VOTERS AND VOTING

Voting is an ancient and modern process by which individuals participate in group decisions. By means of voting, officers and lawmakers are selected to govern and policies may be adopted to guide officers and lawmakers in governing. Under dictatorial rule, it may be a manipulative technique of satisfying the governed by permitting them to approve what is predetermined or inevitable. In democratic government, it is a process by which a majority of the many decide issues and bestow both power and responsibility upon the few of their own choosing. More citizens take part in voting than in any other phase or feature of democratic government. This mass participation, particularly in America, is centrally regulated by constitutional provisions, statutes, and administrative decrees. Despite centralized red tape and bureaucracy, however, actual voting is decentralized. Polling facilities, in city and country, are distributed among convenient locations in such a way that neighbors cast ballots under the supervision of neighbors.

Voting as a function of government

Under our constitution there is no such thing as *national* right to vote. Like many other features of American government, voting qualifications are determined separately by each state, subject to a few important national checks or reservations. The Fifteenth Amendment prohibits the denial of the vote to American citizens "by the United States or by any State on account of face, color,

107

108 or previous conditions of servitude." The Fourteenth Amendment has been used effectively to reinforce the Fifteenth to protect Negro voters as participants in primary elections. The Nineteenth Amendment prevents suffrage discrimination "on account of sex," and World War II was followed by suggestions that the federal Constitution be changed to put the lower age limit for voting uniformly at eighteen. According to Article I and the Seventeenth Amendment, voters for senators and representatives in Congress shall in each state "have the qualifications requisite for electors of the most numerous branch of the State legislature." A degree of indirect control over the suffrage is conferred upon Congress by the provision that each branch shall be judge of the "elections, returns and qualifications of its own members." These national stipulations leave the states wide powers to maintain a broad or narrow suffrage.

Chiefly a state constitutional responsibility

The states fix residence requirements for voting and establish other qualifications, such as ownership of property, payment of a poll tax, or ability to pass a literary test. Even religious tests were applied by a few colonies and states. The democratic expansion of suffrage has essentially been a state movement. Many states had women suffrage prior to the Nineteenth Amendment. The stimulus for wider suffrage has largely come from the West and the large urban centers, from frontier states and industrial states.

The story of suffrage expansion among the American commonwealths parallels the growth of political democracy in the whole Western world. The age of Jackson emphasized the role of the common man and his right to vote without a property qualification. Universal white male suffrage became the vogue in most of the states in this era, although it came about in Rhode Island only after a Dorr's Rebellion jolted the conservative elements to relinquish voting restrictions handed down from colonial times. This general movement toward political democracy more than matched the enfranchisement of men of the middle classes in Great Britain by the epochal Reform Bill of 1832. American Negroes and British laboring classes could lay claim to manhood suffrage by 1870, and fifty years later the women of these two countries as well as of many others were voting. The right or privilege of suffrage, however, was not made absolute in any state. There were conditions to be met and obstacles to be avoided, as will appear in our subsequent look at voting management and procedure.

Development of universal suffrage

The technical establishment of universal suffrage brought new problems to American governments and electorates. Formidable tasks arose in connection with registering voters and supervising voting, particularly in populous areas with high mobility of many classes of people. Furthermore, there is a significant lack of voting in the United States, particularly in local or minor elections and in places or regions where one party or political faction

Nonvoting

predominates. Participation in state and local elections is greater when they happen to be coupled with the election of a president. Those who vote for governor in off-year elections ordinarily number from three-fourths to four-fifths the total of those who vote for governor in presidential years. Table 6-1 demonstrates the disparate drawing power of presidential-year and off-year elections. Many potential voters neglect to register or qualify, and many who qualify often

TABLE 6-1

WEAKNESS OF DRAWING POWER OF STATE CAMPAIGNS: DISTRIBUTION OF 176 GUBERNATORIAL ELECTIONS IN SELECTED STATES, 1926-1952, ACCORDING TO PROPORTION OF POTENTIAL ELECTORATE VOTING, IN OFF YEARS AND IN PRESIDENTIAL YEARS*

Proportion Voting For Governor	Per Cent of Off-Year Elections	Per Cent of Presidential-Year Elections
25-29	2.4	0.0
30-39	16.7	1.1
40-49	26.2	3.3
50-59	32.1	10.8
60-69	17.8	37.0
70-79	4.8	42.3
80-89	0.0	5.4

* The state coverage of the table is: Vermont, North Dakota, Maine, Wisconsin, Michigan, New Hampshire, Pennsylvania, Kansas, Massachusetts, Illinois, Wyoming, Ohio, Colorado, West Virginia, Missouri. The number of elections in off years was 84; in presidential years, 92.

Source: V. O. Key, *American State Politics* (Alfred A. Knopf, Inc., New York, 1956), p. 16, copyright 1956 by V. O. Key, Jr.

fail to go to the polls on election day. Millions who might vote do not vote, even in national elections. The proportion of non-voting is particularly high in some of the southern states. The extent to which Americans fail to exercise their privilege and duty is readily apparent from a contrast between totals of potential and actual voters in a given election.

Much of what we know about voter participation is based on studies of national elections and it may or may not hold true in particular state and local elections. One recent study in Indiana re-examines four familiar propositions on

110 voter participation and suggests the generalizations on national samples may require modification at the state and local level.[1] The four propositions tested in Indiana were that voter participation increases with: (1) the competitiveness of the electoral situation, (2) the degree of urbanism of the population, (3) the prestige of the office, and (4) the totality of the election appeal. The first two were found to be "not necessarily so" in Indiana, where during at least one ten-year period close inter-party races failed to bring out more voters than less competitive races, and where voter participation was found to be greater in rural areas than in metropolitan areas. Greater voting for offices with higher prestige, such as the president or the governor, than for those with lower prestige, such as the prosecuting attorney, was found to be the practice in Indiana. The number of voters attacked by the strange disease of "voters' fatigue" somewhere between the top and bottom of the ballot was not so large as might be expected. The fourth proposition was also substantiated in Indiana — more people vote in state contests if they are held during a presidential election than if not, but, again, the difference is not so great as one might expect.

Studies of nonvoting

No fixed set of reasons can be given for nonvoting.[2] Inertia or indifference to voting responsibility is often the case, especially with citizens who have removed to new scenes or regions and have not "learned the ropes." Some fail to vote because they consider it a futile undertaking, assuming that the "machine will win anyway." Some avoid elections because of confusion over candidates and issues. Some citizens in one-party states fail to vote in the general election on the ground that its result is predetermined in the party primary. In Mississippi's 1959 gubernatorial election only 57,617 voters went to the polls whereas 441,047 voted in the Democratic primary election determining who was to be a Democratic candidate for governor.

Reasons for nonvoting

Even when a close race is predicted, large numbers of potential voters will stay away from the polls if they do not feel deeply about the issues. Crowded conditions and inconvenience at the polls sometimes deter urbanites, including laborers whose working time conflicts with voting hours. This problem is partly avoided in Continental Europe by holding elections on Sunday. But the shorter working day for American employees reduces this obstacle, as does the use of voting machines and other efficient methods of handling voters at the polls.

Voting by Negroes in the South is now rising rapidly after many years of official barriers and unofficial harassment, especially during the period between 1890 and 1920. With the invalidation of the white primary in 1944, the last

---

[1] James A. Robinson and William H. Standing, "Some Correlates of Voter Participation: The Case of Indiana," *Journal of Politics*, XXII (February, 1960), pp. 96-111.

[2] Speculation as to the reasons for our poor voting record continues nonetheless. See, for example, Henry S. Commager, "Why Almost Half of Us Don't Vote," *New York Times Magazine*, October 28, 1956, p. 14.

"fool-proof" method of excluding Negroes from an effective vote was struck down.[3] As Negro registration and voting increase in the South, the degree of increase and the political direction of the "Negro vote" differs sharply both between and within the various states. In Louisiana, for example, Fenton and Vines tested the widely held belief that Negro registration in the South is concentrated in urban areas, and discovered that no clear correlation exists between the degree of urbanism and the extent of Negro registration.[4] They found that Negro registration, if anything, is lower in the large urban centers than in rural Louisiana, and attributed this to several factors: many urban Negroes are rootless and feel little identity with their community or their fellow Negroes; their leadership often works at cross purposes; and interest in registration is probably higher in Louisiana rural areas where the election of a sheriff is an important event. On the positive side, Fenton and Vines investigated the religio-cultural variable and the role of local politicians and concluded that both are extremely important in Louisiana. In French-Catholic parishes the percentage of Negro registration is more than double the percentage in Anglo-Saxon Protestant parishes. They also conclude that where Negro registration is high, the sheriff has almost invariably been friendly to the idea, and their vote seems to be in his factional camp.

Negro voting and non-voting

Negro voting in Texas falls into two sharply different patterns of voting behavior, according to a recent study by Harry Holloway.[5] In the cities Negro registration is high — in Austin their percentage has been higher than for the white population — and seems to approach 50 per cent generally. The city Negroes "form a suprisingly effective, cohesive and stable bloc oriented toward the liberal Democratic candidate, especially if he is strongly pro civil rights. And they decidedly favor candidates of their own race or of Latin (Mexican-American) extraction."[6] A different pattern exists for the rural Negro, however. Holloway suggests that the rural East Texas Negro is still behaving under the tradition of "white paternalism" and is politically manipulated in the caste system of race relations which prevails. Registration is encouraged by white officials so long as he functions as an adjunct to the white vote, but as rural Negroes develop some independence, this encouragement would normally disappear. "Paradoxically, then, the freeing of the rural Negro may well mean some drop in Negro registration in the state's rural countries."[7] A similar pattern

---

[3] *See* Chapter 7 for a discussion of the white primary.

[4] John H. Fenton and Kenneth H. Vines, "Negro Registration in Louisiana," *American Political Science Review,* LI (September, 1957), pp. 707-714.

[5] Harry Holloway, "The Negro and the Vote: The Case of Texas," *Journal of Politics,* XXIII (August, 1961), pp. 526-556.

[6] *Ibid.* p. 527.

[7] *Ibid.* p. 554.

of rural Negro voting in Georgia, in alliance with white factions, is described in a recent study by Bernd and Holland.[8] The first Negro in the Georgia Senate since reconstruction days was elected in 1962 from an Atlanta district.

New federal help to Negroes who had been denied the right to vote was provided in the Civil Rights Act of 1960, enacted after a long and bitter congressional debate. The principal weapon against racial discrimination is an authorization for federal judges to appoint "referees" to determine the voting qualifications of persons local officials refuse to register. If the judge rules that a pattern of discrimination exists in an area, he may name referees to handle voting applications from other persons. Officials refusing to let court-certified Negroes vote are guilty of contempt of court. The law also requires voting records to be kept for 22 months after any election involving candidates for federal office.

Racial gerrymandering

One of the most publicized efforts of a state to prevent Negroes from voting was the action of the Alabama legislature in 1957 in rearranging the boundaries of the city of Tuskegee in such an elaborate manner as to exclude all but four or five of 400 Negro voters, while not excluding any white voters. In the recent *Gomillion* case [9] the U.S. Supreme Court unanimously reversed a lower court ruling and held the Alabama gerrymandering to be an unconstitutional "essay in geometry and geography . . . to deprive colored citizens . . ." of their right to vote in municipal elections. The decision has obvious implications for other types of gerrymandering by state legislatures, making it increasingly difficult to intervene in racial discrimination cases without also intervening in cases of urban-rural discrimination. The Tuskegee decision was thus an important forerunner of the Supreme Court's reapportionment decision in *Baker v. Carr* in 1962.

Proposed remedies for nonvoting

Various remedies have been proposed for nonvoting, which is significantly greater in democratic countries than in modern totalitarian dictatorships. Compulsory voting, with penalties for the negligent, is one suggestion which is occasionally offered. Such remedies have been tried in Australia, Belgium, and a few other small countries with limited success. But America is not moving in that direction. Proposals for compulsory voting have been rejected in a few western states, while the North Dakota and Massachusetts legislatures have failed to make use of specific constitutional power to penalize nonvoting. The American theory is that voting should be voluntary to be worthwhile and that it should be encouraged as both a privilege and a responsibility of citizenship. Civic preaching and energetic campaigning have in recent years succeeded in bringing close to seventy million voters to the polls

---

[8] Joseph L. Bernd and Lynwood M. Holland "Recent Restrictions Upon Negro Suffrage: The Case of Georgia," *Journal of Politics,* XXI (August, 1959), pp. 487-513.

[9] *Gomillion* v. *Lightfoot,* 364 U. S. 339 (1961).

in elections for president,[10] although voting in many local elections is still extremely scant. The problems of voting and nonvoting must not be viewed in isolation. They are to be examined as important parts of a large governmental process and in relation to a group of problems, including the qualifications of voters, ballots and ballot reforms, nominations and elections, the legal regulation of parties and pressure groups, financing politics, and campaign techniques. There is much time and activity between the individual's act of voting and the establishment in office of persons chosen by his vote to govern. It is essential to look at all aspects of the electoral process.

QUALIFICATIONS FOR VOTING

Universal adult suffrage is never quite universal except as a theoretical possibility. In the first place, the age for beginning to vote is fixed at 21 in all the states except four which have a younger minimum age. Georgia and Kentucky have lowered the voting age to 18, Alaskans may begin voting at 19, and Hawaiians at the age of 20. Another requirement not directly connected with personal capacity is that of residence in the state, county, and precinct or other subdivision. The residence requirements vary from six months to two years within the state, from 30 days to a year within the county, and widely for the precinct. A newcomer to Alabama, for example, must reside within the state two years before he can qualify as a voter in any election. Other states which have such a requirement are Mississippi and South Carolina. Twelve states allow voting after residence within the state for a period of six months, and South Carolina provides this privilege to ministers of the gospel and teachers in public schools. Other states have a one-year residence requirement for suffrage.

Age and residence

Until passage of the 23rd Amendment in 1961, *place* of residence, rather than *length* of residence, denied the residents of Washington, D. C., all voting privileges. Ratification of the 23rd Amendment allows the residents of the District of Columbia to elect three electors to the electoral college, but it falls far short of granting full voting rights to D. C. residents. They still have no representatives in Congress, and Congress still controls municipal affairs for the voteless residents of the District.

All states require citizenship as a qualification for voting. There is no

---

[10] The popular vote for president in 1960 was almost 69 million, 64.3 per cent of the adult population. The previous record in modern presidential elections was the 1952 voter turnout of 64 per cent.

national restriction on alien suffrage, and aliens were legally permitted to vote in many states until a wave of native American sentiment called for a change in the 1850's. Several states for some years continued voting by aliens who had formally declared the intention of becoming American citizens, and only within recent times has Arkansas joined all other states in denying the vote to non-citizens. Moreover, citizenship in all states must be without blemish through conviction of serious crime, although a pardon may restore political privileges. Certain states likewise bar recognized paupers and vagrants from voting, but there may be difficulty in determining the facts in the case of persons who are not living in "poor houses" as public charges. In all states the suffrage is denied to the insane and the feeble-minded, but recent studies have raised provocative questions concerning the denial of civil rights to mental patients. In one study[11] a group of patients expressed opinions and interest in political and social issues as readily as the hospital employees did, and, ironically, gave little evidence of being "more illogical, inconsistent, or unprepared to fulfill their obligations as citizens than a similar group of individuals who are not identified as emotionally unstable."

Citizenship without tarnish

The educational or literacy test has been developed partly as a method of restricting certain groups or classes from voting and partly for positive reasons of securing intelligent voting. Much more education is needed in the modern day than in former times because of the multiplicity of offices, candidates, and complex issues for the voter to consider. More than a third of the states have a literacy test, a few of them allowing an alternative in the form of property qualification or an understanding of the principles of republican government. The test prevails most extensively in the South and East, where there is most consciousness of minority groups or the "newer immigration," but it is to be found in all sections of the country. Administration of the literacy test is sometimes characterized by arbitrary abuse or discrimination by local officials, who are often partisan political appointees. Included in such misuses of literacy tests have been instances of "passing" uneducated whites and "flunking" college-trained Negroes in the South, although this type of complaint seems to be on the decline. The New York method of applying the test offers fairly strong safeguards against political abuse. In this state the certificate of qualification is issued by educational authorities, and the requirement is completion of a grammar-school education or a satisfactory examination to provide evidence of literacy.

Educational test

Two vestiges of the property qualification for voting remain. In South Carolina it provides an alternative for persons who cannot meet the literacy

[11] M. R. Hertz, *et al.,* "A Study of Opinions of Mental Patients on Social and Political Issues," *Journal of Health and Human Behavior,* I (Winter, 1960), pp. 251-58.

test. In a few states only owners of property are allowed to vote on public bond issues. Examples of this restriction are found in the West,   *Property test*
although universal suffrage was in part the result of a western movement. The denial of the voting privilege to paupers in a few states is the reverse
application of the respect for the role of property in government.

The poll tax as a requirement for voting bears a kinship to the property
test. It is a per capita tax of something like a dollar or two a year, and it may be
cumulative so that one who skips an annual payment has to pay for two
years in order to participate in an election. It is an absolute requirement,   *The poll tax*
not a substitute for a property, literacy, or other qualification. In 1962
five states still required a poll tax except for persons exempt on account of age
or military service. These states were Alabama, Arkansas, Mississippi, Texas,
and Virginia. The poll tax was adopted throughout the South, during a twenty-
year period ending about 1910 as one of the methods for restricting Negro
suffrage. As a few leaders predicted and a few hoped, it proved effective as a
vote-reducer for both races. More than half the original poll-tax states abolished
the requirement in the first half of the twentieth century, and the resulting
increase in the proportion of voting in these states has provided an invidious
comparison for use by anti-poll-tax forces in efforts to eliminate the restriction
in the states where the tax remains.

As indicated above, concern for voting rights inspired passage of the
Twenty-third Amendment for residents of the District of Columbia in 1961. Voting rights were also the inspiration for the proposed Twenty-fourth Amendment, a
poll tax ban approved by the required two-third vote in both houses of Congress in
1962 after a 23-year-old battle. The poll tax as a requirement for voting would be
outlawed if the proposal is ratified by the legislatures of 38 states within seven
years. Its relation to other restrictions on voting is illustrated by Herblock in
Figure 6-1.

THE REGISTRATION OF VOTERS

It is necessary under modern conditions of society to have a system of
registration for the double purpose of determining who should vote and providing records of those who should vote. The system in each state is set up
through constitutional and statutory provisions along with administrative   *General pur-*
machinery extending from central state and county officials to function-   *pose of*
aries of towns, wards, districts, or precincts. The systems are designed   *registration*
to certify eligible voters and to keep track of such voters by location or residence.
Registration managers check qualifications for suffrage and administer literacy

'I Think Them Feds Got Me, Boys, But I Know
You'll Carry On'

Figure 6-1. Herblock in the Washington Post

tests in most states having such requirements. They make available for use by election officials lists of registered voters at the different polling places. In Arkansas and Texas the records of poll tax payments serve the general purpose of registration.

The method of compiling the lists of registered voters differs among the states and even within a given state. Most states use personal or direct registration, the prospective voter being required to appear in person before the registration board or supervisor to establish his qualifications. A few of the states and less populous jurisdictions use a non-personal or indirect system of registration, registrars being charged with compiling and maintaining the lists of qualified voters. The non-personal method of registration is an obvious convenience for the voter, but it is also an obvious opening for fraud.

The states have two general kinds of voter registration. More than three-fourths have a system of permanent registration in some form. Most of these have this type of registration for all areas and for all elections. The remaining states have periodic registration. A few states vary the regis- *Permanent* tration as between areas or between types of election. The term for *and periodic registration* periodic registration varies widely among the states. A few require annual registration, Nebraska has a six-year period, and South Carolina has ten-year registration. Others have a four-year term. Wyoming requires registration for every general election. Table 6-2 indicates the registration patterns in the different states.

A voter removing from an election unit must transfer his registration to the new area, and permanent registration in certain states may be forfeited upon removal or failure to vote through two elections. It is no easy matter to keep tab on voters who are registered permanently or for a long period. Whatever the form of registration, precautions must be taken to guard against abuses. Otherwise it may be possible for one to vote illegally without serious risk of detection. Registration has become costly and in many jurisdictions burdensome to the point of reducing the electorate.

GENERAL PROBLEMS OF VOTING

The problems of voting have tremendously increased since the Greeks applied the process of casting ballots, or small balls, to express the public choice. The spread of suffrage to the common people brought attention to ways and means of protecting the average voter from direct or indirect coercion, *Secrecy:* whether by candidates, officials, political bosses, employers, or other per- *the Australian* sons of power. One step was to end oral, or voice, voting as well as open *ballot* voting by miscellaneous paper ballots and to adopt a systematic secret ballot. The Australian ballot provided the solution, incorporating new features in the secret ballot, a device which had been known in ancient times and in some of the American colonies. Under the Australian system, each voter on election day receives only one ballot (or set of ballots), which is printed at public expense and which lists all qualified candidates or proposals to be voted for. The ballots are numbered consecutively, private or incomplete ballots are not counted, and no surplus ballots are openly available for fraudulent voting. This system was adopted by Massachusetts in 1888, and subsequently all states except South Carolina have made use of it in one form or another. Henchmen of scheming machines may still sometimes find ways of violating the secrecy or

TABLE 6-2

Type and Coverage of
State Voter Registration Systems

| | Type | | | | | Coverage | |
| | Permanent | | Periodic | | | | |
States	All areas	Some areas	All areas	Some areas	Frequency	All elections	Some elections
Alabama	x[1]	....	....	....	....	x	....
Alaska	....	x	....	....	....	x[2]	....
Arizona	x	....	....	....	....	x[3]	....
Arkansas	....	....	....	....	....	....	....
California	x	....	....	....	....	x	....
Colorado	x	....	....	....	....	....	x[4]
Connecticut	x	....	....	....	....	x	....
Delaware	x	....	....	....	....	x	....
Florida	x	....	....	....	....	x	....
Georgia	x[1]	....	....	....	....	x	....
Hawaii	x	....	....	....	....	x	....
Idaho	x	....	....	....	....	x	....
Illinois	x	....	....	....	....	....	x[7]
Indiana	x	....	....	....	....	....	x[4]
Iowa	....	x	....	x	4 years	....	x[4]
Kansas	....	x	....	x	....	x	....
Kentucky	x	....	....	....	....	x	....
Louisiana	....	x	....	x	4 years	x	....
Maine	x	....	....	....	....	x	....
Maryland	....	x	....	x	....	x	....
Massachusetts	x	....	....	....	....	x	....
Michigan	x	....	....	....	....	x	....
Minnesota	....	x	....	x	....	x[5]	....
Mississippi	x[1]	....	....	....	....	....	x[6]
Missouri	....	x	....	x	4 years	x	....
Montana	x	....	....	....	....	....	x[4]
Nebraska	....	x	....	....	....	....	x[4]
Nevada	x	....	....	....	....	x	....
New Hampshire	x	....	....	....	....	x	....
New Jersey	x	....	....	....	....	x	....
New Mexico	x	....	....	....	....	x	....
New York	....	x	....	x	Annual	....	x
North Carolina	x	....	....	....	....	x	....

TABLE 6-2 (*cont.*)   119

TYPE AND COVERAGE OF
STATE VOTERS REGISTRATION SYSTEMS

	Type					Coverage	
	Permanent		Periodic				
States	All areas	Some areas	All areas	Some areas	Frequency	All elections	Some elections
North Dakota	....	....	....	....	....	....	....
Ohio	....	x	....	x	....	x	....
Oklahoma	x	....	....	....	....	x[5]	....
Oregon	x	....	....	....	....	x	....
Pennsylvania	x	....	....	....	....	x	....
Rhode Island	x	....	....	....	....	x	....
South Carolina	....	....	x	....	Decennial	x	....
South Dakota	x	....	....	....	....	....	x
Tennessee	x	....	....	....	....	x	....
Texas	x[8]	x[8]	x[8]	x[8]	Annual	....	....
Utah	x	....	....	....	....	....	x[4]
Vermont	....	....	x	....	Every elec.	....	x
Virginia	x[9]	....	....	....	....	x	....
Washington	x	....	....	....	....	x[3]	....
West Virginia	x	....	....	....	....	x[10]	....
Wisconsin	....	x	....	....	....	x	....
Wyoming	....	....	x	....	Every gen. election	....	x

[1] Registration is permanent unless removed for cause.
[2] Municipal election.
[3] Except for irrigation district elections.
[4] All except certain minor elections.
[5] Except school district elections.
[6] Registration is for all elections of state and county, but voter must be registered in municipality also to vote in municipal elections.
[7] For all state and national elections.
[8] Constitution provides for registration in cities over 10,000, but no system exists. Poll tax receipts determine eligibility of voters aged 20 to 60 years; exemption certificates for those over 60 in cities over 10,000, and certain others.
[9] Except in some cities.
[10] All elections except special elections.

Source: Adapted from table entitled "Qualifications for Voting," *The Book of the States,* 1962-63, pp. 20-21. Reprinted by permission of The Council of State Governments, Chicago.

integrity of the ballot in order to check on blocs of controlled voters, but the Australian ballot represents a decided improvement over its predecessors.

Secret voting, to be effective, must be accompanied by fairly conducted elections and an open counting of the returns without manipulation. There was a gun battle at Athens in East Tennessee in 1946 on election night when a clique of politicians took the ballots from the polling place to the jail for secret counting without the presence of rival watchers. An alert opposition of young returnees from World War II insisted that the votes "be counted as cast." Election violence has not been limited to rural mountaineers, but such measures are rare.

Honest counting; voting machines

Mechanical voting machines are helpful in regularizing secret voting as well as in facilitating a speedy and accurate tabulation of the results. They remove the problems of spoiled or mutilated ballots and prevent miscellaneous petty frauds. The automatic opening and closing of a curtain for each individual voting operation in the booth make it impossible for one to "stuff the ballot box" without detection. The high initial cost of the machines restricts their use to the more populous areas, although more than half the states have legalized their use. There are old-fashioned city politicians who oppose the installation of voting machines for reasons of their own. Occasional complaints indicate that mechanical voting is not completely fraud-proof, and may have simply inspired more sophisticated devices for adapting manipulation to automation. Administration by honest persons is still the ultimate requirement, if corruption is to be entirely avoided. It is essential, of course, to have fair and honest assistance for persons who cannot perform the mechanical operations because of physical infirmity or incapacity.

Thousands of voters in modern and mobile America are absent from their city, county, or state on election days. To meet this condition, absentee voting has been widely established. The need was first realized during the Civil War, with the taking of a few steps to accommodate the members of the armed forces in the matter of voting. The practice reached great proportions in World War II when Congress and the national government provided cooperative aid to the states in the task of returning votes from the fighting fronts. Most of the states have arrangements for absentee voting, a few providing primarily for persons absent in the armed services. The conditions and methods for absentee voting vary widely among the states. One practice is for an eligible absentee or prospective absentee to apply by affidavit for a ballot during a specified time prior to the election, mark the ballot and sign an accompanying statement before a notary public, and mail the papers early enough that they will reach the proper official at his place of registration in time for the ballot to be opened and counted on election day. Mass "solicitation" of absentee ballots by ward heelers opens the door to a variety of shady

Absentee voting

or fraudulent practices and intimidation of underprivileged voters. Yet the technical safeguards against such fraud and abuse complicate the process, especially for the uneducated voters, who often neglect casting their ballot in this manner.

Many American voters feel burdened with ballot complications, and the intelligent person sometimes finds it difficult to cast an intelligent vote. There are different ways of indicating or emphasizing party nominees of general election ballots. Several states use the Indiana party-column type. This *Ballot com-* provides a separate column for all the candidates of one party, with the *plications* party name and symbol showing at the top. The voter may mark a designated spot at the top to vote the whole party ticket without going down the column to mark each candidate. One master lever on a voting machine casts such a vote. The party-column ballot facilitates and encourages straight party voting, sometimes blind voting. About a third of the states use the Massachusetts, or office-group type of ballot, on which the names of all candidates for a particular office are grouped together with the party designation noted for each name. This makes no provision for straight ticket voting by one stroke, since the voter must make a separate mark for each candidate of his choice. There are modifications of these general types, and sometimes ballots, particularly in local elections, may offer the names of candidates without party classification or designation. Some states and districts confront the voter with more than one ballot at the same general election. There may be one for state officers and one or more for other officers or purposes, especially if there is occasion to vote on a bond issue or a constitutional amendment. Tennesseans go to the polls in August of an election year to mark a state ballot for primary nominations and also a ballot for the final election of county officers. More will be said in the next chapter on the subject of voting in primaries.

The "short ballot" is the aim of a reform movement of fairly long standing for reducing the voter's burden in making his way through the list of candidates and offerings on election day. It is not a superficial paper reform. Supporters of the short ballot have sought to reduce the number *The short bal-* of state and local elective offices to a few of importance and responsi- *lot movement* bility. They emphasize the point that routine and technical positions in government can be better filled by appointment, particularly with the application of merit systems for the selection of civil servants. Studies revealing the advantage to a candidate of having his name near the top of a discouragingly long ballot have given support to the movement.[12] Woodrow Wilson in 1909 became president of the National Short Ballot Organization, which exerted an

---

[12] *See* H. M. Bain and D. S. Hecock, *Ballot Position and Voter's Choice* (Wayne State University Press, Detroit, 1957).

GENERAL PROBLEMS OF VOTING

SAMPLE BALLOT

MARK CROSSES (+) ON BALLOT ONLY WITH RUBBER STAMP; NEVER WITH PEN OR PENCIL
(ABSENTEE BALLOTS MAY BE MARKED WITH PEN AND INK OR PENCIL.)

(Fold ballot to this perforated line, leaving top margin exposed)

GENERAL BALLOT—19th Congressional, 38th Senatorial, 51st Assembly District

INSTRUCTIONS TO VOTERS: To vote for a candidate of your selection for the office of Associate Justice of the Supreme Court, the office of Associate Justice, District Court of Appeal, District One, the office of Presiding Justice, District Court of Appeal, Second Appellate District, Division Two, the office of Associate Justice, District Court of Appeal, Second Appellate District, Division Two, stamp a cross (+) in the voting square after the word "Yes," to the right of the name of the candidate. To vote against that candidate, stamp a cross (+) in the voting square next to the right of the name of the candidate. Where two or more candidates who are to be elected, stamp a cross (+) after the names of all the candidates for that office for whom you desire to vote, not to exceed, however, the number of candidates who are to be elected. To vote for all of the electors of a party, stamp a cross (+) in the square opposite the names of the Presidential and Vice Presidential candidates of that party. A cross (+) stamped in the square opposite the name of a party candidate for President and its Presidential and Vice President candidate, is a vote for all of the electors of that party, but for no other candidates. To vote for those electors who have pledged themselves to vote for a candidate for President and for Vice President of any party not qualified to participate in the election write in the blank names and party of those presidential and vice presidential candidates in the blank space provided for that party. To vote on any measure, stamp a cross (+) in the voting square after the word "Yes," or after the word "No." All marks, except the cross (+) are forbidden. All distinguishing marks or space left for that purpose. To vote on any measure, stamp a cross (+) in the voting square after the word "Yes," or after the word "No," for a person not on the ballot, write his name under the title of the office in the blank erasures are forbidden and make the ballot void. If you wrongly stamp, tear or deface this ballot, return it to the inspector of election and obtain another. On absent voter's ballots mark a cross (+) with pen or pencil.

PRESIDENTIAL ELECTORS
VOTE FOR ONE PARTY

ADLAI E. STEVENSON, for President ESTES KEFAUVER, for Vice President	Democratic
DWIGHT D. EISENHOWER, for President RICHARD M. NIXON, for Vice President	Republican
ENOCH A. HOLTWICK, for President EDWIN M. COOPER, for Vice President	Prohibition
for President for Vice President	

CONGRESSIONAL

United States Senator — Vote for One

THOMAS H. KUCHEL, Republican United States Senator	
RAY GOURLEY, Prohibition Business Man	
RICHARD RICHARDS, Democratic California State Senator	

Representative in Congress, Nineteenth District — Vote for One

CHET HOLIFIELD, Democratic Member of Congress	
ROY E. REYNOLDS, Republican Accountant	

LEGISLATIVE

Member of the Assembly, Fifty-First District — Vote for One

WILLIAM A. MUNNELL, Democratic Member of the Assembly, 51st District, California Legislature	
JOHN R. HINCHEY, Republican Attorney at Law	

JUDICIAL

For Associate Justice of the Supreme Court

Shall MARSHALL F. McCOMB be elected to the office for the term prescribed by law?	YES
	NO

MEASURES SUBMITTED TO VOTE OF VOTERS

FOR THE VETERANS BOND ACT OF 1956. This act provides for a bond issue of five hundred million dollars ($500,000,000) to be used by the Department of Veterans Affairs in assisting California war veterans to acquire farms and homes. — YES

1 AGAINST THE VETERANS BOND ACT OF 1956. This act provides for a bond issue of five hundred million dollars ($500,000,000) to be used by the Department of Veterans Affairs in assisting California war veterans to acquire farms and homes. — NO

2 SCHOOL BONDS. Senate Constitutional Amendment No. 11. Directs issuance and sale of $100,000,000 of state bonds (a) to aid local school districts for school construction in the amount of $90,000,000 and (b) housing and equipment for allocation of money to school districts for schools for physically handicapped or mentally retarded minors. Authorizes legislation providing for allocation for repayment of bonds. Requires legislation for repayment of allocations for other schools, commensurate with districts ability to repay. Declares state policy regarding public school sites and buildings. — YES / NO

3 STATE CONSTRUCTION PROGRAM BONDS. Assembly Constitutional Amendment No. 17. Authorizes issuance and sale of $200,000,000 state bonds to carry out building program contemplated by State Construction Program Bond Act of 1955. Said Act provides for use of the bond money, as appropriated by Legislature, for buildings and building sites for state educational institutions, mental and correctional institutions, and other state facilities. Directs that not less than $60,000,000 of bond proceeds shall be available for state colleges. — YES / NO

4 OIL AND GAS CONSERVATION. Initiative. Prohibits waste, defined as production methods which reduce maximum economic quantity of oil or gas ultimately recoverable by good engineering practices. Provides for unit operation of pools to increase ultimate recovery and lessen waste by lessees of three-fourths of pool. Creates California Oil and Gas Conservation Commission to prevent waste by any necessary or proper orders, including orders limiting production but only to extent necessary to prevent waste. Provides for well spacing; will not prohibit drilling of new wells in new pools. Provides Commission's orders shall protect correlative rights. Provides for enforcement and administration. — YES / NO

5 ALCOHOLIC BEVERAGE ESTABLISHMENTS. Senate Constitutional Amendment No. 2. Eliminates present provision permitting service of intoxicating liquor only in bona fide hotels, restaurants and other public eating places. Permits legislation to separate the service of alcoholic beverages in public premises in which food need not be served; restricts presence of minors in such establishments. Incorporates existing ban on service or sale of alcoholic... — YES / NO

18 INFERIOR COURT JUDGES. Assembly Constitutional Amendment No. 63. Makes judge of a justice court eligible for office as judge of a superseding municipal court established before January 1, even though he is not an attorney, if he has served as such justice court judge continuously since November 7, 1945. — YES / NO

19 STATE BOUNDARIES. Senate Constitutional Amendment No. 1. Empowers Legislature to change, alter and redefine California's state boundaries in cooperation with adjoining states and subject to approval of Congress. Authorizes legislation to adjust property taxes as required by such boundary changes. — YES / NO

COUNTY QUESTIONS

A COUNTY BOND PROPOSITION A. Bonds for Juvenile Detention and Placement Facilities. Shall the County of Los Angeles incur a bonded indebtedness and issue bonds in the sum of Fifteen Million Four Hundred and Fifty-eight Thousand Dollars ($15,458,000.00) for the purpose of providing funds for the acquisition of land and the construction of facilities in various parts of the County for the detention, training or custodial placement of juveniles, and for uses incidental thereto, including the purchase of equipment therefor? — BONDS YES / BONDS NO

B COUNTY BOND PROPOSITION B. Bonds for the Replacement of County Hospital Facilities. Shall the County of Los Angeles incur a bonded indebtedness and issue bonds in the sum of Fifteen Million Four Hundred Thousand Dollars ($15,400,000.00) for the purpose of providing funds for the construction of County Hospital facilities containing approximately 700 beds to replace existing County Hospital facilities at harbor General Hospital, including site development and ground improvements therefor and the purchase of equipment from any funds remaining after construction and other costs have been paid? — BONDS YES / BONDS NO

C SPECIAL COUNTY PROPOSITION NO. 1. Shall the Board of Supervisors of the County of Los Angeles be authorized to adopt the revenue bond method of financing small harbor improvements and a suitable site for public convenience in conjunction therewith, as provided for by Chapter 14 Part 2 Division 2 Title III of the Government Code of the State of California? — YES / NO

D PROPOSED COUNTY CHARTER AMENDMENT NO. 1. Shall paragraph of Section 14 of Article IV of the Charter of the County of Los Angeles be amended to separate the offices of Coroner and Public Administrator by eliminating the requirement that the Public Administrator shall be ex officio Coroner, and to also provide that... — YES / NO

CITY OF MONTEBELLO CITY HALL, POLICE STATION AND CITY JAIL PROPOSITION: Shall the City of Montebello incur a bonded indebtedness in the principal amount of $500,000 for the purpose of the acquisition by said City of certain municipal improvements, to-wit: real property and improvements thereon consisting of a City Hall, City Offices, Police Station, City Jail, and furniture and fixtures necessary therefor?

YES	
NO	

77

---

6 adjacent property necessarily and reasonably needed for and used exclusively for the church parking lot, if such parking lot is required by law and has not been rented or used commercially during preceding year.

NO

STATE LEGISLATURE. Assembly Constitutional Amendment No. 68. Changes name of the Assembly of California Legislature to House of Representatives.

YES
NO

7

LEGISLATIVE BUDGET SESSIONS. Senate Constitutional Amendment No. 4. Requires budget session of Legislature to convene in February of each even-numbered year instead of March. After introduction of Budget Bill permits recess of budget session for period up to 30 days. Provides for expenses of committee members considering Budget Bill during such recess.

YES
NO

8

BOROUGH FORM OF COUNTY GOVERNMENT. Assembly Constitutional Amendment No. 46. Authorizes establishment by county charter of a borough form of government either for all or any part of unincorporated territory of county; any such borough to exercise such county powers and be administered as provided by the county charter.

YES
NO

9

STATE CIVIL SERVICE: CONTRACT ARCHITECTS AND ENGINEERS. Senate Constitutional Amendment No. 6. Provides that civil service requirements shall not prevent Legislature from adopting laws permitting State to employ private architects and engineers by contract when work cannot be performed by state agency staff within the required time.

YES
NO

10

FRAMING COUNTY CHARTERS. Assembly Constitutional Amendment No. 4. Allows one year, instead of six months, for preparation of proposed county charter by board of freeholders.

YES
NO

11

STATE INDEBTEDNESS. Senate Constitutional Amendment No. 7. Sets maximum permissible term of statutory state bond issues at 50 instead of 75 years. Declares that full publicity is given to state bond propositions in ballot pamphlets prepared by Secretary of State; eliminates requirement that such propositions be published for three months in newspaper in each county. Authorizes Legislature to retire authorized bond issue to lesser amount than that fixed by bond proposition.

YES
NO

12

REPEALING ALIEN LAND LAW. Repeal of Initiative Act, Submitted by Legislature. Repeals inoperative law of 1920 which formerly denied aliens ineligible to citizenship the right to hold real estate in California.

YES
NO

13

LEGISLATIVE EMPLOYEES. Assembly Constitutional Amendment No. 9. Authorizes Legislature to provide for selection of legislative officers, attaches and employees, deleting existing limitations regarding method of hiring and amount of daily payroll during sessions.

YES
NO

14

PUBLIC WATER SUPPLIES: MUTUAL WATER COMPANIES. Senate Constitutional Amendment No. 29. Authorizes the State and each political subdivision, district and city to acquire shares of mutual water company stock for the purpose of securing public water supplies. Repeals existing provisions limiting such right to certain public agencies.

YES
NO

15

CIVIL AND CRIMINAL APPEALS. Assembly Constitutional Amendment No. 54. Deletes present time limits within which Supreme Court hearing may be ordered after decision by District Court of Appeal. Authorizes Judicial Council to fix such time limits by rule.

YES
NO

16

CONSTITUTIONAL PROVISIONS RELATING TO JUDICIARY. Assembly Constitutional Amendment No. 53. Repeals a constitutional provision which formerly regulated salaries of superior court and appellate judges. Repeals another provision dealing with the former Supreme Court Commission.

YES
NO

17

Shall WALTER J. FOURT be elected to the office for the term prescribed by law?

YES
NO

For Presiding Justice, District Court of Appeal, Second Appellate District, Division Two

Shall MINOR MOORE be elected to the office for the term prescribed by law?

YES
NO

For Associate Justice, District Court of Appeal, Second Appellate District, Division Two

Shall ALLEN W. ASHBURN be elected to the office for the term prescribed by law?

YES
NO

Judge of the Superior Court Office No. Twenty-Eight

Vote for One

JOSEPH I. CALL
Judge of the Municipal Court

FLETCHER BOWRON
Attorney at Law

influence for the next few years and later was merged with the more comprehensive National Municipal League. In consequence of the movement, the ballot has been shortened or prevented from expansion in many states and municipalities. We have always had a short ballot for national officers. But the long ballot to a large extent continues for county government and plagues the voter in other local and state elections. It contributes to non-voting and makes the outcome of elections more subject to the influence of trivial factors. The long ballot is so stabilized in legal or constitutional provisions and political traditions that shift to the short ballot is a slow and difficult process. The task of the American voter calls strongly for the use of intelligence and information, as will be more abundantly indicated in the following consideration of politics and elections.

SUPPLEMENTARY READINGS

American Council on Public Affairs, *The Poll Tax* (American Council on Public Affairs, Washington, 1940).

Campbell, Angus, *et al., The Voter* (John Wiley & Sons, New York, 1960).

Childs, Richard S., *Civic Victories* (Harper & Row, Publishers, New York, 1952).

Council of State Governments, *The Book of the States,* 1962-63 (Council of State Governments, Chicago, 1960), pp. 16-30.

Fenton, John H., and Kenneth H. Vines, "Negro Registration in Louisiana," *American Political Science Review,* LI (September, 1957), pp. 704-714.

Governmental Affairs Institute, *America Votes: 3,* ed. Richard M. Scammon (University of Pittsburgh Press, Pittsburgh, 1958).

Harris, J. P., *Registration of Voters in the United States* (Brookings Institution, Washington, 1929).

Holloway, Harry, "The Negro and the Vote: The Case of Texas," *Journal of Politics,* XXIII (August, 1961), pp. 526-556.

Lubell, Samuel, *The Future of American Politics* (Harper & Row, Publishers, New York, 1952).

McGovney, D. O., *The American Suffrage Medley* (University of Chicago Press, Chicago, 1949).

MacKenzie, W. J. M., *Free Elections* (Holt, Rinehart & Winston, Inc., New York, 1958).

National Municipal League, *Model Voter Registration System* (4th ed.; National Municipal League, Chicago, 1954).

Porter, Kirk, *History of Suffrage in the United States* (University of Chicago Press, Chicago, 1918).

Price, H. D., *The Negro and Southern Politics* (New York University Press, New York, 1957).

Price, Margaret, *The Negro Voter in the South* (Southern Education Reporting Service, Nashville, 1957).

Robinson, James A., and William H. Standing, "Some Correlates of Voter Participation: The Case of Indiana," *Journal of Politics,* XXII (February, 1960), pp. 96-111.

★ 7 ★

PARTIES, NOMINATIONS

AND ELECTIONS

STATE POLITICS, as distinguished from *national* politics, is probably considered
by many citizens to be in a condition of declining importance against the background of depression, wartime, and space-age issues of national policy.

Persistent importance of state politics
Such a view runs the risk of ignoring the role and importance of state
politics in much the same way that the superficial view of an iceberg
might ignore the dominant seven-eighths of the mass which is submerged beneath the water. Certainly, little or no support for this view
may be found in the writings of political scientists in recent years, whose studies
reflect a contemporary revival of interest in state and local politics. Professor
V. O. Key's *Southern Politics in State and Nation* was a forerunner of many
more studies focusing upon politics and party systems in the states.[1]

---

[1] Alfred A. Knopf, Inc., New York, 1949. Professor Key's *American State Politics; An
Introduction* (Alfred A. Knopf, Inc., New York, 1956), includes states outside the South.
Illustrative of this revival of interest in state politics would be the following recent studies:
Joseph L. Bernd, *Grass Roots Politics in Georgia* (Emory University Research Committee,
Atlanta, 1960); Dean R. Cresap, *Party Politics in the Golden State* (Hayes Foundation,
Los Angeles, 1954); John H. Fenton, *Politics in the Border States: A Study of the Patterns
of Political Organization, and Political Change, Common to the Border States — Maryland,*

126

What explains this new interest in state politics? Undoubtedly the frustration of "party reform" groups interested in changing the character of our national party system has led them to an awareness that in many respects we have 50 party systems in the United States, rather than a single unified national party system. This, in turn, has led to recommendations that more attention be given to studies of political parties at the state level. Much of the problem of developing "a more responsible two-party system," as recommended in 1950 by the Committee on Political Parties of the American Political Science Association, was traced back to the dominant role of the separate state party organizations. As suggested in Chapter 1, American federalism may have withered considerably in the formal constitutional sense, but the strength of state parties continues to give strong life to federalism in practice.

Federalism and state politics

Presidential aspirants in recent years have become painfully aware of the importance of state politics and politicians in their quest for party nomination. The recent Brookings study of presidential nominating politics at national party conventions reveals that the role of governors in this process has come to be more and more important in recent years. In contrast to 1848, when not a single governor was a delegate to the major party conventions, and to 1908, when not quite one-half of the Republican and Democratic governors served as delegates, more than 70 per cent of the Republican and Democratic governors were convention delegates in 1956. Furthermore, of those governors attending the recent conventions as delegates, about three out of four have been chosen delegation chairmen.[2] Senators and congressmen rarely wield as much influence as governors at the national party conventions.

One other factor which seems to be stimulating a new interest in state

---

West Virginia, Kentucky and Missouri (The Hauser Press, New Orleans, 1957); William Goodman, *Inherited Domain: Political Parties in Tennessee* (Bureau of Public Administration, University of Tennessee, Knoxville, 1954); Joseph P. Harris, *California Politics* (Stanford University Press, Stanford, 1955); Warren Moscow, *Politics in the Empire State* (Alfred A. Knopf, Inc., New York, 1948); Stephen B. Sarasohn and Vera H. Sarasohn, *Political Party Patterns in Michigan* (Wayne State University Studies, No. 2; Wayne University Press, Detroit, 1957); Robert Lee Sawyer, Jr., *The Democratic State Central Committee in Michigan, 1949-1959: The Rise of the New Politics and the New Political Leadership* (Michigan Governmental Studies, No. 40, The University of Michigan, Ann Arbor, 1960); Allan P. Sindler, *Huey Long's Louisiana: State Politics, 1920-1952* (Johns Hopkins University Press, Baltimore, 1956).

[2] Paul T. David, Ralph M. Goldman, and Richard C. Bain, *The Politics of National Party Conventions* (The Brookings Institution, Washington, 1960), pp. 97-98. This study points out that a governor may control his state delegation actively even if he is not present at the convention. For example, the Arkansas delegates to the Democratic convention in 1952 are said to have waited for word from Little Rock where the governor kept in communication with the various political forces.

and local politics is a growing feeling among many observers that the traditional image of "bossism," irresponsibility, corruption, and obsession with patronage, is not an accurate reflection of present realities. It might be well first to examine this "traditional image" of party politics, constructing it with assistance from such spokesmen as Lord Bryce, George Washington Plunkitt, Elihu Root, and Theodore Roosevelt.[3] Lord Bryce expressed what we might call the "tweedledee-tweedledum concept" of two parties which have no real programmatic differences between them:

Traditional image of party politics:
(1) lack of program differences

> Neither party has any clear-cut principles, any distinctive tenets. Both have traditions. Both claim to have tendencies. . . . But those interests are in the main interests of getting or keeping the patronage of the government. . . . An eminent journalist remarked to me . . . that the two great parties were like two bottles. Each bore a label denoting the kind of liquor it contained, but each was empty.[4]

The traditional image of the party organization's obsession for patronage probably reached its peak in the "sillygism" of George Washington Plunkitt, a Tammany Hall leader interviewed by William L. Riordin:

(2) dominance of patronage

> First, this great and glorious country was built up by political parties; second, parties can't hold together if their workers don't get the offices when they win; third, if the parties go to pieces, the government they built up must go to pieces, too; fourth, then there'll be h——— to pay.
>
> Could anything be clearer than that? Say, honest now, can you answer that argument? . . . When parties can't get offices, they'll bust. They ain't far from the bustin' point right now, with all this civil service business keepin' most of the good things from them. How are you goin' to keep up patriotism if this thing goes on? You can't do it. Let me tell you that patriotism has been dyin' fast for the last twenty years. Before then when a party won, its workers got everything in sight.[5]

In his oft-quoted speech on "invisible government," Elihu Root pictured the party boss in New York as irresponsible and beyond the reach of the voters:

(3) irresponsibility

> The ruler of the state during the greater part of the forty years of my acquaintance with the state government has not been any man authorized by the

---

[3] The selection of quotations is the same as used by Sawyer, *op. cit.*, pp. 76-77, in a more abbreviated form.

[4] James Bryce, *The American Commonwealth* (2d ed., The Macmillan Company, New York, 1910), II, pp. 21, 24, 29.

[5] William L. Riordin, *Plunkitt of Tammany Hall* (Alfred A. Knopf, Inc., New York, 1948), pp. 18-19.

constitution or the law; and, sir, there is throughout the length and breadth of this state a deep and sullen and long-continued resentment at being governed by men not of the people's choosing. The party leader is elected by no one, accountable to no one, removable by no one.[6]

In addition to the lack of program differences, the dominance of patronage, and irresponsibility, the traditional image of American party politics places strong emphasis on corruption. Theodore Roosevelt once described the boss as

(4) corruption

> . . . a man who does not gain power by open means, but by secret means, and usually by corrupt means. Some of the worst and most powerful bosses in our political history . . . made no appeal either to intellect or conscience. Their work was done behind closed doors, and consisted chiefly in the use of that greed which gives in order that in return it may get. A boss of this kind can pull wires in conventions, can manipulate members of the legislature, can control the giving or withholding of office, and serves as the intermediary for bringing together corrupt politics and corrupt business.[7]

Does this four-fold characterization of American party politics accurately reflect the political realities of the present? One point of view holds that this traditional picture is totally inaccurate because of "a new type of party politics" which is developing in the United States. The idea that the decline of "bossism" has been followed by the growth of a new party politics characterized by responsibility and concern for issues is found in the recent writing of many political scientists, journalists, and at least one novelist.[8] The ingredients of this new party politics have been summarized by State Chairman Neil Staebler of the Democratic Party of Michigan:

A new party politics?

> If I may oversimplify just a little, I'd describe the mainsprings of politics as patronage, money, program and morale. Without minimizing the importance of money and patronage, I would say that the other two, program and morale, which are closely related, are more important.
>
> They are not only more important now; they are becoming steadily more so. There may never be a time when politics can be run without money. . . . But we are in a time of change when the big variable, the big determinant of who will win, the big difference between the Parties is increasingly the difference in Party morale.

---

[6] Robert Bacon and James B. Scott, eds., *Addresses on Government and Citizenship by Elihu Root* (Harvard University Press, Cambridge, 1916), p. 201.

[7] Theodore Roosevelt, *Theodore Roosevelt; an Autobiography* (2d ed.; Charles Scribner's Sons, New York, 1925), p. 149.

[8] *See* Edwin O'Connor, *The Last Hurrah* (Bantam Books, Inc., New York, 1956), pp. 329-331.

130　　This is not necessarily true in every spot. We can all name certain states where patronage is all important. . . . But these areas are shrinking. . . . When the merit system was introduced it gave our political parties a great setback. . . . But it has led to the growth of a new species of Party worker, the volunteer, who works from sheer belief in Party principles and is motivated by this thing I call morale.[9]

It is still too early to know whether a totally new species of party politics in the 50 states is growing up to replace the traditional system of the past century. Probably the most accurate picture is one which recognizes a mix-
Mixture of ture, in varying degrees, of the old and the new. Certainly old-time
old and new bossism and patronage are not what they used to be, but irresponsibility, corruption, and lack of real policy concern have a persistent quality which cannot easily be dismissed. In any case, the modern student of politics should be familiar with all elements in the mixture.

PARTY ORGANIZATION AND OPERATION

Most votes cast in American elections are cast for nominees of political parties, and many nominees appear on ballots in the general elections as the result of being selected in party primaries. Parties and party organiza-
Operational tions affect electoral processes for all units or levels of government,
complexity whether national, state, or local. A political party might be roughly defined as a body of citizens loosely held together by an inner group of leaders and organizers for the purpose of putting its members in office through election or appointment. The party system, in all its aspects, is rather fully treated in courses and texts on American national government.[10] But it is essential at this point to review certain significant state and local features of American politics. The features vary among regions, states, and localities. Party politics is different as between the state and the city of New York, between Mississippi and Minnesota, or between seaboard regions and the hinterlands. The actual power of the major parties is highly decentralized, and sometimes a local unit defies a central committee, whether state or national. Yet the party processes all reflect the historical development of the system, and no political unit is com-

---

[9] Speech delivered to the Woman's National Democratic Club, Washington, D. C., April 18, 1955, as quoted in Sawyer, *op. cit.*, p. 78.

[10] *See,* for example, Chapters IX, X, and XI of H. C. Nixon, *American Federal Government* (Charles Scribner's Sons, New York, 1952).

pletely free from national influences. The ever-changing picture is partly
national, partly federal, and, in part, locally autonomous. It is also largely
illustrative of De Tocqueville's observation that in democratic government "the
members of political assemblies . . . think more of their constituent than of
their party."[11] The analyzer of this political picture must watch his step.

America, in the states as in the nation, has a two-party system with important exceptions and variations. State and local politics in much of the lower
South and in some areas outside the South is based primarily upon a
one-party system, with a frequent two-factional cleavage within the ***Two-party***
dominant party sometimes showing factors much like those of a battle ***system with***
between two major parties. New York City frequently offers the voters ***variations***
the opportunity to vote for one of three party tickets, somewhat in contrast to
the rest of the state. Third parties have at times upset or acquired the balance
of power between the Democratic and Republican parties in Minnesota and
states to the westward. Local voters sometimes disregard party lines and "vote
for the man," as when Little Rock elected a Republican mayor in that Democratic
stronghold or when Milwaukee chose a Socialist mayor. Then there are the
cases of clearly nonpartisan elections of certain officers, notably of members of
school boards and less consistently of judges. The two-party system prevails in
a very loose sort of manner, but it prevails. It is most conspicuous in the most
highly industrialized or urbanized states.

State and local politics, more than national politics, are complicated by
political machines, which may function entirely within one party or may cut
across party lines. The political machine is not limited to any region of
the country, and it may be found under rural as well as urban conditions. ***Political***
It has, however, developed its most striking features in such major cities ***machines***
as New York, Philadelphia, Boston, and Chicago without becoming the
monopoly of one party. It cannot be precisely defined or identified, for a political
outfit may be a legitimate "organization" as viewed by friends or supporters and
a sinister "machine" in the eyes of critics or opponents. The essential operating
"kitty" of a machine may be supplied by various methods, whether fair or foul,
but the solid foundation is an enforced system of rewards and punishments.
Less savory ways of machine financing include assessments on public officers
and employees; kickbacks from public works contractors; bribes or blackmail
from holders of business permits or franchises; contributions from property
owners interested in low tax assessments or lax enforcement of building codes;
protection money from gambling houses, racketeers, and other exploiters of commercialized vice; and kindred methods. Among the machines which have had

---

[11] Alexis de Tocqueville, *Democracy in America* (Alfred A. Knopf, Inc., New York, 1945),
II, p. 90.

leaders entangled with the law, or public investigations, in the middle third of the present century are the Long machine of Louisiana, the Pendergast machine of Kansas City, the Hague machine of Jersey City, and Tammany of New York City. Still other machines have held themselves above criticism on this score for year after year. Machines of both classes are consistently interested in securing and holding political power.

It was often true that a machine was the lengthened shadow of a man, a boss, who was either the founder or an heir in the line of succession. The

Bosses
boss, like the baseball manager, may have been an active participant in the game which he directed with authority, or he may have functioned as an invisible director giving orders from the dugout. Again like the baseball counterpart, he may have been an ex-participant, as illustrated by Boss Ed Crump, of Memphis, a former mayor and a former member of Congress, who mastered the technique of managing mayors, legislators, and governors. Huey Long at the time of his assassination in 1935 was both an active member of the United States Senate and the unquestioned boss of a state machine, playing both visible and invisible roles.[12] The typical boss worked his way up through minor positions in the system to a major place of power in the great game of politics. He was often a man of limited education, but college training proved no handicap to bosses like "Abe" Ruef of San Francisco and Boies Penrose of Pennsylvania. The boss as well as his machine had great power of resilience after defeat at the polls, often surviving what seemed to be their funeral. The development of professional welfare programs made it more difficult for the boss to pose as a benevolent Santa Claus for the city's underprivileged, and the adoption of merit systems, accounting systems, and other administrative efficiencies stripped the state or city boss of much of his old-time power and color. Although bosses have declined in recent years, machines still prevail on the state and local political scene.[13]

Demagoguery sometimes characterizes state politics, and it is by no means divorced from bossism, although the boss was a cool calculator as to what hatreds or prejudices to use in whipping up popular passions. The dema-

Demagogues
gogic play on racial and religious prejudice could not be resorted to by Long in Louisiana in the ways open to a Eugene Talmadge in Georgia

---

[12] See Robert Penn Warren, *All the King's Men* (Harcourt, Brace & World, Inc., New York, 1946).

[13] See Richard T. Frost, "Stability and Change in Local Party Politics," *Public Opinion Quarterly*, XXV (Summer, 1961), pp. 221-235. He reports that the boss is passing in New Jersey, but definitely not the machine. There is a literature of abundance on American political bosses. A classic analysis is that by Lincoln Steffens. See his *Autobiography* (Harcourt, Brace & World, Inc., New York, 1931), much of which is based on his muckraking writings of the muckraking era.

or a Theodore Bilbo in Mississippi. The big city bosses have generally steered clear of this bundle of tricks, although Thompson seemed to please many of his Chicago constituents in talking about hitting the King of England on "the snoot." Demogogic oratory has served at times as a potent weapon for stirring rural and Main Street people to political action against metropolitan interests, "Wall Street," and outlanders in general. But the demagogue may work either side of the fence, pro or con, liberal or conservative.

Reformers and reform movements arise from time to time to challenge the power of boss or machine within or without the party structure of a city or state. Grover Cleveland launched his national career as a reform mayor of Buffalo and then as reform governor of New York. Seth Low became such a mayor of the city of New York around the turn of the century and disrupted the power of the Tammany machine for a season. John Purroy Mitchel accomplished this feat some years later. Governor Ellis Arnall became an important one-term reformer in Georgia and achieved constitutional results, only to see the Talmadge machine return to power. Reform movements tend to die out through apathy of the masses or failure in leadership, or both, unless an able and politically-minded leader takes charge and builds a machine of strength from top to bottom, as did Hiram Johnson in California and the elder Robert M. LaFollette in Wisconsin. Even reformers must play practical politics or soonor or later leave the field. In fact, their category overlaps with those of bosses and demagogues, as was demonstrated by a few southern governors, including J. K. Vardaman and Theodore Bilbo in Mississippi, Huey P. Long in Louisiana, and Charles B. Aycock in North Carolina. Every one of these leaders put through progressive programs in his state, although appealing in part for support to class or racial prejudice in the process. They tempered their sense of idealism or social justice somewhat by the dictates of the possible. *Reformers*

The major parties work through systems of state and local committees in addition to maintaining national committees and a campaign committee for each party in each house of Congress. The national committee of a major party consists of a man and a woman from each state, with additional membership from territories. This national arrangement may aid or influence internal state politics in important respects. But a state committee system has roots and life in its own state and is not under the direct control of any national organization. It is thus part of the workings of federalism in the American party system. State and local committees are most active and effective in two-party regions. Republican committees have limited functions in parts of the South except to render aid to national campaigns and take a hand in federal patronage when their party is in national power. They are non-existent in many southern localities. Political leaders, bosses, and machines *The committee system*

134   may carry on much of their party activity through the committee channels, holding power partly through committee membership and management, or yielding power through loss of committee control. In many cases, however, the men of power may use other methods of operation, leaving routine functions to the responsibility of committees.

The state "central committee" or "executive committee" of a major party varies in composition, organization, functions, and extent of control by law.

State committees   This diversity results partly from the fact that party rules and state statutes on the subject vary widely among the states. Custom and practice also affect the role and importance of the state committee. The membership ranges from about a dozen up to several hundred. The members are chosen through party primaries or by state party conventions, with a few exceptions or modifications. The Democrats of South Carolina pick the members by the county convention method. The unit of selection is frequently the county, but it may be a judicial district, state legislative district, or congressional district, sometimes with the addition of members from the state at large. The officers of the committee, such as chairman, vice-chairman, and secretary, are likely to be important cogs in the system, especially in states where the membership is exceedingly large. The committee chairman customarily is selected on the basis of being satisfactory to the party's candidate for governor. He may be chosen from outside the committee membership.

A state committee which is unwieldy because of large membership finds ways of facilitating its work by delegating much of its power to act to a small executive committee of its own creation. The important work of a large committee is also likely to be planned in advance by a caucus of leaders. An important function of the state committee is to serve as a central coordinating agency for election campaigns. Another is to secure campaign funds. Through its officers, the committee also has duties in connection with arranging and scheduling the state convention, if one is held. In primary elections, the committee has both legal and party duties in making arrangements with candidates as well as with state government officials.

The party picture in the states presents a wide miscellany of local committees. The most prevalent local committee unit for the whole country is the county, but use is also made of such units as town, city, ward, precinct,

Local committees   and district, sometimes including the congressional district. As with the state committee, the powers and functions of these numerous local organizations differ widely under the conditions of two-party or one-party systems, methods of nomination by primaries or by conventions, much or little party regulation by legislation, and other factors. Their official functions are of little importance in local elections which are nonpartisan. The members of a local committee may be chosen by primaries, conventions, or caucuses. These party officials are important agents for getting voters properly qualified and getting out the vote for their nominees on election day. They serve as doorbell ringers, as poll watchers, and as campaigners at the grass-roots or neighborhood level. They cooperate with speakers and candidates as well as with voters, and they overlap with the bosses and machines of their party, if they are not part and parcel of the machines.

It is important to keep in mind the role of the candidates themselves in carrying on the work of the parties to which they belong. They carry much of the brunt of party campaigning, and they provide the leadership for rallying the committee workers. They have much to do with mapping *Candidates* and executing campaign strategy from top to bottom level of the party organization. The work of candidates for important office, along with that of their campaign managers, helpers, and publicity directors, adds much to the life of the party. This work constitutes the chief method of providing or presenting issues for public consideration, even if there is a formal platform offering by the party, which is often not the case. Candidates at times attract the support of ad hoc groups to supplement the activity of the regular party functionaries.

Fischetti

"No Madam, I do not give trading stamps for a vote."

Figure 7-1. Fischetti in the New York Herald Tribune

PARTY ORGANIZATION AND OPERATION

136   In an age of television and other mass media of communication, and of
what the sociologists call "impersonal relationships in a lonely crowd," the
"personal touch" is still very much the basis for a great deal of party

The personal motivation and support. The hand-shaking tour of candidates has be-
touch   come a commonplace part of the American scene, and this kind of
personal attention has become essential both to secure votes and to secure
the loyalty of party workers. Political strategist Jim Farley once wrote about
this aspect of politics:

> . . . I'm an old-fashioned fellow who . . . still believes that the only way to
> get ahead in public life is to understand people and sympathize with their
> viewpoint. It doesn't hurt my feelings when some sophisticated gentleman
> of the writing craft describes me as the kind of fellow who likes to go back
> to the old home town and salute the neighbors by their first names while they
> greet me in return with a hearty "Hello, Jim." The radio is a wonderful
> thing — it has been a tremendous factor in promoting the success of the
> Roosevelt political fortunes — but, to my way of thinking, there is no substi-
> tute for the personal touch and there never will be, unless the Lord starts to
> make human beings different from the way he makes them now.[14]

One of the most perplexing questions which faces the student of politics
is the nature and significance of party competition, especially since genuine
interparty competition at the local level may exist in only a small fraction

Degree of   of elections. What explains why so many districts are always safely "in
inter-party the bag" for one party, and what are the effects of this situation? So
competition little comparative research across state lines has been done on party
competition that it is difficult to generalize. Heinz Eulau concludes from data
gathered in Ohio that there is a correlation between degree of urbanization and
degree of party competition, thus suggesting that advocates of a more competitive party system can take hope in the increasing urbanization of the United
States.[15] This hypothesis found no support, however, when tested by Gold
and Schmidhauser in Iowa. They suggest that degree of urbanization may be
more related to *intra*-party competition than to *inter*-party competition.[16]

---

[14] James A. Farley, *Behind the Ballots; the Personal History of a Politician* (Harcourt,
Brace & World, Inc., New York, 1938), pp. 192-93. For a recent readable account of
politics in Massachusetts, *see* Murray Levin, *The Compleat Politician: Political Strategy in
Massachusetts* (Bobbs-Merrill Company, Inc., Indianapolis, 1962).

[15] Heinz Eulau, "The Ecological Basis of Party Systems: The Case of Ohio," *Midwest
Journal of Political Science,* I (August, 1957), pp. 125-135.

[16] David Gold and John R. Schmidhauser, "Urbanization and Party Competition: The Case
of Iowa," *Midwest Journal of Political Science,* IV (February, 1960), pp. 62-75. For a
discussion of the influence of electoral systems on electoral competition, *see* Charles E.
Gilbert and Christopher Clague, "Electoral Competition and Electoral Systems in Large
Cities," *Journal of Politics,* XXIV (May, 1962), pp. 323-349.

Degree of competition between parties is related to the behavior of legislators, or at least to the "role orientations" of legislators, according to the findings
of a recent study.[17] Data from California, New Jersey, and Ohio seem to support
the hypothesis that legislators elected from competitive districts are more likely
to be district-oriented (as opposed to being state-oriented) than those elected
from one-party districts. Similarly, legislators from one-party districts are more
likely to be state-oriented than those elected from competitive districts.

THE NOMINATING PROCESS

Political evolution and variety characterize the nominating process in state
and local government. John Adams, years before the rise of regular parties,
described a nominating caucus in a "smoke-filled" attic in advance of the
town election. That method is still used in local elections and in con- *Evolution and*
junction with other methods in the making of party nominations. The *variety*
rise of regular political parties brought on the party convention for the
purpose of nominating candidates and drafting party platforms. After several
decades the convention seemed unsatisfactory, at least to democratic reformers,
and the movement for nominating primaries got under way as an accompani-
ment of general adult suffrage. As a result, we find a mixture of caucus, convention, and primary, not only among the states but even in a single state,
as in New York. It is true, however, that party primaries have supplanted or
considerably minimized the party convention in most of the states and local
units of government. It should be mentioned that there still exists a practice of
individual candidacy, handed down from colonial times, by which a prospective office-holder announces for election and gets his name on the ballot independently of party machinery, primary procedure, and caucus endorsement.
Practical and technical problems make this method of self-nomination generally
ineffective in large electorates, but it may be successful in local elections in
small constituencies where personal character and contacts outweigh party influence in the voter's mind. Champions of minor parties and of unpopular
causes sometimes use this techique for purposes of propaganda without any
hope of election.

The caucus method of unofficial nomination was a natural development

---

[17] John C. Wahlke, Heinz Eulau, William Buchanan, and LeRoy C. Ferguson, *The Legislative System: Explorations in Legislative Behavior* (John Wiley and Sons, Inc., New York,
1962), pp. 291-293.

138   with the growth of towns and other large voting units. John Adams, in a classic
       description already referred to, said of the meeting of the Boston Caucus

The caucus   Club in the roomy garret of Tom Dawes, "There they smoke tobacco till
       you cannot see from one end of the garret to the other. There they drink
flip, I suppose, and there they choose a moderator, who puts questions to the
vote regularly; and selectmen, assessors, collectors, wardens, fire-wards, and
representatives, are regularly chosen before they are chosen in the town."[18] This
club operated without legal restriction or regulation, and similar groups operated in this manner for decades afterwards. The congressional caucus for nominating candidates for president followed this plan of eighteenth-century Boston.
Despite its early vogue in high and low places, however, the caucus as the main
or sole reliance for nominating candidates for office came under popular criticism with the rise of Jeffersonian and Jacksonian politics. It was denounced as
unrepresentative and even as corrupt, and caucus by legislators for nominating
non-legislative candidates was objected to as violative of the principle of separation of powers. This method of selecting nominees for president was to end
in the 1820's, but steps were taken earlier to supplant it in the states.

       The delegate convention was resorted to as a more democratic and repre-
sentative method than the caucus for nominating candidates. It also facilitated
       the offering of platform issues to the voters. Delaware adopted the

The con-   convention system during the presidency of Jefferson, and many other
vention   states in the North had gone over to this method by 1830. The nominat-
       ing convention gradually spread over the entire country, with or without
legal regulation. The convention system developed on a hierarchical basis. At
its apex was the state convention made up of delegates from county or town units
which in turn were composed of members from still lower units, such as wards
or precincts. The whole convention system operated under the general direction
of central and local committees. The choice at the level of the precinct unit
could be little more than the work of an old-fashioned caucus, although the
meeting might be designated as a "convention" or "primary." Advantage tended
to rest with the alert insiders, who might meet earlier than the designated time,
might fill the meeting place or bar the door to late comers, and might find other
means of exercising machine control. Then there was the possibility of manipu-
lating the state or county convention in deciding disputes between contesting
delegations in favor of the preferred clique regardless of claims or evidence.
These abuses, great or small, seemed conspicuous in many sections after the Civil
War. They were intensified by the increase in the power and spoils of office
in government, the expansion of which was geared to an expanding economy

---

[18] *The Works of John Adams* (Little, Brown & Co., Boston, 1850), II, p. 144. The citation
is from a diary entry of February, 1763.

with many conflicts of interest. Like the nominating caucus in earlier times, the delegate convention proved unsatisfactory to democratic reformers and yielded to a more direct technique for nominating candidates to office in state and local units.

The primary is a method of making nominations by direct popular action. It is a preliminary election in which groups of voters choose the candidates directly without the use of delegates or representatives in caucus or convention for such purposes. It presumably permits any voter to par-

Rise of the direct primary

ticipate in selecting the candidates to be put on the ballot of his party in the general election. Its first use has been credited to Crawford County, Pennsylvania, where both Democrats and Republicans adopted the practice before the Civil War. The primary spread to other Pennsylvania counties and was used in several states before 1900. In the early years of the twentieth century it was supported by such leaders as Robert M. LaFollette, Theodore Roosevelt, and Charles Evans Hughes as an integral part of the democratic movement of their era. Wisconsin, under the leadership and governorship of LaFollette, in 1903 established by law the first statewide primary election system in the country. Oregon followed the Wisconsin example in 1904, and then the movement spread rapidly among the different states. In 1955 Connecticut lost its distinction of being the only state with no provision for primary elections.[19] In some states, however, the primary is optional with the party committees, and, in certain states, as in New York, it is not employed in choosing candidates for state office or United States senator. In Utah the primary is used only in cities of the first and second class. The Connecticut primary is resorted to only if an unsuccessful convention candidate who polls at least 20 per cent of the convention vote challenges the convention outcome. His challenge is in the form of a petition calling for a primary and signed by a certain number or percentage of party members.

Direct primaries, as generally understood and conducted, are usually distinctly partisan. However, nonpartisan primaries are held in a number of states for local selections and for choosing certain state officers, particularly judges. Minnesota in 1912 applied this type to the selection of

Partisan and nonpartisan primaries

members of the legislature, and Nebraska has prescribed that method for the choice of the members of the state's unicameral legislature. The nonpartisan primary is designed to make local and judicial elections and officers independent of party organizations or machines and national political influence. The candidates are listed on the primary ballot without any party designation or emblem, and a majority vote is sufficient for office without a second election. There

---

[19] *See* Duane Lockard, "Connecticut Gets A Primary," *National Municipal Review*, XLIV (October, 1955), pp. 469-470.

140 must be a second or general election if a divided vote prevents a majority in the first contest. The primary, as thus used, is a preliminary or semi-final general election. The nonpartisan primary frequently does not preclude undue political pressure and machine influence, for candidates may be earmarked and classified by leaders and bosses without the fact being stated on the ballot. Printed slates may be unofficially distributed or published in advance of the polling date. It is difficult to remove national party influence from all local elections, particularly in our largest cities.

Whether partisanship has actually been removed when the nonpartisan ballot has been adopted is the subject of more than one recent study. The result seems to be a variety of patterns in which the role of the party organiza-

Patterns in "nonpartisan cities"

tion varies from a position of recognized dominance to that of almost complete impotence. Professor Adrian suggests the following typology for nonpartisanship in actual practice:[20] (1) cities in which it is normally impossible for a candidate to win without the support of a major party organization (e.g., Jersey City during the time of the Hague machine, and Chicago); (2) cities where both party and nonparty groups compete with slates of candidates on a reasonably equal basis (e.g., Cincinnati, Albuquerque, and Wichita); (3) cities customarily having slates supported by nonparty groups but with little or no participation by party organization (e.g., Kansas City since the fall of Pendergast, Dallas, Fort Worth, Nashville, and many others); and (4) cities in which neither party organizations nor slates of candidates are important. The third and fourth types appear to be far more common than the first two, but the fourth, often based on what Eugene Lee has called a "politics of acquaintance,"[21] may be the most common pattern of all. Under this last system individual candidates typically develop their own organization, financial support, and following on an ad hoc basis.

Primaries, whether optional or mandatory, partisan or nonpartisan, are generally regulated by state law, if one may overlook a few southern attempts to save the "white primary" by processes of de-legalization. Partisan primaries

Legal features of primaries

are usually held on the same day for the different parties at designated voting places. The returns may be canvassed and reported by party officials as prescribed by law. Names of candidates for nomination are placed on primary ballots by various methods, including individual declaration and filing of candidacy, petition by a specified number or percentage of qualified voters,

---

[20] Charles R. Adrian, "A Typology for Nonpartisan Elections," *Western Political Quarterly*, XII (June, 1959), pp. 449-458.

[21] Eugene C. Lee, *The Politics of Nonpartisanship: A Study of California City Elections* (University of California Press, Berkeley, 1960). *See also* James Q. Wilson, "Politics and Reform in American Cities," in Ivan Hinderaker, ed., *American Government Annual, 1962-1963* (Holt, Rinehart and Winston, Inc., New York, 1962), pp. 37-52.

and action through a preprimary convention. The petition method is widely used, sometimes along with others. The aspirant for nomination may be required to pay a filing fee, which varies for different states and offices. This is one way of financing primaries. In the greater number of states a plurality vote is adequate for nomination, but several states, especially in the South, require a majority vote, with a second primary for a "run-off" between the two leading candidates in case no one receives a majority in the first contest. The "run-off" for state nomination in such states as Texas, Louisiana, or Alabama is often a conspicuous battle with manifestations suggestive of a two-party contest.[22] Preferential voting, the casting of first and second choice votes, has been proposed as a means of avoiding the burden of a run-off primary. Adoptions have been few, however, and preferential voting has been used more by sports writers in selecting the top ranking football or basketball teams in the nation than by the states for party primaries.

Partisan primaries are of two types, open and closed. In a majority of the states the closed type prevails. It is based on the theory that only Democrats should vote in Democratic primaries and only Republicans in Republican primaries. Under this method the participant, besides being a qualified voter, is supposed to meet a prescribed test of party allegiance before receiving a ballot at the polls. The test varies from a simple statement of party affiliation to proof by the voter that he has supported the party ticket and expects to support it in the approaching general election. The secret ballot makes it easy in many states for a voter to meet the test without being effectively challenged as a bona fide member of the party.

The closed primary

Court controversies have occurred in parts of the one-party South over a special application of the closed primary. Between 1910 and 1940 movements were undertaken with no little success to bar Negro voters from participation in Democratic primaries. This, in effect, denied them a voice in the election of governmental officers, since nomination in the Democratic primary is tantamount to election in these states. Negroes began to participate rather freely after 1930 in party primaries in portions of the South, particularly in North Carolina, Virginia, and Tennessee. But a series of decisions by the United States Supreme Court was required to break up the "white primary" as contrary to the Fourteenth and Fifteenth Amendments. Southern attempts, especially in Texas, to classify the primary as a private, voluntary

The "white primary"

---

[22] Until 1962 the Democratic state primary in Georgia operated by law as a county unit system somewhat as the Electoral College does in the election of the president of the United States. Eugene Talmadge in 1946 won a majority of the county units and the Democratic nomination for governor with a popular vote second from the top. The rural-cherished county unit system was abandoned after being voided by a three-judge federal court, resulting in the first Georgia primary on a popular-vote basis since 1908.

142 organization, completely nongovernmental in nature, proved of no avail in the end. The Court cut through this subterfuge in the significant case of *Smith* versus *Allwright* in 1944, the last of a series of cases from Texas on the subject.[23] Thus a disguised method of disfranchisement on racial grounds came to an end in the technical and constitutional sense. A substantial participation in primaries and other elections by southern Negroes has followed the outlawing of the "white primary."

The open primary prevails in a few states, including Minnesota, Montana, Wisconsin, Washington, and Michigan. The qualifications for voting in such a primary are the same as for voting in a general election, with

The open primary

no legal way of preventing a Democrat or Republican from voting to nominate a candidate for the other party. In Montana and Wisconsin the voter is supplied with ballots of all parties and instructed to select the ballot of his preference, to vote for the candidates of his choice on that ballot, and to surrender the unused ballots. Minnesota uses a consolidated primary election ballot with the candidates listed in party columns, permitting the voter to choose his column in secret with the restriction that voting for candidates in two columns voids the ballot. The state of Washington has a still more wide-open primary with no semblance of party regularity in the voting booth. This system utilizes a blanket ballot listing all candidates for nomination and permitting the voter to switch freely from party to party in marking his choices. The high man of each party for each office wins the nomination. The open primary, as well as the loosely regulated closed primary, is criticized on the ground that it permits outside voters or interests to raid a party and dictate its nominations, even to the extent of forcing upon the party weak or otherwise unsatisfactory candidates.

Double filing is a system which is closely related in idea and purpose to the open primary. Under this plan a candidate may seek nomination for the same office by two or more parties in the same primary election. This

Double filing

was allowed by California until 1959 and still is by New York. Mayor La Guardia was nominated for his first term by the New York City primaries of the Republican party and the American Labor party. Double filing was limited in New York in 1947 by the legal requirement that candidates be enrolled as members of the party in which they seek nomination unless excepted from the requirement by party authorities. Governor Warren of California was nominated for re-election in 1946 by his own Republican party and by the Democrats in the same primary. In that state a candidate listed on

---

[23] 321 U. S. 649. Other Texas cases involving the issue are *Nixon* v. *Herndon,* 273 U. S. 536 (1927); *Nixon* v. *Condon,* 286 U. S. 73 (1932); *Grovey* v. *Townsend,* 295 U. S. 45 (1935). For an important collateral opinion on the primary not involving the race issue, *see United States* v. *Classic,* 313 U. S. 299 (1941).

in order to make any other nomination effective.

The primary system tends to favor the large parties. A small primary vote tends to serve as an unfavorable opinion poll. In a number of states small parties are denied the use of the system for lack of showing at the polls. Most states prescribe a minimum number or proportion of the votes cast at the last preceding general election to qualify a party to enter the primary. It is 10 per cent in several states, 2 per cent in a few, 25 per cent of the total vote cast for presidential electors in Virginia, 20 per cent of the total vote cast for presidential electors in Kentucky and Oregon, and in Florida on January 1 preceding the primary election the party must have registered to vote as members more than 5 per cent of the total registered electors of the state. The Republican party is out of the primary system in some of the southern states. Weak or new parties may use other means of selecting candidates, but this is likely to call attention to their inferior status.

Appraisal of the primary

The open primary and the nonpartisan primary are criticized as interfering with party discipline or responsibility, and the closed primary is sometimes criticized as entrusting too much public power to party functionaries. The primary has clearly tended to make nominations more democratic than formerly, although it has not met the expectations of its early sponsors. It has increased the number, routine, and expense of elections, with greater burdens for candidates, voters, and election officials, and the result is all too often virtually noncompetitive, deserted primaries. Yet there is little prospect of departure from the use of state and local primaries for the nominating process. The question is more one of change or improvement than of abolition of this method of making nominations for election. The problems of the primary are a part of the general electoral problem, and all of these problems must be considered together.

ELECTIONS AND ELECTORAL PROBLEMS

The general election is the final action in the states and local units in determining who will hold elective office. It is the climax in the great game of politics, and it requires an extensive system of rules, umpiring, and scorekeeping. There is usually an officer, often the secretary of state or a special board, to administer the election laws at the state level. The details, however, are under the charge of local officials, such as the county clerk, city clerk, or special board; and finally there are precinct inspectors, clerks, managers, and returning officers who conduct activities at the polling places. The major parties are generally represented among those conducting elections except

Importance of managing general elections

in areas where only one party prevails. Parties with nominees are allowed to have watchers at the polls. Precinct voting may be held in public buildings, such as school houses, city halls, fire halls, and courthouses, but frequently it is necessary to rent polling places for the day. The hours for voting are determined by law and normally extend from six or seven A.M. to six or seven P.M. After the polls close the votes must be counted, certified, and reported. Local canvassing officials receive returns from the different voting places and report the results to the proper county or state authorities. The results are then officially announced, and writs or certificates of election are issued to the winners. Several days may elapse before the final official results are announced, but usually within a few hours unofficial results are announced to the public.

Unsuccessful candidates frequently contest close elections. The laws for contests vary, but ordinarily the defeated candidate, or in some cases a qualified supporter, may contest an election on claims of miscount, misconduct, fraud, or corruption on the part of election officials; ineligibility of the victorious candidate; illegal votes for the winner; rejection of legal votes for the loser; and bribery or intimidation in such a manner as to prevent a fair and free election. Contests may be heard by an election board or tried by a regular court, according to the law or constitution of the state, with possible appeal to the state supreme court. Denial of national constitutional rights in local elections may lead to cases in federal courts. The exposure of unsavory facts may lead to criminal prosecution of individuals. Legislatures may investigate elections, especially of their own members, and each house of Congress, of course, has full power to investigate state and local elections involving its seats.

Contested elections

The different ways of designating party nominees on general election ballots militate for or against party strength. The Indiana, or party-column type, as noted in the preceding chapter, encourages straight party voting. The Massachusetts, or office-group type, encourages split-ticket voting, or at least equalizes such voting with straight-party voting. There are modifications of both of these general types. Montana has the party column without provision for voting by a single mark. Texas has a column type with the unique requirement that the voter "scratch" the ballot by drawing a line through names of the candidates he opposes, the "unscratched" getting his vote.

Party labels on election ballots

Many methods have been advanced and tried in America and other countries to provide more adequate representation of the minority than is generally found under two-party or one-party systems. Third parties sometimes poll substantial votes only to wind up with no post-election power or voice in government. Several plans have been devised to modify the workings of the simple majority or plurality rule for the selection of

Problems of minority representation

John C. Calhoun anticipated this modern problem in his discussion of the concurrent majority to protect a minority section from the dominance of an arithmetical majority beyond the regional border. Calhoun thought representation should reflect both numbers and interests. Representation of numbers he deemed the absolute majority; representation of interests he deemed the concurrent majority. He maintained that the "more extensive and populous the country, the more diversified the condition and pursuits of its population, . . . the more difficult is it to equalize the action of the government — and the more easy for one portion of the community to pervert its powers to oppress, and plunder the other."[24] It is necessary to guard against both the tyranny of numerical majorities and the tyranny of organized minorities.

Two of the more common proposals for more adequate minority representation are cumulative voting and proportional representation. Cumulative voting is possible in the election of groups or delegations, as when several members to represent a county in the state legislature are to be *Cumulative* selected. It is used in this way to choose members of the lower house *voting* of the Illinois legislature. By this plan a voter may cast one vote for as many candidates as there are members to be chosen from his district or cast his total number of votes for one candidate. Thus a minority group of citizens may concentrate votes on one candidate with the hope of electing him instead of dividing support among a number of sure losers. It is a scheme for facilitating the minority voice within the framework of majority rule.

Other schemes, more mathematically accurate, have been devised for achieving the goal of proportional representation (often called "PR"). One scheme is the List plan, which proportions legislative seats among different lists of candidates on the basis of the relative votes received. It has *Proportional* been used in western Europe and necessitates voting for the party as a *represen-* whole, rather than for individual candidates. American experiments in *tation* proportional representation have been examples or modifications of the Hare system, which was advanced by Thomas Hare, an Englishman, in 1859 and praised by John Stuart Mill. By this method the voter expresses a first choice for one candidate, a second choice for another, and so on for as many as there are positions to be filled. A quota is determined by dividing the total number of valid ballots cast by the number of posts or seats to be filled, plus one, and adding one to the quotient. The quota for a district casting 240,000 ballots for five positions would be $\frac{240,000}{5+1}$ + 1, or 40,001. Candidates receiving 40,001 or more first choices are elected, and, if necessary, their surplus votes as well

---

[24] *The Works of John C. Calhoun* (Appleton-Century-Crofts, Inc., New York, 1853), I, pp. 15-16.

146   as the votes of the weak candidates are distributed among the next ranking candidates to attain quotas. The actual voting procedure is simple, but the counting is a complicated process which confuses many citizens.

Proportional representation has been used in a few American cities for election to the council body, but never for higher legislative chambers as in Europe, Canadian provinces, and Australian states. "PR" is praised as a method of providing representation for minority and occupational groups and for checking local political machines. It is criticized as inimical to the two-party system and as an encouragement to "splinter" parties. It was abandoned by New York City not long after World War II, and one of the arguments used against it in this instance was that Communists could use it to get an official contact with the city government. The dominant party pointed to the 1945 election of two Communists, duly labeled as such on the ballot, to the city's council under the system. The Communists polled 9 per cent of the votes and received 9 per cent of the council's seats.[25]

States have long had laws against such practices as fraudulent voting, buying votes, intimidating voters, providing liquor at polling places, or selling liquor on election days. Modern conditions have called for legislation on

Legislation on corrupt practices

other campaign practices. A number of states prohibit campaign assessments on public employees. There is also state legislation forbidding political contributions by corporations, limiting campaign funds, and requiring reports on sources and uses of funds. This legislation is reinforced in different ways by national legislation on the subject, not only with respect to presidential and congressional elections but also with application to state and local contests. The Hatch Acts, taken together, not only bar federal employees from active official politics but likewise restrict state or local employees receiving any federal funds. They also prohibit political pressure on such employees for campaign contributions. Corporations are barred from contributing to national election campaigns, and federal legislation prohibits corporations, like national banks and labor unions functioning under national protection, from using their regular funds for political purposes.

There is a serious need for revamping and clarifying legislation on the use of money in elections, whether national, state, or local. Substantial funds are necessary in all elections outside of small towns or villages. The

Inadequacy of corrupt practice legislation

electoral safeguards of a frontier democracy are inadequate for the elaborate and high-pressure campaigning in modern America. Extensive use of money in elections might as well be recognized and made allowable

---

[25] *See* Richard S. Childs, *Civic Victories* (Harper & Row, Publishers, New York, 1952), Chapter XXVI, and Belle Zeller and Hugh A. Bone, "The Repeal of P. R. in New York City — Ten Years in Retrospect," *American Political Science Review*, XLII (December, 1948), pp. 1127-1148.

by law. It is a complex task to formulate and apply fair rules for the use of campaign funds by business, labor, agriculture, and professional interests. Low limits for campaign expenditures have led to subterfuge and indirection in the collection and disbursement of funds. It would seem that effective and systematic publicity with respect to all campaign funds is a greater civic need than further restrictions on the size of campaign chests.

SUPPLEMENTARY READINGS

Brogan, D. W., *Politics in America* (Harper & Row, Publishers, New York, 1954).

Childs, Richard S., *Civic Victories* (Harper & Row, Publishers, New York, 1952).

Ewing, Cortez A. M., *Primary Elections in the South: A Study in Uniparty Politics* (University of Oklahoma Press, Norman, Okla., 1953).

Flynn, E. J., *You're the Boss* (The Viking Press, New York, 1947).

Heard, Alexander, *The Costs of Democracy* (University of North Carolina Press, Chapel Hill, 1960).

Heard, Alexander, *A Two-Party South?* (University of North Carolina Press, Chapel Hill, 1952).

Key, V. O., *American State Politics* (Alfred A. Knopf, Inc., New York, 1956).

Lee, Eugene C., *The Politics of Nonpartisanship: A Study of California City Elections* (University of California Press, Berkeley, 1960).

Leiserson, Avery, *Parties and Politics* (Alfred A. Knopf, Inc., New York, 1958).

Levin, Murray, *The Compleat Politician: Political Strategy in Massachusetts* (Bobbs-Merrill Company, Inc., Indianapolis, 1962).

Lockard, Duane, *New England State Politics* (Princeton University Press, Princeton, 1959).

Milligan, M. M., *The Inside Story of the Pendergast Machine by the Man Who Smashed It* (Charles Scribner's Sons, New York, 1948).

Mitchell, Stephen A., *Elm Street Politics* (Oceana Publications, Inc., New York, 1959).

Shannon, J. B., *Money and Politics* (Random House, New York, 1959).

Steffens, Lincoln, *Autobiography* (Harcourt, Brace & World, Inc., New York, 1931).

Van Devander, Charles W., *The Big Bosses* (Howell, Soskin, Publishers, New York, 1944).

Wilson, James Q., *The Amateur Democrat: Club Politics in Three Cities* (University of Chicago Press, Chicago, 1962).

* *8* *

PUBLIC OPINION

AND PRESSURE GROUPS

THERE IS much more to government, particularly democratic government, than the formal processes of nominations, party campaigns, elections, legislation, executive policy, administration, and judicial decision. Social forces, for good or ill, affect all phases, branches, and levels of government. The role

Non-official forces

of public opinion and the press as an influence in American government was recognized by Thomas Jefferson, Alexis de Tocqueville, and James Bryce, not to mention latter-day observers and social scientists. James Madison spoke brilliantly and prophetically in *The Federalist*, Number 10, of "a landed interest, a manufacturing interest, a mercantile interest, a moneyed interest, with many lesser interests" and observed that the "regulation of these various and interfering interests forms the principal task of modern legislation," involving "the spirit of party and faction in the necessary and ordinary operations of government." Madison realized that factional interests are inevitable and cannot be abolished or prevented in any way short of destroying liberty itself. He advanced the opinion that relief is only to be sought in the means of controlling the effects.

Just how important are these organized factional interests or "pressure groups?" The naive citizen may have a totally unrealistic impression of the

148

governmental process consisting principally of well-insulated activities of voting, law making, administration, and court interpretation, and may be strangely unaware of the continuous day-to-day struggle among groups for power and influence over governmental decision makers. At the other extreme, however, perhaps in the name of sophistication, he may have arrived at a cynical view of pressure groups as being all powerful and of politicians and administrators as mere pawns with no real power in their own right. Truth is probably somewhere in between these extremes. A more realistic view of state and local government will strike a balance which includes an understanding of the importance of both the official institutions of government and the non-official forces such as pressure groups.

Two extremes

Certain rights of private and group pressure on government are guaranteed against national intereference by the First Amendment and indirectly against state or local interference by the Fourteenth Amendment. It is possible to regulate and publicize the activities of pressure groups, but the federal government has found such tasks difficult. Lower levels of government have, on the whole, made much less headway than have the central authorities. It should be noted, however, that special interest may balance special interest with incidental results of public good. But there is no standing assurance of such a beneficial balance in specific cases or conditions, as municipalities and counties particularly have discovered in years gone by. The pressure of special interests may be offset by the influence of an independent press and of organized groups of citizens with broad purposes transcending class interests. On whatever score, government is closely linked with organized group power and with the media of mass communication. That linkage is a vital and recognized feature of modern politics.

Pressures exerted by many groups affect both national and state or municipal government in such fields as labor-management relations, taxation, transportation, and conservation. Many pressures are directed primarily at the national government, as is true in matters of foreign policy and international relations. Many special and general pressures are pointed chiefly or entirely at the lower levels of government, as in problems of local health regulation, school improvement, municipal vice or graft, juvenile delinquency, fire prevention, metropolitan growth and adjustment, land-use planning and zoning, and the operation of state, city, or county business. Among the organizations which keep a close watch on state and local government are branches of the League of Women Voters, associations of taxpayers, chambers of commerce, labor unions and councils, teachers' associations, manufacturers' associations, farm groups, leagues of municipalities or counties, and different types of professional groups. Railroad interests and trucking interests are on the job when their franchises, operations, properties,

Types and examples of pressure at state and local levels

and taxes are involved. Newspapers and other vehicles of communication maintain news coverage of all these public activities and at the same time provide channels for shaping opinion on pending issues. Government agencies and administrators also issue statements of information and interpretation concerning their activities, and these statements, whether official or unofficial, are not calculated to cultivate disfavor for the policies of the issuing authorities.

Most pressure groups, exclusive of holders of government jobs and in contrast to political parties, are not directly concerned with winning office for their members. Their primary purpose is to influence government policy, either to achieve something or to prevent something. The influence may *Pressure* *group aims* be applied for the purpose of securing favorable legislation or administrative decision. It may be against a too rigid or too lenient enforcement of a law or regulation where a range of administrative discretion or decision is provided, as in the case of urban zoning, formulating traffic rules, or granting permits for selling and serving beer. It may be for or against expansion of city limits; a proposed administrative reorganization; projected changes in a state constitution; the issuance of county, municipal, or state bonds; and the election of candidates because of their views on issues affecting group interests. A pressure group may have an educational, a religious, a racial, or an economic, purpose, or a combination of purposes. Such a group is by no means detached from politics except organizationally. Its aims are essentially political.

The special and general pressure groups have extensive overlapping of membership and it is frequently the case that an organization or its leadership lacks the support of important blocs of members. We are a nation of *Limitations* *of diverse* *groups* joiners, and many a citizen belongs to many organized groups serving different and even conflicting purposes. Physicians who are members of the American Legion and also of the American Medical Association cannot support both organizations when they clash over policies relating to public health or hospital services. A citizen may not be able to go along with his taxpayers' association on a program of economy and at the same time support his civic group's plan for an expensive civic auditorium. One of the more serious obstacles to the development of a well-informed citizenry, with objective and dependable news sources, is the absence of effective competition between newspapers in many cities. Yet, even in single-ownership communities a newspaper cannot completely ignore or suppress important news and publicity on men and movements it may be fighting bitterly on its editorial page. Huey Long, when governor of Louisiana, made headlines in New Orleans papers which were opposing him. Much of this news was favorable to Long despite slants in writing it. The press ordinarily gives the news, even in a one-paper town, because the economics of newspaper management, if not the ethics of journalism, favors news coverage. There are likewise clear limitations on tendencies toward one-sidedness and partisanship in the uses of radio and television.

What determines the strength or weakness of a pressure group? Perhaps the most obvious source of strength is the number of members (potential voters) which the group can claim, but size alone is not a guarantee of strength. Some groups become increasingly disunited as growth occurs. The larger labor unions seldom exhibit the same cohesion in politics that they do in collective bargaining. When large size is accompanied by unity and cohesion, however, a certain degree of strength is assured. Similarly, the geographic distribution of the members of a political interest group may contribute to strength or weakness, and it would be difficult to state a single rule on the effects of having a scattered membership. A group concentrated in one city, for example, could exert a great deal of influence over the local government of that community. But such a group might well be snubbed by a state legislature as representing only a small sectional interest. Conversely, an influential state-wide organization would be hard put to influence a particular city council or mayor.

Sources of strength:
(1) Size

(2) Cohesion

(3) Geographic distribution

Related to the factors of size, unity, and geographic distribution is the less tangible but equally vital factor of prestige or status. Leaders of the medical profession, the banking association, or the bar association, will usually enjoy more easy access to the decision-making circles of state and local government than will representatives of migratory farm workers, "offbrand cults," or other groups which society has generally branded as having low status. Status is not a permanent thing, nor is it the same from state to state or city to city with respect to similar pressure groups. Leaders of the NAACP do not enjoy the same access to the Mississippi legislature as they do to the legislatures of Illinois, Michigan, and New York. Support of the local Chamber of Commerce may well be the "kiss of death" for a proposal in some city councils, while it may guarantee easy passage in others. Reputations vary with circumstances and there is always the possibility that "abuse of status" may backfire, but a prestigious membership is generally a tremendous asset to a pressure group.

(4) Status

Organization and leadership are other factors which can make or break the power of a pressure group. A decentralized, loosely-knit organization with diversified local power centers may find it difficult to act quickly, to communicate effectively, and to speak with a single voice at the time and place needed. A centralized, tightly-knit organization which concentrates authority in the top leadership can take public stands quickly and is less easily outmaneuvered by opposition groups or by state and local decision makers. The degree of centralization or decentralization in a pressure group may well be the result of the quality of leadership which the group has had over several decades, with the group members and public officials alike looking to a strong leader as the legitimate spokesman for the interests of the group. Thus legislators will come to know that popular, able, Lobbyist X *is* the State Trucking Association, whereas less popular, less able Lobbyist Y is not really

(5) Organization and leadership

152   the League of Municipalities — he must check back constantly with 200 mayors, during which time the battle lines and issues may have changed drastically.

A final characteristic of a pressure group affecting its power position in the state or community, and one which may at times be all important, is the ideological content of the group's program. It is a simple axiom that

(6) Program   a program which fits the prevailing system of values and beliefs of the public at large will have easier sledding than one which runs counter to community values, all else being equal. Granted, a good public relations campaign may make black appear to be white on occasions, but pressure groups cannot afford to put their trust in such manipulative miracles. In spite of widespread Southern acceptance of the Ku Klux Klan's doctrine of white supremacy at one time, the Klan deviated from other community values relating to violence and now has little community respect or support. The brand of "obvious special privilege" on a program will weaken the pressure group, but a clear-cut goal of "fair play," "correcting a wrong," "ending discrimination," or "supporting the weak but worthy," will solidify the support of the group membership and facilitate access to public decision makers.

One other factor which should be mentioned is the political environment in which the pressure group must operate. This is a characteristic of the state or local community rather than of the pressure group itself, but

(7) Political environment   may be an important source of strength or weakness to the group. The contribution to the strength of pressure groups of the separation of powers, a federal system, and weak political parties (by providing such a variety of access points), is discussed in detail in many textbooks on American government.[1] In addition, such factors as the attitude of legislators and councilmen toward lobbying, the relative strength or weakness of the governor or local executives, and the degree of autonomy or integration of the administrative agencies affect the strength of pressure groups and will not produce the same pattern in any two states.

The methods of pressure groups are multitudinous. Many of them work directly to influence party platforms and the selection of candidates. Under the long presidency of Samuel Gompers, the American Federation of Labor

Pressure group methods; party relations   developed an effective policy of endorsing the candidacy and publicizing the records of legislators favorable to labor, regardless of party. Spokesmen of pressure groups are frequently in evidence at party conventions. In fact, an American political party comes close to being a compound of pressure group interests, one group sometimes being more powerful in

---

[1] *See,* for example, Marian D. Irish and James W. Prothro, *The Politics of American Democracy* (2d ed.; Prentice-Hall, Inc., Englewood Cliffs, 1962), pp. 337-338.

property the Homestead exemption - Passed in 1935 - very controversial. This was passed to encourage people to come to the. Now we are being flooded with people. This provision hurts us. Raises 2 classes of people - those who don't pay and those who do. Variate - everyone pays on the 1st $2,000. distribute the tax load and give the H.E. together have a progressive feature. will give $250.00 going to school

C B 3 2 S. The pros & cons of the tax system

11/2/64

C.B. no. 30 - Read - Study pg. 234 - 237.
  "   "   31 - Study
  "   "   - Study
  "   "   - Study

Fla. Handbook - Knows the Supreme Court - compare
with U.S. Supreme Court - Circuit Judges
are imp. - Length of term, retirement, etc.

Essays -
4. Should judges be elected or appointed?

pg. 283
pg. 30, 31.

→ Valuation is irrelevant to the progressive income tax.

Poor 25%
Prop. 25%
25%, 25%
$16.00 Prof. #19.

Most ....

*3. Progressive + Regressive taxation - the tend to be regressive - Motor vehicles wear out ....

Regressive - Motor vehicles wear out. It was only passed because it was a desperate last attempt. The sales tax is fair .....

might go up from 3% to 4% & are might be taxed
pg. 271 *

or progressive and cheap. Severance tax is not one
way's to improve ....
we shouldn't .... This applys to this wealth - underground Business
be very plentiful ....
these outdated .... carry its place - Business goes into these outdated
tax!

Argument for sales tax in the .... the county's pay it. Should legislate about getting rid of sale tax - all of
$20 .... to get rid of sales tax (and have an income tax.

one party and another in the other. The relationship is reciprocal, for a party generally welcomes the civic, financial, and electoral support of powerful pressure groups, although it may seek advantage through criticizing the opposition party for pressure group conections. The support may be open and publicized, as by crusaders against graft or corruption. It may be of an undercover nature, as by gambling interests quietly seeking easy treatment. Invisible electoral pressure may be exerted by other types of vested interest with big stakes and limited popular appeal.

Personal lobbying is an old and continuing method of applying the power of pressure groups. Its importance is by no means limited to the national scene. Its impact is likely to be felt wherever policy-making bodies function. Land lobbies were prominent in the early days of the Republic. *Lobbying* Railroad lobbies became significant in the latter half of the nineteenth century. In this era the Northwestern and Burlington companies, for example, had lobby bosses for work with the Iowa legislature; the Louisville and Nashville used strong pressure on legislative bodies from Kentucky to Louisiana; and Jay Gould made trips to Albany to get what he wanted in the way of favorable railway legislation or non-action on hostile bills. Other public utilities followed the railroads in this activity. The problem of regulating lobbying had to be faced by state legislatures, although with indifferent or varying success, as will be pointed out in the subsequent treatment of legislatures.

The techniques of lobbying are pluralistic. There are professionals and amateurs at the game of making personal and personable contacts with legislators and policy-makers. Bribery and entertainment of lawmakers have been exposed from time to time as reprehensible forms of pressure. Lobbyists have influenced legislation by offering legal fees, retainers, and employment to legislators, their relatives or their firms. Official patronage has been used by lobbyists of the executive branch of government to push administration bills through a legislature. Lobbyists and their sponsors sometimes draft bills to be introduced and supported by their legislative favorites.

Much of the lobbying which goes on is legitimate and even desirable or necessary. It provides valuable information and analysis for lawmakers. Indeed, research has come to be one of the more effective lobbying devices.[2] Facts and views need to be presented from different angles and by different groups in order to provide the whole picture of a complex problem. It is seemingly fair and proper that each group have the opportunity to give its case, if only to counter the bias of other groups. Constructive lobbying has at times led to

[2] See E. F. Cooke, "Research: An Instrument of Political Power," *Political Science Quarterly*, LXXVI (March, 1961), pp. 69-87, a case study of the Pennsylvania Economy League which "has come to wield great influence over the making of public policy instead of being only a research agency."

advances in legislation. It might be observed that pioneer laws for specialized care and treatment of the insane were enacted in several states partly in response to unselfish lobbying by Dorothea Dix (1802-87), a New England schoolmistress turned reformer. Lobbying has its credits as well as its debits on the civic ledger.

Lobbying does not stop when a legislative battle is ended. Whether that battle is won or lost, the effective lobbyist will shift his focus to the administrative arena, or perhaps to the courts or the voters. With the growing importance of administrators in state and local government, especially in increased discretionary powers, the lobbyist's initial legislative defeat may be turned into an administrative victory or a victory may become a defeat. If a pressure group feels that it is not getting a fair deal from a particular agency, it may support legislation to take the agency "out of politics," usually by establishing an autonomous board or commission. This commonly means organizing an agency in such a way that members of the most interested pressure group will control the selection of personnel and the formulation of policy, or, as a second choice, making it more difficult for a competitor pressure group to gain control. Thus, road builders want an autonomous state highway commission, sportsmen want an autonomous game and fish commission, PTA leaders want an autonomous board of education, doctors want an autonomous board of health, and so on *ad infinitum*. To the extent that pressure groups succeed in such efforts to maximize their access to state and local officials by pulling "pet agencies" away from the rest of the governmental structure, the result is fragmented, uncoordinated government, with all of its attendant problems. Most pressure groups would agree that this "isolationist approach" would not be proper for *all* state or local departments, but would insist that "this one function (or agency) is different."

Pressure groups and "administrative autonomy"

Pressure groups of all types are likely to rely heavily upon the use of propaganda, combined perhaps with other methods. Pressure by this method is as old as the "propagation of the gospel." Samuel Adams and his colleagues made excellent use of it in stirring up support for the Revolution, and Tom Paine became an effective pamphleteering propagandist during the Revolution, winning high praise from George Washington for thus stimulating popular morale. Propaganda is used at all political levels — from centers concerned with town politics to groups cultivating opinion in the sphere of international relations. Propaganda may incidentally provide useful information on public matters and contribute to popular education. But it is not primarily designed to educate or stimulate objective thinking. Propagandists seek to utilize or manipulate words and symbols in such ways as to influence belief and action toward predetermined ends. The advertising of merchandise is in reality a special type of propaganda by business interests seeking to influence or pressure prospective customers to buy their products. However, laws and stand-

Propaganda

ards for maintaining truth in commercial advertising are somewhat more enforceable than safeguards against political propaganda. In appealing to human feelings and emotions, political propaganda may skirt away from the truth into realms of half-truths and untruths with a skillful avoidance of technical libel.

Political propaganda has been closely associated with printer's ink, but in modern days it is linked also with the media of radio and television. Candidates may use all the arts of propaganda on the hustings, but the customary label for this as viewed by critics is "demagogy." There were demagogues long before the invention of printing, though printing offered great possibilities for persuasion. Printed propaganda takes various forms, including the distribution of press releases, slanted editorials, editorializing in the news appearing in the regular dailies or weeklies, issuing pamphlets and circulars, publishing organizational journals or periodicals under second-class mailing privileges, displaying slogans on billboards, and purchasing political advertising in newspapers. The effectiveness of these methods is strengthened by the tendency of many people to view the printed word as truth rather than to be skeptical of its validity. The sharp decline in recent years in the number of cities having competing daily newspapers raises important questions about the responsibility of the press in influencing political opinions.[3]

Propagandists and demagogues make use, consciously or unconsciously, of many tricks appealing to prejudice, passion, and other non-rational traits of human nature. They frequently utter glittering generalities, such as emphasizing a stand for "good government," for "honesty, decency, and *Propaganda* morality," or for opposition to "graft and corruption." They resort to *tricks* name-calling, throwing odious terms at the opposition and expropriating lofty terms for their side. They publicize testimony from distinguished or popular characters, testimony favorable to their cause or unfavorable to the opposition, thus seeking to establish praise or blame by association. They know the drawing power of big names is important, as advertisers recognize in using endorsements of merchandise by stars of baseball and the movies. Political testimonials from dead statesmen (Washington, Jefferson, or Lincoln), may be more effective than those from living persons because denials or retractions are impossible — although there is always the risk of counter-quotation by the opposition. They use a mental transfer device, identifying themselves or their leaders with the people, the best people, or the "plain people." Willie Stark, in Robert Penn Warren's *All the King's Men*, illustrated this trick in telling Louisiana rural voters that he was a "hick," they were "hicks," and it takes a "hick"

---

[3] *See* R. B. Nixon and J. Ward, "Trends in Newspaper Ownership and Inter-Media Competition," *Journalism Quarterly*, XXXVIII (Winter, 1961), pp. 3-14. This study of 1,461 American cities reveals that only 61 cities have competing daily newspapers, compared with 552 in 1920.

to help a "hick." Card-stacking arguments and charges show up frequently in political propaganda. An important example of this is the fallacious assumption that events or deeds in a sequential relationship inevitably have a cause-and-effect relationship. Another technique is asking questions having no basis in fact or logic and thus conveying a false implication to minds of the unsophisticated. A classic example of this is, "Have you quit beating your wife yet?" It is said that Al Smith once asked an incumbent opposition leader what he did with the millions of taxpapers' dollars which he claimed to have saved. It is not difficult to inject bias into the meaning and even into the statistical analysis of complex financial data by processes of oversimplification or of deliberate confusion.

The power of the masters of political propaganda to make or mold mass opinion through the expanding media of modern communication and the new political role of Madison Avenue's public relations firms has led certain

Propaganda and democracy

informed observers to despair of democracy for our time. Walter Lippmann[4] is among those who have expressed concern on this point. But there is ground for hope for democracy through diverse propaganda, counter propaganda, and analysis of propaganda. The recognition of propaganda for what it is tends to develop an immunity or resistance to its impact in its extravagant forms. Democratic freedoms permit this development in ways not possible in totalitarian systems of government. American propaganda pressure, on the whole, is greatest in the realm of national politics and policy, although much of it also impinges on federal-state relations. At the same time propaganda is subject to extensive check and scrutiny on the national scene, thanks largely to pressure-group competition and to an able coverage by a variety of journalists and commentators. Propaganda on this large scale is subject to what Woodrow Wilson called "pitiless publicity." It has not always been effectively checked or exposed at state and local levels, as muckrackers and reformers have discovered. But no propaganda engine has quite succeeded in shaping or controlling public opinion in all bailiwicks of a state or region or the nation.[5]

Much money is required to carry on the extensive propaganda and lobbying in America today. Millions of dollars annually are spent for the purpose of influencing opinion and action in matters of government. Additional funds flow partly, incidentally, or indirectly toward the same ends, as in various informational services and publications of private and public bodies. Some of the

---

[4] *See Public Opinion* (Harcourt, Brace & World, Inc., New York, 1922; The Macmillan Company, New York, 1944), and *The Phantom Public* (Harcourt, Brace & World, Inc., New York, 1925).

[5] We are not here concerned with the use of propaganda to solidify opinion for victory in wartime.

most effective lobbying is accomplished by public and private officials who are financed and classified for other functions. The ability to make outlays for political influence and action differs widely among pressure groups, being based largely on the expectations of returns from the funds so expended. On such a basis, it is normally easier to arrange for work and money for special economic purposes than for the general good — for groups of manufacturers, laborers, farmers, and professional men than for all consumers or all citizens, however important may be the interests of all consumers or all citizens. The idea that everybody's business is nobody's business often means that special interests outrank the general interest in financial support for pressure politics, at least in the day-to-day movement of public affairs between elections. Meeting this discrepancy is one of the problems of state and local government, of civic education, and of citizens.

The processes of cultivating opinion and influencing government should not be blindly praised or condemned. They are flexible, yet enduring as the weather. It is important to understand them as phases of political behavior and power. They provide channels of contact between the official *Private or* government of the whole community and a network of unofficial "govern- *fractional* ments" of private groups. The network includes corporation government, *government* labor union government, club government, lodge government, church government, student government, and a miscellany of other unofficial or private governments. These fractional units function in the pattern of social interrelationships and cannot be completely divorced from formal political government to which they are subordinate in final power. A certain amount of politics and political leadership is to be found in the private establishments, which are conducted much like state governments, requiring internal laws, regulations, and prescribed rules of procedure. Intentionally and unintentionally, the fractional groups collectively exert a pressure of large proportions on the government of the community, whether the community be nation, state, city, county, or town. The pressure also moves in the other direction, the spheres of influence of the fractional governments being altered in response to increases in the functions of the state. Our public interests and our private interests are interlinked, for better or for worse. It is necessary and proper to study these interests in their interrelationship, not in isolation.

Bentley, Arthur F., *The Process of Government* (University of Chicago Press, Chicago, 1908).

Blaisdell, D. C., *American Democracy Under Pressure* (The Ronald Press Company, New York, 1957).

Bryce, James, *The American Commonwealth* (3d ed., The Macmillan Company, New York, 1900), II, Part 4.

Frost, Richard T., ed., *Cases in State and Local Government* (Prentice-Hall, Inc., Englewood Cliffs, N. J., 1961); *see* especially Part 2, pp. 41-75.

Hacker, Andrew, "Pressure Politics in Pennsylvania: The Truckers vs. the Railroads," in Alan F. Westin, ed., *The Uses of Power: 7 Cases in American Politics* (Harcourt, Brace & World, Inc., New York, 1961).

Herring, E. Pendleton, *Public Administration and the Public Interest* (McGraw-Hill Book Co., Inc., New York, 1936).

Kelley, Stanley, *Professional Public Relations and Political Power* (The Johns Hopkins Press, Baltimore, 1956).

Key, V. O., *Politics, Parties, and Pressure Groups* (4th ed., Thomas Y. Crowell Company, New York, 1958).

———, *Public Opinion and American Democracy* (Alfred A. Knopf, Inc., New York, 1961).

Lubell, Samuel, *The Future of American Politics* (Harper & Row, Publishers, New York, 1952).

McKee, Elmore, *The People Act* (Harper & Row, Publishers, New York, 1955).

Truman, D. B., *The Governmental Process: Political Interests and Public Opinion* (Alfred A. Knopf, Inc., New York, 1951).

"Unofficial Government: Pressure Groups and Lobbies," *Annals of the American Academy of Political and Social Science,* CCCXIX (September, 1958), entire issue.

Zeller, Belle, *Pressure Politics in New York* (Prentice-Hall, Inc., New York, 1937).

★ *9* ★

THE STATE LEGISLATURE:

GENERAL FEATURES

Tʜᴇ sᴛᴀᴛᴇ legislature, with its colonial origin, is the oldest American instrumentality for the exercise of representative self-government. The colonial assembly played an important role in the course of events leading up to the Revolution, and British interference with local legislative processes constituted *Early importance and* a significant basis of complaint against the colonial governors and the *portance and* Crown. The first half dozen specific grievances set forth in the Declaration *prestige* of Independence concerned the disallowance of colonial laws and the dissolution or disruption of legislative sessions and proceedings. America had already become a land of laws and lawyers, and the idea of legislative supremacy was prominent in the minds of the revolutionists as they undertook to transform the colonies into states. The legislatures, in fact, assumed the chief responsibility for these changes as well as for providing for representation in the deliberative body of the general government.

It was only natural that the idea of legislative supremacy would prevail in the establishment of the Continental Congress and later of the Congress of the Confederation. The patriots entertained strong desires to have a government of laws, not of arbitrary men. It required years of experience for them to get around to the Hamiltonian concept of energy in the executive branch of government. Men like James Otis, Patrick Henry, and Thomas Jefferson served in the legislative body of their state or colony in the course of their public life, seeking through representative law-making the safeguarding of liberty.

The members of a typical state legislature are subject to a large share of the disesteem in which politics and politicians in America are often held today.

Later "de-cline" in stature

There are many possible causes of the seeming decline of this branch of government since the formative years of the republic, and not all of them are related to its eclipse by the rise of the nation and the national Congress. The broadside attacks of the muckrakers at the turn of the century, and their influence on the public image of the legislature, have doubtless lived longer than the conditions which inspired such writing. Typical of this turbulent stream of literature is E. L. Godkin's denunciation of corruption in the New York Legislature in 1898:

> If I said, for insurance, that the legislature at Albany was a school of vice, a fountain of political debauchery, and that few of the younger men come back from it without having learned to mock at political purity and public spirit, I should seem to be using unduly strong language, and yet I could fill nearly a volume with illustrations in support of my charges.[1]

There is a nostalgic assumption by many people that modern legislators lack the goodness and wisdom of their counterparts of olden times when agrarian gentlemen gave their best to the state. This view takes inadequate account of the comparative simplicity of the legislative tasks of early years and also of the shortcomings of legislatures with respect to frauds in dealing with lands, banks, and bonds prior to the Civil War. Accompanying this view, there is a more vigorous and sophisticated complaint that our growing urban centers are underrepresented in state legislatures, requiring urban majorities to appear on bended knee before rural lawmakers or "red necks" and beg for "handouts" from the legislature.

Constitutional restrictions

Legislatures, as noted in a previous chapter, are guided and restricted by state constitutions more than was the case during early statehood. This trend results not only from distrust of legislators, but also from alteration of old constitutions to accord with what the people conceive to be the needs of a technological age. The increase of constitutional clauses has inevitably led to more instances of judicial review of legislation, with the consequence of subordinating the legislature to the judiciary in the public mind.

The executive branch as well as the judiciary shares power and functions with the legislature in ways not anticipated in the simplicity of Jeffersonian

---

[1] Quoted from the New York *Nation* in Ralph Volney Harlow, *The Growth of the United States* (Holt, Rinehart, & Winston, Inc., New York, 1943), II, p. 310.

days. The modern governor has ways of leading and influencing the legislature. Moreover, a vast amount of administrative machinery, partly or largely under direction of the governor, is required in order to implement the work of the legislature, since laws are not self-executing. Administrative activity, furthermore, is constant and continuous, not intermittent like the legislative process. There is meaning in the witticism that "administration is nine-tenths of the law." Executive-administrative leaders may be more responsible and responsive than legislative bodies to the demands of urban citizens, who in most states have a larger voice in choosing the governor and other administrative officers than in determining the legislative majority.

Although the legislature has lost a measure of its comparative supremacy, its "decline" has been more relative and apparent than absolute. This *A more* deliberative body has expanded its functional role within the pattern of *balanced* constitutional and political restrictions. Occasionally a great deal is *view* accomplished in a single legislative session, as is seen in James D. Barber's summation of the work of one state legislature in 1959.

> How . . . does the legislature manage to get anything done? Peopled as it is with those who come to be entertained, those who come to advertise themselves, and those who come to perform a vaguely defined civic duty, the legislature . . . appears more like a clinic than a machine for the production of law.
>
> Yet they did produce. During the five months of the 1959 session, members of the Assembly passed more than 1,450 measures, authorizing the spending of nearly 700 million dollars. They approved nine proposed amendments to the state constitution. They reorganized the state's entire minor court system, replacing 168 local courts with a 44-judge State Circuit Court. They abolished county government — a system in effect for nearly three centuries — and distributed its functions among various state agencies. They became the fourth state legislature to enact a Uniform Commercial Code, covering virtually all commercial transactions. They made major changes in the executive branch, creating new departments of Consumer Protection and Conservation. They authorized the issuance of $345 million in bonds for an immense highway program.
>
> Not all their actions were of such far-reaching significance: they also took time to define the word "stop," to specify the height of junkyard fences, and to establish the Irish Heritage Association. But both critical and enthusiastic commentators agreed that the record of the 1959 legislature was "remarkable" and "historic."[2]

---

[2] James David Barber, *Lawmaker: A Study in Political Adaptation* (forthcoming, Yale University Press, New Haven), pp. 165-166.

THE STATE LEGISLATURE: GENERAL FEATURES

What kinds of people make up the 50 state legislatures? Traditional efforts to answer this question have consisted largely of descriptions of legal qualifications and of statistical studies of such factors as the legislator's age, occupation, income, experience and representational origin. More recent research on state legislatures has begun to suggest new ways of looking at our lawmakers. The old and new in combination go a long way toward presenting a realistic picture of the members of our state legislatures.

Four categories of legislators were discovered by Barber on the basis of their "personal needs and political adaptations" revealed in interviews with members of one state legislature. They are "Spectators," "Advertisers," "Reluctants," and "Lawmakers," whose traits may be summarized as follows:

**Four types
of legislators**

> The passive Spectators, who enjoy watching the legislative show and want to continue on, appear to have been attracted by the prestige of legislative office, thus compensating for feelings of social inferiority. The Advertisers, active but unwilling to return, are out to become known, usually for business purposes, and show occupational insecurity and marked inner conflicts. The Reluctants are legislators under protest, performing a civic duty for their small-town neighbors, but experiencing difficulty in adapting to a strange, fast-moving situation. The Lawmakers, active and tentatively committed to extended legislative service, concentrate on the substantive issues, being freed for this by personal strength and powerful adjustive techniques.[3]

Barber's classification grew out of his effort to discover why so many state legislators do not return to the legislature for a second term, a problem discussed below. He concludes that the non-repeaters tend to be the Advertisers (one session usually meets their need for publicity) and the Reluctants (even one session seems to be too many for many of these). Barber's study is full of interesting *verbatim* accounts of his interviews with legislators. One obviously impressed "Spectator" gave the following account of the governor's tea for the legislators:

> We were very impressed. I mean you couldn't help but be impressed. It's a beautiful home. The Governor and his wife met us graciously and gave us the full roam of the house — "Go ahead, look at anything you want. Make yourself at home. We'll see you later on." And we wandered around. It's a beauti-

---

[3] *Ibid.*, in "Abstract."

ful home. Everything in it is beautiful. And, ah, then tea was served — so we had coffee. (laughs) So we were sitting around, or standing there, and the Governor came by and he talked to everybody, and his wife talked with everybody. So — before that, we drove up in front of the house and a state trooper, there, he opened the car door. The passengers got out. I got out. The state trooper took the car, parked it for me. And, ah . . . so we had tea, and the Governor talked with us. His wife talked with us. And when it came time to leave, we departed. And again, why — a warm handshake. None of this fishy handshake, but a warm handshake. And, ah, they thanked us for coming — whereas normally we should have thanked them for being invited. They thanked us for coming. And we got out there, the state trooper, he opened the car door. And off we go.

Well, as I say, we had a wonderful afternoon there. As I say, we were only there an hour, hour-and-a-half. It was very impressive. You couldn't help but be impressed.[4]

Another way of looking at individual legislators focuses attention on their "political socialization" — the process by which "they selectively acquired the values, attitudes, interests or knowledge that fit them for legislative roles and make them take these roles in characteristic ways."[5] In the four-state study by Wahlke and others, legislators were asked "How did you become interested in politics? What is your earliest recollection of being interested in it?" Responses to these questions reveal a great diversity of roads leading future legislators to an interest in politics. Equally varied is the *time* of political socialization, indicating that politics may become meaningful to a person either early or late in the life cycle. But it was found that the legislator's political interest is more likely to take place at an early age, even in childhood for many of them.

Political socialization of legislators

What are the major sources of political interest for legislators? The summary presented in Table 9-1 gives an indication of the origins of political interest in the states of California, New Jersey, Ohio, and Tennessee.

Sources of political interest for legislators

<u>Primary Group Influence</u>. Already well-established as an important determinant in voting behavior, this was acknowledged by nearly one-half of the legislators as a major source of their political awareness. The law partner who was a city councilman, the grandmother who was a "suffragette," and similarly politically active friends or members of the family are cited by the legislators. Frequently political interest is almost a matter of family inheritance or tradition: "My first recollection of politics was when I was four years old and my father

---

[4] *Ibid.*, pp. 75-76.

[5] Wahlke, *et al.*, *The Legislative System*, p. 70.

COMPOSITION: WHO ARE THE LEGISLATORS?

TABLE 9-1

Major Sources of Political Interest of Legislators
in Four States*

Source of Interest	California	New Jersey	Ohio	Tennessee
Primary group influence (family or friends active or interested in politics)	34%	47%	43%	42%
✓*Political or Civic Participation* (in school, pressure groups, parties; study of politics, etc.)	70	60	49	43
Particular Events or Conditions (Political campaigns; war, depression, state and local conditions/issues, etc.)	42	25	21	18
Personal Predispositions (sense of obligation, admiration for politicians, indignation, power, sociability, etc.)	52	53	52	33
Socio-economic Beliefs (liberal, conservative, religious, etc.)	16	10	6	3

* Percentages total more than 100 since some respondents gave more than one answer.

Source: Adapted from Wahlke, *et al.*, *The Legislative System*, p. 79, by permission of John Wiley and Sons, Inc.

was a member of the House. . . . I played here in this room when I was a little boy."[6]

Political or Civic Participation. This was named more often than any other as a source of political interest, indicating that interest does not necessarily precede activity. The reverse is often true, as in the case of the person recruited into politics by those who sense his potentialities. Classes in civics or politics in school cannot claim large numbers of "converts" among the legislators, but some apparently acquired a *sense* of political participation in the classroom, such as the one who reported: "The man who did the most and stimulated me the most was Dr. X, the head of the government department at the university. He was a Roosevelt New Dealer and I was a good Republican. We had some wonderful fights. I still drop in to see him whenever I'm down that way."[7]

Particular Events or Conditions. Great public events, such as presidential elections and national or local crises like war or depression, have made pro-

---

[6] *Ibid.*, p. 83.
[7] *Ibid.*, p. 86.

found impressions on many of the legislators. The war-time covenant or the prison-camp resolve to return home and "do something about this mess" is familiar political history. The recollection of one legislator is less somber but equally real: "During the Bryan-McKinley campaign I hanged a picture of McKinley on my bedroom wall. My father took it off and I hanged it up again. He took it off and took me to the woodshed. I've been a Republican ever since."[8] Still others cite some local problem or issue as the source of political interest for them: "Our representative bought up and sold it to the state government for deer, fox, and such. Mad foxes were biting families. There were rattlesnakes all over. My friends and businessmen wanted to get the land back."[9]

Personal Predispositions. These were cited in various ways by about one-half of the legislators in response to the question of how they became interested in politics. This could include power predispositions, though few mentioned this specifically, as well as such factors as sociability, indignation, sense of obligation, and the like. It seems to be akin to Barber's "personal needs" concept discussed above. This might suggest that legislators are where they are because at least *some* men are "political animals," but Professor Wahlke and his colleagues warn that, "If there is a personality syndrome of which one may speak as 'political man,' the data do not and cannot reveal its existence among these state legislators."[10] Finally, *socio-economic beliefs* have had a part in stimulating political interest but, with American politics generally being more pragmatic than ideological, it is not surprising that all the evidence points to a relatively minor relationship between beliefs and political interest. As a whole, state legislators are only slightly more concerned about liberalism, conservatism, etc., than the people they represent.

Still another way of describing who the legislators are and what they are like is to discover the legislators' own expectations of what their conduct or behavior should be — their "role-orientations." Making use of "role theory" as developed principally by social psychologists and sociologists, the collaborators in the four-state legislative research project found four "purposive-roles" among legislators responding to the question: "How would you describe the job of being legislator — what are the most important things you should do here?"[11] The four roles which the legislator

"Role-orientations" of legislators

Purposive-Roles

[8] *Ibid.*, p. 89.
[9] *Ibid.*, p. 90.
[10] *Ibid.*, p. 93.
[11] *Ibid.*, pp. 249, 494. The discussion which follows relies heavily on Chapter 11, "The Legislator as Decision Maker: Purposive Roles." The authors' "fundamental working hypothesis" was that "a significant portion of legislators' behavior is role-behavior, that this behavior is substantially congruent with their role-concepts, and that insight into the working of legislative bodies can therefore be gained by ascertaining their role-concepts. The principal objective, therefore, was to discover the main role-orientations of legislators." (p. 29.)

may assume as decision maker are those of *Ritualists, Tribune, Inventor*, and *Broker*.

The *Ritualist* tends to stress the mechanics of the legislator's job, so overwhelming and complex are the formal rules of parliamentary procedure. Preoccupation with legislative maneuvering, the bureaucratic and routinized **"Ritualist"** maze, and mastery of the legislative work-flow chart can become, for the Ritualist, an end in itself rather than a means to an end. Some Ritualists may really be opposed to law-making, as in the case of one who reported, "an old gentleman once suggested to me that all we should do is pass the budget and go home. He didn't like laws. I agree with him in some respects."[12] Of course, the Ritualist's role is essential to the functioning of the legislature, but it is hard to conceive of a legislature composed exclusively of Ritualists.

The *Tribune* perceives himself primarily as the advocate or defender of popular demands and needs. His roots go deep in American political history to the period when the colonial legislature was expected to fight the **"Tribune"** people's battle against the British Crown and his appointed governor. The modern Tribune is not so negative as his colonial predecessor, but he is still principally concerned with knowing the needs, hopes, feelings, and desires of the people, and being their spokesman. Some legislators take the role of Tribune even though they are not *personally* committed to popular views.

The *Inventor* is probably the most frustrated legislator because, in a technological age when the center of gravity for policy formulation has moved toward the executive branch, he still perceives himself as initiator and **"Inventor"** creator of public policy. He focuses attention on what he thinks are the creative aspects of his job, and his self-image is that of the thoughtful, far-sighted legislator of vision and imagination. The Inventor wants to solve the state's current problems — unemployment, mental illness, taxes, and regulation — by inventive effort, and believes the legislator "should be in front of things."

Finally, the *Broker* is consistent with the dominant theme in studies of the legislative process as the struggle between interest groups, constituents, and administrative forces. The Broker's job is to compromise and arbitrate, and **"Broker"** perhaps also to "coordinate and integrate" the demands of conflicting interests. The more naive Broker may think only in terms of an automatic balancing operation achieved by listening to all sides. But the sophisticated Broker sees the need of a tough-minded appraisal of conflicting group interests "in terms of their moral worth, the power potential of the groups in combat, and the political consequences for his own position."[13]

Does each state have the same pattern, proportionally, of Ritualists,

---

[12] *Ibid.*, p. 251.
[13] *Ibid.*, p. 257.

Tribunes, Inventors, and Brokers? Table 9-2 shows the distribution of roles and the variations between the four states. For a detailed analysis the reader should consult the book itself, but the authors' summary gives an indication of the significance of each state pattern:

TABLE 9-2

DISTRIBUTION OF LEGISLATORS' PURPOSIVE-ROLE ORIENTATION*

Role Orientation	New Jersey	Ohio	California	Tennessee
Ritualist	70%	67%	58%	72%
Tribune	63	40	55	58
Inventor	49	33	36	30
Broker	33	48	27	15

* Percentages total more than 100 since respondents could hold more than one orientation.

Source: Wahlke, et al., The Legislative System, p. 259.

In general, then, the data on purposive-role orientations seem to support the assumption that orientations are shaped by both historic conceptions of the functions of the legislature and by contemporary circumstances in the governmental power structure. In all four states, the traditional institutional requirements of the legislative office, centered in the legislative mechanisms, make the Ritualist conception an appropriate orientation in the task of lawmaking. In three states, the Tribune orientation is held widely enough to suggest that the state legislature continues to be an important link between the electorate and the government. The Inventor orientation seems to be relatively unimportant, except in New Jersey where legislature and executive were controlled by different parties and where the legislature may attempt to compete with the governor in the making of state policy. The Broker orientation, probably the most realistic but also perhaps the most difficult to take under modern conditions, was less widely accepted than one might have expected, except in Ohio where economic geography would seem to have made it more salient and central in the total legislative role.[14]

Still other role-orientations play an important part in making the legislator the kind of actor he is in the law-making process. The old brain-teasing question. "What determines your vote — your conscience or your constituents?" gives rise to the threefold classification of representational roles: Trustee, Delegate, and Politico. The Trustee claims to let his conscience and judgment be his guide. The Delegate proposes to follow the in-

Representational roles

[14] Ibid., p. 260.

168 structions and wishes of his constituents or other clienteles. The Politico claims to follow first one, then the other, depending upon circumstances which may require balancing one against the other. Well over one-half of the legislators in California, New Jersey, Ohio, and Tennessee, were found to be Trustees, with the Delegates being least numerous. It is probably true that under modern conditions it is more realistic to be a Trustee, and it may well be a functional necessity rather than a "pious formula."[15]

A problem which has long perplexed legislative reformers is the large percentage of one-term-only members of the legislature. Close to one-half of the approximately 7,600 members are replaced every two years, primarily a result of failure to run for re-election.[16] In his pioneer study of legislative tenure and turnover, Professor Charles S. Hyneman suggests that experience in three sessions is necessary before one can hope to be effective, and concluded:

Legislative turnover

> The real task is to find why so many legislators, senators and representatives alike, choose not to run again. Devices and arrangements which reduce the hazards of an election year to a minimum will still not give us a body of lawmakers rich in the experience of their trade. The state legislator must be made more happy in his career. . . . The key to rehabilitation of the legislative branch is in the nature of the legislator's job and his attitude toward it.[17]

The recent four-state legislative study sheds some light on the problem of explaining withdrawals from the legislature, but no regular pattern for all states was discovered in the reasons given by 220 who expressed unwillingness to run again. "Economic reasons" accounted for 20 per cent; "personal reasons" prevented 18 per cent from running again; 13 per cent considered the job "too demanding"; 12 per cent thought they had "served long enough"; 12 per cent mentioned "political considerations"; and 13 per cent were planning to seek another office. The remainder were either bored or confessed to a feeling of inadequacy.[18] Obviously, returning to the state legislature is not high on the scale of values of these persons.

Reasons for withdrawal

---

[15] *Ibid.*, pp. 281, 286. Other roles studied include "areal roles," "pressure group roles," and "party roles." See also Wilder W. Crane, Jr., "Do Representatives Represent?", *Journal of Politics,* XXII (May, 1960), pp. 295-299; and Thomas R. Dye, "A Comparison of Constituency Influences in the Upper and Lower Chambers of a State Legislature," *Western Political Quarterly,* XIV (June, 1961), pp. 473-480.

[16] Belle Zeller, ed., *American State Legislatures,* Report of the Committee on American Legislatures, American Political Science Association (Thomas Y. Crowell Company, New York, 1954), pp. 61, 65.

[17] Charles S. Hyneman, "Tenure and Turnover of Legislative Personnel," *The Annals of the American Academy of Political and Social Science,* CXCV (January, 1938), pp. 30-31.

[18] Wahlke, *et al., The Legislative System,* p. 127.

But why do the others (252) want to return? The principal reason given was "involvement" in the legislative job, accounting for 58 per cent, while 33 per cent gave "public service" as their reason. Other reasons, including additional ones given by the same legislator, were the status value of holding office (13 per cent), political contingencies (15 per cent), and a variety of "private reasons" such as service to special groups and something approximating "apathy," each of which was mentioned by less than ten per cent. "Responsibility to party" was mentioned by only two per cent. The findings of this study indicates that in states with a more competitive party system the legislators tend to be more committed to running for re-elecion (in New Jersey three-fourths of the members expected to run again), but Barber found no such relationship in his study of legislators.[19] *Reasons for returning*

The picture of our state legislators would be incomplete without a brief look at their socio-economic background. It is always possible to "prove too much" from such studies, especially if it is implied that high-status legislators always support the interests of high-status citizens, or that lawyer legislators always protect lawyer interests. But, viewed with care, such information can be another important tool in understanding legislators and legislatures. *Socio-economic background*

Lawyers tend to dominate the occupational picture of state legislators, to the extent that their critics have been known to poke paraphrased fun at them, saying we have a "government of lawyers and not of men." Farmers have traditionally run a close second to lawyers but in recent years their proportion of the total membership has begun to slip. In the four-state study of 1957 legislatures cited earlier, lawyers accounted for 36 per cent and farmers for only 10 per cent of the members. Almost every significant occupation group was represented, though very few were engaged in occupations demanding manual skills and none at all were in unskilled occupations. Thus, if the unskilled labor force in these four states approximates the national proportion, 20 per cent of the people are "not represented" in the state legislatures in this restricted sense of the word.[20] "Laborers" accounted for 2 per cent of all legislators in a recent study which included all states.[21] Occupationally speaking, state legislators are principally "upward mobile," in that they have tended to take up more prestigious occupations than those of their fathers. *Occupation*

It might come as a surprise to some, but legislators come from the best-

---

[19] *Ibid.*, p. 123, and Barber, *loc. cit.*

[20] Wahlke, *et al.*, *The Legislative System*, Appendix 5, pp. 489-490. *See also* David R. Derge, "The Lawyer as Decision-Maker in the American State Legislature," *Journal of Politics*, XXI (August, 1959), pp. 408-433.

[21] Zeller, *op. cit.*, p. 71.

COMPOSITION: WHO ARE THE LEGISLATORS?

educated sector of the population, with more than three-fourths having been exposed to a college education. The striking contrast between the education level of the total U. S. population and that of the state legislators is demonstrated in Table 9-3. The average starting age for state legislators is in the early forties. Women are no longer "curiosities" in state legisla-

TABLE 9-3

EDUCATION OF LEGISLATORS, COMPARED WITH POPULATION OVER AGE 25

Educational Attainment	Calif.		New Jersey		Ohio		Tenn.		Total U.S.	
	Leg.	Pop.	Leg.	Pop.	Leg.	Pop.	Leg.	Pop.	Leg.	Pop.
Elementary only	—	33%	—	47%	4%	43%	4%	60%	2%	47%
Some high school	15	45	13	38	19	42	22	29	17	37
Some college	31	11	24	6	19	7	28	6	26	7
College graduate	54	8	63	7	58	6	46	4	55	6
Totals*	100%	97%	100%	98%	100%	98%	100%	99%	100%	97%

* Less than 100% because of non-reporting.

Source: Wahlke, *et al., The Legislative System,* p. 489 (Appendix 5).

tures, although the typical picture would be one or two women in a given legislature. Negroes are found in a few of the legislatures, in non-southern states with large urban Negro concentrations. Several southern cities have Negro city councilmen and, with Negro voting on the rise, Negro state legislators can be expected in the South. In 1962 an Atlanta district elected a Negro to the Georgia Senate.

One other social characteristic of legislators — their predominantly rural or small-town origin and outlook — has probably inspired more articles in the Sunday supplements of newspapers than any other facet of the legislature. Accounts of legislative battles with the more numerous "country slickers" putting to flight the outgunned "city yokels" have become commonplace. Strong over-representation of rural districts in state legislatures, for a variety of constitutional and political reasons, is one of the major unsolved problems of state government. This problem, "with its legislative implications," is discussed in detail in Chapter 10.

All American states, except one, have the two-house type of legislature, comparable to the United States Congress. The exception is Nebraska, which followed the advice of the late Senator George W. Norris in passing a constitutional amendment in 1934 to establish a unicameral legislature of 30 to 50 members. Attempts to change to the unicameral system in a few other states have met with failure. *Bicameralism and uni-cameralism*

Bicameralism is traditional among the states. Most of the original thirteen commonwealths came into the Union with the two-house system. Georgia and Pennsylvania, which entered with the unicameral system, soon established two-house legislatures. The state of Vermont made a similar switch after being admitted to the Union. There is little immediate prospect of unicameral expansion among the states, although the Nebraska experiment has won praise, several editions of the Model Constitution issued by the National Municipal League offer such a plan, and unicameralism has proved satisfactory among Canadian provinces, Swiss cantons, and American cities. The bicameral legislature prevails in the United States for historical and other reasons, including the seldom-penetrated wall of political self-preservation, despite strong arguments for the one-house type.

One important argument for the bicameral type of legislature is that it enables one house to check another and thus avoid mistakes. The checking process is supposedly due, at least in part, to the difference in the constituencies of the members of the two houses. The various interests of the state may thus be represented differently in the two houses, so that certain interests may be able to check bills in one house, with certain others holding the reins in the other house. This is a negative argument, which is sometimes countered by the observation that good bills may thus be killed along with the bad. It is also true sometimes that public opinion gets aroused over unpopular bills after the first house passes them, bringing about defeat in the second chamber. *Arguments for the two systems*

Advocates of the unicameral legislature point to the expense and complications of the two-house system with its too prevalent opportunities for lobbying, buck-passing, and miscellaneous scheming to thwart the public will. They emphasize that the single-chamber legislature tends to center and fix responsibility on the legislators, to bring lawmakers and executive together in policy-making, to facilitate the use of competent experts, to avoid legislative delays, and to cut down the cost of legislation. Their arguments are strong but do not prevail against traditional views and ways. Our state legislatures, with their two houses, find coordination of decision and action through different makeshift techniques, including the extra-constitutional and extramural.

Every state legislature, with the exception of Nebraska's chamber of 43 members, consists of two houses of different size and basis of membership. The upper house, or senate, varies from 17 in Delaware and Nevada to 67 in Minnesota. The lower house varies from 35 in Delaware to 400 in New Hampshire. The total number for the 99 legislative chambers runs about 7,600, with additional personnel for staff and clerical work. Most of the states, as shown in Table 9-4, have two-year terms for the lower house, and a majority elect senators for four years. A few southern states have four-year terms for both houses. Re-election is constitutionally permissible and frequently occurs, but a high rate of turnover is a persistent feature as discussed above.

Size

Terms

The 7600-plus state legislators are chosen, not so much to provide the number necessary for the work of lawmaking, but to provide what seems to be the proper representation for the multitude of political units or communities, such as towns in New Hampshire, counties in many states, or districts larger than counties in certain instances. The senatorial districts or units are frequently larger than those for the lower house; but the same basis, say a county, may be used for both houses, with more elected to the lower house than to the state senate if the constituency is populous. While

*Represen-
tational
districts*

TABLE 9-4
THE LEGISLATORS: NUMBERS AND TERMS

State	Senate Members	Term	House Members	Term	Total for Both Houses
Alabama	35	4	106	4	141
Alaska	20	4	40	2	60
Arizona	28	2	80	2	108
Arkansas	35	4	100	2	135
California	40	4	80	2	120
Colorado	35	4	65	2	100
Connecticut	36	2	294	2	330
Delaware	17	4	35	2	52
Florida	38	4	95	2	133
Georgia	54	2	205	2	259
Hawaii	25	4	51	2	76
Idaho	44	2	59	2	103
Illinois	58	4	177	2	235

THE LEGISLATORS: NUMBERS AND TERMS

State	Senate Members	Term	House Members	Term	Total for Both Houses
Indiana	50	4	100	2	150
Iowa	50	4	108	2	158
Kansas	40	4	125	2	165
Kentucky	38	4	100	2	138
Louisiana	39	4	105	4	144
Maine	33	2	151	2	184
Maryland	29	4	123	4	152
Massachusetts	40	2	240	2	280
Michigan	34	2	110	2	144
Minnesota	67	4	135	2	202
Mississippi	49	4	140	4	189
Missouri	34	4	157	2	191
Montana	56	4	94	2	150
Nebraska	unicameral legislature		2 year term		43
Nevada	17	4	47	2	64
New Hampshire	24	2	400	2	424
New Jersey	21	4	60	2	81
New Mexico	32	4	66	2	98
New York	58	2	150	2	208
North Carolina	50	2	120	2	170
North Dakota	49	4	115	2	164
Ohio	38	4	139	2	179
Oklahoma	44	4	121	2	165
Oregon	30	4	60	2	90
Pennsylvania	50	4	210	2	260
Rhode Island	44	2	100	2	144
South Carolina	46	4	124	2	170
South Dakota	35	2	75	2	110
Tennessee	33	2	99	2	132
Texas	31	4	150	2	181
Utah	25	4	64	2	89
Vermont	30	2	246	2	276
Virginia	40	4	100	2	140
Washington	49	4	99	2	148
West Virginia	32	4	100	2	132
Wisconsin	33	4	100	2	133
Wyoming	27	4	56	2	83

Source: Adapted from *The Book of the States, 1962-63*, p. 41.

much attention is given to population as a factor in apportionment, especially in the lower house, this factor is actually combined in different ways with others, such as allowing at least one seat in the lower house to every county in North Carolina or to every town in New Hampshire. Vermont, like New Hampshire, accords every town the right of a representative, and Glastonbury Town, with its population of one, could consequently have its representative. Actually, Victory with a population of 49 is the smallest Vermont town represented.[22]

Technical qualifications for members are comparatively simple. As to age requirements, twenty-one is generally adequate for the lower house and in several states for the upper chamber. A few states have the requirement of twenty-five for a senator. It is quite generally stipulated that a member be an American citizen and voter. The length of residence required varies somewhat among the states, as does the residence requirement for voting. Political tests are more rigid than these official standards, however. It is difficult or impossible for a candidate to win a legislative election without an established residence in the district, town, or county of substantial duration. The importance of party or political connections should not be underestimated, for they are frequently more important than such factors as formal education.

The compensation for members of the legislature varies widely among the states and continues to change from year to year. New York, at the top, has an annual salary of $15,000, with California, Pennsylvania, and Illinois paying $12,000 per year. Massachusetts, New Jersey, and Ohio complete the list of the top seven paying $10,000 or more per year. At the other extreme is New Hampshire, which pays its legislators $200 each for the biennium. The median figure for states paying annual salaries is $3,600. About a third of the states provide compensation only on a per diem basis for legislative service, with no pay for days or periods when the legislature is not in session. As recently as 1943 over half of the states paid their legislators on a per diem basis, so the trend toward the salary basis is clear. The per diem pay is $10 or less in Alabama, Georgia, Idaho, Kansas, North Dakota, Rhode Island, and Tennessee, but is as high as $50 per day in Louisiana. Legislators in many states have their highly unrealistic compensation supplemented by limited allowances for travel and other official expenses. The low scale of compensation is rigidly determined in certain states by constitutional provision. It is clear that many states offer miserly wages for legislative service, but it would be difficult to prove that the standards of performance are proportionately higher where

Compensation and privileges of members

---

[22] See M. J. Dauer and R. G. Kelsay, "Unrepresentative States," *National Municipal Review*, XLIV (December, 1955), pp. 574-575; and U. S. Advisory Commission on Intergovernmental Relations, *Apportionment of State Legislatures* (Washington, D. C., December, 1962).

the pay is higher. Many ill-paid members, however, find sundry ways of rewarding themselves indirectly, if only by putting members of the immediate family, other relatives, or friends on the patronage list, sometimes as legislative clerks with little or nothing to do.

A good scale of compensation is only one of several factors which tend to make a legislative career attractive to citizens of ability and integrity. State legislators have privileges and immunities somewhat like those of members of Congress. The state constitutions generally make these lawmakers free from arrest while attending sessions and going to or from sessions, except for serious crime or breach of the peace. A member thus may not be compelled to leave or miss a session to serve as a witness or answer to a civil suit in court. A member may not be officially questioned in any other place on statements made in speech or debate in the legislature. Of course, his own house may censure him or even unseat him for cause, and a member is always *politically* answerable to critics and constituents as a public figure.

The legislatures of most states are convened and organized in regular sessions biennially, usually in January of odd years. The trend, however, seems to be toward annual sesions. The legislatures in 19 states now meet annually in comparison with four meeting annually in the early 1940's. *Legislative sessions* Most of these have full sessions but some of them are limited to budget matters in the "off" years, in some instances with limited authorization to consider other matters. In those states where the legislatures in the off years are restricted to budgetary matters, there is a possibility that the budget session will gradually be transformed into a full session.

Close to one-half of the states limit sessions constitutionally to 75 days or less. This restriction holds down the pay of members serving on a per diem basis, and it tends to bring on a confusing rush of business during the closing days of a session, sometimes resulting in surprising or unfortunate legislation. Perusal of the legislative output from almost any of these hectic sessions will afford examples of such legislation. Florida, for example, in its 1955 legislative session enacted conflicting laws with respect to the compensation to be paid county commissioners in Okaloosa County. The attorney general rendered the opinion on August 3, 1955, that Chapter 29752 should prevail since it was "the last expression of the Legislature in that its final passage was three days subsequent to said Chapter 29784." Sometimes the clock is turned back at the end of a session to provide time within the constitutional limit for disposal of the cumulative load. Another device is to meet officially for only one or two days a week toward the end of the session, thus leaving many days uncounted and free for clearing up matters through committees and informal adjustment. A method used intermittently by some states with limited success is that of the split session, with a recess of at least 30 days and no bills introduced after the recess except as

176   approved by a three-fourths majority. California was first to adopt it in 1911, but dropped it in 1958. The inadequacy of 60 legislative days for modern needs has brought about an increased reliance upon special or extra sessions, which all states authorize by call of the governor and which may be convened in a few states by concerted action of the members themselves.

The picture of a state legislative organization is similar in broad outline to the congressional structure. There must be standing committees to deal with continuing matters of importance, including finance, taxation, educa-

Organiza-
tional outline
tion, the judiciary, and rules. Special committees are created from time to time for temporary purposes, sometimes for investigative assignments.

Unnecessary committees may be created in order to spread memberships and chairmanships among the legislators for purposes of privilege and publicity. The representatives or assemblymen of the lower house choose a presiding officer, generally with the title of "speaker." A majority of the states have constitutional provisions for an elected lieutenant governor to preside over the senate with a role similar to that of the vice president at Washington. A president pro tempore is available to preside in the absence of the lieutenant governor. The senate in a few states chooses its own regular presiding officer.

In two-party states the majority and minority parties have caucus machinery for organizing the houses, electing officers, and choosing floor leaders to carry on the work. Political factions take over such roles in one-party states, the division sometimes being between the supporters and the opponents of the governor's program and recommendations. The organization at times may be planned and determined by bosses and machines, as exemplified in former years by the Hague machine in New Jersey, the Platt machine in New York, the Long machine in Louisiana, and the Crump machine in Tennessee. Pressure groups may also vitally affect organizational structure of a legislature toward getting the legislation they seek.

The make-up of a state legislature extends beyond the elected membership. There must be clerks, sergeants at arms, doorkeepers, pages, and mes-

Staff and
service
personnel
sengers. Important committees may have expert consultants or investigators on the payroll in order to handle the work with efficiency. The last few decades have witnessed steps to establish systematic services to aid legislators in different ways. Three important types of aids are legislative reference service, bill-drafting service, and the legislative council.

The pioneer example of the first type, starting in 1901, was Wisconsin's Legislative Reference Bureau developed by Charles McCarthy to provide ready and pertinent information for the use of members of the legislature. All but three states[23] have followed this early example, providing in one way or another

---

[23] Idaho, North Carolina, and Utah.

for reference service as an aid to lawmaking. More than a third of the states have taken steps to provide formal assistance in the drafting of bills, which is particularly useful to farmers, businessmen, and other members not versed in law.

Over three-fourths of the states, following the 1933 example of Kansas, have organized legislative councils to give continuous study to legislative problems and legislative planning.[24] The size and composition of the council varies. The membership ranges from five in South Carolina to 260 in Pennsylvania, which is one of the states numbering all members of the legislature in the council. The median size is 15. In some states the governor, other administrative officers, or "citizen" or "public" representatives serve on the council along with legislators. In most of the states the regular membership is restricted to members of the legislature and selected generally by the presiding officers of the legislative houses. In varying degrees, the legislative council facilitates cooperation in policy-making between the chief executive and the lawmakers. It may be divided into committees for division of labor, and it has a supporting staff of research workers and advisers. Some states, with or without a formal legislative council, rely on interim committees of the legislature to serve purposes of research and planning.

The sharp contrasts between various states in legislative working conditions, staff assistance and facilities is presented clearly in the following condensed picture for California, New Jersey, Ohio, and Tennessee: *Working facilities: a comparative picture*

> The California legislature has by far the most impressive working facilities. Each member occupies a modern two-room office suite, with a full-time secretary guarding the outer room, answering mail, keeping track of his bills and making appointments for constituents and lobbyists to see him. A Legislative Council with a staff of 26 lawyers and 22 clerks is available 13 hours a day during the week and eight hours a day on weekends to draft bills or estimate their constitutionality. There is also a Legislative Analyst, with 44 assistants, responsible to the Joint Budget committee for combing the $2 billion executive budget and recommending revisions in line with legislative policy. The University of California Bureau of Public Administration makes long-range studies of specific problems; interim committees with specialized staff work on medium-range ones. The Legislative Bill Room performs prodigious feats of overnight printing to give each member (and lobbyists subscribing) copies of (1) every bill with its latest amendments, (2) a "History" which shows the current progress of all bills, (3) yesterday's "Journal," with roll-calls, and (4) today's agenda (the "Daily File") for both houses and all committees.

> In New Jersey each member receives a small allowance for secretarial help which ordinarily goes to his wife or to his office secretary for keeping track

---

[24] *See* William J. Siffin, *The Legislative Council in American States* (Indiana University Press, Bloomington, 1959).

of legislative affairs from his home or business office. There are no offices for members and few committee rooms in Trenton, but there are caucus rooms — the Senate's air conditioned. This lack of facilities in the Capitol must be seen in the light of the Mondays-only schedule, which makes it possible for members to do the bulk of their homework while they are in their districts. A Law Revision and Legislative Services Commission has research and bill drafting offices, there is a Counsel to the Legislature and a Reference Bureau in the State Library. Records of the session are commercially published.

In Ohio the legislator's desk serves as his office for the session. Here he keeps his files, reads bills, answers mail and interviews lobbyists and constituents. He shares a secretary with a number of other members. A Legislative Reference Bureau, staffed by part-time law students at Ohio State, aids in drafting bills, maintains a file of back measures and also serves as a reference library. A bipartisan Legislative Service Commission consisting of 14 legislators and a professional staff of 12 persons investigates longer-range problems, using the customary power of a legislative investigating committee when necessary. Some subjects are referred to it for study by the Legislature, others originate with the staff or director. Although the choice of subjects bears the stamp of majority-party policy direction, the reports themselves are comprehensive, detailed and "objective." The staff, while outside civil service, is professional and free of patronage appointees.

The Tennessee Legislature operates with a minimum of paperwork. Members work at their desks or in their hotel rooms. They have available for absolutely essential secretarial chores a small pool of stenographers on leave for the session from administrative agencies. The Legislative Reference Service has a staff for bill drafting, but some of the members who feel that omnipresent influence of the Governor here prefer to take their bills to the office of the independently chosen Attorney General. The Legislature provides each member with a subscription to the private "Legislative Service," which daily duplicates copies of general bills and, occasionally, important amendments (but not local bills or resolutions). Floor proceedings are tape recorded, but not transcribed until after the session is over.[25]

POWERS AND FUNCTIONS

The state legislature's most important single function is that of making laws. But it has important powers and functions in other fields. Its role in planning, proposing, or perfecting constitutional revision has already *More than* been discussed in the chapter on state constitutions. It has important *lawmaking* functions in connection with investigating matters bearing on legislation and the operation of state or local government. It has the power to

---

[25] Wahlke, *et al., The Legislative System*, pp. 50-52.

investigate questions of removal of unworthy state officials through impeachment proceedings. The legislature in a few states has the responsibility of
selecting particular state officials, but this role has declined except for selection
of the auditor, as will be noted later, and for rare cases of intervention in disputed
or inconclusive elections. The legislative selection of United States Senators
came to an end in 1913 with the adoption of the federal Seventeenth Amendment. It is usual, however, to require that important appointments by the
governor be confirmed by the state senate, but this process is not applicable to
a large list of civil service appointments made under merit systems, or to officials
chosen by popular election. No state parliamentary body has any special role
corresponding in importance to that of the American Senate with respect to
foreign relations, although action in interstate compacts shows a resemblance
to treaty-making. Most state legislators, moreover, have less time for public
service than members of Congress and likewise less incentive or opportunity to
concern themselves with all phases of the governmental process. Making laws
seems about enough for them.

The state lawmaking power is a broad one, subject, of course, to a few
significant checks and limitations. The legislature must conform to state and
national constitutional provisions or run serious risk of having enactments set aside by state or federal courts. In all states except North Caro-   *Lawmaking*
lina the legislature must guard against a gubernatorial veto or be prepared
to override such a disapproval in the statutory process.

The exercise of a positive legislative role within these limitations applies
to a wide range of subjects under three general classifications. There must be a
large body of statutes on crime and punishment, another set of laws concerned
with civil property relations among persons, and a group of enactments on
governmental functions and units. The work of passing laws on criminal, civil,
and public matters is always with us, and every adjourning legislature leaves in
its wake additional statutes, whether of a general or special type, on the three
subjects. From time to time the session laws are brought together, edited, and
annotated for publication in codified form. Even the codification process is
conducted according to legislation enacted for the purpose. Our 50 state law
factories never completely catch up with their work.

Every legislature has an important role in the field of public finance under
constitutional directions and restrictions. In a strict sense this role falls primarily
under the classification of lawmaking, but in essence it is much more
than lawmaking. It is concerned with the problems of raising revenue   *Financial*
and providing for expenditures, of administering finance and financing   *power*
administration. The legislative power of the purse is a significant power
which has developed through the ages. It was a check on the rule of appointed
governors in the colonial era. This power today calls for fiscal understanding as

180 well as legal learning. It requires close contact and cooperation with the executive branch of government, particularly in budgetry planning and management, as will be emphasized in more detail in the subsequent chapter on state finance.

The two houses of the legislature have different non-lawmaking powers somewhat after the manner of the two houses of Congress. Each is judge of the election and qualifications of its own members, and has disciplinary power

Separate powers of the two houses
over its membership. Each has independent investigative functions, although joint committees of the two houses may be created for such purposes. Each house controls its own organizational set-up, according to constitutional provisions, and makes or modifies its rules of procedure. In impeachment proceedings, the lower house makes the charges, and the other house tries the case, sometimes removing the accused from office and barring him from holding state office in the future. Oregon, a state with provisions for the popular recall of officials, disallows legislative impeachment of state officials. Besides confirming important executive appointments, the senate in a few states exercises approval power over executive dismissals. A number of state constitutions, like the federal document, require that bills for raising revenue originate in the lower house, and this stipulation tends to give that house more initiatory power in dealing with appropriations. The legislative houses function in different ways as forums and mirrors of opinion or group views. Within the scope of their rules and rulings, they are free to adopt independent or concurrent resolutions to support or oppose just about any issue or movement affecting state, nation, or world. They may seek in this manner to influence the outcome of bills pending in Congress. They may call upon Congress to provide for a convention to propose amendments to the United States Constitution, and Congress shall take such a step "on the application of the legislatures of two thirds of the several States." Such a feat has never occurred, although movements to this end have been attempted, particularly for the purpose of limiting national income taxes.

The actual role, power, and restrictions of the state legislative bodies cannot be fully determined or understood by looking merely at the technical structure or constitutional frame of reference. Of equal or greater im-

Power through practice
portance in establishing the position and revealing the picture of the legislature are the political factors, methods, traditions, and accepted practices associated with this branch and the other branches of state government. The legislature gains or loses power and importance partly by the way it works as well as by the way the executive and judicial establishments function. It is now in order to turn to the legislature at work, which will incidentally shed light on the growing problems of organization and procedure on the American state legislative front today.

Abernathy, Byron R., *Constitutional Limitations on the Legislature* (Government Research Center, University of Kansas, Lawrence, 1959).

Council of State Governments, *The Book of the States, 1962-63* (Chicago, 1962), Section II, "Legislatures and Legislation."

Farmer, Hallie, *The Legislative Process in Alabama* (Bureau of Public Administration, University of Alabama, University, Ala., 1949).

Francis, Wayne L., "Influence and Interaction in a State Legislative Body," *American Political Science Review*, LVI (December, 1962), pp. 953-960.

Graves, W. B., *American State Government* (4th ed.; D. C. Heath and Company, Boston, 1953).

Janda, K., *et al.*, *Legislative Politics in Indiana*, (Indiana University Bureau of Government Research, Bloomington, 1961).

Jewell, Malcolm E., *The State Legislature* (Random House, New York, 1962).

Klain, Maurice, "A New Look at the Constituencies," *American Political Science Review*, XLIX (December, 1955), pp. 1105-1119.

Senning, J. P., *The One-House Legislature* (McGraw-Hill Book Company, New York, 1937).

Siffin, William J., *The Legislative Council in the American States* (Indiana University Press, Bloomington, 1959).

Wahlke, John C., and Heinz Eulau, eds., *Legislative Behavior: A Reader in Theory and Research* (The Free Press, Glencoe, 1959).

Wahlke, John C., Heinz Eulau, William Buchanan, and LeRoy C. Ferguson, *The Legislative System: Explorations in Legislative Behavior* (John Wiley and Sons, Inc., New York, 1962).

Zeller, Belle, ed., *American State Legislatures*, Report of the Committee on American Legislatures, American Political Science Association (Thomas Y. Crowell Company, New York, 1954).

(*See also titles* listed for the next chapter.)

* *10* *

STATE LEGISLATION:

PROCESS AND PROBLEMS

THE CHIEF function of the legislature is to legislate. Even those states with
constitutional provisions for direct legislation by state-wide election get most of
their statutes through enactment by lawmaking bodies. In other words,

The **how** *is*
important

the voting citizens do not directly make the laws but choose representatives to adopt the laws. This chapter is concerned with the formal procedure, the institutional controls, the human behavior, and the political
forces and techniques which constitute the state legislative process. It is concerned with the problems of that process as observed in modern times, and with
the various ways and means proposed for their solution. The *how* of the legislative process is both important and at the same time highly complicated. It involves both visible and invisible features or practices. Mastery of the *know-how*
of lawmaking is difficult, not only for the student or observer, but also for the
legislator himself.[1] This inquiry into the actual workings of the legislative mill
at the state level must, therefore, be considered as only suggestive and not
exhaustive.

---

[1] Professor T. V. Smith has graphically explained this point on the basis of his experience as
a member of the Illinois senate. See excerpts and comments in Charles E. Merriam and
R. E. Merriam, *American Government: Democracy in Action* (Ginn & Company, Boston,
1954), pp. 235-237.

An initial word of caution is in order for the student sight-seer who makes the trip to the state capitol to view personally the legislative process. The total legislative process is never on display, not necessarily because secrecy is desired, but because it is never confined to any one place or time. To "see the legislative process" would involve being in scores of executive offices, legislators' hotel rooms, committee rooms, public hearing chambers, pressure group and newspaper offices, capitol corridors, bars, coffee-shop corners, and church vestibules, to name only a few scenes of legislative decision-making. Nevertheless, if all these "feeder points" are kept in mind, a visit to the legislature can be worthwhile, for it is here that all other influences must officially crystallize into laws. It should be remembered that it is both dramatic and dull, but more often dull. The following description of one state legislature might just as easily be of yours:

Caution for "legislative sight-seers"

> The capitol at ——— bears some resemblance to a rococo movie palace. In the Hall of the House, the bright blue rug, the ornate pillars, and the elaborate stained-glass windows create a certain theatrical atmosphere. There were times during the 1959 session when the action matched the setting. One thinks of the stately drama of the inauguration ceremony, the more light-hearted Saint Patrick's Day show, and the sentimental hatchet-burying 'graduation' with which the session ended. Occasionally, debate itself waxed dramatic (as in the struggle to reform the state's court system), or pathetic (as in the attempt to save a local hospital), or comic (as when such questions as deer-hunting with bows and arrows or the operation of barber shops on Washington's birthday were before the House). The original verse recited during the session would fill a small but entertaining volume. For the visiting legislative buff, the session had its moments.
>
> But they were few and far between. Considered as pure entertainment, the day-to-day operations of the Assembly — the perfunctory debates or minor bills and irrelevant resolutions — could not sustain for long the interest of an audience of outsiders. As one who watched a considerable number of House sessions in 1959 (often alone in the gallery), the writer confesses that he often found his attention wandering to the pigeons conspiring on the window-sills. Most of the time — to the mere observer — the proceedings of the House are dull.[2]

FIFTY PATTERNS OF LEGISLATIVE PROCEDURE

Like the human fingerprint, each state legislature is unique. It has formal and informal configurations of power and procedure all of its own, like other

---

[2] Barber, *op. cit.,* pp. 56-57.

184

*Unique con-
figurations
of power and
procedure*

states in some respects but totally different in others. It is only one part of the structure of power in the state's political system and is thus functionally interdependent with four other *major* political variables: the executive establishment, political parties, pressure groups, and the legislators' constituencies.[3] It is essentially this web of relationships, unique in varying degrees in each state, which explains the state's legislative decision-making process. Your own state legislative pattern depends upon a number of "ifs." *If* the governor dominates, the legislature may be principally a ratifying agency or may be preoccupied with checking executive usurpations. *If* the political parties are strong and policy-oriented, the legislature may function primarily as an arena for disciplined partisans to support the majority or minority leaderships. *If* the constituencies are effectively assertive, the legislature tends to focus on carrying out popular mandates. *If* pressure groups dominate, the legislature may function as an institution for compromising and integrating group conflicts. Of course, to these "ifs" must be added various constitutional requirements and limitations as well as a backdrop of history, customs, and traditions.

The four-state legislative study by Wahlke, Eulau, Buchanan, and Ferguson provides an excellent illustration of interstate variations in the legislative process. Notice the differences in what are judged to be the "essential elements" in each state's legislative system:[4]

> *California:* (1) the vast number of bills; (2) the essential part played by the author; (3) the open committee hearing and the overt part taken by lobbyists in decision-making; (4) the "automatic calendar" which gives every bill some consideration if the author asks it; (5) the importance of the floor vote; (6) the wide range within which the outcome of any given issue is unpredictable, depending as it does upon the actions of certain members who remain until the last essentially free agents; and (7) the irrelevance of political parties.

> *New Jersey:* (1) the small size of the legislature; (2) the strength of partisanship; (3) the dominant part played by the majority caucus *as a group;* (4) the irrelevance of committees; (5) the impersonalism achieved by rotation of members in the Assembly and officers in both chambers; and (6) the inability of the minority to make a responsible contribution to policy development.

> *Ohio:* (1) the complete fusion of chamber and majority party leadership, administered by presiding officers; (2) the smooth functioning of this leadership to the point where it is secure enough to treat the opposition permissively on occasion; (3) the importance of committees as the heart of the legislative process; (4) the general resemblance to congressional procedures; and (5) the formalization of structure and process required by the size of the lower house.

---

[3] This discussion is based upon the analysis in Wahlke, *et al., The Legislative System,* p. 245.

[4] *Ibid.,* pp. 61, 62, 64, 65.

Tennessee: (1) high turnover and brief sessions; (2) initiative almost entirely in the hands of the Governor, represented by his floor leaders; (3) the importance of floor action as the central point of decision; (4) the amount of time and attention devoted to local bills in a variation of the "unanimous consent" procedure; and (5) the negligible part played by political parties.

State legislatures also differ in the type of conflicts which consume the members' energy and dictate their rivalries and alignments. For example, striking differences are shown in Table 10-1 between the Ohio and New Jersey legislators' concern for "regional conflicts," which are very impor- ***Types of*** tant to the former, but relatively unimportant to the latter. Party con- ***conflicts*** flicts rank quite low in importance in California and Tennessee and exceptionally high in New Jersey. The urban-rural conflict is the only type rated important by over half of the legislators in all four states. Conflicts with the governor are ranked high in New Jersey and Tennessee but much lower in California and Ohio. In the description of state legislative procedure which follows, an effort is made to focus attention on both the similarities and the differences between states, insofar as they seem significant.

TABLE 10-1

IMPORTANCE OF LEGISLATIVE CONFLICTS IN FOUR STATES

Type of Conflict	Per Cent Declared "Important"*			
	California	New Jersey	Ohio	Tennessee
Urban-Rural	65%	53%	79%	91%
Party	26	96	49	23
Governor	18	76	36	89
Liberal-Conservative	58	22	52	29
Labor	65	18	61	54
Regional	69	18	17	13

* Figures are for members of lower house only, in each state.

Source: Adapted from Wahlke, *et al., The Legislative System,* p. 425.

FLOOR FORMALITIES AND ACTIVITIES

It takes a vast amount of talk and manipulative tactics to translate democratic will and policy into law in representative assemblies, wherever those assemblies are located. Much of the debate and discussion is essential to free

186 government, as emphasized by John Stuart Mill and many others.[5] Much of it
is likewise unessential, if not definitely detrimental in itself, but partly
unavoidable. Similarly the miscellaneous tactical maneuvers are employed
constructively and otherwise, both to accomplish and to prevent the taking of steps, whether for public or private interest. Through such a combination of talk, action, and compromise thousands of bills are adopted into statutes in the fifty states each biennium, while many more thousands of introduced bills are sidetracked along the legislative way, never to become law. Some idea of the magnitude of the legislative load is afforded by consulting *The Book of the States'* biennial inventory of the number of legislative introductions and enactments in regular and extra sessions. Well over half of the legislatures will introduce more than 1,000 bills in the regular session, with New York leading the way with over 8,000 each year. Very few states actually enact as many as a thousand bills into law in one session; only seven did in the 1960 and 1961 sessions with Florida's 3,031 topping all others.[6]

Talk, tactics, and legislation

In this complicated process, significant technicalities and formalities are observed to systematize the lawmaking game. The average state legislature thus functions with a continuous mixture of inefficiency and discipline, with somewhat less systematic performance than is to be observed in Congress. It is more amateurish than the national legislative branch.

The question or problem of a quorum may arise in any type of deliberative body, public or private. All members cannot be present all the time, and yet regular business presumably cannot be carried on with too few present. Hence a quorum must be determined or defined in proportion to the total membership, or as a fixed number of members who must be present for official action or decision. Such a stipulation is designed to insure representative government against minority rule. The customary requirement parallels the provision in the federal Constitution that a majority of each house of Congress "shall constitute a quorum to do business; but a smaller number may adjourn from day to day, and may be authorized to compel the attendance of absent members, in such manner, and under such penalities as each House may provide." There are exceptions to the majority requirement, however, as exemplified in the Tennessee constitutional provision that two-thirds of the membership be present for a quorum. A provision like this may at times enable a stubborn minority through concerted absenteeism to block majority action. Even though a majority of the membership favor and can pass a bill,

The quorum and majority

---

[5] T. V. Smith, *The Legislative Way of Life* (University of Chicago Press, Chicago, 1940), deals with the relationship between talk and legislation in America.

[6] The others were: California (2,232), Delaware (1,362), North Carolina (1,298), Indiana (1,197), New York (1,098 and 970 in its two annual sessions), and Alabama (1,045). *See* the *Book of the States, 1962-63, op. cit.,* pp. 56-57.

two-thirds of the members must be present under such a rule to permit action. **187**
There are stories of Tennessee legislators breaking a quorum and delaying the
legislative game by crossing the near-by Kentucky border to become immune
from arrest for non-criminal conduct. Normally the lack of a quorum is cor-
rected by calling in absentees from adjacent rooms or neighboring quarters or
having them brought to the floor by sergeants-at-arms. But raising the question
of a quorum, with consequent roll calls and rounding up of members, is one
of the techniques for carrying on a legislative filibuster.

The passage of a bill, according to the state constitution, may require
affirmative action by a majority of a quorum, as in Congress, or it may require
a majority vote of the total membership, as in Iowa and Tennessee. Kentucky
requires an affirmative vote by two-fifths of those elected and a majority of
those voting. In the New Hampshire house a majority constitute a quorum, but,
if less than two-thirds of the elected members are present, two-thirds of those
present must assent to render any action valid. A roughly similar rule governs
action in the New Hampshire senate. Non-controversial bills and resolutions
are often passed by a one-sided voice vote without a large attendance and
without any check or challenge as to the matter of a quorum or a constitutional
majority. This is particularly likely to occur in the case of local bills, in which
only the members from the communities involved have an interest.

No proposal becomes a bill for official consideration by a legislative
chamber unless it is formally introduced by a member, group of members, or
committee of that house or is received with a certificate of adoption from
the coordinate house of a bicameral legislature. Non-members, even *Introduction*
high state officials, have no technical power to introduce bills, however *and readings*
much initiative and influence they may exercise in preparing drafts of *of bills*
laws and pushing them to adoption through a variety of means, including at
times actual lobbying on the floor. Any member may introduce bills without
limit, regardless of actual authorship, even to the extent of tossing in crackpot
proposals "by request," but with no assurance that his offerings will get beyond
the introductory stage. According to the practice in the state, a member intro-
duces a bill by speaking from the floor or by filing it in the "hopper" to be
announced in due course by the clerk or presiding officer, who assigns it to an
appropriate committee.

On its sojourn through one house a bill is given three readings, actual
or nominal, unless it becomes stranded along the way without reaching the point
of decision for adoption or defeat. A few states, Nebraska and the Dakotas
included, have reduced the requirement to only two readings. Separate readings
on separate days are required in all states, either by constitutional provision or
by rules of procedure. Full oral readings were essential and also feasible in
the days of simple government when convenient facilities for printing and dis-

tributing copies of pending bills were lacking. But such ample renderings on the floor are neither necessary nor feasible for handling the mass of complicated proposals, which the modern lawmaker must ponder and study for himself or in consultation with experts to approach an understanding of the problems involved.

The first reading, customarily by title only, occurs when the bill is introduced or is announced as having been introduced. The second reading, either in full or by title, is part of the process of considering the bill as reported by the committee to which it was assigned. This reading is usually accompanied by debate, perhaps by committee of the whole house, and this is the appropriate time for offering amendments. In many states the crucial vote on a bill is at some stage in the second reading. After passing the second reading, with or without change, the bill is ready for its third reading but must normally await its turn. At the last reading, debate is not customary but may take place with attention centered on the measure as a whole. The proposal of amendments at this stage requires unanimous consent. After passing the third reading, whether by title or in detail, the bill is engrossed and put in form for the certification signature of the presiding officer. It is now ready for consideration by the other house, or, if it has come from the other house in identical form, it is ready for its way to the governor's desk and most likely the statute books.

Legislative bodies conduct floor activities normally in accord with orders of business and calendars, making exceptions and digressions through unanimous consent, special orders, and the like. The daily order of business includes *Orders of business and calendars* such items as the prayer by the chaplain, roll call, corrections of the journal, petitions and memorials, reports of committees, introduction of bills, bills on first reading, bills on second reading, bills on third reading, special business, unfinished business, and miscellaneous business.

The calendars are really lists of bills completed by committees to be taken up in sequence on designated days. Local bills, for example, may be placed on a separate calendar and be considered exclusively on specified days, as Mondays. There may be calendars for general bills, for unanimous consent items, and for other matters. Urgent or favorite bills may get top priority through unanimous consent or through special rules of a powerful rules committee, steering group, or informal majority leadership. This special treatment, in effect, reduces the priority of other bills and also reduces the likelihood of their getting attention by the deliberative body. But this discretionary treatment is part of the process of legislative politics, and it frequently is necessary for the passage of constructive legislation and avoidance of chaotic conditions near the end of a session.

Legislative houses cast votes on bills and motions in different ways. One method is by unanimous consent, with the raising of no voice of opposition and announcement by the presiding officer that the point is carried or ordered.

Another is the voice vote (*viva voce*), with the chair judging whether the yeas or the nays have a majority. If there is doubt, there may be a show of hands to be counted or a division, with members passing by tellers in two groups to be counted. There are legal and constitutional ways for requir- *Voting* ing a vote by roll call, with every member present responding to be recorded as voting for or against the motion or as being present but not voting. This is a slow process unless electric devices are used. A number of states have installed electric voting systems, with push buttons at each member's desk and with a scoreboard to flash each vote as well as to indicate the results. This method preserves a mechanical record of the voting proceedings.

There are ways of regulating and limiting debate in legislatures in order to get the work done. This is more noticeable and necessary for assemblies of large membership than for the small bodies. Most of the state senates and Nebraska's unicameral legislature fall in the latter classification, but *Floor man-* the lower houses generally operate under procedural regulations that may *agement;* be highly restrictive of freedom of discussion. The rank-and-file member *the speaker* of a lower chamber is likely to find it difficult at strategic times to get the oppor- tunity to speak. Also he is likely to find his time limited to a few minutes when he does get the floor. Not only does the lower house make more use of rules limiting debate than the upper house; the speaker of the house is often in a position to exercise more power and partisanship than the presiding officer of the senate.

The speaker of the lower chamber is invariably chosen from the member- ship. He becomes the chief spokesman for the majority party, group, or faction of the house over which he presides, keeping in intimate contact with the other leaders of the majority. That majority may be further strengthened through political line-up with executive leadership as exemplified by the governor. Under such circumstances, it is not easy to overrule the speaker. He has an effective power of recognition, with no little discretion to give the floor to friends and withhold it from enemies. He has the important power to appoint the members of standing committees and to assign bills to committees for study and report. He is in a position to make partisan interpretation and application of the rules in doubtful or border-line cases, although custom, politics, and majority opinion are checks on excessive abuse of this power. The speaker may rank next to the governor for his role in state political management.

It might be said that all rules of legislative procedure are made to be broken. This observation applies to upper and lower houses. There are rules for breaking rules, for suspending them by unanimous consent or by a two-thirds vote. Even if rules are set forth in the state constitution, there *Rule-break-* are ways of adopting special orders that such rules have been applied *ing and jour-* when, in fact, they have not been applied. It is a type of legal fiction to *nal-keeping* record three readings for a bill when there may have been no actual readings. It is a further fiction, as is sometimes the case, to assume that the readings occurred on three separate days when the so-called readings were rushed through in one day. There are also fictions as to the presence of a quorum contrary to the facts. It is an undisguised fiction at the end of a session to turn the official clock back and hold it short of midnight while the planet perhaps makes a complete revolution on its axis. These fictions are written up and authenticated in the journal of the house concerned as if they were not fictions. And the law is what the journal says is the law when the session ends, and the members go home, sometimes to discover in leisure what they did in haste. It is, furthermore, the practice of courts and attorneys general to accept the certified journals at face value, refusing to go behind them to check the process of a separate branch of government. Nevertheless, fiction, including the legislative variety, need not be inherently detrimental. There is hope that it may serve useful public purposes.

UNOFFICIAL "RULES OF THE GAME"

Legislative procedure involves far more than written rules. Some unwritten rules are more important than official ones and the consequences of their violation may be a great deal more serious. The four-state legislative study provides an interesting catalog of such rules-of-the-game described by legislators themselves. The rules are grouped into six categories according to their primary function.[7]

(1) *Rules Primarily Intended to Promote Group Cohesion and Solidarity.* Respect for other members' "legislative rights" ranks high among these rules ("support another member's local bill if it doesn't affect you or your district"; "don't steal another member's bill"; "accept the author's amendments to a bill"). Another rule is that of impersonality ("don't deal in personalities"; "oppose the bill, not the man"; "don't criticize the moral behavior of members"). Others related to promoting group cohesion and solidarity include the rule of modesty ("don't be a prima donna"; "don't talk for the press or galleries"); the rule of respect for other members' "political rights" ("respect the incumbent-status of

---

[7] The discussion which follows is adapted from tables in Wahlke, *et al., The Legislative System,* pp. 146-147, and pp. 160-61. The material has been greatly reduced but much of the language is theirs. The authors are indebted to Professors Wahlke, Eulau, Buchannan, and Ferguson and to John Wiley & Sons, Inc., for granting permission to use it in this form.

other members"; "don't embarrass him in his district"); and the rule of institutional patriotism ("defend the legislature and its members against outsiders").

(2) *Rules Which Primarily Promote Predictability of Legislative Behavior.* Ranking above all other rules in frequency of mention is the rule of performance of obligations ("keep your word"; "abide by your commitments"). Related to this is the rule of advance notice of changed stand ("notify in advance if you can't keep a commitment"). Two rules concerning predictability relate to openness — openness of aims ("be frank in explaining bills"; "don't conceal real purpose of bills or amendments"); and openness in opposition ("don't conceal your opposition"; "notify in advance if you're going to oppose or introduce amendments").

(3) *Rules Which Primarily Channel and Restrain Conflict.* Perhaps the best example of rules to ameliorate conflict is the rule of conciliation ("be willing to compromise"; "don't be a perfectionist"; "accept half a loaf"). Closely related are the rules of seniority ("respect the seniority system"); and of apprenticeship ("respect older members"; "don't try to accomplish too much too soon"). In the states with more competitive party systems frequent mention was made of following caucus or conference decisions and observing "senatorial courtesy" in the more narrow sense of controlling appointments.

(4) *Rules Which Primarily Expedite Legislative Business.* The most obvious rule to expedite legislative business, and one which ranked high in frequency of mention, is self-restraint in debate or, simply, "don't talk too much." Related to this is restraint in opposition ("don't fight unnecessarily"; "don't be opposed to everything"). Others deserving some mention include application ("don't leave after your own bill has been considered"); restraint in bill-introduction ("don't introduce too many bills or amendments"); and commitment to job ("take the job seriously").

(5) *Rules Which Serve Primarily to Give Tactical Advantages to Individual Member.* Some rules relate not so much to group purposes as to the personal self interest of the legislator. Examples of these are courtesy, sociability, gracefulness in defeat, caution in commitments, negotiation, and self-restraint in goals.

(6) *Desirable Personal Qualities Cited as Rules.* Some legislators, when asked to name the unofficial rules-of-the-game, mentioned various personal qualities which did not fit readily into any of the above categories. Ranking first is integrity, followed by personal virtue, objectivity, ability and intelligence, and non-venality.

UNOFFICIAL "RULES OF THE GAME"

192   Possibly more significant than the rules-of-the-game are the methods legislators have of punishing those who fail to comply. Sanctions for enforcement are shown in Table 10-2, ranked in order of their frequency of mention by legislators in the four states. The arsenal of weapons is imposing, with obstruction of the non-complying legislator's own bills being most frequently mentioned. Ostracism, mistrust, loss of political perquisites and rewards, denial of special privileges, and public ridicule, are all recognized in lesser degrees of strength. Reprimand in party caucus is apparently significant only in states such as New Jersey where party discipline is high.

COMMITTEES: ACTIVE AND INACTIVE

      Legislative bodies rely heavily upon committees of different kinds and sizes for much of the actual work of investigation and lawmaking. They use committes to originate, revise, and report bills as well as to pigeonhole

Indispensa-bility of committees
or bury numerous proposals, thus preventing them from reaching the floor for time-consuming consideration. The committee system provides a division of labor among legislators, opens official ways for engaging the services of non-member experts and advisers, and affords direct opportunity for individuals and groups to present pertinent facts and opinions on pending bills with which they are concerned. The system has superfluities but is, nevertheless, indispensable for modern democratic government.

      There are several types or classes of committees and committee functions. The most general is the *standing* committee for the consideration of all bills and matters in a particular field of interest, such as revenue, appropriations,

Types of committees
labor, or the judiciary. There may be *special* or *select* committees to look into temporary problems, such as election frauds or civil disorders or administrative scandals, to make reports and recommendations, and to pass out of existence when the special task is completed. There may be *interim* committees to make studies or investigations between sessions of a legislature. It becomes necessary to set up a *joint conference* committee, with members from both houses, to iron out differences when a bill passes both houses but in different form or language, and the house of first passage will not accept the changes. This is sometimes the only way of obtaining inter-house unity of action on significant measures in such fields as financial policy, administrative reorganization, or regulation of economic enterprise. Several states, for example, Maine, Massachusetts, and Connecticut, make use of standing joint committees to consider bills in the first instance to minimize deadlocks between the two houses.

TABLE 10-2 193

SANCTIONS FOR ENFORCING RULES-OF-THE-GAME PERCEIVED
BY LEGISLATORS IN FOUR STATES

Sanction	Proportion of Legislators Naming Each Sanction in			
	California	New Jersey	Ohio	Tennessee
OBSTRUCTION OF HIS BILLS: abstain or vote against him: bottle up his bills in committee; amend his bills; pass them only if of major importance to general welfare.	55%	42%	57%	72%
OSTRACISM: give him the "silent treatment"; subtly reject him personally.	24	14	31	29
MISTRUST: cross-examine him on floor, in committee; don't put any trust in him.	34	14	25	12
LOSS OF POLITICAL PERQUISITES, INDUCEMENTS & REWARDS: Take away patronage, good committee assignments; report to constituents, local party organization.	15	9	19	4
DENIAL OF SPECIAL LEGISLATIVE PRIVILEGES: denial of unanimous consent; otherwise delaying bills.	9	8	4	2
REPRIMAND: in caucus, in private.	—	12	*	1
OVERT DEMONSTRATIONS OF DISPLEASURE: ridicule, hissing, laughter, etc.	3	1	2	3
MISCELLANEOUS OTHER SANCTIONS	5	12	*	3
NO SANCTIONS PERCEIVED	7	14	11	10

* Less than 1%.

Source: Wahlke, *et al., The Legislative System,* p. 154.

COMMITTEES: ACTIVE AND INACTIVE

194

Multiplicity and size of committees

Many state legislatures have excessively numerous standing committees, particularly in the lower house, with more than 50 for Arkansas and Florida. A few senates have large numbers, Mississippi topping the list with 46 and several having just under 40. Counting the house, senate, and joint standing committees, the number runs above 100 for Mississippi. Several states have but little less. The smallest number is unicameral Nebraska's 14. A survey by the Council of State Governments indicated that the median number of house standing committees dropped from 39 in 1946 to 23 in 1961, while the median for the senate committees dropped from 31 to 20. According to the study made by the Committee on American Legislatures of the American Political Science Association, it would be feasible for state legislatures to limit the number of standing committees to about 12.[8]

Many of the committees have large memberships. North Carolina's 82 committees range from 6 to 62 members. At the other extreme are several states, among them Wisconsin and Massachusetts, where there are committee memberships of less than 5. New Jersey has 16 General Assembly committees with 7 members each, 16 senate committees ranging from 5 to 7 in membership, and 4 joint committees with 12 members each.[9] Large memberships provide committee representation for various groups and regions of a state, but such memberships in combination with numerous committees inevitably entail an extensive duplication of members, often making it impossible for a legislator to attend all of his committee meetings, even if he can keep up with when and where the meetings are to be held.

The committee process

The *modus operandi* of standing committees varies somewhat among legislatures and among the committees of any particular legislature. The rules committee, because of its continuous connection with house proceedings, invariably has the prerogative of meeting at any time of the day or night. Most or all other committees are generally required to avoid conflict of time with the regular floor sessions, except for urgent reasons and with special house permission. They are expected to meet evenings, mornings, or over weekends, leaving the regular afternoons clear for attendance on the floor. In considering bills, important committees hold public hearings and also meet in executive session to prepare reports on their assignments. Unimportant and "graveyard" committees sometimes rock along for months or more without meeting or report, particularly if a dominant chairman is opposed to

---

[8] Belle Zeller, ed., *American State Legislatures,* Report of the Committee on American Legislatures, American Political Science Association (Thomas Y. Crowell Company, New York, 1954), p. 100.

[9] *See* Table, "Legislative Procedure: Standing Committees and Hearings," *The Book of the States, 1962-63,* p. 49, for number and range in size of standing committees in the various states.

action. It becomes common knowledge that legislatures are equipped with "hot-running" committees and "cold-running" committees, with "committee stacking" as the method of determining committee temperature on specific questions.[10]

A large committee with heavy duties has certain characteristics of a legislative chamber at work, with a schedule or calendar of items for consideration and, perhaps, with a division of functions among subcommittees for investigation and report to the full committee. The chairman of such a committee often exercises significant powers to divide up the work and to guide, speed, or delay attention to measures assigned to his group. A committee hearing may take less than a day or may extend over several days or weeks, with all sides on pending proposals having their say and with members putting questions and arguments to the different advocates.

One-third of the states require every committee to report on every bill referred to it, whether the report be favorable, unfavorable, or without recommendation. This stipulation tends to prolong legislative sessions. The remedy in many states for committee neglect is to discharge a committee from handling a bill and recall the bill to be placed on the calendar of the chamber for debate and vote. The step for recall may be taken by majority action or petition. Such a move, however, is not easy and is no guarantee of final passage when the showdown comes. An unfavorable report by a committee may be counteracted by a motion to substitute the original bill or a minority report for the committee version, but this strategy is likewise no guarantee of adoption. The rank-and-file member might conclude from the fate of his bill that the Ark would not have been built if Noah had depended upon a committee and a legislature.

The work of legislative committees varies widely in quality, and different opinions of the same committee work doubtless vary. One of the less favorable appraisals of committee work is found in a legislator's statement reported *Quality of* in Barber's legislative study: *committee work*

> I've seen different members of the committee — not that I'm knocking them personally, but this is just a broad statement — they got holes in their shoes. Their heels are run down. Their ties got spots on them. And the way I visualize it, now, you see, you see them sitting there, so austere, listening to a (high official) making counter-claims about these points, and you know they probably haven't got a dime for a cup of coffee. (laughs) Yet they're to judge, or pass favorably on these matters that go into millions of dollars![11]

High quality is said to be more likely in legislatures with few and rela-

---

[10] *See* Loren P. Beth and William C. Havard, "Committee Stacking and Political Power in Florida," *Journal of Politics*, XXIII (February, 1961), pp. 57-83.

[11] Barber, *op. cit.*, p. 67.

196 tively small committees which can be streamlined for the exercise of both power and responsibility with less opportunity for bypassing the public interest. The streamlining of committee functions is not only meritorious in itself; it is also an index of general concern for streamlining and strengthening the legislative process, as evidenced in Nebraska, Maine, and Massachusetts. Committee work has been facilitated and improved through the rise and expansion of expert assistance. As pointed out in the preceding chapter, this assistance includes bill-drafting service, legislative reference service, and legislative councils. But the quality of work of legislative committees can rise no higher in the long run than the quality of the legislature itself.

THE ROLE OF PARTY

If someone asked you which political party has the majority of members in your state legislature, you probably could answer quickly. But if you were asked *how important* party membership is in the legislative process in

Question of party's importance

your state, you might have a more difficult time answering. Political scientists specializing in the legislative process find it very difficult to generalize on the legislative role of parties for all fifty states, and even within individual states this can be a hazardous job. The ascribed role of party in one legislative session may come unglued one or two sessions later.

Statistical studies of party membership of legislators do give *some* answers. Many states, most of them in the South, are one-party states. In some respects they become *no-party* states because there is no reason for tight party disci-

Two-party, one-party, and no-party legislatures

pline to protect partisan control of legislation such as might be expected in competitive two-party states. Four state legislatures[12] consisted entirely of Democrats in 1961 and six others were more than 90 per cent Democratic.

As mentioned in the previous chapter, legislative organization in such states tends to follow factional lines rather than party lines. Several states are considered strongly Republican, but no state legislature is wholly Republican and only one state, Vermont, was as much as 80 per cent Republican in 1961. Two states, Minnesota and Nebraska, require non-partisan election of their legislators.

Statistics on nominal party membership, however, cannot tell who are "party men" in the legislature and who are not. Recent studies reveal wide

---

[12] They were Alabama, Louisiana, Mississippi, and South Carolina. *See The Book of the States, 1962-63, op. cit.,* p. 41.

variations in the extent of partisanship in legislatures, not only between states but also between houses and between parties within one state.[13] *Party influence on legislative behavior* The device used in the four-state legislative study to tackle the question of party influence was to seek an evaluation by the legislators themselves. Their own ratings, summarized in Table 10-3, show a striking contrast between strong influence in New Jersey, moderate influence in Ohio, still less influence in California, and the least influence in Tennessee. The

TABLE 10-3

EVALUATIONS OF PARTY INFLUENCE ON LEGISLATIVE BEHAVIOR, BY STATE

Evaluation	New Jersey	Ohio	California	Tennessee
Much/considerable inflence				
Republicans have	37%	34%	1%	16%
Democrats have	22	1	5	3
Both parties have	33	16	—	1
Some/increasing influence				
Republicans have	—	7	5	16
Democrats have	1	6	15	4
Both parties have	—	5	34	3
Little/no influence				
Republicans have	1	2	8	2
Democrats have	—	17	—	4
Both parties have	6	12	32	51

Source: Wahlke, *et al., The Legislative System,* p. 355.

relatively high rating given Republican influence on legislative behavior in Tennessee reflects a feeling that the Republican minority occasionally swings the balance of power between Democratic factions on such issues as redistricting or segregation. As some Democrats expressed it: "You never thought about the Democratic Party unless the Republicans were trying something — for example,

---

[13] *See,* for example, W. J. Keefe, "Comparative Study of the Role of Political Parties in State Legislatures," *Western Political Quarterly,* IX (September, 1956), pp. 726-742; Warren Moscow, *Politics in the Empire State* (Alfred A. Knopf, Inc., New York, 1948); and W. Duane Lockard, "Legislative Politics in Connecticut," *American Political Science Review,* XLVIII (March, 1954), pp. 166-173.

198 reapportionment;" or "Some few Republicans think they can join up with the niggers to beat us."[14] A different pattern appears in Ohio where the minority party in a two-party competitive legislature is rated low in influence on individual members. As one House member described it:

> No one has told me to vote for or against something because I'm a Democrat. I don't know, though; it may be different with the Republicans. I think that they are closely associated with their party because they are in control. No one bothers us (i.e., the Democrats) because they know that the Democrats can't deliver.[15]

On the whole, a kind of quasi non-partisanship seems to exist for the *majority* of state legislatures for *much* of the time, certainly more so than for Congress. The frustrating efforts of Professor Wahlke and his colleagues *Quasi non-* to find a demarcation line between the "party man" and the "inde-*partisanship* pendent" or "maverick" in the legislature led them to the conclusion *of legis-* that "ambivalence and uncertainty about the meaning of 'party' is a *latures* fact of political life, felt by the legislators themselves; it is not just a reflection of the state of political research."[16]

PRESSURE GROUPS AND LOBBYISTS

The popular stereotype of lobbying in the state legislature is a picture of legislative weaklings engaged in daily "surrender exercises" to merciless attacks from marauding bands of wicked lobbyists whose weapons are principally *Exaggerated* money and the power of political reprisal. That this is gross exaggeration *stereotype* in the contemporary state legislature should be obvious to the conscientious student of politics. What, then, is the role of pressure groups and lobbyists in the state legislative process? Much of the answer was supplied in Chapter 8, but it may help to consider the question again from the legislator's point of view.

Facilitators, The friendliness or hostility of legislators toward pressure groups, and *Resistors,* awareness of them, were measured in the four-state legislative study and *and Neutrals* legislators were classified into three groups:[17]

---

[14] Wahlke, *et al., The Legislative System,* p. 359.

[15] *Ibid.,* p. 357.

[16] *Ibid.,* p. 376.

[17] *Ibid.,* p. 325.

(1) Facilitators: Have a friendly attitude toward group activity *and* relatively much knowledge about it.

(2) Registers: Have a hostile attitude toward group activity *and* relatively much knowledge about it.

(3) Neutrals: Have no strong attitude of favor or disfavor with respect to group activity (regardless of their knowledge of it), or, have very little knowledge about it (regardless of their friendliness or hostility toward it).

An almost equal number of Facilitators and Neutrals were found, 36.5 per cent and 36.7 per cent respectively, with the remaining 26.8 per cent being Resisters. The realism of this classification is supported by the response of legislators to the question of why they thought the legislature might work better or worse in the absence of pressure groups. Although 63 per cent of the Facilitators considered pressure groups indispensable to the legislative system, only 14 per cent of the Resisters held this opinion. (See Table 10-4.) Resisters were the

TABLE 10-4

USEFULNESS OF PRESSURE GROUP ACTIVITY IN THE LEGISLATIVE SYSTEM,
AS RATED BY LEGISLATORS IN FOUR STATES

Most Favorable Opinion Expressed	Role Orientation of Legislator:		
	Facilitator	Neutral	Resister
1. Groups are indispensable	63%	39%	14%
2. Group activity is in general good, though certain "bad practices" of groups are undesirable	23	41	46
3. Other less favorable opinions: e.g., group activity may be objectionable but one ought not interfere with the democratic right to be heard; group influence is over-rated, it is not an important factor; group activity is a wholly disruptive force which ought to be eliminated.	14	20	40
	100%	100%	100%

Source: Adapted from Wahlke, *et al., The Legislative System,* p. 326.

group most frequently expressing less favorable opinions, including the view that pressure group activity "is a wholly disruptive force which ought to be eliminated."

Although legislators disagree on how influential lobbyists are, few feel that the omnipotent-devil stereotype is an accurate picture of lobbyists. The four-state study found that most would go no further than the legislator

**Legislators'
views of
lobbyists'
influence**

who said, "Lobbyists do affect the vote. Maybe they don't change your vote — lobbyists are only effective with those who are undecided — but they can sure make you bleed."[18] While most legislators were found to agree that pressure groups can, on occasion, make them "bleed," ultimate influence of the lobbyists is downgraded by such statements as:

> Legislators aren't really influenced much by lobbyists in the way people think. We go to their parties because we like free meals and parties. But no one expects that to affect your vote. I don't know that any lobbyist ever really could buy anything.[19]

The authors of this four-state study do not reject the proposition that one of the central functions of the legislature is the "accommodation of interest group demands." Their findings add further weight to it but suggest, in addition, that in "refereeing" the group struggle, legislators may view the pressuring lobbyists with a much more impartial or "public minded" eye than is generally believed. Concerning the quotation above alleging that free meals and parties do not really buy votes, Professor Wahlke and his colleagues concluded:

> Cynics will no doubt write off such comments as platitudinous talk for public consumption, but the impression of interviewers in all four states was that such views represent genuine convictions. Legislators themselves seem to be not only much more sophisticated in their estimates of the relative power and merits of various groups than they are generally given credit for, but also much more adept at parrying the thrusts of these groups and devising their own counterpressures against them.[20]

The frequent call to "do something about lobbyists" probably comes as much from disgruntled groups nursing wounds from a legislative defeat as from a legislative defeat as from any other source. Their lobbyists may

**Regulation
of lobbying**

have lost to other lobbyists. But the call to regulate lobbying has received strong popular support from time to time, particularly as some

---

[18] *Ibid.*, p. 340.

[19] *Ibid.*

[20] *Ibid.*

example of abuse is brought to light. The problem of preventing abuses while protecting the right to be heard is not a simple one. The legislature is intended primarily to serve the public interest; yet it is composed of private persons and is steadily confronted with urgent pressure from private groups. The private pressures are concentrated, while pressure for the public interest is likely to be diffused. Moreover, private interests have the constitutional rights of speech, press, and petition, and lawmakers cannot be shut in, like a trial jury, and shielded from contact with interested parties. They certainly cannot be shielded from contact with the governor and other executive officers, who may lobby or exert other types of pressure. Pressure through propaganda and appeals to public opinion cannot be checkmated except through exposure or counter propaganda. But further measures may be offered to check personal lobbying around legislatures. At times there have been more private lobbyists than public legislators at a state capitol, and such conditions have provoked severe criticism for their actual or alleged influence in corrupting the lawmakers. As in many other ventures, individual states preceded the national government in seeking to regulate or restrict lobbying activities. Georgia, in 1877, adopted a constitutional provision declaring that "lobbying is a crime." Massachusetts and Wisconsin pioneered with legislation on the subject prior to 1900, and more than 30 other states have subsequently adopted statutes to combat the evils of the "third house." Wisconsin passed a new lobby control law in 1957, one of the strictest in existence. It prohibits the buying of meals, drinks, or anything of value for a legislator, thus attacking head-on the problem of where to draw the line between harmless courtesies and corrupting favors.

Important features of lobbying laws require the registration of paid lobbyists, the names of the sponsors, and the terms of compensation. Failure to comply with the requirements may subject the violator to fine, imprisonment, and denial of registration. The legislation has proved difficult to enforce, although it is said to have improved the practice of lobbying in a few states like Wisconsin. There are sundry and subtle ways of evading the regulations or secretly violating them. There is no legal method, for example, to prevent the election of a powerful lobbyist to the legislature, where he can ply his trade with skill. Nominally unpaid lobbyists cannot be easily exposed or restricted, particularly if they are also important political bosses. There is a degree of hope for the public good in the diversity of purpose and competitive balancing of power among the special interests seeking legislative blessings through lobbying and other pressure tactics. Employers and employees may battle as lobbyists. So may railway and trucking spokesmen. Group may balance group and unintentionally promote the public interest, partly by exposing each other to the public eye. Lobbyists cannot completely disregard the effect of public opinion.

H. L. Mencken, in one of his rare lapses into optimism, once predicted that the "rotten borough" could not last. Writing in 1928, he observed that, "The yokels hang on because old apportionments give them unfair advantages. The vote of a malarious peasant on the lower Eastern Shore counts as much as the votes of 12 Baltimoreans. But that can't last. It is not only unjust and undemocratic; it is absurd."[21] If Mencken could have seen the Maryland legislature and its apportionment in 1961, and that of the great majority of other states, he would have discovered that the rotten borough not only survived but, in the face of the rising tide of urban growth, thrived in more extreme circumstances than ever. A state senator from one Eastern Shore county (Kent) in 1961 represented 15,481 Marylanders, but one from Baltimore County represented 492,428. Over three-fourths of Maryland's population in 1960 lived in the four largest counties plus Baltimore City, but they elected only one-third of the members of the upper house of the state legislature.

Aggravation of the rotten borough

Maryland provides merely one example of the rotten borough — a term originally applied to certain British districts prior to the parliamentary Reform Bill of 1832. Legislative malapportionment in 1961 existed in different degrees in nearly all of the fifty states. Only two states, Wisconsin and Massachusetts, had rural and urban representation approximating the democratic ideal of "one man, one vote," according to Gordon E. Baker in his study of urban-rural imbalance.[22] The 1960 census indicated that urban under-representation was getting worse rather than better, especially in those states deliberately basing their representation on land area or something else besides number of people. In California the 6,038,771 people in Los Angeles County were represented by one state senator, the same representation granted to the mountain peaks of the Sierra Nevada and the 14,294 people living in that district. The nearly 2,000,000 increase in Los Angeles County's population between 1950 and 1960 had no effect on its representation in the state senate — no effect, that is, except to dilute it still further. California's ten largest counties all suffered in this re-

---

[21] Quoted by Anthony Lewis, "On the Trail of the Fierce Gerrymander," *New York Times Magazine*, February 19, 1961, p. 17.

[22] Gordon E. Baker, *Rural versus Urban Political Power* (Doubleday and Company, Inc., Garden City, 1955). See also such studies of individual states as E. H. Hobbs, *Legislative Apportionment in Mississippi* (Bureau of Public Administration, University of Mississippi, University, Miss., 1956).

spect, having over three-fourths of the state's population in 1960 (11.9 million out of 15.7 million) but only one-fourth of the members of the state senate. New Jersey's Essex County, with its 923,545 people, had only one state senator, while Cape May County's 48,555 people were also repre- sented by one senator. Georgia's lower house makeup has been fairly *Limits on big city rep- resentation* well publicized, whereby the 159 counties were divided into three categories: the eight largest were given three representatives apiece, the next 30 received two and each of the remainder received one. Fulton County, with more than a half-million people, had more than one hundred times the population of rural Marion County (5,477 in 1960) but had only three times its representation in the Georgia lower house.

The fine art of gerrymander provides another method for bolstering rural legislative supremacy, with boundary lines of multi-county districts drawn to suit special needs. Muscogee County, Georgia (containing the city of Columbus) was the victim of a party tradition of "rotating" the nomination for state senator among the three counties of the district. Two rural counties (Chattahoochee and Marion) were joined to Muscogee County in Senate District 24 and each was given the privilege by the state Democratic party of nominating the senator once every three legislative sessions. The people of the other two counties were not even permitted to vote in that primary. The 1960 population of the three counties was as follows:

County	Population	Per Cent
Marion	5,477	3.2
Chattahoochee	13,011	7.3
Muscogee	158,623	89.5
Total	177,111	100.0

With nearly 90 per cent of the district's population, Muscogee County had no real senate representation in two sessions out of three, thanks to a gerrymandered district plus party rotation rules in a one-party state.

Some states have been even less subtle in their method of limiting urban representation than the above examples of representing area or governmental units rather than people. A few state constitutions specifically limit the representation of the most populous county to prevent its dominating the state legislature. For the three countries of Delaware, representation in both houses of the legislature was frozen in the constitution of 1894 and has remained the same ever since. New Castle County, with a two-thirds "majority" of Delaware's population, has a permanent two-fifths minority status in the legislature specified in the constitution.[23] Cook County, with over half of Illinois' popula-

---

[23] Actually, 7 of 17 senators and 15 of 35 representatives.

204   tion, is given 24 of the state's 58 senators. In Hawaii the island of Oahu (Honolulu) has close to 80 per cent of the total population of our fiftieth state, but the new constitution specifies that Oahu's representation in the senate shall be a permanent minority of 40 per cent.

Probably the most frustrating cause of under-representation for urban people is simply the failure of the legislature to obey a constitutional requirement for reapportionment after each census. By 1961 six censuses had

Balking legislatures

come and gone since legislators last reapportioned the states of Alabama and Tennessee, even though it is clearly required every ten years.

Indiana and Louisiana had not reapportioned since 1921 and many others were not up-to-date with the letter of their constitutions. Far more were out of step with the *spirit* of their constitutions, having carried out "token" reapportionment without making a genuine adjustment for population changes.

The foregoing discussion of the extent and methods of reapportionment was, of necessity, written in the *past* tense because of the revolutionary changes now taking place since the Supreme Court's 1962 reapportionment decision in *Baker v. Carr.* Events since then may make H. L. Mencken more of a prophet than once seemed likely. The picture of malapportionment prior to 1962 is still relevant, however, because it provides the essential political backdrop for the Court's historic decision reversing its tradition of denying jurisdiction in such cases. Before considering the decision itself, it is important first to examine the results of malapportionment and to trace the long and winding path of groups seeking change in apportionment.

What have been the results of this fairly consistent pattern of over-representation of the rural areas within states? The answer rural people give is obviously different from the answer of urban people. To rural people

Results of malapportionment

the result seems to be the preservation of state government sympathetic to rural needs and interests, and the prevention of domination by city people who have no understanding of their problems. To urban people the argument is the converse, except that they can claim that if one group *must* be governed without sympathy or understanding, it should be the minority and not the majority which is thus overruled. While there is merit in arguments to protect minority groups from oppression, it is difficult to conceive of continued rural domination of state legislatures in a democratic nation now 70 per cent urban. In the final analysis, most arguments for continued over-representation for farmers, pastures, counties, and land area generally, boil down to a defense of rural people as "better" or "safer" citizens than city people.

City people contend, with a considerable amount of evidence, that rural legislators frequently vote against legislation desired by large cities, such as governmental reorganizations, increased taxing power, urban-type regulatory authority, daylight savings time, and welfare legislation. Some southern cities have had their "moderate" approach to racial problems wiped out by rural segregationists dominating the legislature. The greatest amount of friction may be found in the division of the state's tax dollar, particularly in such matters as rural versus urban highways. State legislatures have been very reluctant to share with the cities the revenue from motor vehicle taxes, and have tended to appropriate it for use outside cities. This has compelled cities to finance their streets and expressways from the over-burdened property tax, even though the bulk of motor vehicle use may be inside the large cities. President Kennedy, while still a candidate for Democratic nomination in 1959, took notice of this problem and stated that ". . . our state legislatures, still rural-dominated in most states, will neither expand municipal taxing powers nor distribute to our cities and suburbs a fair share of the taxdollars collected within their boundaries."[24]

Several recent studies have suggested that the importance of urban-rural conflict in legislatures may have been exaggerated. David Derge found that conflicts between core city and suburbs, between parties, and between factions, are more common in the Illinois and Missouri legislatures than urban-rural conflicts.[25] Although Professor Robert Friedman finds that "urbanness and ruralness" are much less useful in explaining American politics than "more detailed interest groupings," he concludes that because legislators still *think* in terms of urban-rural conflicts, they must, by definition, be included as an important part of the political process.[26] M. C. Havens studied urban-rural cleavage in the Alabama legislature and found that urban-rural alignments do take place to a significant extent, though not on the majority of roll-call votes.[27] However, in a recent study of Florida, one of the most extreme cases of malapportionment, Havard and Beth conclude that any correspondence between legislative acts and the will of the majority of the people is largely accidental.[28]

The inadequate representation for urban people is often distasteful to the leaders of organized labor and to other groups opposed to rural guidance. The under-represented groups often seek results through the legislative power of the governor, who most likely appreciates urban votes. For important types of

---

[24] Address before the 1959 American Municipal Congress, Denver, Colorado; quoted in *Tennessee Town and City*, XI (February, 1960), p. 6.

[25] David R. Derge, "Metropolitan and Outstate Alignments in the Illinois and Missouri Legislative Delegations, *American Political Science Review*, LII (December, 1958), pp. 1051-1065.

[26] Robert Freidman, "The Urban-Rural Conflict Revisited," *Western Political Quarterly*, XIV (June, 1961), p. 495.

[27] M. C. Havens, *City Versus Farm?* (Bureau of Public Administration, University of Alabama, University, Ala., 1957). *See also* Table 10-1 on this point.

[28] William C. Havard and Loren P. Beth, *The Politics of Mis-Representation; Rural-Urban Conflict in the Florida Legislature* (Louisiana State University Press, Baton Rouge, 1962).

legislation and investigation, urbanites may skip an unsympathetic state government entirely and look to Congress for action, perhaps under the interstate

Malapportionment and centralization commerce power. According to the President's Commission on Intergovernmental Relations, the unrepresentative character of state legislatures is exerting a centralizing influence on the American federal system. Legislative neglect of the under-represented urban communities "has led more and more people to look to Washington for more and more of the services and controls they desire."[29] The Commission notes that "The same shift of population which has resulted in State legislatures becoming less representative of urban areas has had the effect of making the United States Senate more representative of these areas, because Senators, elected at large, must depend heavily upon urban voters, even in predominantly rural States."[30]

Why was it impossible, at least prior to *Baker* v. *Carr,* to reapportion state legislatures to reflect twentieth century realities in population? The answer is found in a combination of obstacles to change: the vested interest of

The politics of apportionment legislators, economic and sectional interests that cut across urban-rural cleavages, abnormal restrictions on revising old constitutions, and public apathy. The desire of legislators to preserve the status quo is well known. Professors Steiner and Gove report that legislators, even when forced to act (as in the case of Illinois in 1955), still can be expected to work on behalf of the following vested interests:

1. Individual preservation, the desire to be in a "safe" district.
2. Mutual preservation, the willingness of members to cooperate with each other in protecting incumbents against potential challengers.
3. Political party preservation, the desire of the leaders of each political party organization to maximize its strength in the legislature.
4. Bloc preservation, the desire of members of voting blocs — whether based on geographic, economic, or ideological cohesion — to retain existing personnel and strength. Such blocs are often bipartisan, and their membership is relatively small.[31]

The politics of reapportionment is not simply a rural versus urban conflict. Urban business groups sometimes oppose reapportionment and the resulting increase in urban legislative strength because of a preference for the more

[29] Commission on Intergovernmental Relations, *A Report to the President for Transmittal to the Congress* (U. S. Government Printing Office, Washington, 1955), p. 39.

[30] *Ibid.,* p. 40.

[31] Gilbert Y. Steiner and Samuel K. Gove, *The Legislature Redistricts Illinois* (University of Illinois, Institute of Government and Public Affairs, Urbana, 1956), p. 71.

conservative policies of rural legislators. As a Salt Lake City businessman, opposed to reapportionment in Utah, explained, "It's better the way it is. People from the country are less radical."[32] Even the leader of the normally urban-minded AFL-CIO in a southern border state maintained that he received more sympathetic consideration from "intelligent rural legislators" than from the "bums" elected at-large from the metropolitan counties.[33] Geographic and partisan factors may also work at cross purposes with simple urban interests. Highly urban San Francisco once helped reject a proposal which would have increased its strength in the California senate, fearing the additional consequence of multiplying the legislative strength of Los Angeles and Southern California. The urban push for reapportionment often loses steam when it is discovered that the principal benefits will go to the opposition political party, currently in a minority status. Such is the case in Tennessee where much of the gain would go to solidly Republican East Tennessee.

Economic and sectional cross-currents

A seemingly inevitable result of repeated frustration of reapportionment efforts, whether at the hands of a recalcitrant legislature or of a rigidly unchanging constitution, is creeping public apathy. Even under the most favorable conditions, representation and apportionment issues compete poorly with such hardy perennials as schools, roads, pensions, and taxes. Nevertheless, in some states — e.g., Oregon, Washington, Colorado, Minnesota, Illinois, and New York — the public interest in this issue has been aroused to a considerable degree.[34] In several states political frustration has led to court action, in an attempt to compel the fulfillment of a constitutional obligation. Early results of such efforts were not encouraging, with the judiciary refusing to dictate to its "sister" under the doctrine of separation of powers. The plaintiffs were given the hollow prescription that the only remedy is to elect a legislature that will perform its duty, and have called it a political question, not a judicial one.[35]

Public apathy

Courts and reapportionment

More recent court action concerning reapportionment has been more bold and imaginative. A federal district court in Minnesota in 1958 accepted jurisdiction in a case demanding at-large election of legislators because of failure to reapportion since 1913. With a veiled threat of subsequent action, the court

---

[32] Ernest H. Linford in Robert S. Allen, ed., *Our Sovereign State* (Vanguard Press, New York, 1949), p. 350.

[33] Wilder Crane, "Tennessee: Inertia and the Courts," Chapter 17 in Malcom E. Jewell, ed., *The Politics of Reapportionment* (Atherton Press, New York, 1962), p. 317.

[34] Gordon E. Baker, *State Constitutions: Reapportionment* (National Municipal League, New York, 1960), p. 39. *See also* his study, *The Politics of Reapportionment in Washington State*, "Eagleton Case Studies in Practical Politics" series (Holt, Rinehart and Winston, Inc., New York, 1961).

[35] *Colegrove v. Green,* 328 U. S. 549 (1946).

postponed a decision to afford the legislature another opportunity to "heed the constitutional mandate to redistrict."[36] This unusual assertion of judicial power was followed by a long legislative struggle and finally by passage in 1959 of the first redistricting bill in Minnesota in 46 years. Though the bill fell far short of the prescribed population basis, it offered substantial improvement for the urban areas, and especially for the five-county Twin City metropolitan area.

The Tennessee legislature met in 1961 under the threat of U. S. Supreme Court action, but failed to follow the Minnesota legislature's example. The almost immediate result was a 6-to-2 landmark decision reversing the no-jurisdiction precedent of *Colegrove* v. *Green*, but leaving to the lower federal courts the task of deciding whether actual discrimination exists in violation of the Fourteenth Amendment. The case of *Baker* v. *Carr* set forth three main propositions: (1) voters may sue for relief from any unconstitutional interference with their right to vote, (2) a complaint that discriminatory and arbitrary state apportionment violates the Fourteenth Amendment, whether well-founded or not, is a claim falling within the jurisdiction of the federal courts, and (3) merely because such a claim raises a political question is not sufficient cause for dismissing such a case.

Baker v. Carr and aftermath

Reaction to this decision was electric, varying from the charge by more than one Southern senator that it was a "death blow" to states' rights, to the prediction that it would so reform state government that the "look-to-Washington" trend will grind to a halt. Justice Frankfurter, the only remaining member of the Court who cast one of the four majority votes in the 1946 Colegrove decision, wrote a vigorous dissent in the 1962 case, calling it "a massive repudiation of the experience of our whole past in asserting destructively novel judicial power." While arguments and counter-arguments were still ringing, however, politically starved cities lost no time in moving through the judicially opened door. Rural-minded state legislatures shook off a half-century of lethargy and began frantic explorations in special sessions to discover whether limited concessions to the cities might stave off more drastic judicial action. The unprecedented activity during the six months following *Baker* v. *Carr* included the adoption of reapportionment laws by eight legislatures in special sessions, the filing of 48 law suits in 30 states, the handing down of 41 lower court decisions, and the initiation of ten constitutional amendments affecting reapportionment. A special session of the Tennessee legislature made modest changes in a reapportionment act, but a three-judge federal court held that it still failed to comply with even the State constitutional requirements. They reserved final judgment on all issues until the 1963 legislature had had the opportunity to try again.

---

[36] *Smith* v. *Holm*, 220 Minn. 486 (1945), quoted in *Magraw* v. *Donovan* (Minn. Fed. Dist., 3d Div.), Civil 2981 (July 10, 1958).

There can be little doubt that the Tennessee case will have far-reaching effects on legislative apportionment at all levels of government. It is still too early to sound the death knell for rural power in state legislatures, however. The Supreme Court did not decide the major question of the kinds of apportionment which will be approved as constitutional. Will geographic representation, as distinguished from population representation, be approved by the Court when duly specified in state constitutions? Will the "federal analogy" argument, patterning state senates after the U. S. senate, be accepted as valid? Will rural legislatures be able to "get around" court decisions by "token" reapportionments, at least for many years to come? These and many other devices for retaining rural control will be available for use, but the long-term outlook is not encouraging for rural interests.

Questions remaining undecided

Before leaving the subject of apportionment, it should be noted that population changes reported in the 1960 census have taken an ironic twist as they have affected the legislative representation of the core cities in some of the larger metropolitan areas. Chicago, for example, which lost population between 1950 and 1960 for the first time in its history, is now better represented in the state senate than is suburban Cook County. The Chicago metropolitan area as a whole, however, still is under-represented. Baltimore City showed a population decrease in the 1960 census, and its legislative representation is not nearly so diluted as that of Baltimore County, whose population almost doubled in the last decade. Professor Robert S. Friedman called attention to this development even before the 1960 census, citing the rise of suburbia as a new bone of contention in the struggle for fair apportionment.[37]

Suburbia and apportionment

DIRECT LEGISLATION: THE
INITIATIVE AND REFERENDUM

The legislative process is not necessarily a *representative* process, as we are constantly reminded by ballots greatly enlarged by the "initiative and referendum" in many states. Popular dissatisfaction with legislatures during the muckraking days brought about a movement around the turn of the century for direct methods in the lawmaking process, particularly in the West. With the reformist zeal of the Progressive era carrying the day, almost half of the

---

[37] "Reapportionment Myth," *National Civic Review*, XLIX (April, 1960), pp. 184-188.

states adopted constitutional provisions for supplementing or restricting the legislative program through the widely heralded initiative and referendum, generally coupling this weapon with a direct recall of important executive officers. As the Progressive movement slowed up, so did adoptions of "I and R," and only Alaska has adopted them since 1917.

This system of legislation by direct democracy calls for a vote by the electorate to pass on a proposed law or constitutional matter if a petition is properly presented with a sufficient number of voters' signatures, say 8 or 10 per cent of the number participating in the last preceding election. An initiative petition asks for a vote on a proposed law in the face of legislative neglect or opposition. The initiative in some states is *indirect,* with the proposal going first to the legislature and not to the electorate unless the bill is not passed by the legislature. In the *direct* initiative the proposal goes straight to the voters, bypassing the legislature completely. A referendum petition asks for a popular vote to give the people a chance to reject or accept some legislative enactment. This is sometimes called the *protest* referendum, in contrast to the *compulsory* referendum on constitutional amendments or other issues which the legislature is required to submit to the electorate, and the *voluntary* referendum which may or may not be called for by the legislature in its discretion. Examples of the latter would be a "right to work" bill or a large bond issue considered "too hot" for the legislators to handle by themselves. In such circumstances there is a fine line of distinction between a genuine desire to let the people rule and the urge to "pass the buck."

The critics of direct legislation are numerous, arguing that to bypass the legislature actually weakens the legislature and confuses legislative responsibility, that such a device assumes more expertness and interest on the part of the voters than realism would support, that an already long ballot is made much longer, and that in practice "I and R" have given undue advantage not to "the people" but to well-organized and well-heeled pressure groups. Contemporary proponents, while recognizing that the high hopes of its originators have not been fulfilled, defend these direct methods as a kind of shotgun over the door available to the people in our pluralistic political structure when all else seems to fail. It seems clear, in any case, that those states using direct legislation are not inclined to abandon it. As an impact on the legislative process, it has hardly equalled the modern governorship, which is our next subject for consideration.

Baker, G. E., *Rural Versus Urban Political Power* (Doubleday & Company, Inc., Garden City, N. Y., 1955).

————, *State Constitutions: Reapportionment* (National Municipal League, New York, 1960).

Beth, Loren P., and William C. Havard, "Committee Stacking and Political Power in Florida," *Journal of Politics,* XXIII (February, 1961), pp. 57-83.

Bosworth, K. A., "Lawmaking in State Government," in The American Assembly, *The Forty-eight States: Their Tasks as Policy Makers and Administrators* (Graduate School of Business, Columbia University, New York, 1955).

Buck, A. E., *Modernizing Our State Legislatures* (American Academy of Political and Social Science, Philadelphia, 1936).

Breckenridge, A. C., *One House for Two* (Public Affairs Press, Washington, D. C., 1958).

Dauer, M. J. and R. G. Kelsay, "Unrepresentative States," *National Municipal Review,* XLIV (December, 1955), pp. 571-575.

Derge, David R., "Metropolitan and Outstate Alignments in Illinois and Missouri Legislative Delegations," *American Political Science Review,* LII (December, 1958), pp. 1051-1065.

Jewell, Malcolm E., ed., *The Politics of Reapportionment* (Atherton Press, New York, 1962).

"Legislation," continuing article in *The Book of the States* (Council of State Governments, Chicago).

"Legislative Reapportionment," *Law and Contemporary Problems,* XVII (Spring, 1952).

Neuberger, R. L., *Adventures in Politics; We Go to the Legislature* (Oxford University Press, New York, 1954).

Reed, T. H., ed., *Legislatures and Legislative Problems* (University of Chicago Press, Chicago, 1933).

Smith, T. V., *The Legislative Way of Life* (University of Chicago Press, Chicago, 1940).

Walker, Harvey, *The Legislative Process* (Ronald Press, New York, 1948).

(*See also* titles listed for the preceding chapter.)

* *11* *

THE GOVERNORSHIP

THE GOVERNORSHIP might be described in many respects as a small-scale edition of the American presidency. It has standardized features with a margin of fluctuation according to the state, the time, and the man on the job. It is a venerable American office, stemming from colonial times and characterizing the state establishments from the beginning. Restrictions on the office by the makers of the first state constitutions on the basis of bitter experience with colonial governors did not prevent social prestige and distinction from becoming attachments of the chief executive. This was true in the early national period when the governorship was held by men like Thomas Jefferson and Edmund Randolph in Virginia, John Hancock in Massachusetts, and George Clinton in New York. It became no less true in later eras when the office was to constitute a marker on the road to the White House for such leaders as Grover Cleveland, Woodrow Wilson, Theodore Roosevelt, and Franklin D. Roosevelt.[1]

General importance and prestige

There is more than chance in the fact that between the presidencies of Generals Grant and Eisenhower, every winner of two elections to the White House was a man who had served as governor, one of these governors winning

---

[1] *See* Figure 1-2 in Chapter 1.

212

four national elections. The role of the governor has increased contemporaneously with that of the president and largely for the same reasons of governmental expansion. If the early governor had prestige, the present governor has acquired substantial power, sometimes without real prestige and sometimes exercising that power in accord with the wishes of a boss or machine behind the scenes. The expansion and reorganization of the executive system in many states since 1910 has put more power and more responsibility in the gubernatorial office, as will be explained in the next chapter.

Governors have been strong and weak, competent and incompetent, leaders and followers, honest and dishonest. Many have acquired permanent nicknames, such as "Soapy" Williams, "Kissin' Jim" Folsom, "Ma" Ferguson, and Huey "Kingfish" Long. There have been clowns, dictators, demagogues, and grafters, even with the federal prison opening and closing the door for more than one in the current century. But who would contend that the majority have been any less honest and capable than the executives of American business, labor, or other institutions? Many have been strong leaders, as indicated by those who became president and by others like Hiram Johnson of California, Frank Lowden of Illinois, Harry Byrd of Virginia, Robert La Follette of Wisconsin, Gifford Pinchot of Pennsylvania, Alfred E. Smith of New York, and more recently Thomas E. Dewey of the Empire State. Most of these exemplified mastery of both the political and the administrative spheres of state government, although in distinctly different ways. *Various types of individuals*

On the whole the accent is increasingly on youth among the state governors, with a median beginning age of 47 during the decade of the 1950's compared to a median of 51 during the 1940's. According to a study of 157 governors during the 1950's, 24 became governors in their thirties in contrast to only 10 elected at this age in the 1940's.[2] The largest number of governors (68) were in their forties, with 41 in their fifties, 17 in their sixties, and 4 in their seventies. The formal education of governors has continued its steady rise with over 90 per cent having attended college. The legal profession is the dominant vocation of men who became governors, accounting for 84 of the 157, with the teaching profession perhaps suprisingly in second place. *Accent on youth*

The turnover in the office of governor is rather extensive in most of the fifty states. The reasons for this are historical, constitutional, and political. A number of the states have a two-year term for the office, although a majority have a four-year term. About half of the states providing for a four-year term, however, forbid a regular incumbent to succeed himself. Factors other than technical often contribute to compulsory retire- *Turnover; exgovernors*

---

[2] Samuel R. Solomon, "State Governors, 1950-1960," *National Civic Review*, XLIX (September, 1960), pp. 410-416.

ment after one term, even for excellent performance. Many have found the office a blind alley with respect to a political future. Only a few from a few states can entertain hopes of candidacy for president. A governor may go to the United States Senate, but, if so, he is likely to hold the seat for a long time, leaving little oportunity for another governor to move in this direction. A few former state executives become state or federal judges, and a few are appointed to important administrative posts in state or nation. Some become lobbyists. Many return permanently to private life and enterprise, often in law or business.

The annual salary of the governor ranges upward from $10,000 in Arkansas and North Dakota to $50,000 in New York, not including the governor's mansion and certain expense funds. Besides the requirements of *Aspects of the* citizenship and residence, a minimum age of 30 is usually stipulated, but *governorship* for political reasons one almost necessarily needs the experience of more than 30 years to win a governorship. Candidates for the office are nominated by party primaries in most of the states, although a few states, including New York, still cling to use of the party convention for this purpose. The Democratic nominee in Georgia is selected through a party primary but with the results determined on a county units basis somewhat as state votes are determined in the Electoral College. This Georgia plan minimizes the proportionate weight of cities in the primary decision. The final choice of the governor is by direct popular vote in all states except Mississippi, which uses a county unit system. The Mississippi scheme for the general election has little significance, however, since the real choice in that state is made in the Democratic primary.

The governor's role embraces a broad range of powers and functions, although it is generally hedged with more restrictions and division of authority than the role of the president. The governor is the ceremonial and tra-*General role* ditional head of the state, and he speaks officially for the state in important relations with other states or the national government. He is commander-in-chief of state troops when they are not in national service, and there have been constitutional provisions for him to command the "navy" of the commonwealth. Under his responsibility for law enforcement, he may order out state troops to preserve order; and, under the federal Constitution, he may request and receive military aid through order of the president to check "domestic violence." He has powers of appointment and removal of officers or employees as prescribed and limited by constitutional and statutory provisions of his state. In a majority of the states the governor has broad or restricted powers of pardon, parole, and commutation of sentence except in impeachment cases. In a few states he is an important member of a board having jurisdiction in such matters. The governor has a measure of supervisory power over central administration, but this power varies widely from state to state, partly according to whether the executive branch is integrated under him or shared with a number of other elected officers. This phase of state administration will be considered in the next chapter. The governor has a miscellany of powers to issue proclamations, orders, rules, and regulations, to call special elections as necessary and required, and to serve as an ex officio member of sundry boards or commissions. He is in a position to exercise important powers and employ strategic methods in formulating and initiating policy, including the making and blocking of legislative policy.

THE GOVERNOR AS LAWMAKER

The governor has distinct constitutional powers enabling him to influence the legislature, provided he has the personal capacity and political arrangement or apparatus to utilize them. The powers to call special legislative sessions, to recommend measures by speech or message, and to veto bills belong technically to the weak governor as well as to the strong one, but ability and skill are necessary to make effective use of these techniques. The convening of special sessions is normally more important for the governor than for the president, since state legislators spend much less time than congressmen in regular session. The governor in about a third of the states has the additional power of exclusively specifying legislative matters for consideration by a special session.[3]   *Constitutional powers*

Of the 49 states with provision for the governor's veto, about one-fourth allow the "pocket" veto at the end of sessions and more than three-fourths have the item veto, which came into practice after the Southern Confederacy adopted it in the Civil War. Under the "pocket" veto a bill fails to become law unless signed by the governor before a specified time after adjournment of the legislature. The item veto enables the governor to prune individual parts or figures from an appropriation bill without rejecting the whole measure. Most states providing for the item veto restrict it to appropriation bills. The veto power is of particular importance to the governor as unfinished business piles up for a legislature at the end of a session with little or no time for repassage of bills rejected by the chief executive. Sometimes popular but questionable legislation is passed and sent to the governor in order to saddle him with the "rap" for disapproval. Studies and observations[4] indicate that less than five per cent of

---

[3] The subjects are stated in the call, which, however, does not bar the legislature from undertaking impeachment proceedings under the constitution.

[4] See F. W. Prescott, "The Executive Veto in Southern States," *The Journal of Politics,* X (November, 1948), pp. 659-675, and F. W. Prescott, "The Executive Veto in American States," *Western Political Quarterly,* III (March, 1950), pp. 98-112.

bills passed by the legislatures are vetoed by governors and that less than ten per cent of vetoed bills are subsequently enacted.

The affirmative vote necessary to override the veto varies. Some states apply the congressional pattern of requiring a two-thirds majority of each house. Requirements in other states range through a clear majority, a three-fifths majority, and two-thirds majority of the membership of each house, a simple majority and a three-fifths majority of those present.

The governor has extra-constitutional ways of influencing lawmakers. He may strike bargains crudely or constructively by exercising or not exercising his technical legislative as well as his patronage powers. He may find

Extra-consti-tutional ways other influential methods for throwing his executive weight around for legislative purposes. He may come into office with a well-formulated and much-publicized program and steadfastly insist upon translating it into law and fact. He may make effective appeal to public opinion through speech and press for support of his program, particularly if the offerings meet recognized needs. He may devote the major portion of his work to the problems of legislation, which Theodore Roosevelt said he found to be necessary as governor of New York. He may step forward as the actual as well as the nominal boss of his party in his state. Woodrow Wilson gave advance announcement of such leadership in his election campaign for governor of New Jersey and followed up this notice by attending the legislative caucus of his party contrary to expectation and without invitation. In spite of the division of authority with other elected officers, the governor may unify his party or faction more than the president, who must build his program upon the diverse interests of his continent-wide backing. Going beyond his party or political faction, he may shrewdly divide the power and balance the interests of pressure groups in order to attain his objectives. He may also resort to the strategy of composing or reconciling the demands of different geographic regions of the state, for his constituents are not limited to one political subdivision as are those of a member of the legislature. Governors like Huey Long in Louisiana have been known to discriminate in their legislative influence against sections or cities which furnished heavy opposition to their election. If not a political weakling or a subservient tool of invisible spoilsmen, the chief executive may speak to and for the people in advancing state policy. He may utilize his station to transmit expert knowledge on important subjects of public concern. Despite the circumscription of his power and the onerousness of his office, the governor is in a better position than any other in his state to speak as the chief lawmaker for all — as the tribune of the people.

The influence of a strong and purposeful governor over the legislative process may be seen in a case study of New York Governor Nelson Rockefeller's experience with a special session of the state legislature.[5] The two main proposals of a controversial nature on the agenda for the special session were a multi-million dollar program of state aid to help schools and colleges to build fall-out shelters and a reapportionment bill for the state's Congressional districts. New York's constitution permits the governor to call the legislature into special session only "on extraordinary occasions," and Warren Weaver, Jr., suggested in the *New York Times* that: *The governor and the special session*

> There were few compelling reasons offered this week, however, as to why the shelter program and reapportionment could not have been postponed for seven weeks, to await the convening of the regular session. There remained only the purely practical reason that it was a lot easier to pass these controversial bills intact by the convenient and somewhat ruthless mechanism of the special session.[6]

Why should it be easier to pass the governor's proposals in a special session? More than anything else the factors of time and publicity work against the deliberative role of the legislature during special sessions. The text of the shelter bill, 38 legal-sized pages long, was not made public until mid-morning on Wednesday before the opening session on Thursday. Although copies were sent special delivery to the senators and assemblymen, many who left home early for the trip to Albany saw the bill for the first time Thursday morning before the session convened at noon. A general outline of the shelter plan had been made public three weeks earlier, but withholding the full details of the legislation made it less likely that substitutes or amendments might be drafted. While there is no constitutional obstacle in New York to prolonging a special session for a week or more to consider amendments to the governor's proposal, most legislators are anxious to return to their homes and are reluctant to go beyond a day or two for the special session. Thus, the governor called the signals with the shelter bill and the pressure of time tended to produce a "take it or leave it" situation. This was most effective in its   *Pressures of time and publicity*

---

[5] See the excellent summary by Warren Weaver, Jr., "The Governor's Show," *New York Times*, November 13, 1961, which the authors have relied upon for these paragraphs.

[6] *Ibid.*

218 impact on the Republican legislators, of course, for any action resulting in pushing the session over into the next week would appear to be disloyalty to Governor Rockefeller.

The governor's hand was also strengthened by the publicity circumstances peculiar to a special session. The public spotlight was clearly aimed at the legislature, and, even more significant, such scrutiny was easily focused on the legislator's vote on a single issue. The normal committee delays and procedural red tape so common to a regular session were not available to dissipate the public awareness of what was going on. Perhaps most important of all, Governor Rockefeller was able to call the session at such a time, and define the issue in such a manner, that some luke-warm legislators felt that a vote against his shelter bill might well be considered by the public as a vote against protecting school children's lives. The bill passed intact after brief debate.

The governor enjoyed similar success with the reapportionment proposal, a much more partisan measure. The 26-page bill and accompanying maps of the new districts were made public just as the special session convened on Thursday. The bill became a law on Friday, slightly more than 24 hours later. Amendments were even less likely than in the case of the shelter bill because the task of drawing congressional district boundary lines is a highly technical process, even under more leisurely conditions, and the Democrats had little chance to alter a measure adopted on straight party lines.

If the shelter and reapportionment bills had been submitted to a regular session of the legislature, there can be little doubt that both would have received extensive study and some revisions at the hands of both Republicans and Democratic legislators. In the circumstances of a special session, however, the legislative initiative and key controls were shifted into the hands of a resourceful governor.

PROBLEMS OF VACANCY AND SUCCESSION

How vacancies occur; how filled

Vacancies occur in different ways prior to the expiration of a governor's term, and sometimes the succession is associated with bitter politics and controversy. The governor may die or may become incapacitated for duty, although the latter status may be difficult to determine. He may resign or be removed through impeachment proceedings. In certain states he may be recalled by a popular vote in a special election. If the state has the office of lieutenant governor, that officer succeeds to the vacant governorship except in cases of popular recall. In the ten states without a lieutenant governor the presiding officer of the senate or the speaker of the house normally becomes the chief executive for the unexpired term. As in the national government, there may be a further line of succession for possible emergency. The successor may serve as "governor" or as "acting governor" according to constitutional language and interpretation. The lieutenant governor has a regular administrative post, with commensurate salary, in Indiana, but in most states he is primarily a contingent executive except for instances of membership on boards or councils. Presiding over the state senate, with or without committee appointment power, is his usual function. In many states he serves as acting governor during the governor's absence from the state. There have been occasions when the acting official upset the executive apple cart under such circumstances, by the dramatic pardoning of long-term prisoners or other action contrary to the wish or policy of the absent governor. Governors at times have hesitated to leave the state even for a short period, not wishing to turn the reins of government over to the personal or political opposition. The Alabama constitution protects the governor during his temporary visits beyond the border by providing that there be a 20-day absence before the lieutenant governor exercises the higher authority.

Absence of any procedure for determining inability of the governor in Louisiana in 1959 proved to be a source of embarrassment and, doubtless, of entertainment, to the people of the state and the nation. Governor Earl Long was taken, against his will he alleged, to a mental clinic in Galveston, Texas, and when released he was committed to a state mental hospital in Louisiana on court order obtained by his wife. Long was released in subsequent court action and proceeded to dismiss the state police chief, the head of the state department of hospitals, and the director of the hospital to which he had been committed. Although the attorney general gave an opinion during the month of these events that the executive power resided with the lieutenant governor, he refused to assume such powers.[7]

The governor resigns sometimes for straightforward reasons and sometimes for purposes of political strategy. An example of the former was the resignation of Governor Earl Warren of California to accept appointment by President Eisenhower as Chief Justice of the Supreme Court. An **Resignation** example of finesse would be the resignation by a governor under an agreement or cordial understanding in advance that his successor will reciprocate by appointing him to a vacant seat in the United States Senate. This is not an unusual occurrence. Early in his political career, A. B. ("Happy") Chandler switched from the governorship of Kentucky to a senatorship in this manner.

---

[7] See Bennett M. Rich, *State Constitutions: The Governor* (National Municipal League, New York, 1960), p. 11.

There have been resignations under embarrassing circumstances, as when an Indiana governor a few decades ago surrendered office to serve time in the federal pentitentiary at Atlanta for conviction of fraud.

Provisions for impeachment proceedings against the governor and other officials are found in the constitution of every state except Oregon, which relies entirely upon the recall process for removal. In most states the impeach-

Impeachment ment pattern approximates the formula provided for dealing with officers of the national government. The lower house of the legislature adopts charges of impeachment, generally on the basis of a committee investigation and report. This adopted statement then goes to the senate, which conducts a trial, hearing testimony and argument from both sides, with the lower house providing the prosecution and the defendant utilizing counsel in his own behalf. In the end the senate decides the question, usually under the requirement of a two-thirds vote for a verdict of guilty. The punishment consists of removal from office and disqualification as to subsequent holding of state office. Any conviction for prison sentence must be through a separate trial before a tribunal of the judicial branch. There have been only a few removals of governors by impeachment trials in the twentieth century, including one in New York, one in Texas, and two in Oklahoma. A few impeachments have failed to result in removal, including three in Oklahoma and one in Louisiana. In these cases the senate votes for conviction were below the required total. The successful action in Texas against Governor James Ferguson in 1917 had a bizarre sequel in the subsequent election of the ousted official's wife, Miriam ("Ma") Ferguson, to the office in a campaign which heard the slogan, "Two governors for the price of one." Mrs. Ferguson was not a career woman and was considered a proxy.[8]

Twelve states have provisions for the recall of the governor and other state officials by popular vote. The recall is a method of holding an election for the removal of an officer in response to a petition by a designated per-

The recall centage of voters. Oregon, first to adopt state recall (1908), requires the signature of 25 per cent of the voters for an election; Kansas requires only 10 per cent; the others approach Oregon rather than Kansas. The petition contains a statement of reasons or claims justifying the recall. The election is held within a specified time, and the results of the balloting determine whether the officer relinquishes or retains office. In several states simultaneous voting provides for a contingent successor, but three states require a subsequent election in case of removal. Only one governor has been removed through a

---

[8] More than 3,000 pardons were granted in her two-year term, often with her husband as legal spokesman for the applicant. Pardon columns appeared in the press. The Fergusons had an agrarian reformist appeal.

stirred up opposition over agrarian reforms. Soon after his removal in 1921, he was elected to the United States Senate. The recall has been less effective at the state level than impeachment proceedings. It has found more use in local government. It is not a judicial process and imposes no punishment of disqualification.

The full annals of the American state governorship would cover exciting controversies over titles to office affecting a tiny few of the many hundreds of individuals who have held that public position. The Dorr rebellion in Rhode Island over outmoded suffrage restrictions brought about a clash *Disputed* in 1842 between two governors or would-be governors prior to collapse *titles to* *the office* of the Dorr movement. Duplicating claims to the governorship in Louisiana and in South Carolina were ended in 1877 when President Hayes withdrew federal troops from those states, letting political nature take its course. When a North Dakota governor became involved in a federal trial in the 1930's, the lieutenant governor undertook to administer the office, and the state supreme court ousted the governor. Following the ensuing election, the residential qualifications of the winner were challenged shortly after he assumed office. A court decision again disqualified a governor, and again a lieutenant governor took charge, giving the state four governors in less than a year.[9] Georgia presented a more explosive case in 1947, following the death of Eugene Talmadge, the governor-elect, on the eve of his inauguration. M. E. Thompson, the newly elected lieutenant governor, undertook to assume the governorship, and so did Talmadge's son, Herman, who had been counted in as second in the race for the governorship as the result of precautionary write-in votes. Backed by state troops and legislative action, Herman Talmadge exercised control of the office and moved into the governor's mansion. His men made short shrift of outgoing Governor Ellis Arnall's gesture toward retaining power pending the constitutional determination and qualification of a successor, but Thompson was able to use a capitol office as president of the senate. The state government, except for routine matters, marked time for two months before the Georgia supreme court resolved the Talmadge-Thompson duel in favor of Thompson. Young Talmadge then moved out but won the next election for a return engagement.

---

[9] R. L. Miller, "The Gubernatorial Controversy in North Dakota," *American Political Science Review*, XXIX (June, 1935), pp. 418-432.

The multiple roles of the governor have increased in the twentieth century both through determinism and design. More people with more occupational interests inevitably called for more government at all levels, including the state level. The trend toward increased government emphasized centralization or partial centralization of many functions, as in the administration of education, highways, and law enforcement, with the governor sharing in much of this administration through appointive or supervisory powers.

Reasons for an increasing role

Theodore Roosevelt as president emphasized the importance of the role of the governors individually and as a group in intergovernmental cooperation. The cooperation may be interstate or between the states and the national government in tackling common problems such as conservation. That general policy of cooperation has continued in many ways, as exemplified by the annual sessions of the Governors' Conference and by regional conferences.

State legislatures, like Congress, have discovered that all the details of modern government cannot be put down specifically in statutes and that a degree of operational choice or discretion must be left to the executive, particularly the chief executive. There developed the parallel necessity for legislative reliance upon the governor and his aides to formulate or recommend policy in the complex technical matters of modern government. Part-time legislators cannot master the intricate problems confronting the states today, and an able governor may provide answers to the problems, becoming the chief lobbyist among lobbyists.

The governor has gained power in varying amounts through governmental reorganization in more than half of the states in the last 50 years. Three states, New York, Virginia, and Massachusetts, achieved reoragnization by constitutional amendment. Many others, notably Illinois, made sweeping reorganizational changes through legislative enactment, with stimulative leadership by governors supported by effective research on the subject. Under the influence of Governor Lowden, Illinois in 1917 scrapped more than 100 agencies and offices and allocated the functions among nine departments, although not touching the constitutionally elective offices. This definitely increased the power of the governor both through appointment and through supervision. Virginia and New York went further toward a short ballot for state officers and toward establishing the governor at the top of an administrative hierarchy. The governorship has found new strength in the spread to three-fourths of the states of executive budget-making and fiscal control, particularly where reorganization has become most extensive and effective. The

Gains through reorganization

flexible role of the governor in this field is further considered in the subsequent chapter on finance.

The reorganizational movement is continuous, and the governors are in a position to sponsor and utilize studies by professional experts on the subject. The movement has not led, in the main, to major alteration of state governmental structure in the post World War II period. But studies continue to be authorized and afford grist for the mill of political pressures for strengthening administrative structures. It is not an extravagant observation to say that reorganization and modernization of state administration have transformed and continue to transform the governor "from figurehead to leader." [10]

SUPPLEMENTARY READINGS

Abernathy, Byron R., *Some Persisting Questions Concerning the Constitutional State Executive* (University of Kansas Government Research Series No. 23, Government Research Center, Lawrence, Kansas, 1960).

Brooks, Glen E., *When Governors Convene* (The Johns Hopkins Press, Baltimore, 1961).

Cross, W. L., *Connecticut Yankee: An Autobiography* (Yale University Press, New Haven, 1943).

Governors' Conference, *Proceedings* (Chicago, annually).

Hutchinson, W. T., *Lowden of Illinois* (University of Chicago Press, Chicago, 1957).

Lipson, Leslie, *The American State Governor: From Figurehead to Leader* (University of Chicago Press, Chicago, 1939).

Macdonald, A. F., *American State Government and Administration* (6th ed.; Thomas Y. Crowell Company, 1960), Chapter 7.

Perkins, J. A., "American Governors, 1930 to 1940," *National Municipal Review,* XXIX (March, 1940), pp. 178-184.

Ransone, Coleman B., *The Office of Governor in the United States* (University of Alabama Press, University, Ala., 1956).

Schlesinger, J. A., *How They Became Governor* (Bureau of Social and Political Research, Michigan State University, East Lansing, 1957).

Smith, Alfred E., *Up to Now: An Autobiography* (Viking Press, New York, 1929).

Spicer, G. W., "Gubernatorial Leadership in Virginia," *Public Administration Review,* I (November, 1941), pp. 441-457.

(*See also* rules listed for the next chapter.)

---

[10] On this point *see* Leslie Lipson, *The American State Governor: From Figurehead to Leader* (University of Chicago Press, Chicago, 1939).

* *12* *

THE GOVERNOR AND

ADMINISTRATION

THE GROWING strength of the governor is more manifest in the field of administration than in any other area of his activities. The most significant twentieth-
century changes in the role of the governor have taken place in his re-

*The
governor's
new role*

lationship to law enforcement and program execution rather than in his
position as chief legislator, chief ceremonial representative of the state, or
political chief of the state's majority party or faction. As our state governments have become financial giants, governors are more and more finding it impossible to shut off from their concern the administering of the state's affairs as "mere
work for the clerks." The political-minded candidate of today who campaigns
successfully for the office of governor finds himself — often unhappily — suddenly transformed into a chief administrator responsible for day-to-day managerial decisions.

THE GOVERNOR AS GENERAL MANAGER

Prior to 1900 most governors had little to do with administration. This
resulted in part from the early preference of the people for the legislative branch,

in part from the highly decentralized character of state administration; *Early em-* and in part from the fact that administration was not on a very large *phasis on* scale. Governors themselves were chiefly interested in the legislature, *non-admin-* politics, and party leadership, and the usual grant of "executive power" *istrative* found in the early state constitutions offered them little opportunity to *functions* behave any other way. Constitutionally, the governor was made "head of state" with miscellaneous powers on ceremonial occasions as well as the pardoning power and control of the militia, but he was certainly no "head of administration." Administration was left vaguely responsible to the state legislature, and later directly to the people, but not to the chief executive. This scanty administrative power and the lack of coordination of independent offices and agencies were observed by De Tocqueville in his American travels in 1831.

About the turn of the century, as popular demands upon government increased, it began to be recognized that there was a serious discrepancy between the constitutional or legal picture of the governor and the picture of the governor as seen by the people generally. The popular notion *Constitu-* of the governor was that he had all the power necessary to see that the *tional* laws of the state were enforced, but prior to the turn of the century, *limitations* Woodrow Wilson described the administrative weakness of the governor:

> The governor . . . is not the 'Executive'; he is but a single piece of the executive. There are other pieces coordinated with him over which he has no direct official control, and which are of less dignity than he only because they have no power to control legislation, as he may do by the exercise of his veto, and because his position is more representative, perhaps, of the state government as a whole, of the people of the state as a unit. Indeed it may be doubted whether the governor and other principal officers of a state government can even when taken together be correctly described as 'the executive,' since the actual execution of the great majority of the laws does not rest with them but with the local officers chosen by the towns and counties and bound to the central authorities of the state by no real bonds of responsibility whatever.[1]

Wilson's description of the constitutional position of the governor is still valid in many states, although statutory changes and other factors have tended to make the formal constitutional picture unrealistic today. Even so, the legal position of the governor in most states is much weaker than that of the president in the government of the United States, in that the governor shares responsibility for the executive branch of the government with several other elected executives.

---

[1] Woodrow Wilson, *The State: Elements of Historical and Practical Politics* (Rev. ed.; D. C. Heath and Company, Boston, 1909), p. 330.

226   The extraordinary expansion of governmental activities and the growing
importance of the administrative side of state government have made changes
in the administrative role of the governor inevitable. The powerful

The emerg-
ing general
manager

forces of scientific management in industry and crusading reform in
municipal government spilled over into both state and national levels
of government with the result that on the state level, during the past
half-century, the governor has begun to secure recognition as the "general manager" of state government. The state reorganization movement, based on the
necessity for unity of command, effective coordination, internal responsibility,
and administrative leadership, has undertaken to provide for the entire executive
establishment in state government a general manager in the person of the
governor. The governor's increasing managerial responsibilities have now been
recognized in most states, and the states seem slowly but surely to be granting
additional administrative power to the governor for performing his new job.

THE GOVERNOR'S
ADMINISTRATIVE POWERS

Although most state constitutions vest the governor with "the supreme
executive power," little if any definite authority is conferred on the governor by
this provision because state courts have applied the rule of strict con-

Strict
construction
on powers

struction to the powers of the governor much more than have the federal
courts in the case of the president. Only specific grants of authority are
recognized. Differing court interpretations of seemingly equal grants of
authority in the various states make it hazardous to generalize on the basis of
constitutional and statutory provisions alone. Other variables of even greater
importance, such as the effect of political strength, personal appeal, or custom
upon the administrative power of a governor, make it obvious that no single
pattern can be said to describe the governor's administrative power. Nevertheless,
three major administrative powers are possessed by every governor in varying
degrees: (1) the power of appointment and removal, (2) the power of fiscal
management, and (3) the supervisory power. These are the principal means by
which the governor makes his impression on the administration of state affairs.

The power of appointment is one of the most important powers possessed
by the governor, not only in his control of the administrative branch but in his
relations with the legislature as well. No governor can have complete

The power
of appoint-
ment

confidence in subordinates whom he has not selected, nor can he properly be held responsible for the actions of such persons. Personal appoint-

ment of subordinates does not guarantee their responsibility, but it makes the probability considerably greater. Exercise of the appointing power is not so simple as it might seem. Appointments are frequently made under a great deal of pressure of many kinds. There is the practical requirement that the winning candidate for governor must choose most of the people who will help him operate the state government even before he takes the oath of office. He realizes that, although no one of his appointees can make a success of his administration, any one of the many persons appointed can seriously damage his administration by incompetence or dishonesty. There is seldom a shortage of applicants for the various positions, but salary limitations and insecurity of tenure make it exceedingly difficult to find capable men for the jobs. Few department heads can expect to serve longer than the limited tenure of the governor.

All states are generally agreed in the strict construction of their constitutions that the appointing power is not inherently and exclusively an executive function. The history of court interpretation of the governor's appointing power reveals the predominant opinion that such power must be expressly granted in the state constitution or by statute. In the first *Appointing power not inherent* state governments the power to appoint administrative officers was largely in the hands of the legislature, and early in the nineteenth century choice of such officer was transferred to the electorate. The governor was looked upon as a political figure, in whom the power of appointment did not rest any more properly than in other divisions of the government. Since state constitutions generally have made little mention of the governor's power of appointment, recent increases in this power result from legislative action creating the many new offices and boards. Furthermore, the state reorganization movement has increased the governor's appointing power over department heads in many states.

In spite of the increase in the governor's power of appointment in recent years, there are many restrictions upon this authority. In most states a large number of important appointments are made subject to confirmation by the senate. This restriction is defended as requiring the governor to make *Restrictions on appointing power: senate confirmation* better appointments since they will have to run the gauntlet of legislative scrutiny. In practice, however, no such superiority has been demonstrated under this system, and there is considerable evidence that the confirmation requirement serves to destroy the personal responsibility of the governor for appointments.

Another restriction on the appointing power of the governor is the practice of writing into the law special qualifications for an appointee to a certain office. For example, the law may specify that each member of a board must represent a different geographic area of the state or that an officer *Legal qualifications* must possess certain professional qualifications, such as five years of experience in banking for one to be appointed bank commissioner. Some years ago the Arkansas legislature passed a bill stipulating that the governor's appointees to the five-member hospital board had to be a doctor, a lawyer, a farmer, and two businessmen, but Governor Ben Laney vetoed it, on the ground that it would be unwise to limit membership on the board to a few professions and occupations.

Another common restriction on the governor's appointing power, particularly in states which have no merit system to prevent the ravages of the spoils system, is the "buffer board" created with long and overlapping terms of office in the hope of taking an agency or institution "out of politics." The governor's influence is usually limited to the appointment of one board member each year, although a strong governor finds many devices for arranging for more than one vacancy. Buffer boards serve, where effective, to prevent clear-cut change in state policy. The influence of the outgoing governor lingers after his departure, and the only consolation for the new incumbent is recognition of the fact that his influence will also grow and ultimately confront his successor with the same deterrent to change.

Buffer boards

Civil service laws constitute a limitation on the governor's appointing power only to the extent that the merit system may effectively diminish pressure and influence in those areas where the governor would otherwise make or influence appointments. Here again, the strong governor is able to find and use many loopholes, and it should be remembered that the civil service laws do not apply to the higher ranking bureau and department heads and to other exempted categories of positions.

Civil service

One other restriction on the governor's appointing power, a serious limitation in some states, is the popular election of many other administrative officers besides the governor. At its worst this practice saddles the governor with a cabinet of department heads not of his own choosing who manifest varying degrees of hostility and aloofness from the governor's administrative leadership. Such elective administrators may even conceive of themselves as rivals to the governor and pursue alternative policies in order to impress the public with their fitness to succeed or perhaps to replace him. The long ballot, which results from the election of administrative officials, dates back to the second quarter of the nineteenth century, when the Jacksonians considered it self-evident that government could be derived from the consent of the governed only if the people elected their administrative officials as well as their legislature. It was not until many years later that the problem of fixing the responsibility for the conduct of big government began to make evident the necessity for the short ballot. Some states have been able to limit this restriction on the governor's appointing power by retaining only one or two elective officials in addition to the governor. In New Jersey the only other elective officer is the auditor, and he is elected by the legislature. The two newest states, Alaska

Elective administrators

and Hawaii, have limited the number of popularly elected administrative
officials to two and three, respectively. Other states have simply bypassed the
elective officers by giving important responsibility to the newer appointive officers
while at the same time whittling away the powers of the independent officers,
leaving many of them mere figureheads. This is often the practical substitute
for a constitutional amendment altering or abolishing an office which retains
the sentimental support of the people.

The following states are the most serious offenders in extending the list
of elected officers beyond the governor and lieutenant governor:[2]

State	Number of Elected Department Heads	State	Number of Elected Department Heads
Mississippi	13	North Carolina	9
Oklahoma	13	Alabama	8
Louisiana	11	Arizona	8
Michigan	10	Nebraska	8
North Dakota	10	New Mexico	8
West Virginia	10	South Carolina	8
Georgia	9	South Dakota	8
Kansas	9	Texas	8
Kentucky	9	Washington	8
Nevada	9	Florida	7

The governor's power of removal is the indispensable counterpart of the
power of appointment. One without the other is of doubtful potency for purposes of administrative control, since the appointing power cannot be
exercised when no vacancy exists. As a general rule, the power of removal   *The power*
must be specifically provided by the state constitution or statutes,   *of removal*
since state governors are held not to acquire a power of removal from
their general executive power or their power of appointment. There is no
"Myers case for states" which gives to the governor extensive removal power over
administrative officials in the way in which that 1926 Supreme Court case
did for the president. Two states, Missouri in 1945 and New Jersey in 1947,
provided in their constitutions extensive power for the governor to remove
appointive state officials, but this does not apply to boards and commissions in
New Jersey.

The most common statutory and constitutional provision dealing with the
governor's removal power is the requirement that removals must be "for cause
only." Although this undoubtedly serves to deter a governor somewhat,   *Regulation*
since courts have generally held it to require a definite statement of   *of removals*

---

[2] Adapted from table, "Constitutional and Statutory Elective Administrative Officials," *The
Book of the States, 1962-63*, pp. 140-141.

THE GOVERNOR'S ADMINISTRATIVE POWERS

230   charges and an opportunity for a hearing, it is the governor himself who has full power to decide whether the evidence sustains the charges. In practice, the governor's removal power is frequently much stronger than the constitution, statutes, and court decisions indicate. In states where a newly elected governor is usually strong politically, there is always a large group of holdover officials who voluntarily resign when the new governor takes office. Furthermore, the governor may request an official to resign, whether he was appointed for a definite term or not and whether the governor has the removal power or not, and such a request may be honored in preference to the probability of an unhappy and prolonged "cold war" existence in the state government. As a final resort, the determined governor who controls the legislature may oust the uncooperative official by the device known as the "ripper bill" — a legislative act abolishing the office or agency and creating a new one, usually with only a slightly altered name.

Few governors have gone so far as Governor Eugene Talmadge of Georgia, who demonstrated how members of one of that state's most independent boards, the state highway board, might be removed. In April, 1933, he

Removals in practice

tried to have certain highway department employees fired, and in order to achieve this he omitted their names from the quarterly budget which was sent to him for approval. The chairman of the board protested this act, and in June, 1933, Governor Talmadge invoked martial law and removed the chairman and one member from the board, with state troops escorting the chairman from his office. The remaining member of the board was placed in charge and the governor appointed two other persons to fill the vacancies. The ousted chairman and member of the board brought suit, but they were unsuccessful. The case is obviously not typical, but it serves as a reminder that realistic appraisal of the governor's power of appointment and removal must include not only constitutional and statutory provisions but also such factors as the governor's personality and political strength and the traditions and practices which have developed in the state.

Because available financial resources set a maximum limit on all that state government can do, the management of finance becomes an inescapable responsibility of the governor. Fiscal management, broadly conceived,

Power of fiscal management; early history

consists of budget making and budget execution, and the first hundred years of our nation's history in these two fields witnessed expansion of fiscal machinery without any significant modification of the ideas on which that machinery was originally based. The center of gravity for the whole system continued to be the legislature. But even within the legislature there came to be such a scattering of responsibility among various legislative committees and subcommittees that pork-barrel and other wasteful appropriations were made easy, and a general view directed toward financial planning was made impossible. Dispersion of financial responsibility in the administrative branch was even worse. The traditional fiscal officers — assessors, collectors, treasurers, comptrollers, and auditors, all jealous of their independence — usually devised their own bookkeeping methods without regard for the needs of other fiscal offices. With the creation of new, uncoordinated agencies, separately concerned with particular taxes, debt, investment and the like, it became increasingly difficult in matters of state finance, if not impossible, for the right hand to know what the left hand was doing.

Since about 1920 there has been a reversal of the trend toward financial dispersion and a steady movement in the direction of consolidation. Improvements in both legislative and executive organization and procedure have gone far toward creating an orderly and responsible financial system. *Recent fiscal trends; budget making* Probably the most significant development of all has been the increased role of the governor in both budget making and budget execution. The "executive budget," making the governor the budget-making authority, has been adopted in 44 states, and in five other states the governor is chairman of a budget board or committee. In Arkansas the legislative council is the authority for budget recommendations, but the governor's appointive comptroller takes an active role in preparation of the budget in actual practice. Budget making involves the bringing together of estimates of total requirements of the government, comparison of estimates with past and present expenditures, calculation of probable income, preparation and submission of the budget document to the legislature, adoption of the budget, and enactment of bills designed to carry it into operation. Budget formulation is the basic instrument for statewide planning, and the manner of its use, misuse, or neglect by the governor is crucial in determining his success or failure in office.

The theory and practice of budget execution — controlling state expenditures — have undergone changes equally as fundamental as those in budget making. Before three or four decades ago, an appropriation was considered an *order* to spend the amount appropriated to a department. However, this doctrine has gradually been replaced by the principle that an *Budget execution* appropriation is an *authorization* effective only so far as necessary, and subject to the specific or general authorization of the governor. It is now standard practice to vest the governor with one or more control devices intended to insure proper use of funds already duly authorized by the legislature. Some of the more common devices for executive control of expenditures include the administrative pre-audit or control through accounting, the quarterly allotment system, central control of purchasing, and approval of transfers from one appropriation item to another. Different states give the governor these control devices in differing combinations and in varying degrees of strength. For example, the administrative pre-audit may be very weak, primarily checking

232 illegality, or it may be exceptionally strong, authorizing disallowance of expenditures which seem unwise. No realistic appraisal of a governor's administrative power can be made without careful examination of his role in fiscal management.

A power as essential to a governor as to any business executive, but one which receives little formal recognition by state constitutions, is the supervisory power. The governor is not an operating official in the sense that he *The super-* actually executes the law himself, but it is his constitutional job to "see *visory power* that the laws are faithfully executed." He must oversee and direct the administrative process, fixing the major policies supplementary to legislation and directing the operations of state agencies. Many areas of authority already discussed relate to the supervisory power, such as appointments, removals, and finances, but there is more to it than this. In essence, it is the governor's power to make his wishes known and secure acquiescence in them, a power that varies according to his ability to use certain methods or devices for supervision and direction. These devices include the requirement of information, informal investigations, individual and group conferences, orders and directives, approval of administrative acts, and the use of staff agencies. While the constitutional and statutory provisions relating to the supervisory power of the governor are important, and while it cannot be denied that most states need better legal recognition of the governor's supervisory role in administration, in the final analysis no amount of enabling legislation can make an effective supervisor out of a personally weak or disinterested governor. Individual case studies of the governors reveal that such factors as personality, prestige, personal interest in administration, and political power are strong determinants of the supervisory power.

In this connection a word should be added concerning ministerial and discretionary powers. The governor's powers are either ministerial, in which *Ministerial* case he has no choice in the manner of exercising them or whether *and discre-* to use them, or discretionary, in which case he may decide whether, *tionary power* when, and how to exercise such powers. The more difficult it becomes for the lawmakers to spell out in the constitution and statutes the exact circumstances when a governor should act and the specific action which he should take, the more prevalent becomes the practice of granting discretionary powers to the governor.

In a different and practical sense every governor demonstrates the discretionary nature of executive power when he crusades for vigorous law enforcement in one or two "pet fields" about which he may have campaigned for reform, while permitting administrative relaxation in certain other departments of state government. In effect, every governor has the discretionary power to pick and choose from among the state laws those which will receive special

attention, with the result that a state may have few if any arrests for violation   233
of truck weight limits under one governor and drastic enforcement of such
measures under another. This is actually an extra-legal type of discretionary
power, but no picture of the governor's role in administration is complete
without it.

PRACTICAL RESTRAINTS UPON
THE CHIEF ADMINISTRATOR

The discretionary power in the office of governor calls to our attention
an additional dimension of the governor's role in administration. Simply to
describe the administrative powers of the governor is not enough. Even
when his extra-legal powers are considered, one still does not have a *Importance*
realistic view of the actual governor, but only of the potential governor. *of other*
factors
Whether the powers are utilized, how they are utilized, and the practical
obstacles to their utilization are equally important parts of the picture of the
governorship. The performance of the governor depends upon such additional
factors as demands on the governor's time, his ability, personality, background,
training, and interest in politics as compared to administration.

No single fact is more apparent from an intensive study of the work of
the governor than the insistent demands made upon his time by non-administrative activities. A study of the persons and groups that called on the
governor of Arkansas during four reasonably typical days produced *Demands on*
the following classification of purposes of calls.[3] *governor's*
time

Purpose of Call	Per Cent of Total Number of Calls
Requests for jobs	23
Requests for special favors	13
Requests from civic, church, and school organizations	12
Problems of administrative officials	10
Criticisms of governmental policy or actions	7
Social calls	6
Reporting confidential information	5
Requests for clemency	4
Requests for extradition	2
Miscellaneous and unknown purposes	18
	100

[3] Daniel R. Grant, "The Role of the Governor of Arkansas in Administration" (Unpublished Ph.D. dissertation, Northwestern University, 1948), pp. 30-39.

234   Over 60 per cent of the conferences which occupied this governor's time concerned such matters as requests for jobs and special favors or consisted of social calls and visits by representatives of civic, youth, and church organizations. The requests for jobs presumably would be fewer in a state with a merit system, but, if the total for these non-administrative matters amounted to no more than half of the calls, it would still constitute a very important drain on the time of one charged with responsibility for directing the administrative process of state government. It will be noticed that conferences with administrative officials accounted for only 10 per cent of the callers received by the governor, ranking fourth in the list of groups seeing the governor.

Administrative duties overshadowed

Another "time and motion" study of a governor in action was made by the New Hampshire "Little Hoover Commission" covering three weeks during 1949 for Governor Sherman Adams. The demands of interviews, meetings, writing and making speeches, correspondence, phone calls, and travel required work weeks of 68, 67, and 56 hours. Although department heads and officers in New Hampshire seemed to fare better than those in Arkansas in point of time with the governor, such interviews still accounted for less than 7 per cent of his work week. Coleman B. Ransone, Jr., who includes this and other analyses in his book on the governorship, concludes that by far the most time-consuming function of the governor is his many-sided job of public relations, with the result either that his roles as policy maker and general manager are crowded out or that he carries an almost impossible burden of work.[4]

Predominance of public relations

In addition to the diversion of competing demands, a governor's lack of interest in his role as general manager may result in a virtually headless administrative establishment, even though the legal framework provides for a strong chief administrator. Many governors have had exclusively legislative or judicial experience, and it is safe to say that their primary concern is with legislation and traditional politics rather than with what they consider to be the less political area of administration. Such political activities can be particularly time-consuming for a governor who combines his normal political role with aspirations for further office-holding or who conceives his governorship as a stepping-stone to another office.

Preoccupation with politics

The activities of New York's Governor Harriman for three months following adjournment of the state legislature in 1955 indicate the time and interest which a governor may give to politics and public relations. He made at least 49 public appearances outside of Albany in 91 days, including a trip to

---

[4] Coleman B. Ransone, *The Office of Governor in the United States* (University of Alabama Press, University, Ala., 1956), pp. 152-154.

Florida, four trips to Washington, D. C., three to Buffalo, two to Syracuse and Suffolk, and at least one each to Nassau and Westchester counties and the cities of Massena, Ogdenburgh, Lake Placid, Bear Mountain, and Olean, as well as frequent shuttling between Albany and New York City. He met with Adlai E. Stevenson at least four times, conferred with the visiting prime ministers of Thailand and Italy and the foreign minister of France, addressed nine political fund-raising dinners, and spoke at three college commencements. Travelling by trains, automobiles, commercial airlines, National Guard planes, the Conservation Department's fish-stocking plane, and by helicopter, he still was surpassed in his travels by New York governors Al Smith, Franklin D. Roosevelt, and Thomas E. Dewey, when they were campaigning for the presidency.[5]

Many other factors may operate to make the actual role of the governor different from the potential role pictured by his legal powers and responsibilities. None is more important, however, than the personal qualities of the man himself. Ability or lack of ability, forcefulness or weakness, and ambition for higher office or the absence of such ambition, all are important de- *Personal* terminants in the governor's performance. In addition, the customs and *qualities* expectations of the people help condition the governorship, as well as such circumstances as depression, prosperity, war, and peace.

All of these are factors complicating, if not frustrating, the role of the governor in administration. Demands on the governor's time, pre-eminent concern for political matters and public relations, and the lack of previous experience in public administration make some analysts doubt whether *Proposals for* the elective governor can perform effectively as the general manager of *improvement* state administration. The most frequent proposals for improvement are to increase the governor's professional staff assistance to make his time count for more in the administrative field, or to create the office of assistant governor. This official would be, in effect, a highly-paid director of administration responsible to the governor. Occasionally a "state manager plan" is proposed along the lines of the council-manager plan for cities, but the motion has had few seconds. Coleman B. Ransone may well be right in concluding that the most fruitful approach probably combines the elimination of certain of the lesser functions of the governor, reduction in the time spent on other functions, and provision for more adequate professional staff assistance in carrying out his many responsibilities, particularly with respect to administration.

---

[5] Leo Eagan, "Harriman Gets Around," *New York Times,* July 5, 1955.

Alexander, Margaret C., *Development of the Power of the Executive in New York* (Smith College Studies in History, Northampton, 1917).

Fairlie, J. A., "The Executive Power in the State Constitution," *The Annals of the American Academy of Political and Social Science,* CLXXI (September, 1935), pp. 59-73.

Faust, M. L., *Manual on the Executive Article* (Missouri Constitutional Convention of 1943, Columbia, 1943).

Graves, W. B., *American State Government* (4th ed.; D. C. Heath and Company, Boston, 1953).

Highsaw, Robert B., "The Southern Governor — Challenge to the Strong Executive Theme?" *Public Administration Review,* XIX (Winter, 1959), pp. 7-11.

Kammerer, G. M., "The Governor as Chief Administrator in Kentucky," *Journal of Politics,* XVI (May, 1954), pp. 236-256.

Mitau, G. Theodore, "The Governor and the Strike," in Richard T. Frost, ed., *Cases in State and Local Government* (Prentice-Hall, Inc., Englewood Cliffs, 1961), pp. 207-218.

New York State Constitutional Convention Committee, *Problems Relating to Executive Administration and Powers* (Albany, 1938).

Ransone, Coleman B., *The Office of Governor in the South* (Bureau of Public Administration, University of Alabama Press, University, Ala., 1951).

Rohr, C. J., *The Governor of Maryland; A Constitutional Study* (Johns Hopkins Press, Baltimore, 1932).

Ruskowski, C. W., *The Constitutional Governor* (Bruce Humphries, Inc., Boston, 1943).

Scace, H. E., *The Organization of the Executive Office of the Governor* (Institute of Public Administration, New York, 1950).

(*See also* readings listed for preceding chapter.)

· *13* ·

PROBLEMS OF ORGANIZATION
AND PERSONNEL

THE THREE major elements of administration which concern state and local executives are organization, personnel, and finance. Each of these affects the others to such an extent that it is difficult and somewhat misleading to discuss them separately, but each has had its own peculiar historical development which constitutes an essential part of the understanding of state and local government. This chapter deals with organization and personnel, and the next chapter is devoted to finance.

The "big three" of administration

Some people are afflicted with the habit of assessing the relative importance of organization and personnel as they relate to public administration, and organization usually comes out a poor second in such comparisons. Effective administration undoubtedly depends in large measure upon the skill, integrity, and energy of the individual persons who make up the public service, but it is actually not fair to try to calculate this value in contrast to that of the structure within which the personnel operate. It is like comparing the relative merits of the contributions of oil and water in the operation of a steam engine — each is essential in its own way. In spite of the importance of personnel, it would certainly be naive to conclude that forms of government have little effect on administrative efficiency. Not only does the form of organization

Organization vs. personnel

237

238   help or hinder able administrators, but certain forms of organization tend to attract capable personnel while other forms tend to discourage their entry into the public service.

ADMINISTRATIVE ORGANIZATION
AND REORGANIZATION

One of the outstanding developments in the history of state government is the multiplication of state functions and activities and the accompanying growth in number and scope of administrative agencies. Because of this expansion, problems have arisen which were never dreamed of by those who were originally responsible for the administrative systems in our states. As early as 1900 many states possessed no less than 100 officers, boards, and commissions, most of them independent and uncoordinated. Some states had as many as 200 such agencies, and a recent study of California revealed a total of 360 administrative boards, commissions, and agencies, ranging from the Board of Guide Dogs for the Blind to the Yacht and Ship Brokers Commission. This expansion of governmental machinery was carried out in an unplanned, haphazard fashion, with the spoils motive frequently dominating. After their creation these officers, boards, and commissions tended to magnify the importance of their activities with requests for increased staffs and higher appropriations and to seek to preserve their independent status.

Multiplication of activities and agencies

Initial efforts to reform state administrative organization got underway a decade or so after the turn of the century, with most of the concentration upon a set of defects found in varying degrees in the administrative set-up of all of the states. The problem primarily singled out for attack has been the dispersal of the administrative structure. Instead of all activities or services of the same functional character, such as public welfare, or public works, being combined, each activity or service was separate and distinct, with little or no relation to other like activities or services. Typical was the administration of activities related to agriculture in Virginia in 1910, which was carried on by five independent agencies instead of a unified department. The legislative practice of creating new departments for new activities, with no reference to their proper relationship to others, inevitably resulted in a planless structure of numerous uncoordinated agencies.

Dispersed administrative structure

Another practice which has been strongly criticized is the extensive use of boards and commissions for "purely administrative" or ministerial activities.

The plural-headed agency is said to be characterized by slow action, lack of iniative, and lack of professional competence. Furthermore, the use of boards and commissions either constitutes a limitation upon the governor's power of direction or provides a perfect "cover-up" for passing the buck through the scattering of responsibility. *Boards and buck-passing*

The long ballot, resulting from the large number of elective state administrative officials, has been criticized as much for its effects upon the administrative structure of the state as it has for its contribution to nonvoting or uninformed voting. Some elective officials are specifically provided for in the state constitution, particularly such older offices as secretary of state, attorney general, treasurer, auditor, and superintendent of public instruction. The duties of the secretary of state are mainly ministerial in character, though quite numerous, and consist of a miscellany of functions varying from affixing the great seal of official state documents to certifying election results. The attorney general has the twofold task of acting as legal counsel to state officials, including the governor, and representing the state in civil suits and occasionally in criminal cases. Both the treasurer and auditor head clerical and accounting offices whose work is largely routine in nature, and only in the case of the auditor does logic indicate independent status. The superintendent of public instruction is less commonly elected, but this method of selection still remains in about half the states. *The long ballot; constitutional officers*

The constitutionally elective officers, along with those made elective by legislative act, have become in many cases administrative "touch me nots" in terms of their relations with the governor. This confronts the governor with subordinates who are not actually subordinate, making it totally unrealistic to speak of a governor's cabinet in the sense of the president's cabinet. The existence of such elective offices renders administrative coordination difficult and creates areas of unaccountability within the executive branch of state government. The same result is achieved frequently by the practice of fixing terms of state officers so that they do not coincide with the governor's term of office. Mistakenly considered to be a means of "keeping politics out" of particular agencies, this practice more often has the effect of prolonging the politics of a defeated regime for several years. *Administrative "touch me nots"*

Other problems on which the state reorganization movement focused attention have been defects in the organization for financial administration and, to a lesser extent, for personnel administration. The basic organizational weakness in the fields of finance and personnel is little different from that in other fields, but the impact of multiplication and dispersion of independent officers and agencies in these fields is undoubtedly greater. The dollars-and-cents cost of a dispersed state fiscal organization became more and more obvious, and state surveys did not fail to point out this cost. *Poor fiscal organization*

240   The movement for state administrative reorganization is usually said to have received its start about 1909 or 1910. The People's Power League of Oregon published a plan for reorganization of the state government in 1909 and again in 1911. The plan provided for concentration of executive power in the hands of the governor, subject only to the check of an independent auditor, and closer relations between the governor and legislature. In 1910, Governor Charles Evans Hughes of New York stated in his annual message to the legislature:

Beginnings of reorganization

> It would be an improvement, I believe, in state administration if the executive responsibility were centered in the governor who should appoint a cabinet of administrative heads accountable to him and charged with the duties now imposed upon elected state officers.

The proposal for reform of the national administration made by President Taft's Economy and Efficiency Commission in 1912 caused the state reorganization movement to gain momentum. Although Congress took no action on this report, several state legislatures were influenced by it to such an extent that they immediately established efficiency and economy commissions to study their state administrative organization and methods. By 1935 more than thirty states had made investigations and recommendations.

Federal stimulus

The first comprehensive reorganization plan was adopted by Illinois in 1917. Under the leadership of Governor Frank O. Lowden, the legislature abolished more than one hundred separate offices, boards, and commissions, consolidating their activities in nine functionally organized departments. A similar effort in New York had failed at the polls two years prior to the Illinois reorganization. Massachusetts in 1918 and 1919 was next to reorganize, followed by Idaho and Nebraska in 1919, and Washington and California in 1921. In 1923 reorganization plans were adopted in Tennessee, Maryland, Pennsylvania, and Vermont. By 1938 26 states had more or less remodeled their administrative structures, three of them by means of constitutional revisions and the others by statutory changes.

The example of Illinois

New impetus was given to the reorganization movement by the 1937 report of President Roosevelt's Committee on Administrative Management which gave its blessing to the principles upon which state reorganization had proceeded. Reorganization continued throughout World War II and after, although somewhat less sweeping than in the early period of the movement and consisting in some cases of "re-reorganizations" in states which had been overhauled previously. Numerous "little Hoover" commissions were created in the late 1940's and 1950's to pave the way for additional reorganizations. Taking their cue from the 1947 Commission on

Continuation of movement; "little Hoover" commissions

many states authorized administrative surveys of various types in 1949 and subsequent years. The flood tide for such surveys was reached by 1952 when a total of 33 states had set up "little Hoover" commissions.

This movement has been based upon principles or standards which are considered worthy aims with respect to the organization and integration of state administration. It is contended that these standards are no longer theoretical, but are based upon experience and supported either partially or entirely by actual practice in a number of states. Although no exact classification of these basic standards of reorganization has even been agreed upon, probably the first most commonly accepted standards are the following: (1) functional departmentalization of administrative agencies, (2) concentration of administrative authority and responsibility in the governor, (3) the undesirability of boards for the purely administrative work, (4) establishment of staff and auxiliary agencies responsible to the governor, and (5) provision for an independent audit. *Standards of reorganization*

According to the principle of functional departmentalization, state agencies performing similar or closely related activities should be organized and operated within the same department. Such consolidation would eliminate overlappings and effect savings by reducing the number of employees needed. Moreover, reduction of the hundred-odd virtually independent agencies into a dozen orderly departments would remove one of the greatest obstacles to central administration of all agencies by the governor. *Functional departmentalization*

Probably the basic standard of the reorganization movement, and the one upon which most of the others rest, is the concentration of authority and responsibility in the governor. It is considered not only unwise administrative practice but also unjust to impose a duty upon the governor or any other official without giving him authority commensurate with that responsibility. It is contended that the proper way to hold the administration accountable to the people is to center authority and responsibility at a single point, so that both deeds and misdeeds may be credited to the proper place. This principle requires elimination of most elective administrators, extension of the governor's appointing power to include all department heads, provision for a governor's cabinet, and establishment of a four-year term of office for the governor and other state officials. Consistency would also require the elimination of restrictions which prohibit a governor from running for re-election, since the governor is otherwise insulated from this important democratic device for reward or punishment. *Concentrated authority and responsibility*

Boards or commissions are deemed undersirable for "purely administrative" activities, because they are generally found to be inefficient. The single-headed agency is preferred for greater initiative, professional competence, quicker action, and clear location of responsibility. It is conceded, how-

Undesirabil-
ity of boards

ever, that boards or commissions may be attached advantageously to departments which are required to perform duties of a policy-determining, quasi-legislative, or quasi-judicial character.

In keeping with the expanded administrative role given to the governor, it is recommended that the various staff and auxiliary services of administration be coordinated and made responsible to the governor. According to this

Coordinated
staff services

principle the well-equipped governor will have adequate assistance in personal office staff, a planning agency, and central offices for the budget, accounting, purchasing, and personnel administration. During the past decade a trend has developed in the direction of uniting many of these functions in a single state department of administration and finance.

Most of the state reorganization survey groups have recommended a complete separation of the functions of financial control and accounting from those of independent auditing and review. This recommendation is based on

Independent
audit

the assumption that the control and accounting functions are executive in character and should be performed by an officer directly responsible to the governor, while the functions of post-audit and review belong to the legislature.

One suggestion for accomplishing administrative reorganization is to grant power to the governor, similar to that possessed by the president, to initiate reorganization proposals subject to subsequent disapproval by the leg-

Executive ini-
tiative in re-
organization

islature during a specified period of time. A few states have adopted such authorizations by statute in recent years, and Alaska became the first and only state to incorporate such a plan in its constitution. Such provisions make it clear that the legislature retains authority over the powers and functions of departments, however.

Efforts for administrative reform at the state level have been matched by similar movements aimed at county and city governments, with some significant differences. The assumptions of the reorganization movement at the

Parallel
movements
in cities
and counties

local level have been virtually the same as at the state level, including much the same arguments for integration of the administrative structure, as well as similar forces contributing to separatism and dispersion. Reorganization of city government has often revolved around the proposal for a complete change in form of government, such as the commission plan or the council-manager plan. This is partly true in the case of county reorganization, which has recently focused on the adoption of a county-manager system or the provision for a "chief administrative officer." County reorganization has proceeded at a snail's pace, easily the slowest of all levels of government, occurring primarily in the highly urbanized counties. Problems of administrative organization uniquely related to cities and counties are discussed subsequently in special chapters on these local units.

The reorganization movement has not been without its critics. Although most political scientists have been in general agreement with the standards of reorganization and the movement as a whole, there has been criticism of both the practice and the theory of the reorganization movement. One frequent criticism, which occasionally finds much popular support, is the contention that reorganization would concentrate too much power in the hands of the governor. Abolition of the constitutionally elective officers is condemned as undemocratic, and the proposal to make the governor responsible for every administrative agency is said to stake too much on the ability of one man.

Criticisms of reorganization: governor too powerful

Many have criticized the efforts to abolish boards and commissions. It is said that the best work often comes from private individuals who feel an urge to serve and that many boards have been characterized by this spirit of voluntary service. Other arguments put forth in defense of boards and commissions are that a board will keep politics out of a department, that where its members' terms overlap it guarantees continuity, that group decision is frequently indispensable and that a board meets the need for group and sectional representation.

Boards defended as valuable

The contention is made that the spoils system is nourished rather than eliminated by reorganization. According to this argument the governor's control of the spoils system is consolidated by his increased appointing power over higher administrative officers. Not only is the control of spoils, formerly scattered among independent agency heads transferred to the hands of the governor but he is in a better position to bypass civil service restrictions simply because of the added influence which his new powers under reorganization have given him.

Spoils system strengthened

The charge has been made that many reorganizations have been only "paper reorganizations" characterized by reshuffling of bureaus rather than genuine consolidation. As a result, there has been no reduction in agencies, personnel, or expenditures. Examples are cited of groups of miscellaneous state agencies which have been thrown together loosely into a new department, solely for the sake of paper symmetry. In New Jersey the courts have even recognized the nature of paper reorganization by declaring that even though the New Jersey Turnpike Authority is placed by law in the State Highway Department, it actually is "in but not of" the Highway Department.[1]

Reshuffling of bureaus

---

[1] Bennett M. Rich, *The Government and Administration of New Jersey* (Thomas Y. Crowell Company, New York, 1957), p. 256.

ADMINISTRATIVE ORGANIZATION AND REORGANIZATION

The criticism has been made by others, particularly by line officials, that the staff agencies are too strict. It has been said that the reorganizers have instituted excessive financial control especially through budget bureaus and that the finance officers have been given too pre-eminent a position.

Another criticism, less frequently voiced but in many ways more serious, concerns the wisdom of compelling the governor to perform the functions of chief administrator or general manager of the executive branch when his chief interest, his capabilities, and even the major demands of his constituents, all direct him toward political, legislative, and ceremonial leadership. The tendency of non-administrative functions to monopolize the governor's time and interest casts some doubt upon the assumptions of a movement which undertakes to make the politician a general manager. These critics would say that "you can lead a political horse to administrative water but you can't make him drink."

*Governor not
interested in
adminis-
tration*

Finally, there is a very large group, particularly among political scientists, which makes the single criticism that the reorganization movement has not gone far enough in its changes. In effect, it does not attack the principles upon which the reorganization movement is based, but it contends that there has been an inadequate application of these principles. This group points out that no state has adopted all the component parts of the reorganization program in their entirety. They would be the first to admit further that many reorganizations have resulted merely in a shuffling of bureaus on paper, rather than in genuine integration of administrative agencies.

*Half-a-loaf
reorganiza-
tions*

These criticisms of administrative reorganization, coupled with the opposition of those having vested interest in the status quo, have made progress rather slow. Probably no force has been stronger in defeating reorganization proposals or in effecting compromises than the constitutionally independent officers and the personnel of independent boards and commissions. The attitude of the forces opposed to administrative reorganization is exemplified by the following historical account of the 1931 defeat of a reorganization plan in Arkansas. The description was written by the secretary of the Arkansas History Commission.

*Opposition
from affected
agencies*

Slick brain trusters of the National Institute, Inc. [sic] plainly had the governor sold wholeheartedly on this plan of theirs which looked, on paper, like the setup of an ideal plan of government. . . .

Governor Parnell's faith in this new streamlined system as a cure-all of much that is complained of as ill in government is not to be questioned. Deceived by his own naive enthusiasm, he thought he might induce the Legislature to submit the plan to a referendum vote of the people as proposals for amending the constitution. However, the Legislature was cold to the scheme as a contrivance calculated to put it in the power of the governor to make himself a dictator. Once that impression got around, the majority would have no part of that which the New York doctors of political science had prescribed.[2]

The one-sided nature of the state historian's account of the fate of reorganization in Arkansas can be explained in large measure, perhaps, by the fact that the proposed functional departmentalization would have swallowed up the state history commission, eliminating its status as an independent agency. While each state has had its own peculiar circumstances leading to the defeat of reorganization proposals, this distrust of "slick brain trusters" and fear of dictatorship undoubtedly are shared by a large segment of the legislators and voters. *Defense of status quo*

In spite of criticism and opposition, few people in those states which have experienced major reorganization now desire to return to the conditions existing before reorganization. The accomplishments of the state reorganization movement cannot be evaluated fully until more adequate, comprehensive analyses have been made of the results of reorganization, but there is agreement on at least a few of its accomplishments. It is generally agreed that responsibility can be more easily located in the reorganized administrative system, and many would cite this as the principal benefit attributable to reorganization. In terms of economies, it is difficult to show actual dollars-and-cents savings, but there can be little doubt that reorganization has resulted in more and better service per tax dollar. One of the inevitable results of increased public confidence in government in a reorganized state is the demand for new services or for expansion of existing services, making tax reductions impossible. Finally, the administrative work of the reorganized state is undoubtedly better planned than that of the unreorganized state, and the credit rests with the governor's new-found executive leadership. The governor finds it less difficult to take an all-embracing view because of the more simplified structure of government and the assistance of new staff agencies. Information is more easily obtained, and long-range planning becomes attainable. *Accomplishments of reorganization*

THE CIVIL SERVICE REFORM MOVEMENT

Structural reform in state and local government was actually preceded by civil service reform in the beginning, although the two movements have pro-

---

[2] D. T. Herndon, *Annals of Arkansas* (Arkansas History Commission, Little Rock, 1947), p. 272.

246 ceeded at about the same pace since 1900. There can be no doubt at all that the finest organization conceivable is doomed to failure if it is manned by un-

Importance of personnel

trained, unscrupulous, and undependable employees. There *should* be no doubt that such an organization will also fail under the ever-increasing demands of modern society even if it is manned by honest, mediocre and half-trained employees, although some still have the notion that the public service can get along all right with well-meaning "second raters." Experience has increasingly demonstrated that the public service in the mid-twentieth century demands the best personnel that can be found.

A history of personnel management in state and local government has been until recent years primarily a history of the "spoils" system. Although Andrew Jackson is sometimes blamed for introducing the spoils system into Ameri-

Origins of spoils system

can politics, many made use of the system before he did. Even colonial America operated under a spoils system of a sort. Colonial governors tended to treat public office as a special preserve of a privileged class — the British aristocracy — and this became the source of friction between the colonial legislature and the royal governor concerning his appointing power. After the Revolution the short terms and rotation of office prevalent in state governments made possible a new kind of spoils system long before Andrew Jackson was elected president. The statement of Senator Marcy of New York in 1832 that "to the victor belongs the spoils" signaled not the beginning of the spoils system but merely its spread from state and local government to the national level. Aaron Burr, the first "boss" of Tammany Hall, had applied it most skillfully in New York City after defeating Alexander Hamilton in 1800. Thus, while spoils activity was relatively insignificant at the national level from 1800 until 1829, it flourished vigorously at state and local levels. From 1829 to 1883 the doctrine of party monopoly went virtually unchallenged at all levels of government.

The spoils system at its worst has had a disastrous effect on the efficiency of state administration. At best it has been a crude and frustrating mechanism for selecting and supervising public administrative personnel. With

Evils of spoils system

party activity the chief criterion for selecting employees, state and local employment became a temporary and uncertain occupation which the most capable persons had no desire to enter. The spoils system had a demoralizing effect on administration, with the quality of personnel caught in a downward spiral of short tenure of office, high labor turnover, and a general public inclination to think of public employees as incompetent and lazy. Low prestige contributed to still greater labor turnover which, in turn, contributed to still lower prestige.

The spoils system has been both a blessing and a curse to the governor and to the mayor. As a means of strengthening party or faction, of insuring the

PROBLEMS OF ORGANIZATION AND PERSONNEL

loyalty of the public service, and of giving the chief executive strong bargaining power with his legislative body, the spoils system was defended for years as essential to democratic leadership. As the tasks of public administration became increasingly technical in character, however, the effects of the spoils system not only became more damaging to the administrative process, but they became an increasingly serious burden upon the governor in his new role as chief administrator of a multi-million-dollar public business. Governors began to find it intolerable to spend the greater part of each working day speaking to the many friends of the previous campaign who had "clients" in need of a job. This was all the more serious because the greatest pressure always came during the first few months of the governor's term of office, when most of his time was needed for consideration of the important initial decisions of his administration. A comparison of governors' inaugural addresses with their farewell addresses reveals an interesting contrast in their recommendations concerning patronage. The silence of the incoming governor is followed by statesmanlike pronouncements from the outgoing governor on behalf of a strengthened civil service.

Dissatisfaction with the spoils system grew during the post-civil war period, but did not find tangible expression until 1880 when the New York Civil Service Reform Association was organized. It later became known as the National Civil Service Reform League and is now the National Civil Service League. Civil service reform was given a dramatic push in 1881 by the assassination of President Garfield by a disappointed office seeker. This incident mobilized strong support for a federal law, which was passed in 1883, requiring examinations to test the abilities of job applicants. The law was very inadequate by present standards, but it was a beginning and eventually it had a far-reaching influence. Later in 1883 the state of New York established a civil service commission with authority to administer competitive tests for state employment, and Massachusetts followed in 1884. Although these two states were the only ones to adopt the merit principle for more than twenty years, by 1900 there were 85 civil services in the cities of the nation.

Beginnings of reform

Early in the present century (1905) Wisconsin and Illinois began a new era of civil service reform by setting up civil service commissions. Colorado and New Jersey followed in 1907 and 1908, and by 1920 Connecticut, California, Ohio, Kansas and Maryland had fallen into line. Another lapse in activity followed and it was not until 1937 that new converts to the merit system began to appear. In that year five states adopted the merit principle for state employment, and subsequent adoptions brought the total number of states to more than half of the fifty. In addition to these states, which have what the Public Personnel Association terms "general coverage," the remainder of the fifty have complied with a 1939 federal requirement by enact-

Extension of civil service

THE CIVIL SERVICE REFORM MOVEMENT

248 ing civil service laws applying to state workers associated with certain of the federal grant-in-aid programs.

Some of the states listed in the general-coverage column have experienced difficulty in continuing to manifest genuine conversion to the merit principle.

Circumvention of civil service

Many have accepted the merit principle in name only and have devised numerous ingenious means of continuing patronage appointments. Temporary and interim appointments, tampering with examination scores, coercion to secure waivers from the top candidates, and exemption of particular classes of appointments are just a few of the possible methods of defeating the intent of a civil service law. Other states have "fallen from grace" or "backslidden" by repealing their civil service laws after only a brief trial period, as in the case of Arkansas (1937 to 1939) and New Mexico (1939 to 1941). Louisiana, which first established a civil service commission in 1940, returned to the spoils system in 1948, but was officially reconverted to the merit principle in 1952 by a popularly approved constitutional amendment. New Mexico returned to general coverage in 1959. In spite of occasional defections from the ranks, the general trend has been clearly in the direction of tightening up and extending the scope of state civil service laws. Counties have lagged far behind the cities and the states, however, in adopting civil service systems.

The original emphasis of the civil service reform movement was largely negative — that is, its design was to "keep the rascals out" by means of a watchdog type enforcement of competitive entrance examinations. Other aspects

Essentials of personnel management

of personnel management were neglected or omitted from the functions of the civil service commission. The merit system has come to mean far more than keeping the spoilsmen out of office, however, and the modern personnel department is engaged in a wide variety of activities aimed at recruiting, selecting, supervising, and promoting the best qualified persons for the public service. Its many responsibilities include recruitment, examination, certification, position classification, pay policy, in-service and other training programs, performance evaluation records, discipline and removals, safety and welfare programs, and many other related activities.

Recruitment, examination, and certification are the first functions of personnel management in the chronology of a person's entry into the public service.

Recruitment, examination and certification

Recruitment, still a neglected phase of personnel management in many states, includes all activities aimed at attracting candidates for public employment. Too often recruitment amounts to little more than posting an unattractive mimeographed announcement of examinations on the same bulletin board which contains reward notices for fugitive criminals. In recent years the more progressive cities and states have adopted "positive recruitment" programs utilizing a variety of modern methods to seek actively the best qualified persons for state employment.

almost the exclusive personnel function, continues to be of vital importance to the merit system. Examinations for applicants may be oral, written, or a test of performance, where physical skill or strength is involved; they may test achievement, aptitude, or physical fitness; they may be competitive or "pass," and assembled or nonassembled. In the assembled examination the candidates are brought together in one or more examining rooms to answer specific questions in writing, but the unassembled examination involves more personal and individual evaluation of education, experience, and qualifications, where the number of applicants is small and the position is in the higher grades. Examinations are essential aids in judging their probable future success or failure in the public service.

Following an examination, the civil service commission does not make appointments. Instead, most states provide for certification by the commission to the appointing authority of the three highest on the eligible list, from which he makes his selection. This "rule of three" is defended as allowing discretion for the appointing officer while at the same time providing a deterrent against partisan appointments.

In many ways position classification is more appropriately the first function of personnel management than the preceding ones, at least in providing the foundation on which most other personnel activities must rest. Although considered highly technical and mysterious by some employees, *Position classification* it simply consists of grouping positions with similar duties into classes which permit uniform treatment. Without a position-classification plan, employees performing essentially the same duties in several different departments of state government may be on different salary scales, depending on the department's political power and prestige and similar factors. A position-classification plan not only makes possible equal pay for equal work, but it has many other uses. It provides the information necessary for intelligent recruitment and examination. Increasing information on the qualifications necessary for the higher positions in the state public service facilitates transfers and promotions within the service. Mobility of personnel is seriously limited without a classification plan. On the basis of the classification plan, in-service training programs are inaugurated, designed both to improve employees' performance and to prepare them for higher positions. Probably the fundamental rule in position classification is the fact that it is the *position* which is classified — not the person who fills the position. Thus the determining factors are the duties actually required by the job, and not the exceptional talents of the person who happens to be filling the position when it is classified.

Discipline in the public service varies from comparatively mild measures, such as warning or reprimand, to more stringent forms, such as suspension or

250 dismissal. Between these extremes are such alternatives as loss of seniority, de-

Discipline and dismissals

merits from efficiency ratings, loss of privileges, and demotion in rank. The desire to protect employees from unwarranted dismissal — particularly political removal — has led in many jurisdictions to the enactment of elaborate appeal procedures which make the civil service commission a quasi-judicial agency. Some kind of hearing is guaranteed to employees dismissed in such cases, and it often takes on the appearance of a formal trial, complete with legal counsel, testimony, cross-examination, and jury decision (by the commission) of guilty or not guilty. Such an appeal procedure is defended as essential to protect the innocent from the onslaught of the spoils system, especially during the formative years of a civil service system. These protective measures have been criticized, however, both for being ineffectual when a strong mayor or governor seriously wants to fire an employee and for imposing too much "red tape" upon administrators genuinely interested in removing unsatisfactory employees. The natural inclination of an administrator is to retain an incompetent employee indefinitely rather than to risk open combat in a public hearing in which all the dirty linen of the department might be washed. In spite of this unfortunate result, there seems to be no way to move from the spoils system toward the merit system in city or state government without reasonable safeguards against arbitrary dismissals.

The importance of a service-wide retirement program for public employees is perhaps best indicated by reference to the state of affairs existing prior to adoption of a pension system. In the absence of adequate retire-

Retirement

ment benefits for public employees, the tendency has been to keep employees on the payroll long after their usefulness has come to an end. This understandable reluctance to dismiss persons with long years of faithful service not only clogged up the payrolls with the over-aged and incapacitated, but also clogged up promotional ladders, put off salary increases, and discouraged the entry of young men and women into state and local employment. A two-fold motivation — a combination of humanitarianism and administrative self-interest — prompts development of an adequate program of compulsory retirement and pensions.

Few states or major cities have not adopted a comprehensive pension system for all state employees, although some of the systems adopted depend upon the financially unsound "cash disbursement" plan which makes no attempt to establish adequate, actuarially determined reserves. The "actuarial reserve" plan takes the guesswork out of the annual requirements of the pension fund and does not leave this to the vicissitudes of legislative economy drives. Although the old age insurance plan enacted by Congress in 1935 specifically excluded employees of state and local governments, subsequent legislation permits these groups to participate in the federal social security system.

The movements in state and local government for administrative reorganization and for civil service reform seem to contradict each other in one respect. The movement for administrative reorganization strongly recommends increased appointing power for the chief executive, while the *Reorganization, civil service, and the governor* movement for civil service reform strongly recommends reduced appointing power for the chief executive. On the surface it seems that the "reorganizers" favor strengthening the administrative position of the governor or mayor by giving him more appointing power, while the civil service reformers favor weakening him by divesting him of great portions of his appointing power. To complete the picture, it should be noted that most textbooks in the field of state and local government appear to give strong support to *both* movements.

Actually, there is at least a partial explanation for this seeming contradiction of recommending more and less appointing power for the chief executive at the same time. The explanation lies in the types of appointments which are referred to in each case. The state reorganization movement is primar- *Different types of appointments* ily concerned with giving the governor the power to appoint the heads of the important departments and bureaus of the executive branch, in order that he may fulfill the constitutional mandate to see that the laws of the state are faithfully executed. The civil service reform movement, on the other hand, is primarily concerned with insuring non-political appointments of clerks, technicians, and professional employees at a level lower than department or bureau head. Furthermore, civil service reform has been more concerned with the method of appointment than the source of the appointing power, although the latter is naturally involved.

Just what should be the organizational relationship of the whole function of personnel administration to the governor? This question poses one of the most perplexing problems facing those interested in improving state government. In one corner stand those who favor a strong and inde- *The strong and independent commission* pendent civil service commission, isolated from the office of governor in order to prevent his meddling in appointments and removals simply to pay his political debts. This independent status for the civil service commission is usually achieved by providing that the members of the commission shall have longer terms of office than the governor and that their terms shall not expire at the same time. Insulation from the governor's influence is further provided in some states by requiring that the governor fill vacancies on the commission only from nominees submitted from independent groups, such as specified university presidents. Advocates of the strong and independent civil service commission regard it as an essential part of our system of checks and balances to prevent the governor and his department heads from abusing their power.

In the opposite corner stand those who favor an integrated personnel department as one of the principal staff arms of the governor. Proponents of the integrated department point out that the governor's new role as administrative chief of the state, added to his older roles as political and ceremonial chief, make it essential for him to have authority over personnel management. It is argued that to deprive the chief executive of authority over personnel management is to send the soldier to battle with one arm tied behind his back. One of the strongest arguments advanced for the integrated personnel department is the contention that it is essential before the states can begin to move away from the negative, keep-the-rascals-out philosophy of personnel management, to the more positive philosophy of a merit system. It is said that so long as the personnel program is not the program of the governor and the department heads, the independent civil service commission will never obtain more than begrudging and half-hearted compliance from line officials who must, in the final analysis, carry out the program.

The integrated personnel department

What is the answer to the dilemma? The doctrines of modern "positive personnel management" seem to dictate that the chief executive should have authority over the personnel department, but practical experience with the spoils system seems to dictate that the governor needs an independent check in this area. In actual practice, most states seem to be moving toward a compromise between these two extremes.

While most states cling to the idea of a commission rather than a single head for the personnel agency, there is growing recognition that most of the work in personnel management is detailed administration, rather than rule-making and adjudication. Increasing authority is being placed in the office of director of personnel, with the civil service commission being retained primarily as a rule-making and disciplinary body. Such an arrangement permits a close relationship between the governor and the personnel director, while retaining the independent status of the commission. But the answer does not lie in a single organizational pattern. Each state will require a tailor-made plan, with due consideration to whether the office of governor in that state has outgrown the necessity for an independent watchdog to keep the spoilsmen out. Some states obviously have not outgrown this necessity. Advocates of the council-manager plan can claim with some justification that their system of government for cities is more conducive to the merit system than one under a popularly elected executive.

Compromise in practice

One other problem should be mentioned as having been aggravated by the administrative reorganization movement, but it is actually as old as government itself. This is the problem of how the governor, who has come to be a powerful figure in even the most unreorganized states, can be controlled by the people so as to avoid hamstringing a "good governor," while

Gubernatorial accountability

keeping a "bad governor" checkmated and harmless. The administrative reorganization movement has made it clear that an impotent governor cannot
adequately perform the tasks assigned to him in modern state government and
recommended greatly increased administrative powers. Probably the most serious
omission of the reorganization movement, some would contend, has been an
equal concern for a strengthened system of holding the governor and administration accountable to the people. This is probably an unfair criticism, however,
for many of those who advocate reorganization of the executive are also proponents of modernizing the legislature. Reorganization of the legislature along
lines laid down by modern principles would sharpen this time-honored instrument for control of the executive and render it abler to insure accord between
the action of the executive and the popular will. In any case, the new growth of
administrative power certainly merits thoughtful consideration of new and
sensible methods of control over this power.

A close examination of the methods available to the people for controlling
their state governor will reveal that in many states the system of continuing
accountability of the governor — either to the legislature, the courts, or
more directly to the people — is seriously ineffective. A case study made *Inadequate*
by one of the authors indicates that controls existing in Arkansas are not *methods of*
adequate for holding the governor accountable for his conduct of admin- *control*
istration in that state.

> The legislative controls are subject to the limitations of a sixty-day biennial
> session and are often made ineffective because of the submissiveness of the
> legislature to the governor. There is no independent audit of expenditures
> subject to the legislature. The court will not compel the governor to perform
> either his discretionary or mandatory duties, and its chief restraint upon the
> governor lies in declaring acts to be unconstitutional. The biennial election of
> the governor has proved to be a slender reed on which to rely for obtaining
> responsible administration, and there is no provision for the recall. Finally,
> pressure groups, including political factions, wield a substantial amount of in-
> fluence upon the governor, but there is no assurance that such groups represent
> the people as a whole.[3]

It was the quest for a system of strong but responsible state administration
which undoubtedly led to the suggestion of a state manager plan many years ago
by Harvey Walker[4] and the proposal by William Y. Elliott and others for a

---

[3] Daniel R. Grant, "The Role of the Governor of Arkansas in Administration" (Unpublished
Ph.D. dissertation, Northwestern University, 1948), p. 334.

[4] Harvey Walker, "Theory and Practice in State Administrative Organization," *National
Municipal Review*, XIX (April, 1930), pp. 249-254.

responsible executive on the model of English cabinet government.[5] Both
proposals probably deviate too far from American governmental tradition

Toward a
stronger state
legislature

to offer much hope in the foreseeable future.

The most feasible approach to a solution at present probably lies in
strengthening the state legislature so that it can adequately fulfill its function of controlling the purse strings and supervising the administration. This does
not mean reliance upon the legislature as the only form of control over the governor. It simply means that the legislature seems best suited to become the bulwark of an effective system of control. Responsible administration cannot be
realized without a legislature capable of efficiently handling the task of appro-
priating funds for administration, of controlling expenditures by means of a
regular audit as well as investigations, and of being general guardian of the
administrative interests of the people.

SUPPLEMENTARY READINGS

Bollens, J. C., *Administrative, Reorganization in the States since 1939* (Bureau of
Public Administration, University of California, Berkeley, 1947).

Bosworth, K. A., "The Politics of Management Improvement in the States," *American
Political Science Review*, XLVII (March, 1953), pp. 84-99.

Buck, A. E., *The Reorganization of State Governments in the United States* (Columbia University Press, New York, 1938).

Carpenter, W. S., *The Unfinished Business of Civil Service Reform* (Princeton University Press, Princeton, 1952).

Civil Service Assembly of the United States and Canada, *Readings in Public Personnel Administration* (Civil Service Assembly of the United States and Canada, Chicago, 1942), and other reports by this organization, now known as
the Public Personnel Association.

Council of State Governments, *Reorganizing State Government* (Council of State
Governments, Chicago, 1950).

Fish, C. R., *The Civil Service and the Patronage* (Harvard University Press, Cambridge, 1920).

Frost, Richard T., "The New Jersey Institutions Case," in *Cases in State and Local
Government* (Prentice-Hall, Inc., Englewood Cliffs, 1961), pp. 219-236.

---

[5] William Y. Elliott, *The Need for Constitutional Reform* (McGraw-Hill Book Co., Inc.,
New York, 1935).

Heady, Ferrel, *State Constitutions: The Structure of Administration* (National Municipal League, New York, 1961).

Hyneman, C. S., "Administrative Reorganization: An Adventure into Science and Theology," *Journal of Politics*, I (February, 1939), pp. 62-75.

Stahl, O. Glenn, *Public Personal Administration* (4th ed.; Harper & Row, Publishers, New York, 1956).

Wilbern, York, "Administration in State Governments," *The Forty-eight States: Their Tasks as Policy-Makers and Administrators* (The Graduate School of Business, Columbia University, New York, 1955).

$\star$ *14* $\star$

FINANCE

I⊤ ɪs not wise to learn public finance from the typical "economy candidate" who runs for the office of governor. His glib promises of greatly increased governmental services without corresponding increases in state taxes simply

Financial
demagogy

brand him as one of two things — a demagogue or an ignoramus. Many a victorious gubernatorial candidate in recent history has faced the prospect of unanticipated (and unpromised) new taxes or an unbalanced budget immediately upon taking office. He can usually be depended upon to speak differently about financing state government in the next election, having learned about state finance by the rigorous, school-of-hard-knocks method.

Public finance, with its concern for expenditures and revenues, is a two-edged sword which cuts across every major program and problem of state and local government. It is difficult to think of any administrative or political

Importance
of finance

act which does not have financial implications. Whether it is the employment of a new engineer in the state highway department or a newspaper editorial urging replacement of a dilapidated and unsafe wing of a local hospital, money is involved.

How much money do state and local governments spend and for what is it spent? What is the comparative cost of different government programs? Who decides where the money goes? Where does the money come from, and

256

what are the major problems in extracting it from citizens? What is happening   257
in state-local financial relationships? The answers to these and other questions
are essential to an understanding of the role of finance in state and local government.

EXPENDITURES

All levels of government — federal, state, and local — spent approximately
165 billion dollars in 1961, and of this amount over 67 billion dollars, more than
40 per cent of the total, were spent by state and local governments.
Except for national defense spending, which accounted for a lion's share   *Increased*
— 49.4 billion dollars — the federal government actually spent less than   *expenditures*
the total for state and local governments. State governments, which spent
less than 500 million dollars in 1915, increased their expenditures five-fold to
2.5 billion dollars in 1930, and by 1954 the 1930 amount had increased five-fold
to more than 13 billion dollars. In 1961 their expenditures amounted to 24.6
billion dollars. In addition, the amount distributed by state governments to local
governments each year (10.1 billion dollars in 1961) has been increasing even
more rapidly than the state governments' own direct expenditures.

While there can be no doubt about the great increase in state expenditures, it is misleading to speak of a 5,000 per cent increase in the past half-century
as proof of waste and extravagance. Increase in population and decrease
in the purchasing power of the dollar must be credited, at least partially,   *Causes of*
for causing increased expenditures. Inflation makes it especially hazardous   *increase*
to compare annual statistics on public expenditures. When "constant
dollars" are used rather than "current dollars," the percentage increase in state
expenditures during the past decade is very nearly cut in half. Much of the
increase, however, must be attributed to expansion of state functions, through
steadily broadening old services, provision of new services, and state assumption
of services provided previously by local governments. Those concerned about
the increase may be reassured by the knowledge that the ratio of state and local
taxes to net national product has remained fairly constant since 1940. Taxes for
state and local governments have amounted to no more than 5 to 8 per cent of the
net national product during this time.

For what is the money spent? At the state level the three big functions
of highways, education, and public welfare account for well over one-half
of annual expenditures. The predominance of the cost of education over all   *Objects of*
other functions of government does not appear from state expenditures   *expenditure*

258   alone. This predominance becomes apparent in the figures on local government expenditures or in combined totals for state and local government. In terms of state expenditures alone, education ranked second to highways in 1960 and ranked only slightly above public welfare. However, when the 15.5 billion dollars spent on education by local governments is added to the 3.6 billion dollars spent at the state level, the total of 19.1 billion dollars exceeds the combined total spent on highways and public welfare by state and local governments together. Highways and public welfare accounted for 9.4 and 4.5 billion dollars respectively in state and local expenditures in 1960. Health and hospital costs ranked fourth with 3.8 billion dollars, followed by police (1.8), sanitation (1.7), natural resources (1.2), fire protection (1.0), housing (0.9), and parks and recreation (0.8).[1]

Total figures for expenditures of the 50 states may imply a uniform expenditure pattern in each state, while actually there is a considerable amount of variation from state to state. The variation is especially apparent in *Variation among states* any state-by-state comparison which excludes local government expenditures, because state-aid programs to local governments differ greatly among the states. Even so, it is a rare thing if expenditures of a state government for education, highways, and public welfare, do not account for between one-half and two-thirds of that state's total budget. The dominant position of these three functions is indicated by the listing in Table 14-1 of expenditures for these and total state functions for the several states in 1960.

The question of where the money goes is not answered simply by an indication of the cost of particular governmental programs. Government expenditures may be classified according to current operations, capital outlays, *Character of expenditures* and other objects. Considered in this light, state and local expenditures for 1960 are presented in Table 14-2.

What part of state and local expenditures goes for salaries and wages of government employees? The total payroll in 1960 was 24.5 billion dollars, nearly 40 per cent of total expenditures. Payrolls for public school teachers and *State and local payrolls* other employees in the field of education accounted for more than 40 per cent of all state and local expenditures for personal services. This is simply another indication of the dominant position of public schools in the requirements and problems of public finance. The gubernatorial candidate who promises to improve the financial status of school teachers is biting off a very sizeable hunk of the total budget for state and local government. By the same token, the candidate who criticizes the "wasteful expenditure of vast sums of the taxpayers' hard-earned money" is very likely to be revealing his ignorance concerning the objects of state and local expenditures.

TABLE 14-1   259

STATE EXPENDITURES IN 1960, FOR THE THREE MAJOR FUNCTIONS
(In thousands of dollars)

State	Total General Expenditure	Education	Highways	Public Welfare
All states	$27,228,429	$8,856,702	$7,316,737	$3,703,761
Alabama	497,867	174,281	150,148	1,216
Alaska	49,871	21,930	4,301	4,368
Arizona	240,378	82,847	62,641	25,165
Arkansas	246,945	74,530	72,856	46,437
California	3,050,525	1,243,318	555,918	434,734
Colorado	309,915	90,299	75,067	80,756
Connecticut	389,686	90,675	116,077	53,350
Delaware	113,181	50,931	26,814	7,721
Florida	724,491	259,999	219,434	78,698
Georgia	530,357	202,378	131,281	92,347
Hawaii	182,435	52,340	20,464	9,678
Idaho	111,987	29,237	44,236	11,233
Illinois	1,210,986	302,873	426,023	232,731
Indiana	609,029	223,199	206,819	37,316
Iowa	430,366	99,405	169,771	54,390
Kansas	313,136	89,985	105,581	40,992
Kentucky	406,185	113,275	152,707	58,783
Louisiana	785,602	242,240	184,176	162,554
Maine	145,290	28,485	54,311	22,336
Maryland	432,901	119,461	121,715	27,305
Massachusetts ...	787,350	105,408	176,531	140,772
Michigan	1,341,386	519,279	349,135	132,502
Minnesota	580,080	224,210	156,484	57,937
Mississippi	335,696	123,440	93,198	52,030
Missouri	519,725	142,247	136,126	140,675

[1] U. S. Bureau of the Census, *Summary of Governmental Finances in 1960* (August 18, 1961), p. 17.

TABLE 14-1 (*continued*)

State	Total General Expenditure	Education	Highways	Public Welfare
Montana	126,625	36,578	45,333	13,464
Nebraska	168,232	34,537	72,679	20,801
Nevada	68,514	23,278	21,604	4,520
New Hampshire .	93,322	16,498	43,011	8,835
New Jersey	517,184	147,947	136,621	54,731
New Mexico	211,059	96,636	52,052	25,865
New York	2,772,336	815,475	543,082	308,981
North Carolina ..	604,190	264,256	138,685	59,695
North Dakota ...	146,162	39,058	55,124	13,358
Ohio	1,242,688	293,221	465,246	177,431
Oklahoma	435,569	131,294	103,648	127,496
Oregon	359,915	108,722	109,274	42,797
Pennsylvania ...	1,602,830	566,527	369,258	195,860
Rhode Island ...	127,346	22,995	32,265	23,158
South Carolina ..	315,260	110,481	92,151	30,170
South Dakota ...	115,002	26,483	50,061	13,257
Tennessee	459,618	149,184	162,913	58,994
Texas	1,224,910	487,237	395,349	176,694
Utah	166,763	73,094	46,473	17,755
Vermont	81,040	17,905	35,823	8,117
Virginia	454,640	157,103	126,441	25,967
Washington	620,344	254,642	115,995	111,292
West Virginia ...	276,743	98,304	89,922	39,374
Wisconsin	597,080	149,950	159,342	54,930
Wyoming	95,687	29,025	43,570	4,493

Source: Adapted from the Bureau of the Census, *Compendium of State Government Finances in 1960.*

TABLE 14-2

261

STATE AND LOCAL EXPENDITURES BY CHARACTER AND OBJECT: 1960
(*In millions of dollars*)

Item	State and Local	State	All Local
Total expenditure	61,384	31,596	39,280
Intergovernmental expenditure	——	9,283	209
Direct expenditure	61,384	22,313	39,071
Current operation	36,560	9,694	26,866
Capital outlay	15,232	6,607	8,625
Construction	12,480	5,509	6,971
Land and existing structures	1,560	802	758
Equipment	1,192	296	896
Assistance and subsidies	3,518	2,015	1,503
Interest on debt	2,043	536	1,507
Insurance benefits and repayments	4,031	3,461	570
Exhibit: Total personal services	24,445	6,055	18,390

Source: Taken from U. S. Bureau of the Census, *Summary of Governmental Finances in 1960,* August 18, 1961, p. 15, Table 2.

REVENUES

Most of the money required to finance the ever-growing activities of state and local governments comes, of course, from taxation — federal as well as state and local. Taxes are compulsory contributions exacted by governments for public purposes. State and local taxes include levies on property, general sales and gross receipts, motor fuels, income, motor vehicles, alcoholic beverages, tobacco, corporation franchises, and estates and inheritances. A big revenue producer, sometimes omitted from lists of tax sources because of its special purpose, is the payroll assessment for the state unemployment insurance. When the three levels of government are considered separately, state government leans heavily upon three big tax sources — general sales, motor fuels, and income taxes — which accounted for 60.7 per cent of state tax collections in 1961. (*See* Figure 14-1.)

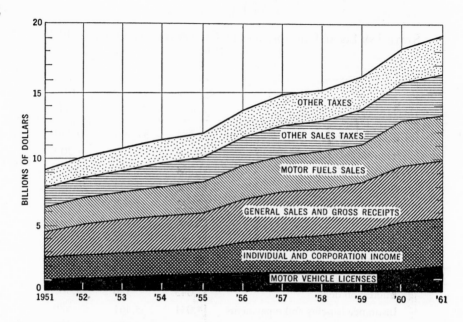

Source: "State Tax Collections in 1961," *The Book of the States, 1962-63*, p. 234.
Figure 14-1. State Collections: 1951-1961

Both the federal and local governments rely on one big revenue producer, with 80.8 per cent of federal tax collections coming from the income tax (individual and corporation) and 87.5 per cent of local tax collections being derived from the property tax.

Governmental revenue from all sources in 1961, federal, state, and local governments, totaled 158.7 billion dollars. About 65 per cent of this 1961 revenue was collected by the federal government, with the state and local levels dividing the remaining 35 per cent on an almost equal basis. Actually, about one-fifth of the grand total of governmental revenues came from nontax sources, with about 116.3 billion dollars being the total revenue from taxes at all levels of government. When taxes only are considered, federal collections accounted for 66 per cent of the total for all levels of government, with the state and local levels collecting the remaining 34 per cent in nearly equal proportions. The tax totals for the three levels of government in 1961 were 77.5, 19.1, and 19.8 billion dollars respectively, excluding the payroll taxes for old age and unemployment insurance.

These are the totals, but what are the trends? It should be apparent that

Revenue totals

the over-all trend has been upward. Probably the most significant trends over the past 50 years are the changes in relative position of the three levels of government in their percentage of total tax collections. Beginning with 23 per cent in 1916, the federal government rose to a peak of 65 per cent in 1920, dropped back to 22 per cent by 1932, rose to an even higher peak of 82 per cent in 1945, by 1955 had dropped to 71 per cent, and continued its decrease to 66 per cent of all governments' tax revenues in 1961. *Trends in tax totals; absolute and relative*

The percentages for local governments have followed the federal pattern in roughly inverse proportion, beginning with a very high 65 per cent of the total in 1916, dropping to 28 per cent in 1920, rising steadily to a peak of 56 per cent in 1932, falling to the all-time low of 9 per cent in 1945, and rising with some fluctuation to 15 per cent in 1955 and 17 per cent in 1961.

State governments' proportion of the total tax collections, however, has changed the least of the three levels of government, beginning with 12 per cent in 1916 and, after less drastic fluctuations, rising only to 14 per cent in 1955 and 17 per cent in 1961. The states' proportion dropped to 7 per cent in 1918 and reached a peak of 25 per cent in 1940.

The trend in dollar totals from taxes during the past half-century is very clearly upward, whether the different levels of government are considered separately or together. Total local government tax collections have risen from 2.0 billion dollars in 1916 to 19.8 billion dollars in 1961. For state government the increase during this period was from a much smaller beginning of .4 billion dollars to 19.1 billion dollars. The federal government, *Dollar increases at all levels* also collecting less than local governments in 1961, rose from .7 billion to 77.5 billion dollars in 1961. Total tax collections for all levels of government thus increased from 3.1 to 116.3 billion dollars in a little less than 50 years.

Before considering separately some of the more important taxes at the state and local level, it is important to note some of the constitutional restrictions — both federal and state — which limit the taxing power of state legislatures. The federal Constitution prohibits states, without the consent of Congress, *Federal restrictions on state taxation* from levying tonnage duties or placing duties on imports or exports. By implication, it prohibits a state from using its taxing power to evade constitutional restrictions. Thus, a state may not use its taxing power to impair the obligation of a contract or to violate the equal protection of law and due process clauses of the Fourteenth Amendment.

Many state constitutions restrict the taxing power far more than the federal Constitution does. Some place a maximum limit on the rate of taxation, especially property taxation. Many have tax uniformity clauses which, if strictly interpreted, mean more than merely fair play and equity in *Restrictions in state constitutions* taxation throughout the state, requiring that all property, personal or real, income-producing or satisfaction-producing, be taxed at a uniform rate. Such restrictive clauses may prevent a classified property tax, or progressive income and inheritance tax rates. Other state constitutions specifically prohibit certain taxes, such as an income or sales tax. In addition, most state constitutions stipulate the conditions under which the state or local governments may borrow money.

General property tax

As recently as the period immediately preceding World War I the general property tax was the principal source of revenue for state as well as local governments, accounting for more than one-half of all state revenue and virtually all local revenue. Now the general property tax has dropped almost completely out of the picture as a source of revenue for state governments, producing only 3.4 per cent of total state tax collections in 1961, with many states having abandoned it altogether. Or the other hand, the property tax remains the major source for local governments, accounting for 87.5 per cent of local tax revenues in 1961. The virtual disappearance of the property tax at the level of state government is attributable in part to the serious problems involved in the administration of this tax and its deviation from generally accepted principles of sound taxation.

Defects in the property tax

The property tax applies not only to *real* property, such as land, buildings, and other improvements, but also to *personal* property. Personal property consists of both *tangible* property, which includes things of intrinsic value such as jewelry, clothing, or automobiles, and *intangible* property, which includes evidences of wealth such as mortgages, stocks, bonds, and currency.

In actual practice, most personal property escapes taxation. Most locally elected assessors find it expedient to permit self-assessment in the case of personal property, placing a premium on the dishonesty or temporary loss of memory of the taxpayer. Even that property which does end up on tax rolls, real property for the most part, is notoriously under-assessed and unequally assessed, varying from as low as 10 per cent of its fair and reasonable market value to as much as 60 or 75 per cent — though not often the latter. Many other criticisms have been made of the property tax, but probably at the root of most of these criticisms is the outmoded structure of county governments in the United States, which remain the "dark continent of American politics" and which retain a firm grip on the age-old ways of assessing and collecting the property tax.

Possibilities for reform

What can be done about the sad state of affairs into which the property tax has fallen? One thing that has been done in many states is simply to abolish it as a source of revenue at the state level, leaving it exclusively for the local governments. For a time, this took away some of the incentive for one county to assess its property at a much lower percentage of true value than another. However, the steady increase in state aid to local governments, with larger grants to the poorer counties, has made it important to avoid rewarding a county which feigns poverty simply by reducing its property assessments. Thus the problem of equalizing assessments remains. Some things which could be done to improve the administration of the property tax include the improvement of recruitment and training of personnel, development of procedures which can be applied to achieve uniform results, and supervision of local assessments by the state revenue department or board of equalization. The property tax is a stable and productive source of revenue and such improvements in its administration could go far to reduce its defects.

The general sales tax

The general sales tax has come up rapidly as a source of revenue until it is now the principal revenue producer at the state level. It yielded more than 4.3 billion dollars in 1960 for the 35 states levying some form of general sales or gross receipts tax. In 1961 Texas became the thirty-sixth state to levy such a tax. It is a tax at uniform rates upon the sale of a wide variety of commodities. It may include personal services and may extend to transactions by wholesalers as well as retailers. Strong opposition to the general sales tax has come from those who point out that it is regressive in effect, imposing a relatively heavier burden upon the poor than upon the rich. Nevertheless, one state after another, in time of financial crisis, has looked in desperation to the example of West Virginia which in 1921 became the first to adopt the general sales tax as a major revenue source. In addition to its use by the states, it is levied by more than 300 cities.

Sales taxes on specific articles

Preceding the general sales tax in historical origin are the sales taxes on specific articles, such as gasoline, liquor, and tobacco. The gasoline tax has been adopted by every state and runs the general sales tax a close second in percentage of total tax collections. The tobacco tax accounted for 5 per cent of 1960 state tax collections, and taxes on alcoholic beverages brought in less than 4 per cent. All states have alcoholic beverage taxes, and 47 of the states levy a sales tax on the various forms of tobacco.

Income tax

Close to three-fourths of the states now have an income tax, but most of them have been enacted during the past two or three decades. Although Virginia had an income tax as early as 1843, it was not until Wisconsin adopted it in 1911 that it became apparent that it could be made administratively workable at the state level. It was the search for new revenue sources during the early depression years of the 1930's which led many other states to accept it. Although most of the states make it applicable both to corporations and individuals, a few limit it to one or the other. This tax conforms to the principle of taxation in proportion to one's ability to pay, even though the rates which the states levy are much less progressive than those of the federal government. It ranks third in importance as a revenue producer for the states, accounting for 18.8 per cent of their total tax collections in 1960, a moderate increase from 15.7 per cent in 1955. An increasing number of cities have begun to make use of an income or payroll tax, commonly using it as a device to tax

266   suburbanites who work inside the central city but reside outside.

Inheritance or estate taxes, although providing only about 2 per cent of total state tax collections, are levied by every state except Nevada. The latter state has not yet yielded to the "incentive plan" provided by the federal

Inheritance taxes

government in 1924 which in effect penalizes any state not taxing inheritances. Congress amended the federal inheritance tax in 1924 to permit deductions to be made from the federal tax, up to 80 per cent, if the state collects such a tax. Florida had no inheritance or estate tax for many years, much to the unhappiness of neighboring states which were losing wealthy retired residents to Florida, but in 1930 it finally levied an estate tax to claim the revenue which would otherwise go to the federal government.

There is no "business tax" as such, but a variety of taxes are levied on business concerns in addition to those on property and income. Special taxes are levied on incorporation or entry into the state based upon a variety of measures. The franchise tax is collected in every state but in revenue cannot compare in importance with the various consumer taxes. Unincorporated businesses are also taxed in special ways, the most common being the license to do business, whether for the barber, physician, peddler, newsstand, or drugstore. In addition to business taxes there are motor vehicle taxes — primarily licenses — and such levies as poll taxes, and severance taxes on the extraction of natural resources.

Federal grants-in-aid constitute important nontax revenue for state and local governments, totaling almost 7 billion dollars. (See Figure 14-2.) The fiscal importance of these federal grants is indicated by the fact that it

Nontax sources: federal grants in-aid

would have required an over-all increase of 19 per cent in state and local taxes in 1960 to replace this money if the grants had been eliminated. In more than a dozen states the increase in state taxes required to replace federal grants would have been above 50 per cent. The states of Wyoming and Alaska received more from federal grants in 1960 than they raised from state taxes. In contrast to this, the total of federal grants to state and local governments seems hardly more than a drop in the bucket in terms of the federal government's total financial picture, the 7 billion dollars granted in 1960 amounting to 9.0 per cent of its tax revenue or 6.9 per cent of its total revenue.

Although grants-in-aid are found in a wide variety of forms, the common characteristic of all forms is that the central government provides aid for a particular service without supplanting the recipient units of government

Nature and scope of grants

which actually perform the service. Grants are usually made in the form of money, although the early land grants were an exception, as are some present grants of agricultural commodities. Most grants-in-aid are continuing arrangements, but there have been a few single-action grants.

Although the federal grant program viewed as a whole may seem to be a

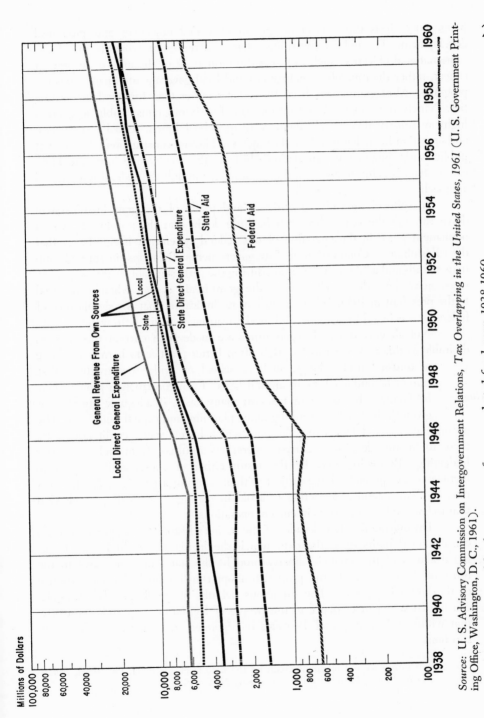

Millions of Dollars

Source: U. S. Advisory Commission on Intergovernment Relations, *Tax Overlapping in the United States, 1961* (U. S. Government Printing Office, Washington, D. C., 1961).

Figure 14-2. State and local government finances: selected fiscal years 1938-1960

hodgepodge, it is the natural outgrowth of varied objectives and piecemeal development. The federal government has used the grant primarily to achieve some national objective, such as to get the farmer out of the mud or to prevent cancer, rather than merely to help states and local governments finance existing programs. Most grants have been for services rather than for regulatory activities. Ninety per cent of all federal grants is for six programs: public assistance, highway construction, employment security, school lunch, school construction and operation in "federally-affected areas," and hospital construction. The largest public works program in our nation's history, the 40,000-mile interstate highway system, is being financed and administered through the federal grant-in-aid approach.

In spite of intermittent criticism and praise of the grant-in-aid system down through the years, there can be little doubt that the system has won a permanent place in the operation of our federal system. It is significant that the (Kestnbaum) Commission on Intergovernmental Relations, in spite of ominous sounds and a "show me" attitude during the early stages of its investigations, recommended no drastic changes in the grant-in-aid system when it reported to the president in 1955. There is little or no indication that the significance of federal grants-in-aid to our state and local governments is likely to wane.

Not all governmental expenditures are made from current revenues, as desirable as this may seem to be. It is often better practice to borrow for large or unusual undertakings, such as school or bridge construction, that *Public* cannot be budgeted on an annual basis. Even construction projects may *borrowing* be financed from current taxes in many cases, if adequate attention is given to the necessity for long-range planning and capital budgeting. The unfortunate cases of borrowing, the ones which hurt a state's credit rating, are those to finance deficits in current operations resulting from lack of proper budgeting. Borrowing may be the result either of statesmanlike action to finance an exceptionally large project without causing a greatly fluctuating tax rate, or of unstatesmanlike action to avoid increasing taxes during an election year to finance increased costs in current operations.

During the first few decades of the nation's history the states imposed no constitutional limits upon the debt which the legislature might incur. Legislative abuses of this financial liberty brought the states in some cases to the brink of disaster and led the people to adopt constitutional clauses restrictive of the borrowing power. The numerous defaults of the 1840's, for example, constituted sufficient evidence to the people of legislative ineptitude, or worse, that within a 15-year period 19 states incorporated such clauses in their constitutions.[2]

---

[2] For an interesting account of public credit on the state level, *see* B. U. Ratchford, *American State Debts* (Duke University Press, Durham, N. C., 1941).

In spite of state constitutional limitations on borrowing and on total debt,
state and local indebtedness has been increasing fairly steadily. Indebtedness of
all local governments is now close to three times as great as that of state
governments, although the ratio was more than seven to one in 1929. *Borrowing*
Local indebtedness increased from 11.6 billion dollars in 1929 to 51.2 bil- *totals and*
lion dollars in 1960. State indebtedness was 1.6 billion dollars in 1929 and *trends*
has risen more rapidly, percentagewise, to a total of 18.5 billion dollars in 1955.
Alarmists concerning public indebtedness should take comfort in the fact that
total state and local indebtedness amounted to a lower percentage of the "net
national product" in 1960 than in 1929.

Public borrowing is usually accomplished through bond issues, which
may be for terms of from 10 to 40 years or even longer. Longer terms are discouraged, because the interest to be paid over such periods becomes excessively burdensome, and because it is considered unwise to extend the *Forms of*
term of the bond beyond the anticipated life of the improvement which *borrowing*
the bond issue is to underwrite. Many cities today are paying interest and
principal on bonds for streets long since worn out and repaved.

The two principal forms of bonds are sinking-fund or serial bonds. In the
first type, a sinking fund is established with annual payments adequate for
payment of the debt on the date the bonds mature. The plan is not infallible,
however, as it is not unusual for states to delay their contributions to the fund
so that unsound debt management results. In the serial bond issue a certain
number of bonds mature each year and are paid off until all of the bonds are
retired. No sinking fund is required, and it becomes more nearly a self-enforcing
system for regular retirement of the bonded debt. The use of serial bonds is
generally replacing sinking fund bonds.

The bonds which governments issue may also be distinguished as general
obligation bonds and revenue bonds. General obligation bonds are supported
by the taxing power of the government concerned, thus constituting a
lien on the property of the taxpayers, while revenue bonds are retired *General obli-*
only from the revenues of a particular governmental enterprise, such as *gation bonds*
a city water department or power distribution department, or a state *vs. revenue*
toll highway. General obligation bonds tend to secure a lower interest *bonds*
rate, thus costing the taxpayer less, but in recent years their use has been ham-
pered by legal debt limits. Since the debt limits do not apply to revenue bonds,
issuance of the latter has become a common method of circumventing such
restrictions.

Other nontax revenues for state and local governments include income
derived from sale of portions of the public domain and from operation of various
public enterprises. Sale or lease of mineral rights, rental of camp sites, and
sale of timber from public land produce this kind of revenue. The principal

Other nontax revenues

state-operated enterprises providing revenue are alcoholic beverage, monopoly systems, toll bridges, and port facilities. A little more than one-third of the states now have entered the wholesale and retail liquor business. At the local level the municipally operated water systems, power distribution systems, and bus or trolley systems are among the most common public service enterprises.

Regardless of the level of government, the more generally accepted principles of sound taxation are the following: (1) the tax should have a reasonable relationship to one's ability to pay; (2) it should be a reasonably convenient tax to pay; (3) it should be characterized by certainty, that is, it should be generally clear to the taxpayer how much he must pay and the basis on which it is figured; and (4) it should be an economical tax to collect, requiring minimum administrative costs. Many of the problems of our tax systems stem from failure to measure up to these standards suggested by Adam Smith many years before our time. By these standards it must be recognized that the general sales tax and the property tax, the principal sources for state and local governments, respectively, can hardly qualify as "sound taxation." By the same token, the income tax, which plays a lesser role than those two on the state and local levels, nearly qualifies in all respects.

Principles of "sound taxation"

The quest for an improved tax structure for state and local government reveals many serious revenue problems. One of the most perplexing is the growth of double and overlapping taxation between the different levels of government. There was a time when revenue sources were rather clearly segregated for the federal, state, and local levels, so that each level of government tended to avoid disturbing the others. During the depression scramble for new revenues, however, the states invaded the federal government's field of income taxation, and the federal government invaded the states' field of gasoline taxation. Many more duplications followed, and it is extremely doubtful that it will ever be possible to segregate tax sources according to governmental level again. The principal alternatives currently being discussed by tax administrators are a system of federally-collected, state-shared taxes, or a system whereby each level would continue to collect its own taxes but make some reciprocal arrangement for distributing the revenue. The latter plan would not eliminate the cost of duplicating collection facilities, but it would avoid the dispute over possible surrender of the states' taxing power to the federal government.

Overlapping taxation

Many state and local governments are plagued with the problem of the "earmarking" of revenue sources for specific objects. Nothing can be more frustrating to effective budgeting efforts than a conglomeration of taxes which are required by law to be spent for specific purposes. The practice of earmarking has a very natural origin in the desire of a pressure group interested in a single function of government to secure with certainty more money for that particular function; e.g., to designate that all revenue from the gasoline tax be spent for highway purposes. It is also the only way, on *Other* occasions, to make a tax increase palatable to the public. Earmarked taxes *revenue* in the long run make it exceedingly difficult to adapt the revenue pro- *problems* gram to changing needs.

    Another problem facing every governmental jurisdiction is the extensive concession of tax exemptions, not only for educational, religious, and charitable institutions, but for other governments, homesteads, and veterans. Although such exemptions make the taxes higher for other people, they are defended as essential for the encouragement of worthy causes and seem to be well established. Some modification in practice has been obtained by means of voluntary "payments in lieu of taxes" by some govermental juridictions.

STATE-LOCAL FINANCIAL RELATIONSHIPS

    The picture of state and local finance is not complete without a few comments on trends in the financial relationships between state and local levels of government. During the past few decades, state supervision and control over local finances has been steadily expanded until it covers in *Scope of* varying degrees nearly all phases of financial administration. This may *state supervi-* include supervision of tax assessment and collection, limitations on the *sion of local* kinds and rates of taxes, control over budgets and expenditures, limita- *finances* tion on the procedure and maximum total of debt incurrence, supervision of accounts, conduct of audits, and financial assistance in the form of shared taxes or grants-in-aid.

    Of all of these areas of state-local fiscal relationships, undoubtedly the one of greatest change is that of shared taxes and grants-in-aid. Especially since the end of World War II, local governments have been caught in the squeeze between increased costs for public education and other func- *Shared* tions and the exhaustion of local taxing and borrowing powers. State *taxes and* legislatures have responded increasingly to pressure from local govern- *grants-in-aid* ments by voting new grants-in-aid and providing for state-administered, locally-shared taxes. A distinction is usually made between grants-in-aid and shared taxes, although the distinction occasionally becomes blurred. As a general rule, shared taxes have few if any "strings" attached and retain their identity as coming from a specific tax. Grants-in-aid are made for a particular activity, without regard for the origin of the funds, and frequently impose a matching requirement.

    In all, the local governments received 9.4 billion dollars from the states in 1960, almost one-fourth of the total revenue of the local governments in that

272   year. (*See* Figure 14-3.) Education has been the most important single object of state aid to local governments, with the purpose being to improve teachers' salaries, to construct buildings, and to improve standards in general. More than one-half of total state aid to local governments in 1960 — over 5.3 billion dollars — was for education.

Some impli-
cations of in-
creasing state
assistance

There can be no doubt that the substantial state assistance in recent years has resulted from such factors as the fiscal inadequacy of local units of government and the increasing demand for higher minimum standards of service within the various states. However, one question which has not been adequately answered as yet concerns the effect of this increased aid upon the degree of honest effort by local units to raise funds locally. Is the increased aid causing some cities and counties simply to reduce the financial effort they were formerly making? Some states have already found this to be true and have taken the next logical step of tying state assistance to a formula which measures local effort. This, of course, requires accurate state information on actual local assessment levels, and further centralization in state-local financial relationships is made inevitable. Related to this problem, but more fundamental in its implications, is the question of whether state aid is not actually serving to perpetuate marginal and submarginal units of government which are in serious need of consolidation or elimination.[3]

FINANCIAL PLANNING

The budget:
a financial
plan

Something must be said about the crucial role of financial planning or budgeting in state and local government. A budget is simply a financial plan, and the budgetary process is simply the planning process in public finance. It is the process whereby resources are apportioned among competing demands. If there is any single document which tells what a government plans to do, it is the budget. It is the major device through which responsible leaders in government plan and ultimately decide what facilities and services should be provided and when.

The budget is a twentieth-century phenomenon in America. New York City is credited with pioneering public budgeting in this country in 1907, followed by many of the states and larger city governments after 1910. The

---

[3] For detailed analysis of state-local financial relationships, see three studies by the U. S. Advisory Commission on Intergovernmental Relations: *Local Nonproperty Taxes and the Coordinating Role of the State* (September, 1961); *State Constitutional and Statutory Restrictions on Local Government Debt* (September, 1961); and *State Constitutional and Statutory Restrictions on Local Taxing Powers* (October, 1962).

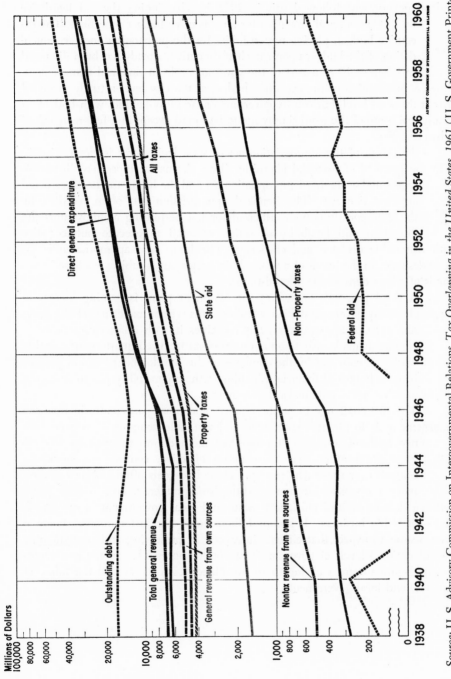

Millions of Dollars

Source: U. S. Advisory Commission on Intergovernmental Relations, *Tax Overlapping in the United States, 1961* (U. S. Government Printing Office, Washington, D. C., 1961).

Figure 14-3. Sources of local government financing: selected fiscal years 1938-1960

274 federal government followed suit in 1921 by abandoning the old legislative
budget system and providing for an executive budget procedure. The ex-

Growth of
the executive
budget

ecutive budget, placing responsibility for the preparation and recommendation of the budget upon the chief executive, already has been discussed
in Chapter 12 as a part of the governor's role in financial management.
Progress in adoption of the executive budget at the city level actually preceded
that at the state level, but county governments lag sadly behind, with budgeting
in any real sense of the word simply not to be found except in a few reorganized
urban counties.

The form of the appropriation act of state legislatures is closely tied in
with the problem of financial planning. Two alternative types have been the
segregated or itemized appropriation act and the lump sum or unrestricted

Itemized vs.
lump sum ap-
propriations

appropriation act. The itemized appropriation act, often required by
the state constitution, is criticized for not permitting administrators the
discretion and flexibility of action essential to execute public policy
with reasonable dispatch and efficiency. The lump sum appropriation is far
more desirable in the hands of a wise administrator but is subject to abuse in the
hands of a less dependable administrator.

A third proposal, known as the allotment plan, is gaining increasing
support in many governmental jurisdictions. This system makes use of the lump
sum type of appropriation, but combines it with quarterly or monthly

The allot-
ment plan

allotments made only upon approval of an itemized quarterly or monthly
work program. Again, the emphasis of this development in fiscal practice
is upon improved financial planning with responsibility placed upon the
chief executive of the state or local government.

The real challenge in public finance, and more particularly in financial
management, is to attain a reasonable and workable compromise between the
two goals of applying "business-like methods" to the management of

Two-fold goal
in public
finance

government affairs, yet maintaining effective, continuing, democratic
controls over those who govern. These two goals often pull our government in opposite directions, and the basic problem is how to effect peace
between democracy and efficiency. State and local government is not child's
play — it is big business. It spends billions now, not just millions. There is
every reason to expect that citizens interested in preserving and strengthening
the sub-national levels of government can build successfully on the movements
already begun toward weaving these two objectives together into the fabric of
our state and local governments.

Blakey, R. G. and Gladys M. C. Blakey, *Sales Taxes and Other Excises* (Public Administration Service, Chicago, 1945).

Buck, A. E., *The Budget in Governments of Today* (The Macmillan Company, New York, 1935).

Burkhead, Jesse, *Government Budgeting* (John Wiley & Sons, Inc., New York, 1956).

Commission on Intergovernmental Relations, *A Report to the President for Transmittal to the Congress* (U. S. Government Printing Office, Washington, 1955).

Council of State Governments, *Federal Grants-in-Aid* (Council of State Governments, Chicago, 1949).

Groves, H. M., *Financing Government* (3d ed.; Henry Holt & Company, Inc., New York, 1950).

Kilpatrick, Wylie, *State Supervision of Local Finance* (Public Administration Service, Chicago, 1941).

Lutz, H. L., *Public Finance* (4th ed.; Appleton-Century-Crofts, Inc., New York, 1947).

Maxwell, James A., *Tax Credits and Intergovernmental Fiscal Relations* (The Brookings Institution, Washington, D. C., 1962).

McKinley, J. R., *Local Revenue Problems and Trends* (Bureau of Public Administration, University of California, Berkeley, 1949).

Municipal Finance Officers' Association of the United States and Canada, *Financial Planning for Governments* (Municipal Finance Officers' Association of the United States and Canada, Chicago, 1949).

U. S. Advisory Commission on Intergovernmental Relations, *Tax Overlapping in the United States* (U. S. Government Printing Office, Washington, D. C., 1961).

―――, *Coordination of State and Federal Inheritance, Estate and Gift Taxes* (U. S. Government Printing Office, Washington, D. C., 1961).

―――, *Measures of State and Local Fiscal Capacity and Tax Effort* (U. S. Government Printing Office, Washington, D. C., 1962).

U. S. Bureau of the Census, *Summary of Governmental Finances in 1960*, August 18, 1961.

⋆ *15* ⋆

THE JUDICIARY

Courts constitute one of the three basic divisions of state government, as of the United States national government. The state judiciary may restrain or support the role of governor or legislature, approving or disapproving

Significance of state courts

policies through the exercise of the power of judicial review. More state laws have been set aside by state courts as contrary to state constitutions than have been invalidated by the United States Supreme Court under terms of the federal Constitution. Moreover, state judges are bound by the "supreme law of the land" clause of the federal document, regardless of state laws and constitutions, and they occasionally rely upon this provision for invalidating state action.

Along with the role of constitutional interpretation, state courts, centrally and locally, provide a wide spectrum of governmental contact for citizens. They exercise an important function in the affairs of men, often having the final word in regulating or umpiring the relations of man to man and of man to the state. Collectively they try many more cases than do the federal courts, and within any one state the state courts try more cases than do the federal courts within that state. They handle more human drama, whether the issue be property or crime. Theodore Dreiser's *An American Tragedy* reaches its denouement in a state court.

The broad jurisdiction of state courts in subject matter stems from constitutional and historical factors. In the American system of federalism as stipulated in the Tenth Amendment these courts are not restricted to delegated or enumerated powers, as is the federal judiciary. They have wide functions and responsibilities in the field of police power, which was described in the fourth chapter. Much more than the federal courts, they have served *Reasons for broad jurisdiction* as vehicles for transplanting and perpetuating the principles and practices of British jurisprudence in America, as is exemplified by the use of common law and equity and by the institutionalized justice of the peace. It is significant that the American Revolution wrought no fundamental change in our judicial institutions and ways of justice. The state courts became direct heirs of the colonial courts and grand-heirs of the British judiciary.

COMMON LAW AND EQUITY

The origin and development of our state systems of courts and jurisprudence cannot be understood without taking account of the growth, application, and meaning of the English common law, which has spread to the United States, Canada, and other countries. That body of law has vitally affected the legal commandments of all of our states except Louisiana, *The rise of common law* which was influenced by the Napoleonic Code and its antecedents. Even in Louisiana there has occurred a partial fusion of English and French doctrines, particularly in criminal law. It is difficult to convey in a few words the concept of common law as expounded by such men of legal learning as Coke and Blackstone in England and Kent, Story, and Holmes in America. Elements of the common law came into vogue as early as the thirteenth century through the formulation by judges of rules based on recognized customs common to the realm. These rules served for the trying of cases involving points and issues not covered by the prevailing statutes. The decisions and commentaries constituted efforts to apply established principles and common sense to civil and criminal matters. The system grew with time as judges relied upon former court opinions, thus adding precedent to precedent. This body of judge-made law had reached a high stage of crystallization when it became doctrinal baggage for export to America. But it had attained a wide scope which was to prove more suited to the functions of the state judiciaries than to the prescribed jurisdictions of our federal courts.

It should be noted that statutes, as they come into existence, take precedence over the common law in case of conflict or discrepancy. That has been

true in both England and America. Statutory law may duplicate, amplify, mod-
Common law ify, or displace common law. This encroachment varies among the states
and statutes according to the completeness or comprehensiveness of statutes and codes,
but common law seems never to perish. A change in common-law doctrine
by state legislation is exemplified in the industrial era by the legislative
requirement for compulsory compensation to workers for accidents incurred on
the job. The statutes relieve the employee of much of the burden of proving
damage and take from the employer much of the immunity handed down
through the common law of a simpler society. Modern state constitutions
also contain many provisions that deviate from the precepts of common law.
The common law, however, has strongly influenced the applied meaning of
state statutes and constitutions as interpreted by the courts, both state and
federal. State laws and court opinions have been upheld by the Supreme Court
of the nation on the basis of being in tune with the common law and thus
not violative of the federal Constitution. This point was set forth both before
and after the adoption of the Fourteenth Amendment.[1]

Both state and federal courts try cases in equity, although state suits of
this type are far more numerous. Equity applies to civil matters, not directly to
criminal cases. It too originated in England, and it arose through the crystallization of the common law by the judges. The rigidities of common law became
inadequate for settling unprecedented disputes and for dispensing preventive
or corrective justice not measurable in legal or monetary terms. For more flexible remedies Englishmen turned to their king, who found it convenient to
leave such matters to the royal chancellor, who thus became known as "the
keeper of the king's conscience." The practice expanded into a separate system
of jurisdprudence and came under the administration of a chancery court. The
development of this type of justice brought forth a body of chancery rules,
based partly on the principles of Roman law and Canon law. The system
eventually facilitated the just settlement of complicated cases without the use
of juries. Equity expanded by the time of Shakespeare to the importance of
the common-law jurisprudence, and it accompanied the latter system to the
New World, where both were to become essential features of the American
pattern of justice.

Equity proceedings in England and America today are circumscribed
and regulated by statutory provisions, but nevertheless they serve modern needs
flexibly. Equity hearings and decrees frequently offer the best or only means of
satisfying the miscellaneous interests of a group of adult and minor heirs to
an estate not covered by a will. Equity writs of injunction serve definite pur-

---

[1] Supreme Court opinions on this point are cited in Chapter 4 in the discussion of police
power.

poses of preventing property damage by one person to another. In past years such writs have been applied rather extensively to labor disputes, but this use has become somewhat limited by legislation, especially by laws permitting collective bargaining and peaceful picketing. It should also be remembered that equity decisions may be appealed from the trial court of a state to higher courts for proper reasons and even to the United States Supreme Court, should a national constitutional right be involved. Equity suits in federal courts between citizens of different states may also be appealed on constitutional grounds. It might be said that the equity process is, in a sense, extra-legal, but, in its flexibility, it may not become illegal or unconstitutional. Only a few states, Arkansas, Delaware, Mississippi, and Tennessee, have separate chancery courts and chancellors. The others have law and equity jurisdictions in the same courts, as is true of the federal judiciary. Thus equity has been considerably reduced as a separate procedure in America, although certain of its features remain significant. It is an integral part of the system of justice.

THE JUDICIAL HIERARCHY

The state judiciary roughly duplicates the federal judiciary in hierarchical features of centralization and decentralization. No sharp example of autonomy is to be found at any point from bottom to top, although there are wide variations of actual merit and method among the states and among the courts. The trial judge with the smallest territorial basis of selection and jurisdiction is always an arm of the law and the state. In that capacity *One process, central and local* he is subject to higher authority in his dispensation of justice. He is part of a system which is one in its central and local applications. The prosecuting "party" of a murderer in any original trial court, for example, is not the "county" or the "city" but the "state." The highest points of constitutional interpretation may be raised and applied or rejected in the trial court, with or without the possibility of appeal.

The state judicial systems embrace three or four classes of courts, as shown in Figure 15-1, with additional types for special purposes in the larger states and in important urban centers. At the bottom are minor courts presided over by justices of the peace, other local magistrates, or police *Lowest of the classes of state courts* judges, frequently without the qualification of formal legal training. These courts function without juries and dispose of no major matters, either civil or criminal, although they may conduct preliminary hearings to determine whether an accused person shall be held in jail or placed under bond for a jury trial for homicide.

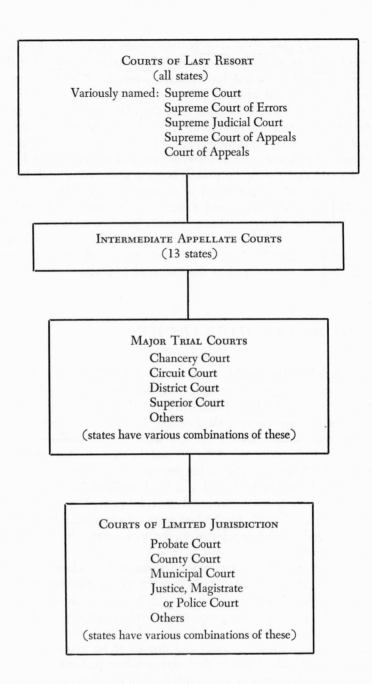

Figure 15-1. The state and local judicial hierarchy

The justice of the peace ("J.P.") once performed useful functions in rural neighborhoods and villages prior to the existence of speedy transportation and communication. But this part-time officer has been subjected to criticism in recent years, sometimes for operating "marriage mills" at convenient points or near a state line and sometimes for improvising a fee racket. There have been complaints of cooperation between justices of the peace and rural constables in "speed traps" for collecting advance fees and fines from passing motorists who could not tarry for court proceedings in a country home, store, or shop.[2] Since the party starting a suit before a justice of the peace often wins the case, it has been cynically observed that "J. P." signifies "judgment for the plaintiff." The makeshift minor courts, rural and urban, have bred distrust in many instances for reasons of inadequacy, subservience to the fee system, and connection with unsavory politics.[3] The dissatisfaction has led to their being supplanted or supplemented in a number of states and cities with more systematic courts and professional judges that exercise somewhat greater authority and serve larger territorial jurisdictions. These improved tribunals have such designations as municipal courts, general sessions courts, and courts of common pleas.

Between the courts of minor jurisdiction and the appellate courts are the regular trial courts, or tribunals of "first instance," in which most American suits of importance begin and end. Cases are sometimes shunted to these intermediate courts from the minor courts, and a number of cases are appealed for one reason or another to higher courts, but the work *Intermediate or regular trial courts* of these state courts stands as the main component of our administration of justice. Officially these courts are classified as "circuit," "district," or by other designations. Juries are used in these courts, and each trial is presided over by a single judge. The geographical jurisdiction is customarily limited to a county or city, although in rural regions of limited needs a judge may "ride circuit," holding sessions in county after county in rotation. Lawyers may also "ride circuit" along with the judge, as did Abraham Lincoln. There is often a separation of functions in populous centers between criminal and civil courts, regardless of whether equity is in a different jurisdiction. Where there is too much work for one judge, a court may have two or more divisions, with a trial judge for each. The judges are almost invariably qualified lawyers, both because of technical necessity and because bar associations insist upon professional training for the bench.

---

[2] For an account of one "speedy" trial in which a homemade grocery table served as a judge's bench, *see* James P. Economos, "Justice, Safety, and Traffic Courts," *State Government*, XXV (January, 1952), pp. 9-11, 20-21.

[3] In Leon County, Florida, for example, candidates for justice of the peace have won regularly on the platform promise that they will do nothing in the office.

Every state has a highest court of appeals, which is generally called the Supreme Court, although other titles are used in New York, Massachusetts, and a few other states. This court consists of from three to nine judges,

Higher courts the number often being five or seven. Most of its work is devoted to cases coming up from lower state courts, although it has original jurisdiction in special types of cases in a few states. It sits without a jury. In many states it has the responsibility of formulating rules of procedure for the whole judicial system of the state within the framework of constitutional and statutory provisions. In a few states the supreme court may be required to render advisory opinions on vital matters, such as the constitutionality of pending legislation, if requested by the governor or the legislature. There is no appeal from this state court, except to the United States Supreme Court on federal constitutional grounds. To relieve the highest court of excessive burdens, many of the more populous states maintain other courts of appeal, which constitute a class or grade above the trial courts and have the final word of review in many cases or types of cases. Large questions of state constitutionality, however, can hardly be put at rest until the supreme court renders opinion. The high state courts may be called upon to test the constitutionality of statutes and the legality as well as the constitutionality of administrative performance.

Some idea of work loads of the highest appellate courts in the states is afforded by a survey conducted by the Chief Justice of the Supreme Court of Florida. The average number of cases disposed of by supreme courts during 1954 was 334.4, with 187.8 by written opinions and 146.6 by orders on motions, certiorari or otherwise. The total number of cases disposed of by the Florida Supreme Court was 1,251, the heaviest load of any state, which explains the interest of the Florida Chief Justice in such a survey. In six states the supreme court handles less than 100 cases during the year.

Special courts of different kinds are to be found on the fringe of the hierarchical system, notably in highly urbanized regions. These courts may handle such matters as domestic relations, juvenile delinquency, proba-

Special courts tion of wills, small claims, and the like. Much of their work is of an informal nature and partly free from battles by attorneys, although through proper channels it may be reviewed for possible reversal by higher courts. It is also true that in modern state government, as in the national government, there are administrative bodies with power to conduct hearings and render decisions which are binding in the regulation of civil affairs unless invalidated upon review by a judicial court. Administrative tribunals and administrative law are essential to all levels of government. This type of adjudication may be applicable to such problems as tax disputes, intrastate or local utility rates, urban zoning, licensing and location of liquor stores, enforcement of health and sanitary measures, abatement of smoke evils, and removal of fire

states, including Missouri and Tennessee, although most of their functions are
not judicial or even quasi-judicial in nature.

THE JUDGES

About three-fourths of the states choose judges by popular election, which
is in striking contrast to the method used for the federal bench. Many bar
associations oppose selection by popular vote as an interference with
the independence and continuity of the judiciary. But lawyers individu-   *Method of*
ally and collectively often exercise a strong influence for the election of   *selection*
qualified judges. Many groups, including workers, farmers, and crusaders
for direct democracy, insist upon making the choice by popular vote as the best
means of checking the influence of special interests. A few states have election
of judges by the legislature, and others have appointment by the governor with
confirmation by legislature, senate, a council, or a commission. California
adopted a constitutional amendment in 1934 to combine the methods of appointment and election for putting judges on the supreme and appellate courts.
Under this plan a vacancy is filled for an initial term through appointment by
the governor with the joint approval of the chief justice, another judge, and
the state attorney general. Successive terms are won by election, with no opposing candidates on the ballot but with voters having opportunity to approve or
disapprove. In a way the judge runs on his record, and, if he is rejected,
gubernatorial appointment of another judge is in order. The Missouri constitution, adopted in 1945, contains provisions approximating the California plan but
requiring the governor, in making an appointment, to select from a list of three
submitted by a commission consisting chiefly of judges and lawyers of the state
or district.

The state constitutions and statutes give rather limited attention to judicial qualifications aside from matters of age, citizenship, and residence.[4] There
are general or indefinite requirements that judges have legal knowledge
or experience, but these standards are more contingent upon popular   *Qualifica-*
and professional opinion than upon technical stipulations. In many ways   *tions, tenure,*
and in many states it is essential that a prospective judge have political   *and compen-*
insights and connections to win a place on the bench. The political fac-   *sation*
tor does not in itself exclude professional competence.

The length of terms for which judges are chosen varies among the

---

[4] For individual state requirements *see* Table 3: "Qualifications of Judges of State Appellate
Courts and Trial Courts of General Jurisdiction," *The Book of the States, 1962-63,* p. 125.

284 states and also sometimes among classes of courts. For the highest court the term is only two years in Vermont, six years in eighteen states, and seven or more in the others. It is twenty-one years in Pennsylvania, until the incumbent is seventy years old in New Hampshire, for life in Massachusetts, and for the "term of good behavior" in Rhode Island. It is customary in many high and low jurisdictions to re-elect short-term judges who have given satisfaction and retained the confidence of the legal profession.

The salaries of judges are fixed sometimes by constitutional provisions but more frequently by statutory enactment, and the scale in most states ranges rather generally below the compensation in the federal judiciary. The annual compensation for members of the highest court ranges from $10,500 in Vermont to $36,500 in New York. Many states pay the chief justice more than the associate justices, with $500 and $1,000 being the most usual additional compensations. Salaries received by intermediate appellate judges range from $12,500 in Tennessee to a maximum of $36,500 in New York. Justices of the peace and certain other minor court magistrates rely, of course, upon fees for compensation.

Judges, like other officials, may be removed in one way or another for sufficient cause or demand, although this is not a common occurrence. There is the slow and cumbersome method of impeachment. Eight states have the possibility of the recall of judges by popular election. Some states provide for removal by the governor at the request of the legislature, and in others a joint resolution by the two houses of the legislature is effective for removal. Judges, moreover, are not technically immune from prosecution for crime. Removal has in rare cases been accomplished indirectly by legislative manipulation of a judge's jurisdiction.

Removal of judges

JUDGES AND POLITICS

Are judges just as much "in politics" as mayors, councilmen, or governors? To say that we have "a government of laws and not of men" often leaves the impression that courts and judges perform a cut-and-dried operation of applying unambiguous and impartial law to human situations in a way that places it outside the boundaries of the arena of politics. An increasing number of political scientists are moving in the direction of correcting this highly unrealistic picture of the judicial process by studying the courts as a part of the political process. This does not mean that there are no distinguishing features of the judicial process and judicial institutions, but it does mean that judicial decisions involving money, office, votes, services, life,

Courts in political process

and liberty, determine in part who gets what, when, and how, in our society. The courts are thus unavoidably enmeshed in politics.

Professors Sayre and Kaufman, for example, in their excellent book *Governing New York City*,[5] describe the governmental process in New York City as a "contest for prizes," and point to the judges as important participants in the contest. Their role is usually, though not always, that of umpire rather than of player, but the outcome of a contest is in large measure dependent on what the umpires do. Sayre and Kaufman point out *Judges as political umpires* that in settling disputes judges do much more than affect the immediate litigants — they are determining the "rules of the game" for all kinds of present and future power struggles involving upsetting state legislation, local legislation (much more frequently), or administrative rules, regulations, and specific actions. They settle election contests with far-reaching effects and decide whether to invalidate inequalities in legislative representation. The rewards in the power struggle to influence the decisions of government — the "contest for prizes" — are distributed in a manner strongly affected by what judges say the rules of the game are.

Judges in and from New York City, 315 of them, are involved in the political struggle in another way, according to Sayre and Kaufman. They are the formal appointing officers for the nonjudicial staffs of the courts, involving several thousand employees. Many of these are subject to civil service and other legal and practical restrictions, but the judges still run a sizable job-dispensing operation and many of the jobs are considered to be highly desirable.

Even though judges are in many respects like all other participants in the contest for the stakes of politics, Sayre and Kaufman warn against the possibility of overstating the case and of overlooking some important differences. For example, the Anglo-Saxon tradition of juridical independence is reflected in many devices which reduce considerably the accountability of the courts to elected legislatures and executives and grant some degree of immunity to pressure and retaliation. Furthermore, the avenues of access to, and bargaining with, judges by various political groups are restricted by such factors as the formalized procedure of adjudication, the strong weight given to legal precedent, and the ethical norms of the profession. But, on the whole, Sayre and Kaufman are more fearful that the student of politics will fail to recognize judges as participants in the contest for the rewards of politics, than that he will fail to recognize certain differences between judges and the various other participants. *Political distinctives of judges*

---

[5] Wallace S. Sayre and Herbert Kaufman (Russell Sage Foundation, New York, 1960). The authors have relied heavily on their discussion found on pp. 528-531 and 536-538. *See also* W. J. Keefe, "Judges and Politics," *University of Pittsburgh Law Review*, XX (March, 1959), pp. 621-631.

The importance of viewing the behavior of judges in the broad political context is illustrated by the recent study of the political involvement of judges in Louisiana by Herbert Jacob and Kenneth N. Vines.[6] In studying the selection of judges in Louisiana, Vines discovered that over 80 per cent of the judges had held political office (usually elective) before coming to the court. Although the state constitution requires that judges be "learned in the law" and that they have experience in legal practice in the state, only a minority of them had actually pursued a substantial career in private law practice. Instead, Louisiana judges came to the bench after political careers as state legislators, as state law enforcement officials or as parish and municipal officials. Vines concludes that these judges bring their political values and viewpoints of state politics to their performance on the courts.

Although a tradition of reelection and long tenure in most cases has given Louisiana judges relative freedom from the cares and costs of campaigning, there is still the practical possibility that a judge will have to face opposition if he does not give continuous and careful attention to state politics. Professor Vines discovered that the Louisiana Supreme Court had abundant opportunities to "take sides" in intra-party and factional disputes in that one-party state, with a total of 204 cases involving such matters as elections, the appointment and removal of governmental officials, and disputes among governmental agencies during twelve selected years. In deciding these cases the Court made important determinations affecting the allocation of power and personnel in state politics. When Huey Long successfully dominated the state from 1928 to 1935, the State Supreme Court helped him at critical points by deciding in favor of Long-backed candidates in election contests and by backing Long in disputes with state officials.

Two cases will help to illustrate the relation of the Louisiana Supreme Court to the creation and domination of the Long faction. The first was decided following the death of one of the anti-Long justices, and the Court helped maintain a voting majority of four justices favorable to the Long faction. Governor Huey Long is reported to have promised John B. Fournet a place on

---

[6] *Studies in Judicial Politics* (Tulane Studies in Political Science, Vol. VIII, New Orleans, 1963). The authors are indebted to Professors Jacob and Vines for permission to make liberal use of their material for purpose of this summary. Two selections by Vines, "The Selection of Judges in Louisiana," and "Political Functions of A State Supreme Court," and one by Jacob, "Politics and Criminal Prosecution in New Orleans," have been used in these paragraphs.

the Supreme Court as a reward for having helped quash the removal proceedings against Long when Fournet was Speaker of the House of Representatives. The death of an incumbent judge, Winston Overton, just two days before his bid for reelection in the Democratic primary in 1934, provided the opportunity, but not without some unusual assistance from the Court. The only opponent to Overton was Thomas Porter, an anti-Long candidate, and a Louisiana statute clearly prohibited the entry of any new candidate within three days of the election. The election was held as scheduled and Porter received well over a majority of all votes cast. Instead of declaring Porter the party nominee, however, the party committee called for a second primary one month later. Fournet qualified for this primary and defeated Porter by a slight majority. The State Supreme Court became involved when Porter sought an injunction against Fournet's running. With three judges dissenting the Court refused to grant the injunction, claiming that the Court had no jurisdiction and that the party committee's decision had to be followed.

Some four years earlier, the Louisiana Supreme Court helped Long keep control of the state after he moved from the governor's office to the United States Senate in 1930. Following Long's election to the Senate, Lieutenant Governor Cyr took the oath of office for governor as provided in the state constitution. Long did not accept this, however, and had Alvin King, president *pro tempore* of the Senate, take the oath for governor. Cyr filed suit for intrusion into office and received a favorable decision in district court, but the State Supreme Court overruled and held that the courts were without jurisdiction in the dispute. Judges were thus the instruments for Long to continue his domination of the office of Governor.

A different facet of Louisiana judicial politics, the politics of criminal prosecution in New Orleans, was examined by Professor Jacob. A study of political influences bearing upon judicial discretion in the disposition of criminal cases revealed different patterns of leniency, depending on which political faction was in power. Jacob discovered that a district attorney backed by the traditional political machines of New Orleans, the "Old Reglars," was tougher and less lenient in his handling of cases than a district attorney supported by a middle-class reform movement. Also studied was the impact of increased racial tensions on the prosecution of Negroes in New Orleans between 1954 and 1960. Based on dismissal of cases because of non-prosecution or dismissal of the affidavit, Jacob discovered not only that Negores were treated more harshly than Whites in the criminal courts, but that the harshness of the treatment (compared with the treatment of White defendants) increased as racial tensions grew between 1954 and 1960. Thus, whether one looks at intra-party factional politics or at racial politics, one can expect to find extensive judicial involvement.

Judges are officially the central figures in courts and court proceedings, but the drama of justice requires a cast of many other characters for formal performance in all hearings above the level of minor tribunals. It might

Participants and roles

be said that in trial courts the participants ordinarily appear in person, but in an appeal the higher courts rely primarily upon transcription, examining the script, as it were, and hearing arguments over its correctness in applying legal or constitutional standards to the factual story. The initial suit opens with one party against another, that is, plaintiff versus defendant or "state" versus defendant. Normally each party has a lawyer or a team of lawyers, the prosecuting counsel in criminal cases being known by some such title as "district attorney," "state's attorney," "solicitor," "attorney general," or "assistant" officer. Each party is entitled to have witnesses, whether experts or laymen with direct knowledge. Affiliated with the courts are enforcement or administrative officers to serve papers, announce court, maintain order in court, guard prisoners, bring in witnesses, and wait upon juries. In important trials, exclusive of equity cases, there are trial juries unless the right of jury hearing is mutually waived. There are clerks and stenographers to handle records, documents, and correspondence.

The right of trial by jury has been handed down for centuries. It is designed to insure amateur and indigenous qualities in the performance of justice and prevent external or tyrannical professionalism. The trial jury,

The trial jury

known as petty or petit jury, usually consists of twelve persons drawn from the jurisdiction of the court. Potential jurors are selected somewhat by lot from a large list of eligible voters, freeholders, or taxpayers, with some gaining automatic excuse or discretionary excuse from the judge for occupational or urgent personal reasons. Further screening is undertaken for a particular trial, eliminating those with formed opinion or known prejudice in the case as well as those with interest in the outcome through kinship or other close affiliation with a party to the suit. An avowed opinion against capital punishment bars one from service in a murder case which might lead to capital punishment. Finally each side is allowed a limited number of peremptory challenges for disqualification, and this prerogative is often exercised to the full extent by the counsel on each side in important criminal trials. Days may be required in the process of selecting and qualifying a jury for a highly publicized criminal trial. The trial jury exercises the important role of passing upon the truthfulness and weight of the evidence for the determination of the verdict, with guidance from the judge as to the meaning of the law and the significance of the evidence in so far as the jury finds it to be true. The jury, not the judge, establishes guilt or innocence and in civil cases grants or denies the claims of the plaintiff. Traditionally the jury verdict must be unanimous, but unanimity has been removed in several states for civil cases and in a few for criminal cases. A few states require a unanimous verdict only for sentence of death or life imprisonment. If a jury fails to reach a required unanimous verdict, the result is a mistrial, with choice to the prosecution of retrying or dropping the case.

The grand jury is also a feature of our system of justice as inherited by way of the English common law. Its work actually precedes that of the trial jury in criminal procedure. It is selected in a manner much like the method used in choosing members for the trial jury but without challenges as to qualification by opposing attorneys. It varies in size up to 23 members. It is *The grand jury* an investigative body, not a trial board, and much of its work is performed in secret. It looks into specific and general matters of crime and misconduct within the jurisdiction of the court it serves. Since its members are normally laymen, it is largely dependent upon the prosecuting attorney for advice and guidance in considering cases for possible indictment or "true bills." It may indict a person and thus require a trial without unanimous agreement. It may report a "no true bill" for a person held for grand-jury investigation if the facts clearly point to such a conclusion. The Fifth Amendment of the national Constitution provides that no person, except in the armed forces, "shall be held to answer for a capital, or otherwise infamous crime, unless on a presentment or indictment of a Grand Jury." The Supreme Court of the United States has never held this provision to be a requirement that the states restrict themselves to indictment by grand jury, however, and many states provide constitutionally for trial of criminal cases on an affidavit or information by the proper prosecuting attorney in the jurisdiction of the trial court. Thus the grand jury is only an alternative method of bringing an accused to trial in a number of states, especially for cases not involving felony. The grand jury works somewhat less expeditiously than an expert prosecuting staff in rounding up criminals, and, whatever the method of presentment, the accused still has the protection of a jury trial and a defense lawyer when he appears in the "court of first instance." The grand jury may still perform useful functions in checking the work of local government officials, whether for indictment, general criticism, or exoneration. In special or unusual crime waves, special grand juries may be called into session for speedy action, and such bodies sometimes take effective initiative in civic house-cleaning, working secretly to provide a grist of indictments for the mills of the trial courts.

The appellate process is by nature a technical game, and its roster of participants consists primarily of judges and lawyers. A losing or disappointed party to a civil suit or a party convicted in a criminal case may wish to appeal to a higher court. The "state" or prosecution has no appeal from

290 a verdict of acquittal, although a chronic criminal may be held for a subsequent trial for another alleged violation. The seeker of appeal may not get it, and, if he gets it, he may still lose his case. His counsel prepares motions and

Hearings papers for appeal and argues the case in the higher court, if the latter

of appeal allows the hearing for legal or constitutional reasons. The appellate court always functions with a plurality of judges, and one of them writes the opinion of the court in each case. There may be dissenting opinions. The court may uphold or reverse the ruling of the lower court and put an end to the case unless there can be appeal to a still higher tribunal. It may find errors in the lower ruling and send the case back for a retrial by the first court. Its disposition of the case accords with its interpretation of points involved in the record, the law, and the constitution. There have been exceptional instances of cases reaching appellate courts two or three times, with trial and retrial in the court of original jurisdiction. Much of this type of procedure, however, has been eliminated in civil cases by the systematic administrative handling of many damage matters, as in the automatic compensation for injury to industrial or corporate employees. Civil cases are sometimes settled "out of court" by mutual agreement between the parties, thus terminating the litigation. But the "law's delay" still characterizes our state justice in more ways than one, as will be subsequently noted.

PROBLEMS OF MODERNIZATION

The judiciary constantly faces problems of adjusting old principles to new conditions, of maintaining old wine in new containers in a new age. Such problems confront the courts more than other branches of government,

Dilemma of and they confront the state courts more sharply than they confront the

old and new federal judiciary, which has concern with a smaller variety of cases and powers. The problems of adjustment are also more difficult for the state systems, because the state courts function generally within a much greater circumscription of constitutional and statutory regulations than do the federal courts. These outside regulations may tell the state judge not only what to do but how. The state trial judge normally exercises somewhat less mastery in directing and expediting proceedings in his court than a comparable member of the federal bench. He plays a much less forthright role than a regular trial judge in England, where court procedure has been simplified and technical manipulations have been reduced. The American state courts offer more opportunities than others for field days for lawyers, with comparative costs of litigation running high, particularly in long-drawn-out civil cases. Yet lawyers have voiced much of the criticism of outmoded features of these courts.

Movements for statutory or constitutional reform or improvement of the judicial systems of the several states have been in evidence throughout most of the present century. The early call for overhauling organization and procedure was high-lighted by Roscoe Pound, a Nebraska lawyer and law professor, who was to continue and expand his influence for improvement after becoming dean of the Harvard Law School. Criticisms and proposals *Reform movements* for change have come from the American Bar Association, the American Judicature Society, the publications of the American Academy of Political and Social Science, and other sources. Social workers and social reformers have exerted pressure for certain types of judicial specialization, notably in the realm of juvenile delinquency, in which Judge Ben Lindsey became a constructive influence and authority through more than a quarter-century of service as juvenile court judge in Denver.[7]

General dissatisfaction over enlarged and crowded dockets has lent emphasis to the demands for injecting leavening elements of expertness, unity, and system into the state judicial processes, especially in populous urban regions. More than half of the states, with Ohio and Massachusetts as pioneers, have set up judicial councils, somewhat analogous to legislative councils, to make studies and recommendations with a view to improving or streamlining court organization and procedure. These bodies usually consist of judges and lawyers and function mainly for the purposes of research and advice, thus offering hope on a limited or gradual scale.

New Jersey has been a leader in seeking to coordinate and modernize the units of its judiciary through constitutional provisions adopted in 1947. As a result of these changes that state has a regular administrative director of courts, and his annual reports provide information on the status and dockets of the courts from local to supreme. The constitutional changes have tended to speed the work of the higher courts, although backlogs of cases still confront lower courts, particularly with respect to civil cases. That the effort is worthwhile is indicated by Chief Justice Vanderbilt's statement that "in our Supreme Court we have reduced the time between argument and decision from an average of 105 days under the old system to 31 days under the new, and in our intermediate court of appeals from 113 days to 23 days."[8] At the end of the third year under the new constitution the number of cases on the

---

[7] See R. G. Caldwell, "The Juvenile Court: Its Development and Some Major Problems," *Journal of Criminal Law, Criminology and Police Science,* LI (January-February, 1961), pp. 493-511.

[8] Arthur T. Vanderbilt, "Clearing Congested Calendars," *NACCA Law Journal,* XIV (November, 1954), p. 335.

calendar of New Jersey's courts was the smallest in 20 years despite increases in the number of cases being initiated.

The results achieved in New Jersey are attributed by Chief Justice Vanderbilt to several factors. Popular sentiment demands high performance of the courts, and judges and lawyers strive to realize the popular expectation. Introduction of a simple system of courts is almost equally fundamental. Assignment of judges to the kind of judicial work in which they excel, whether it be appellate, criminal, civil, equity, probate, or matrimonial judicial work, maximizes the performance of the court system. Assignment or administrative transfer of judges to jurisdictions where there is work to be done permits concentration upon congested dockets and insures that one judge does not sit idle while another has too much to do. The requirement of reports on work accomplished and distribution of summary reports to all the judges helps to realize a fair division of work among the judges. Standardization of rules through promulgation by the highest court of rules applicable to the entire judicial hierarchy reduces confusion and abuse of procedural technicalities. The use of pretrial conferences serves to reduce the element of surprise in trials and also to produce voluntary settlements by agreement of the parties. Finally, limiting recourse to a referee reduces the time required to secure a judgment.[9] New Jersey's achievement warrants careful study.

Growth of business seems to entail growth of litigation. Thomas E. Dewey, when governor of New York, asked for a "truly twentieth-century court system" to clear up a lamentable congestion of delayed cases. Important authorities have observed that constitutional provisions must be combined with constructive legislation, competent judges, and prevention of cases through zealous administration of the law, if justice in the states is to be adequate and expeditious.[10]

The states are finding various ways of reducing or avoiding the prolonged handling of controversies by the regular courts. A number of states have provided for the issuance of declaratory judgments by the courts for the benefit of potential litigants, who may thus get points of law determined in advance on the basis of facts presented and come to common understanding without further suit. Small claims courts reduce the cost and trouble of litigation for miscellaneous small matters, at the same time reducing the dockets for the regular courts. Legal aid clinics in important large

Auxiliary features

---

[9] Arthur T. Vanderbilt, *The Challenge of Law Reform* (Princeton University Press, Princeton, 1955), pp. 85-93.

[10] *See* A. Leo Levin and Edward A. Wooley, *Dispatch and Delay* (Institute of Legal Research, University of Pennsylvania Law School, Philadelphia, 1961); S. H. Hofstadter, "Traffic Jam in the Courts," *New York Times Magazine*, February 21, 1954, p. 14; and E. S. Greenbaum, "A Plea for Court Reform Now," *New York Times Magazine*, February 27, 1955, p. 12.

centers facilitate the adjustment of claims and cases for citizens of limited means, sometimes using voluntary leg-work by law-school students. Improvement, clarification, and acceptance of performance by regulatory bodies may prevent many court cases from arising, both civil and criminal.

The corrective processes, to which the courts contribute, are not necessarily ended when judges, juries, and appellate bodies dispose of cases. Performance in compliance with a court decision may be a long or difficult role for parties concerned, whether in civil or criminal matters. A long term in prison may be the inevitable consequence of arrest and conviction for serious crime. In such a situation, the executive arm of government, which brought the accused to trial in the first place, undertakes to administer the punishment to the guilty according to law and court decree. Thus both court and administration are concerned with the old and new problem suggested by the slogan, "Let the punishment fit the crime." It is not easy to solve this problem for the quarter of a million inmates of the state and federal prisons of America. How and how much to modernize penitentiaries are as difficult questions as those of improving the state courts. Prison riots on a large scale have occurred in the sixth decade of the century in such different and distant states as Massachusetts, Michigan, Texas, and Washington. Preventing violations of law, apprehending violators, and managing convicted violators are large orders in our government and society. These subjects are discussed in Chapter 19, after some of the unique aspects of the units of local government are considered.

"Let the punishment fit the crime"

SUPPLEMENTARY READINGS

American Bar Association, *Journal* (Chicago).

America Judicature Society, *Journal* (Chicago).

Beaney, W. M., *The Right to Counsel in American Courts* (University of Michigan Press, Ann Arbor, 1955).

Cardozo, B. N., *The Nature of the Judicial Process* (Yale University Press, New Haven, 1921).

Frank, Jerome, *Courts on Trial* (Princeton University Press, Princeton, 1949).

Haynes, Evan, *The Selection and Tenure of Judges* (National Conference of Judicial Councils, Newark, 1944).

Hurst, J. W., *The Growth of American Law* (Little, Brown and Co., Boston, 1950), Chapters 5, 12, and 13.

Kaplan, Benjamin and Livingston Hall, eds., "Judicial Administration and the Common Man," *The Annals of the American Academy of Political and Social Science,* CCXXCVII (May, 1953).

Keeney, B. C., *Judgment by Peers* (Harvard University Press, Cambridge, 1949).

Mayers, Lewis, *The American Legal System* (Harper & Row, Publishers, New York, 1955).

Murphy, Walter F., and C. Herman Pritchett, *Courts, Judges, and Politics* (Random House, Chicago, 1961).

Pound, Roscoe, *Organization of the Courts* (Little, Brown and Co., Boston, 1940).

Radin, Max, *The Law and You* (Mentor Books, New York, 1948).

Vanderbilt, Arthur T., *The Challenge of Law Reform* (Princeton University Press, Princeton, 1955).

Vanderbilt, Arthur T., *Minimum Standards of Judicial Administration* (New York University Law Center for the National Conference of Judicial Councils, New York, 1949).

* 16 *

LOCAL GOVERNMENT:

THE COUNTY

LOCAL GOVERNMENT has come into view frequently in the preceding chapters, for that government is constitutionally and functionally interwoven with state government in important ways, including local channels to federal agencies and federal funds. No unit of government is an island and inter- *Local govern-* governmental relationships become more extensive and intensive with *ment not* modern times and modern needs. The student should guard against *isolated* any isolationist concept of the local unit or process as attention is centered somewhat briefly upon some of the more specific and unique features of local government.

The county, with its political subdivisions, is geographically the most universal jurisdiction of local government in America; and, with the New England town, it exemplifies a heritage and a continuity from British and colonial self-government. All states but three are composed of *Importance* counties, the exceptions being Connecticut, Rhode Island, and Alaska.[1] *of the county*

---

[1] Counties in Connecticut, already in a state of "withering away," were abolished in 1960. "Boroughs" are authorized in Alaska, but had not been established by 1962. The use of the word "borough" was for the purpose of getting away from the implication that it is primarily created for state purposes, rather than for local purposes, and to avoid "importing" to Alaska the judicial decisions relating to counties in other states.

Another exception is found in Louisiana, where counties are called parishes, but the exception is more in name than in actual character. The inhabitants of most cities are also inhabitants of counties and subject in various respects to county authority.

Although common to virtually all the states, the county is by no means a standardized unit of government. It has consistently and historically been more important in institutional life in the South than in New England, partly for reasons of geography and different types of colonial civic development. The states of other regions have tended somewhat to fluctuate in the development of county government between the southern emphasis and the New England de-emphasis.

In the absence of urbanization, the county most likely becomes an important core of grass-roots government and community. The county as a political entity and going concern registered a definite imprint in the wide hinterlands as those regions provided territory after territory and then state after state in the dozen decades following the adoption of the Constitution. In these hinterlands the county, with subdistricts and townships, served as a base for bringing people and government together in such essential matters as maintaining law and order, providing schools and roads, holding elections, and legalizing land deals, mortgages, wills, and marriages. The competition between communities hoping to be designated the county seat was sometimes fierce, because such stakes as the county fair, increased retail trade, and greater social and political prestige usually went to the winner. The county constitutes the locale of identification for many Americans of rural residence or background, as is illustrated by the memoirs of former President Truman and others. The counties themselves bear many beautiful Indian names as well as names of early national leaders, notably of Washington, Jackson, and Jefferson. A vast amount of American human history is associated with counties and county annals.

The more than 3,050 counties in the United States, an average of 65 per state, are difficult to defend in terms of administrative or economic needs. Many of them are small in area or population or both. In days of transportation by horse and buggy over dirt roads it was a civic convenience to have the county small enough in area so that the courthouse would be not much more than a dozen miles distant from the homes of any of the citizens of the county. The farmer was thus able to do the morning milking, hitch up the buggy, drive to the county seat, transact business, and return to his home in time for the evening milking. The creation of new counties in formative eras was also sometimes stimulated by the expectation of increased opportunities for public office, improvement contracts, and official printing. Historical evidence points to such perquisites as having motivated the establishment of counties in different states of the South and Middle West. These

Multiplicity of counties

considerations and other factors, constitutional, political, and traditional, offer
almost insurmountable obstacles to the consolidation of counties, even in Texas
where there are more than 250 or in Georgia where there are more than 150.
Except in rare cases, the arguments of administrative efficiency and economy
are of no avail for the reduction of the number of small counties throughout
the land.

The counties bear testimony that Americans have been largely a people
of rural birth or heritage despite the present high proportion of urban population. Although many counties are sufficiently populated to be classed
as urban or semi-urban, a majority of them are primarily rural or small- ***Rural***
town in composition and retain patterns of government that were created ***heritage***
by an agrarian society. Counties provide civic links between rural citizens
and the outside world. County government continues to reflect no little acceptance of the idea of performance by laymen or amateurs rather than by experts
or professionals, unless politicians be classed as professionals. Much of it is
more personalized than systematized. Ministering to the public needs of a
rural county differs from the governmental administration of a big city about
as much as the management of an old-fashioned country store differs from the
operation of a modern department store or chain market system in a metropolitan center. Rural county officials, like rural merchants, are doubtless convinced
that they need not conform completely in organization or administration to the
city model in order best to serve their purposes.

Many rural-oriented county governments in recent years have been confronted with the perplexing fact that most of their citizens are city residents
rather than "country folks." Some 300 urban counties now govern more
than two-thirds of our nation's population. The movement from rural ***Schizophrenia***
to urban areas in the United States between 1950 and 1960 caused ***in the urban***
1,536 counties to lose population, while close to the same number were ***county***
increasing in population and becoming more urban. (*See* Figure 16-1.) Urban
and suburban demands for municipal services have caused many governments to develop a kind of split personality with a variety of symptoms of
rural-urban cleavage. The rural heritage and outlook of the county is not easily
or quickly cast off, with a resultant schizophrenic urban county today behaving
much as "new wine in old wineskins."[2]

Counties, unlike cities, are not incorporated, and, unlike states, have no
sovereign powers. With few exceptions, there is no chief executive corresponding to a mayor, city manager, or governor. Almost universally the main governing authority of a county is a body of elected members with the official title of

[2]*See* William N. Cassella, Jr., "County Government in Transition," *Public Adminis*
tration Review, XVI (Summer, 1956), pp. 223-231.

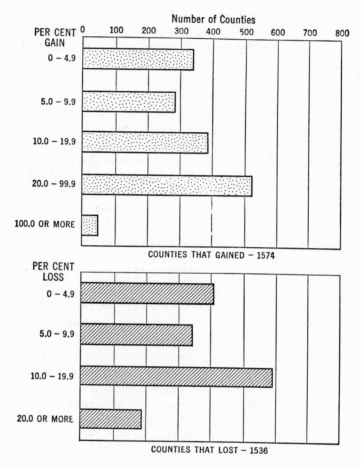

Source: U. S. Bureau of the Census, U. S. Census of Population, 1960.

Figure 16-1. Number of counties by per cent of change in population: 1950-1960.

"board," "court," "commission," or other title. The number of members ranges mainly from three to nine but extends up to 30 or more in some instances

Main features and officers of county government and more than 100 for Wayne County, Michigan, in which Detroit is located. The members hold such titles as "commissioner," "supervisor," or "magistrate," and, in Louisiana parishes, "police juror." The presiding officer has no regular vote or veto, and his status as chairman is decided sometimes by the members and sometimes by the voters. He has a measure of administrative authority in applying the decisions and orders of the body.

LOCAL GOVERNMENT: THE COUNTY

The chairman in a few states has the title of "judge of the county court," as in the case of Harry Truman when he headed the governing board of Jackson County, Missouri.

The county board is both a policy-making and an administrative agency. It normally has responsibilities for the construction and maintenance of county buildings and roads, the management of miscellaneous equipment and property, and the letting of contracts on behalf of the county. It has important financial powers and duties, subject to constitutional and statutory provisions. It often has actual or adjustment powers with respect to tax rates and assessments. It may have regulatory jurisdiction over various matters. The place of the county in wide functional processes is touched upon in other chapters, including those on highways, education, agriculture, courts, and law enforcement, as well as more general subjects.

UNDERSTANDING THE COUNTY BOARD: A CASE SUMMARY

Understanding how the county board behaves is not easy for the student of local government, and understanding *why* is even more difficult. An analysis by Professor Wilder Crane of his experiences as a member of the Chippewa County (Wisconsin) Board of Supervisors should help the student to understand why many county boards seem to be automatic rubber stamps on the "really big issues," while endlessly debating and bickering over picayune, insignificant matters.[3] In his first meeting as a member of the 45-member county board, Supervisor Crane was "completely confused at first by the process . . . of having a clerk drone through the reading of various legal-sounding documents followed by a roll call in which everyone was expected to say 'aye' when his name was called." He was initially assured that these matters, related to determining the budget, setting the tax rate, enacting ordinances, and authorizing payment of claims, had been investigated by committees prior to the board meeting. However, after serving two two-year terms he still had not realized his ambition to learn what the board was actually called together to approve. He was even more disturbed to know that few of his colleagues had the desire to know what they were validating with their "aye" votes. His initial comfort in the assurance that at least the committee had looked into these matters was shattered by his serving on committees "whose

Reflections of a County Board Member

---

[3] This case summary is based on the article by Wilder W. Crane, Jr., "Reflections of a County Board Member," *The County Officer,* XXI (September, 1956), pp. 202-205, and is used in this condensed manner by permission.

sole function was to devote hours to passing hundreds of documents around a table for the signature of each member."

Supervisor Crane finally decided that his first impression of confusion was more accurate than he had realized. In reflecting on why a county board meeting had "come to be regarded by its members as a process of ratifying fate," he gave three reasons. (1) The board is required to spend so much time approving purely ministerial, routine matters, such as claims already paid, that there is a predisposition to rubber-stamp even those matters over which they could exercise discretion. (2) Some matters are so complex, and involve such long documents in abstruse legal phraseology, that few board members understand them and most board members are predisposed to cover their ignorance by voting "aye." Thus the highway department is in effect regularly delegated the authority to spend hundreds of thousands of dollars for equipment because of a complicated revolving fund for machinery, whereas many board members would quibble over delegating their authority to make $30 purchases because a $30 purchase is understandable. One of the most enlightened debates of the Chippewa County Board preceded a vote on closing the courthouse on Saturdays. (3) Finally, Crane felt that federal and state grants-in-aid had resulted, in effect, in abdication of county control over welfare and highway programs because of non-discretionary regulations prepared in the state and national capitals.

Causes for confusion

Assuming the likely prospect that Wisconsin will keep its large county board system, what could be done to alter the pattern of the board's simply "ratifying fate"? Professor Crane suggests that intelligent reforms "would be directed toward duplicating the conditions which characterized the discussion of office hours in the courthouse for more important matters." Two elements characterized the debate on the Saturday closing of the courthouse — clear-cut awareness that the matter is within their authority, and an understanding of the issue. To accomplish this result, Crane recommends such procedural reforms as relieving the board of much of its routine, purely ministerial work, and several devices for assisting board members to understand the more important policy questions to be decided. Concerning grant-in-aid programs he concludes that the county would do well to withdraw authority "over matters which it cannot effectively control."

Reducing routine, and increasing understanding

OTHER COUNTY OFFICERS AND AGENCIES

Turning from the county board to the other county officers, those who are generally elected include the sheriff, tax collector, tax assessor, treasurer, county attorney, coroner, and school board. A number of states provide for the election of a county school superintendent, but many having this officer provide for his appointment by the county school board. The county must have a clerk or officer to keep official records as well as to record deeds, mortgages, marriage certificates, wills submitted for probate, and other legal instruments. This officer may also have charge of issuing such licenses as those for marriage, conducting particular businesses, owning automobiles, and other matters unless provision is made for special agencies to handle them. He sometimes serves as secretary of the governing body, which may appoint him if he is not an elective official.

It would be impossible to list all types and titles of officers or agencies in the thousands of American counties. No county or state contains all varieties. Counties have created or expanded agencies to distribute funds under state and federal programs, as, for example, in the field of welfare. Many populous counties have separate officials or establishments for specialized functions, which may lie within the province of the central governing body in the smaller counties. Examples are election commissions, planning commissions or offices, budget and accounting authorities, and boards for reviewing tax assessments. There may be a health board or health officer, according to the size of the county. It may also be necessary to have a county engineer for duties in connection with roads and public buildings. The engineer or a county surveyor may be called upon to establish land lines for real estate owners. Many of the miscellaneous functions of government in small counties are performed by part-time officers, whether the officers are elected or appointed. This is particularly true of the coroner or medical officer, and the prosecuting attorney in a rural county may carry on a private law practice along with his official duties.

Miscellaneous officers and agencies

The counties contain many thousand political subdivisions, such as districts, precincts, and townships. The township, as developed in a number of states from New York to the Dakotas, reflects a mixture of the New England town and the southern county. As a civic unit it must not be confused with the "township" as a land measurement and identification term handed down from the federal public land office, although the civic and the land units may sometimes coincide.

Political subdivisions

These sub-units of different labels serve as geographical centers or areas for schools, elections, road work, tax administration, jurisdiction of justices of the peace, and the like. A great proportion are rural. The tendency is for these units to become more and more mere outlets for the administration or distribution of county government. In the past many have had internal civic activity, but they have all but lost community identity through consolidation of schools, discontinuance of magistrates' courts, and the transference of district controls to the central government of the county. With speedier transportation and communication than in early days, rural people easily turn to officials at the county courthouse for matters of local government instead of using or supporting neighborhood functionaries for such purposes. The federal government has incidentally conformed to the changing pattern in discontinuing most rural post offices and providing mail service through rural free delivery.

In the general centralization process, functions pass, in part, from state to nation, from county to state, and from community to county, with nothing left for the last outlying civic unit to absorb or centralize. With this loss of neighborhood identity the county has a greater role than ever in serving rural constituents, developing wider community interests, and facilitating citizens' participation in government.[4]

COUNTY REFORM EFFORTS

For decades the county has been criticized as the scene of the most backward and inefficient administration of government, as was pointed out in the first chapter of this text. It is criticized for having an unsystematized jungle of offices without a definite executive authority, for having too many elective offices, and for being at the mercy of "courthouse rings" in the distribution of patronage and contracts. In many counties fees instead of salaries still constitute coveted features of important offices, sometimes providing the object of bitter contests between rival groups. Conditions, on the whole, are not so unsavory as they have been. But, aside from questions of abuse or graft, county government is too often in serious need of constructive reform to improve or increase its role in public service, to secure a higher degree of administrative efficiency, and to avoid waste of the taxpayers' money. With a few exceptions, modernization or reorganization of county government has trailed that of city, state, and national units.

Criticism of county government

The proposal for improving county government through consolidation of the smaller counties reached the stage of serious discussion about 1930 and was given attention by a few state leaders, including Al Smith when he was governor of New York. A few state constitutions permit consolidation. But results have been rather meager. Tennessee eliminated a little county, merging it with Hamilton County, which contains the city of Chattanooga. Georgia reduced the number of its counties from 161 to 159, one of the mergers being in the Atlanta metropolitan area. Consolidation

The county consolidation movement

---

[4] The problem of rural community decline is discussed by H. C. Nixon, *Possum Trot* (University of Oklahoma Press, Norman, 1941). Several states have abolished township governments or reduced them in number.

of particular functions or departments of two or more county governments has occurred in a few instances through legislative or contractual arrangements. Several counties in New Jersey, for example, have a joint sewage disposal system. Minnesota permits consolidation of health departments of counties as well as of cities and counties. During World War II southern counties sometimes pooled activities or services under the impact of national defense establishments. But the general status and identity of the numerous counties are little disturbed.

The overlappings between county government and city government in the same geographical areas raise many problems and stimulate many proposals in the fields of law enforcement, education, taxation, public utilities, and other matters. In New Orleans there is one administration *City-county* for the city and the coterminous parish of Orleans. In particular cases *relations* in a few states cities have been detached from counties for governmental purposes, as will be described in the chapter on metropolitan problems. Consolidation of functions and offices occurs more frequently, however, than the complete merging or the complete separation of city and county units. Rural and suburban citizens, along with their political spokesmen, hesitate to surrender their county prerogatives to city regimes, and thus they limit the streamlining of city-county government. Local political machines not infrequently play significant roles in the harmonious and discordant relations between city and county governments. City-county relationships are discussed in greater detail in relation to metropolitan problems in Chapter 18.

Counties normally have not been governed under charters or by chief executives, as have cities. But proposals to put county administration under stronger executive control have met with a measure of success, especially in highly urbanized counties. In some counties the cumbersome *Improvement* governing board has been replaced with a small commission of members *in adminis-* elected at large instead of by geographical divisions. Virginia authorizes *tration* the popular election of a chief executive, and a few counties of that state have made use of this provision. Some states — Virginia among them — permit counties to have managers chosen by the governing boards.[5]

An increasing number of urban counties in the country have adopted the manager or chief executive type of government, and some use a modified or limited example of the plan, as illustrated by the role of a "chief administrative officer" in the counties of Los Angeles and San Diego in California. Whereas a manager possesses direct, individual authority over all administrative affairs, the CAO is the agent of the governing board, appointed by it, and

---

[5] See G. W. Spicer, *Fifteen Years of County Manager Government in Virginia* (University of Virginia, Charlottesville, 1951).

performing in the name of the board the administrative duties assigned to him by the board. The CAO generally has more restricted powers reflecting the board's unwillingness to relinquish control over such matters as the appointment of personnel, but practice in given jurisdictions may blur theoretical differences between his position and that of a manager.[6] Petroleum County in Montana is a conspicuous example of a small rural county with manager government. McMinn County in eastern Tennessee came under a special manager plan through special state legislation in consequence of a serious incident at Athens, the county seat, on the night of the local election in 1946, when an armed posse of aroused citizens intervened to secure a fair count of the ballots and to dislodge what they considered to be an entrenched political machine.

Constitutional barriers in many states make county-manager rule impossible or difficult. Urban counties here and there have reorganized their government on an executive basis through the process of special legislation, and others, by law, regulation, or practice, have turned the headship of the governing board into an approximate executive office. There has been less demand in counties than in cities for state-wide provisions for local home rule to permit administrative reorganization.

Over-all merit systems exist in only a small percentage of the nation's counties, and what little progress there has been in this respect is to be found in the populous or urban counties or in administrative operations subject to state and federal standards. A few states have provisions for state assistance or supervision in administering local merit systems on a county optional basis. Among these states are New York, New Jersey, and California. An example of the merit system under special or local legislation is to be found in Jefferson County, Alabama, which contains the city of Birmingham. In many rural or isolated counties it would be impossible, even with full legal or constitutional power, to inaugurate a real merit or personnel policy without reliance upon imported experts and applicants. But rural folkways may permit the development of a rule-of-thumb competence that smacks neither of expertness nor of pure spoils.

Merit systems

The funds flowing annually through the government of a large county today approximate the amount required in a year by the United States government when George Washington was president. The counties which have improved their personnel and executive systems have also generally modernized their financial management, giving attention to such features as budgeting, accounting, and central purchasing as well as more efficient

County finance

---

[6] *See* J. C. Bollens, *Appointed Executive Local Government: The California Experience* (Haynes Foundation, Los Angeles, 1952), Chapters 1 and 5, for a consideration of the theoretical and practical differences between these two offices in the light of Californian experience.

methods of taxation. The California county of Los Angeles, with a larger annual budget than that of the city of Los Angeles, is one of those that might be cited for more effective financial organization. Many counties, however, remain behind the times in financial structure, except for accountability and regulations enforced in connection with the use of funds from the state or federal government.

Much of the revenue for county expenditures consists of allocations from federal grants or from state taxes, notably from state sales taxes, for the support of public schools and other purposes.[7] The trends toward centralizing the financing of phases or projects of local government are examined elsewhere in chapters on state and local finance and functions. In this centralized process a poor county with a relatively large population may receive more funds from the state treasury than its taxpayers pay into that treasury, while the citizens of a wealthy county pay state taxes in excess of the receipts from that state government by their county government for public purposes. This public equalization is somewhat similar to the policy of the national government in much of its aid to the states.

In addition to actual money, counties get other types of aid and technical assistance from their state governments. State planning agencies often provide useful information and technical advice to counties and cities. So do state offices concerned with schools, libraries, welfare, highways, parks, conservation, and other activities. Such assistance sometimes comes from the national government also, as exemplified in agricultural service, school lunch programs, welfare, and FBI cooperation. The Tennessee Valley Authority is a regional agency of the national government which has pioneered in different ways in cooperating with counties and other units and institutions in extending technical service and assistance.

Counties are subject in many ways to the impact of the changing states and the changing cities. County government, like the area in which it operates, is less isolated and less autonomous than once was the case. Although it retains a heritage of self-rule from other centuries, in much of its contact with the governed in our time it functions partly as a sort of middle agent for dispensing public services as prescribed and provided by larger centers of authority. It is other-directed as well as inner-directed, passive as well as active with respect to its role and destiny. Its defenders would contend that, in the interest of balanced governance and local initiative, those larger centers should guard against neutralizing all the power and responsibility for decision at the

Retaining the old along with the new

---

[7] *The County Officer*, journal of the National Association of County Officers, published a revised "Federal-Aid Guide" in February, 1962, describing some 17 programs of federal aid for which counties are eligible. The revision was made because of "unprecedented demand" for an earlier Federal-Aid Guide printed in 1958.

COUNTY REFORM EFFORTS

county level in sacrifice to the gods of efficiency. By so doing, it may be possible to preserve a flexible union of tradition and progress at this grass-roots scene of government.

THE NEW ENGLAND TOWN

A vestige of direct democracy

As indicated earlier, the importance of the county as a unit of local government varies between geographical regions; New England is one region in particular where another governmental unit is closer to the people and more prominent in the public mind than the county. This unit is the New England town, long cited by philosophers as the ideal form of direct democracy, as distinguished from representative democracy. The term "town," as used in this part of the United States, refers not only to an urban area but also to the surrounding rural area, and its origins go deep into the colonial heritage of New England. The early settlement pattern of small villages surrounded by farms, coupled with common problems of severe winters and potential Indian attack, resulted in the creation of "natural" governmental areas with boundary lines generally dictated by those of the economic, social, and "military" community. This is considerably different from township boundary lines which have so often followed the arbitrary square pattern of the surveyor's lines.

Town meeting government

Although not created as municipal corporations, the New England towns have been given municipal-type functions from time to time by state legislatures, as well as certain judicial functions. The "trademark" of the New England town is the "town meeting" of all qualified voters, an institution which levies taxes, makes appropriations, determines basic policy, and elects officers. The annual town meeting is traditionally held in March, with such additional meetings as may be necessary. Besides electing the board of selectmen and the town clerk, it directly elects many other officers, though not so many as in the days when fence viewers, surveyors of hemp, surveyors of boards and shingles, sealers of leather, cutlers of staves, hogreeves, and scavengers were elected.

Modern variations of town government

The town meeting has lost much of its virility and feasibility in many areas because of urbanization, apathy, and the unwieldy size of such a meeting if all qualified voters should actually attend. Several variations in this form of government have been adopted in different areas, such as a *representative* town meeting based on a limited number of voting delegates but with continued right of all citizens to attend and participate in debates. An increasing number of towns have adopted a modification of the council-manager plan by providing for a town manager, chosen by and responsible to the board of selectmen. The pressure on the towns to provide new services and perform new functions has resulted in not infrequent legislative action to sew new patches and appendages to this old institution which is seeking to adjust to an era of rapid change.

SUPPLEMENTARY READINGS

Alaska Legislative Council and the Local Affairs Agency, *Final Report on Borough Government* (Local Affairs Agency, Juneau, Alaska, 1961).

Bebout, John E., *Model County Charter* (National Municipal League, New York, 1956).

Bollens, J. C., *Appointed Executive Local Government: The California Experience* (Haynes Foundation, Los Angeles, 1952).

Bromage, A. W., *American County Government* (Sears Publishing Company, New York, 1933).

Commission on Intergovernmental Relations, *An Advisory Committee Report on Local Government* (U. S. Government Printing Office, Washington, 1955).

County Officer (National Association of County Officials, Washington, D. C., monthly).

Gittell, Marilyn, "The Metropolitan County in New York State," *The County Officer*, 27 (February, 1962), pp. 60-61, 99-101.

Lancaster, L. W., *Government in Rural America* (2d ed.; D. Van Nostrand Co., Inc., New York, 1952).

National Civic Review (National Municipal League, New York, monthly except August).

Pate, J. E., *Local Government and Administration* (American Book Company, New York, 1954).

Snider, C. F., *Local Government in Rural America* (Appleton-Century-Crofts, Inc., New York, 1957).

Spicer, G. W., *Fifteen Years of County Manager Government in Virginia* (University of Virginia, Charlottesville, 1951).

Wager, Paul, ed., *County Government Across the Nation* (University of North Carolina Press, Chapel Hill, N. C., 1950).

Wells, R. H., *American Local Government* (McGraw-Hill Book Co., Inc., New York, 1939).

★ *17* ★

LOCAL GOVERNMENT: THE CITY

T HE AMERICAN city is a modern example and adaptation of an old pattern..
There were organized centers of people, wealth, and culture in ancient Egypt,.
Phoenicia, Greece, and Italy, where the Romans effectively applied the·
An ancient   institutional concept of the corporate municipality.[1] Cities and city states;
pattern   of later ages provided checks or fortresses against feudalism and servile·
society. Transoceanic transportation and commerce stimulated a new·
urbanism and a new capitalism in the Western world after the discovery of a
great frontier by Christopher Columbus. Dominant cities like London and Paris
became capitals of great national states which supplanted the political power
of a feudal network of landed lords and vassals. The city, in western Europe
and eventually in America, came to be associated with sophistication and progress,
even with the hope of democracy.

Yet agrarian gentlemen were often inclined to pass unfavorable judgment upon the man-made concentrations of trade, industry, and society. Thomas
Jefferson recognized differences between rural and urban ways of life, consid- ·
ering the former as the more natural and the more conducive to happiness and
hoping that his countrymen would never "get piled upon one another in large

---

[1] *See* W. B. Munro, "City," *Encyclopaedia of the Social Sciences* (The Macmillan
Company, New York, 1930), III, pp. 474-482.

cities, as in Europe." This Jeffersonian viewpoint was prophetic of later cleavage and friction between "city slickers" and rural "hicks" and of subsequent difficulties in maintaining mutually satisfactory relations between urban and rural constituents. The city-county cleavage continues even in the face of the increasing synthesis of rural and urban living under modern conditions, including common facilities of transportation and communication.

City government in America is an intensive and really expansive pattern, but primarily it supplements rather than supplants other patterns. It lacks the feature of sovereignty of state or nation. It lacks the national, state, and county characteristics of geographical coverage, being applicable only *A supplementary pattern* to spots on the continental landscape. The municipal corporation is *tary pattern* called into being when a community desires certain services or controls not normally provided by the county or other units of local government. It has been subjected wisely and unwisely to external centralized controls, sometimes at the dictate of rural political pressure.[2] It has been frequently subjected to stresses by the rapidity of urban or metropolitan growth, by the mobile influx of masses of nonvoters or passive voters, and by the resulting creation of problems faster than they could be solved.

City government, under these conditions, has evolved its own politics and political machines, types which were to be limited and modified by civic reforms, constitutional change, and reorganizational legislation, but nevertheless were to remain as unofficial essentials of the general pattern. American municipal government has registered vast improvements in both ethical and administrative standards since James Bryce wrote of its conspicuous shortcomings or since Lincoln Steffens and other muckrakers wrote of its corruption. But city political machines have undergone processes of refinement rather than of death.

CITY CHARTERS

American cities are incorporated under charters, or organic documents, which provide for boundaries, governmental powers and functions, methods of finance, election and appointment of officers and employees, and miscellaneous matters. Certain of these provisions in reality authorize a city *General* to exercise governmental functions in the name of the state; others confer *features* proprietary power. A city in its proprietary capacity, as operator of waterworks and other utilities, bears points of resemblance to a private company. In connection with such proprietary functions, a city is not immune to suit by private persons for claims or damage.

---

[2] *See* the discussion on this point in Chapter 3.

Municipal charters largely consist of laws which have been adopted by legislatures under constitutional authority or of local provisions adopted under legislative and constitutional authority. Different portions of a charter may represent adoptions at different times and in different ways. The portions may or may not be assembled in one book, but they are often voluminous, New York City's running to several hundred pages. City charter powers, furthermore, must be interpreted and applied in the larger contexts of state and national powers. They are not to contravene the constitutional rights of persons, for example, or to offer unreasonable obstruction to the national regulation of interstate commerce.

Charters are sometimes classified according to the methods by which they are formulated and put into effect. These methods of adoption may be indicated be designating charters as special-act, general-act, home rule, classified, and optional. Different methods or combinations of them may be used in the same state and cumulatively for the same city. There is, furthermore, no necessary difference between one method and another as to the actual form of municipal government resulting from the process. A mayor-council government, for example, might function under a charter adopted or modified by any method or any combination of methods.

Types of classes of charters

The special-act charter is of long standing and is still widely used, involving a piece of legislation naming a specific city and prescribing its charter. It is not subject to any compulsory consideration of general standards of uniformity for municipal government in the state. Within constitutional limits and political sanctions, this charter process permits the widest variations among the cities of a state. It has been criticized by municipal reform groups for more than a century as being too much at the mercy of vindicative political machines controlling the legislature, as leading often to extensive logrolling manipulations among the legislative delegations from the important cities of a state, and as consuming a large amount of the official time of lawmaking bodies without attracting the serious attention of legislators or citizens in general. Cities resented and sought to resist what they considered to be unwarranted interference by the state legislature in the purely local affairs of individual cities.

Special-act charters

The general-act charter grew out of this dissatisfaction with special-act charters, with some states (Ohio and Indiana as early as 1851) outlawing special legislation by constitutional amendment. Under this technique general municipal legislation became a sort of standard charter for all the cities of a state, at least for the regular functions of local government. As a scheme for correcting the abuses and haphazard nature of special-act charters, it proved objectionably rigid and failed to allow for local differences in needs and desires of cities. In practice the general laws were frequently sup-

General-act charters

plemented by exceptions or modifications through special legislation. The mixture of general and special features offered one way of avoiding too little and too much uniformity between cities.

Other ways to achieve a blend of order and flexibility were sought in plans for classified and optional charters, especially where constitutional provisions severely restricted special legislation. In order to get around constitutional requirements for charters by general legislation, many states provided for charter differences on the basis of the population of the city. *Classified and optional charters* The classified system provides for a series of general charters, with each class applicable to all cities within a prescribed population range. If a leading city is in a distinct census class by itself, it may have the equivalent of a special charter without the name or constitutional obstacle. In some cases the courts have been so generous in approving single-city population classes that the practice of passing special-act charters has in effect been smuggled back into the state legislature.

The optional charter system is somewhat like the numbered combination of offerings on a restaurant menu. The state, perhaps through constitutional provisions, offers a number of standard form charters, allowing a municipality its choice from the published menu. The alternatives usually include the mayor-council, commission, and council-manager forms of government, plus certain variations of these forms. New Jersey in its Optional Municipal Charter Law of 1950 established an interesting procedure for municipalities considering adoption of optional plans. The law provided for election of a charter commission, the function of which is to study the form of government of the municipality, to compare it with other forms available under New Jersey law, and to recommend and explain to the community the option most suitable to its needs. The optional process is actually an exercise of limited municipal home rule. As in other processes, special legislation may be permissible and necessary or desirable to amplify or supplement optional charters, notably for large centers in highly urbanized states.

Home rule, as the term indicates, is designed to confer powers of initiative upon the local political unit with respect to the establishment or modification of the framework of local government. This incidentally reduces the burden of the state legislature in the sphere of local legislation. Home *Home rule* rule may result from constitutional power or legislative enactment or both, and it may apply to city charters as well as to particular changes in municipal-county or county government, including the consolidation or joint operation of political subdivisions. Legislative home rule is a less secure grant of power to municipalities than constitutional home rule, since any subsequent legislature could retract the grant if it so desired.

More than half of the states have general, limited or conditional provisions for city home rule, and some two-thirds of the cities over 200,000 in population have home rule. The movement has been rather intermittent since Missouri adopted a constitutional measure for such government in 1875. Home rule movements were most active at about the turn of the century and prior to World War I. Thereafter interest declined until the period following World War II when it registered a strong upsurge. Several states, among them being Georgia, Louisiana, Maryland, Rhode Island, and Tennessee, adopted constitutional amendments in the 1950's to permit or increase home rule in their cities. Cities with home-rule charters are found chiefly in the West, the Middle West, and the state of New York, with New England and much of the South relying on the older legislative methods of managing city charters.

Some states have constitutional provisions making all cities eligible for home-rule charters. Others have arrangements for applying the system to cities of specified population range, as over 3,500, over 10,000, or over 50,000. *Scope and limitations of home rule* Some states require gubernatorial or legislative approval to make the adoption of home rule effective for a municipality. Michigan authorizes a governor's veto of home rule adoptions. Sometimes home-rule constitutional provisions are not self-executing without legislative action, which may not be forthcoming, as was discovered by Philadelphia which had to wait 27 years for legislation implementing the "permissive" amendment.

The expansion of home rule is partly checked for political considerations, sometimes by party interests and pressure groups with more power in the legislature than in the city. An agrarian legislature may hesitate to reduce its power over a large city of a different political complexion. Urban legislators are often sent to the state capital from counties rather than from cities. They may relish the continuous exercise of local power through special legislation, preferring not to grant home rule. Many cities may not feel "threatened" by the state legislature, particularly when the controlling local faction is a part of the controlling group at the state level.

Moreover, home rule, when granted, is never absolute and never establishes a "free city." It may stimulate local democracy, but it provides no necessary reduction of state administrative centralization, which may render any city financially dependent regardless of its type of charter. Other aspects and difficulties of home rule for cities and other units will be indicated in the next chapter, dealing with metropolitan problems.

FORMS OF CITY GOVERNMENT

Every American city charter, however adopted, provides for one of three general forms of municipal government, although for each form there are adaptations or variations. The three, in chronological order of origin, are the mayor-council, commission, and council-manager forms. The first is the most widely used. It constitutes the only form in vogue for American cities with a population of a million or more, and it easily dominates the choice of small cities and towns which must rely largely upon part-time officials rather than full-time administrators. The other forms have been accepted for hundreds of large or middle-sized cities below the million population limit. Since World War I commission government, as strictly understood, has ceased to make gains and has even declined slightly, while the manager form has become widely attractive to cities of the middle bracket. The council-manager type rapidly supplanted or supplemented mayor-council government in the second quarter of the twentieth century, becoming the form most widely used by cities between 25,000 and 500,000 in population. The number of adoptions of the council-manager plan stood at about 500 in 1940, had doubled to approximately 1,000 by 1950, and had reached 1,800 by 1962. The trend has tended to match the growth or advancement of expert management in business and industry. Table 17-1 gives the forms of government in cities of over 5,000 population.

Rise of three forms

City government by mayor and council is the nearest approach to the separation of powers or functions between legislature and executive in the old-fashioned way. It stems by title at least from cities of Britain or Europe, being an adaptation of the form which the colonists knew in their native land. It is defended as suitable to American urban politics, whether for good or ill. It might be described as the "most politicalized" type of urban government and, largely because of that characteristic, is not easily changed or replaced.

Mayor-council government

Many cities which retain this form, however, have found ways of modifying and modernizing it. Only a few of them now use the bicameral council which once was in fashion, and the one-house council sometimes consists of a small membership. Nine is the number of councilmen for Pittsburgh and Detroit, where they are chosen at large, but Chicago holds to an old-style membership of 50, elected by wards. Well over half of the cities with a population over 5,000 now have councils elected at large, and the percentage is much greater for the smaller cities. This poses a problem of minority and area representation and, to some extent, the citizen's feeling of loss of direct contact with "his" councilman. Proportional representation for council membership has been urged for some years by reformers for effective representation of minority groups and as a check to boss rule, but it has made little headway except in a small way with cities having council-manager government.

Only in the largest cities are councilmen found who are devoting full time to the city's business, and even then many divide their time between

TABLE 17-1

FORM OF GOVERNMENT IN CITIES OF OVER 5,000 POPULATION BY POPULATION GROUPS

Population Group	Total Number of Cities	Total Number of Cities in Table	Mayor-Council		Commission		Council-Manager	
			No.	Per Cent	No.	Per Cent	No.	Per Cent
Over 500,000	21	20	16	80	0	0	4	20
250,000 to 500,000	30	30	13	43	5	17	12	40
100,000 to 250,000	80	80	31	39	10	13	39	49
50,000 to 100,000	192	190	69	36	24	13	97	51
25,000 to 50,000	406	392	137	35	50	13	205	53
10,000 to 25,000	1,033	1,015	495	49	104	10	416	41
5,000 to 10,000	1,292	1,284	861	67	66	5	357	28
All cities over 5,000	3,054	3,011*	1,622	54	259	9	1,130	38

* Not included in this table are Washington, D. C., 19 cities with representative town meeting government, 15 cities using town meeting form, and 9 other cities for which no information was available.

Source: "Governmental Data for Cities over 5,000 Population," *The Municipal Year Book, 1962* (International City Managers' Association, Chicago, 1962), p. 100.

being a councilman and a businessman. A likely hypothesis concerning the kind of person attracted to the council is that the less time required for the councilman's job, the more likely it is that the community's most respected civic leaders will be found on the council. Generally speaking, smaller cities will have councils more nearly composed of leading citizens than will larger cities, but advocates of the council-manager plan contend that relief of councilmen from routine and time-consuming administrative detail is equally important in attracting community leadership to the council.[3]

It is customary for textbooks in local government to classify the various mayor-council systems in the United States as either the weak-mayor type or the strong-mayor type, with some adding a third category called the hybrid type. To accept these categories uncritically is to run the risk of over-simplifying forms of city government and of neglecting the importance of the informal, "real power" picture of a city's government. Nevertheless, the classification is useful in differentiating the extremes of the power continuum for the mayor if these limitations are kept in mind.

The weak-mayor plan inherits the spirit of Jacksonian democracy which calls for the splintering of government into many small parts, none of which can do a great deal of good or evil. Strong reliance is placed upon the council, not only for making policy, but for handling many administrative matters. The mayor is little more than a figurehead, competing as he does with other elected city officials and a variety of independent boards, commissions, committees, and officials who look primarily to the council for administrative direction and control. Although the mayor usually is weak in policy making, the greater weakness is in administrative power, for he is denied the important managerial tools of organization, finance, and personnel. Unless a mayor is able to change drastically the formal structure of power by such means as a strong political position or a forceful personality, the incumbent under the weak-mayor plan is doomed by and large to the role of ceremonial head of the city. Figure 17-1 depicts the weak-mayor type of mayor-council government.

The weak mayor

The development of the strong-mayor form of government has never been conceived of as a new creation in governmental forms, since it differs primarily in degree from the weak-mayor type. Its development has had both formal and informal contributions. Like other public executives, many a technically weak mayor has discovered informal political ways of making himself strong, partly through civic necessity and partly

The strong mayor

---

[3] For an analytical view of a city council in action, *see* J. Leiper Freeman, "A Case Study of the Legislative Process in Municipal Government," in John C. Wahlke and Heinz Eulau, eds., *Legislative Behavior: A Reader in Theory and Research* (The Free Press, Glencoe, 1959), pp. 228-237.

MAYOR-COUNCIL FORM

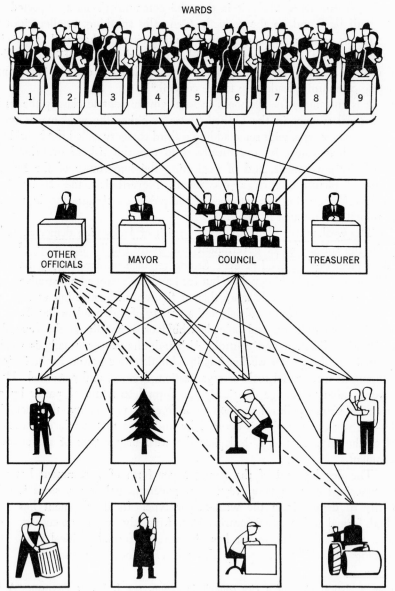

Source: National Municipal League. Reproduced by permission of the National Municipal League.

Figure 17-1. Chart of mayor-council form of city government

LOCAL GOVERNMENT: THE CITY

through a natural cultivation of power. If not strong in his own political right, such a mayor may derive seeming power from a dominant political machine. Chicago's mayors often provide effective executive government, for example, through inherent political leadership or machine support while dealing with a council which is not only legally powerful but also large. In many cities administrative reorganization has strengthened the hand of the mayor as a genuine executive clothed with power as well as responsibility for the conduct of city affairs. An increasing number of weak-mayor cities have evolved into strong-mayor systems resembling a model of the national government with the administrative departments clearly under the control of the President. Council surveillance over administrative details is diminished as the mayor is equipped with authority and staff assistance for administrative supervision. This includes extensive powers of appointment and removal, budget preparation and execution, day-to-day supervision, and the veto power. More recently some of the largest cities have added by charter amendment or ordinance a new feature to the strong-mayor form. They have created the position of "chief administrative officer," a kind of deputy mayor in charge of many of the more technical aspects of modern administration. The power of the "CAO" varies a great deal from city to city, but the idea is to meet the criticism that few mayors can succeed both as political leader and expert administrator, and possibly to meet the popular challenge of the council-manager plan.

Most mayor-council cities fall somewhere in between the weak-mayor and strong-mayor plans, so that the most prevalent form might well be called the hybrid type. Neither the Jacksonian tradition of extreme dispersion nor the modern model of administrative integration can be said to dominate, although some elements of each can be found in most mayor-council cities today. Most cities have moved in the direction of central budgeting, purchasing, and personnel controls, but still remain a patchwork structure of independent boards and commissions not responsible to the mayor. *The common mixture*

The commission form of city government was designed to avoid the defects of unwieldy councils and the divided responsibility of hide-and-seek politics often involved in the old form of mayor-council government. (*See* Figure 17-2.) It got off to a dramatic start at Galveston in 1901, although approaches toward it had previously been made by other cities. A tidal wave engulfed that Texas city in 1900, entailing loss of life for thousands and property damage of many millions of dollars. Taxes could not be paid, and city services were disrupted. A huge task of reconstruction and reorganization had to be faced, and inefficient or corrupt government-as-usual was out of the question. A group of businessmen moved into the domain of public affairs, and part of their work consisted of getting a new charter from the state legislature to facilitate their emergency undertaking. Commission *Commission form*

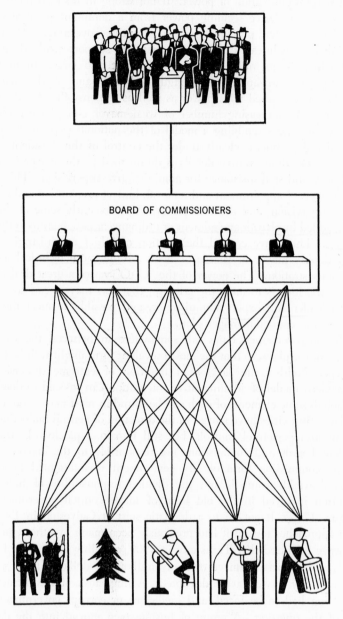

Source: National Municipal League. Reproduced by permission of the National Municipal League.

Figure 17-2. Chart of commission form of city government

LOCAL GOVERNMENT: THE CITY

government was the result, and the new form, although established for temporary purposes, became permanent and provided an example for other cities, including many of smaller size as well as larger ones like Birmingham and Des Moines.

The city commission consists of three to seven members, usually five, who are elected at large, one of them being chairman and nominally the mayor. The commission as a deliberative body formulates policy much in the manner of a council, and each member is administratively responsible for the management of a specific department, such as finance, public works, or public safety. Thus the same men make policy and execute it. As long as all are in agreement, government may run smoothly, but deadlocks can be unfortunate and disrupt leadership. Moreover, commissioners may tend to trade votes for the advantage of the departments over which they preside, and, where this is done, the result may be extravagant budgeting or imbalance in over-all program. It is sometimes observed that the membership of a city commission, which has both legislative and executive functions, is too small for the former and too large for the latter. These shortcomings became more noticeable as a newer form of municipal government began to attract attention. Reformers and reorganization experts turned from commission to city manager as a more efficient way of meeting the growing demands made upon the American city. Galveston, birthplace of the commission plan, abondoned it in 1960 in favor of the council-manager plan.

Something akin to council-manager government was established in Staunton, Virginia, in 1908, but the plan was grafted upon the mayor-council form and retained a bicameral council. Sumter, South Carolina, adopted a clear-cut council-manager form in 1912, and authorities are divided on whether Staunton or Sumter should be counted the first council-manager city. But the spread of the council-manager form dates from 1914, when Dayton, Ohio, became the first large city to come under this form of municipal rule. Dayton, like Galveston earlier, had to meet sudden problems caused by a devastating flood. Civic leaders of the Chamber of Commerce, however, were already working on plans for municipal reorganization to remedy conditions of graft and inefficiency. The flood emergency intensified their effort and gave it national attention. The new charter and the new experiment lent popular impetus to the city-manager movement.

Council-manager form

This system of municipal government recognizes the separate but coordinate functions of politics and administration. It provides for the adoption of policy, approval of financial plans, and enactment of ordinances by a council normally consisting of five to nine members elected at large on a non-partisan ballot. The council chooses the manager, who may or may not be a resident of the city at the time of his appointment. The manager is responsible to the council, which controls his tenure and which, in turn, is responsible to the voters for the proper government of the city. All or most of the branches and agencies of the city administration, except the board or department of education,

320 operate under the general direction of the manager, who has power to hire and fire personnel within the scope and limits of a merit system. The council's role in administration is limited to selecting and dismissing the city manager, and it is prohibited from exercising direct authority over city employees. A mayor is usually selected by the council to serve only as a ceremonial officer. Figure 17-3 depicts the organization of the council-manager type of city government.

Many claims have been made to support adoption of the council-manager plan; so many in fact, that over-enthusiastic proponents sometimes run the risk of serious disillusionment by the citizenry when *all* problems of a community are not actually solved. Two features of this form of government stand out above all others, however, as within the realm of reasonable expectation. One is the bringing of a professionally trained, career-oriented administrator to the position of top management in municipal government, in contrast to non-professionalism in the other forms. The other outstanding feature is an institutional guarantee against stalemate between the executive and legislative branches of government, since the manager serves only at the pleasure of the council. Many other features usually associated with the manager plan, and hotly debated in campaigns for adoption, are not the exclusive property of the manager plan and it is not unusual to find them incorporated in mayor-council charters. To mention a few, the short ballot, administrative integration, non-partisan elections, a small council elected at large, and a council freed from petty administrative routine and detail, are not at all incompatible with the mayor-council plan.

Unique features

Probably the most controversial part of the manager plan, both for governmental theory and practical politics, is the role of the manager in policy leadership. Statements made earlier about the theory of the council-manager plan, some by implication and others explicitly, called for a manager whose role was strictly policy execution, not policy formulation. This raised a serious question concerning the source of policy leadership, no longer provided by an elective mayor, and many argued that councils could not be expected to lead themselves and that a political vacuum existed under the manager plan. This whole controversy has been modified, though not ended, by more systematic research which examines the council-manager plan in practice as well as on paper. A study by Professor Charles Adrian of policy leadership in three middle-sized council-manager cities in Michigan revealed that the manager and administrative departments are the principal sources of policy innovation and leadership—even though the manager avoids a *public posture* of policy leadership.[4] Adrian reports other significant findings: the councilman designated as mayor is not likely to become a general policy leader for the council; individual councilmen step forward as policy leaders more in isolated

Whence comes political leadership?

---

[4] Charles R. Adrian, "Leadership and Decision-Making in Manager Cities: A Study of Three Communities," *Public Administration Review*, XVIII (Summer, 1958), pp. 208-213.

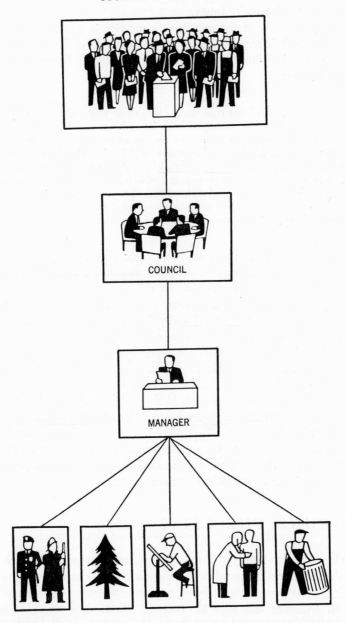

Source: National Municipal League. Reproduced by permission of the National Municipal League.

Figure 17-3. Chart of council-manager form of city government

322 instances than as general leaders, and even then more in *opposition* to particular proposals than as advocate or innovator.

The policy role of the manager in practice is confirmed by Kammerer and DeGrove in their recent study of tenure problems of Florida city managers.

The manager as policy leader They conclude that the manager is a political figure of considerable importance:

> Nine out of ten of our case study cities show that citizens, civic leaders, and councilmen identify managers, both incumbents and their predecessors, with certain policy stands on many of the questions just listed. Some managers, for example, were identified as major "builders" of significant public improvements in the sense that these works stood more or less as their programs. Others were cited as the promoters and defenders of strict zoning programs to preserve a certain type and style of life. Yet others were thought of as stimulators of industrialization efforts. Some were vetoers of public construction or spending programs and defenders of the status quo.[5]

Any evaluation of the council-manager plan must recognize this ambivalent position of the manager with respect to political leadership. Some argue that he cannot be a strong leader, and for this reason oppose the manager plan, particularly for the largest cities, where policy matters loom so large. Others criticize the manager plan as primarily "businessmen's government," which is not so responsive to the "labor viewpoint." Minority groups and areas at times complain that their interests are overlooked by a small council elected at large and a manager responsible to such a council. On the other hand, proponents of the plan can and do marshall an imposing array of arguments, usually centering on the idea that the proof is in the pudding—that in fact the manager plan *has* provided progressive leadership for cities and continues to meet with widespread public acceptance. Relatively few municipalities have taken steps to abandon it after trying it. City management as a career continues to grow, with an increasing number entering the field by way of graduate training and internship experience in municipal administration.

WHO RUNS THE CITY?

The discussion thus far in this chapter has dealt primarily with the legal roots of the municipal corporation and the more visible aspects of governmental

---

[5] Gladys M. Kammerer and John M. DeGrove, *Florida City Managers: Profile and Tenure* (Public Administration Clearing Service, University of Florida, Gainesville, 1961), p. 29. See *also* Clarence Ridley, *The Role of the City Manager in Policy Formation* (International City Managers' Association, Chicago, 1958).

structure commonly called "form of government." It is quite possible to be a master of these subjects and still be unable to answer even in general terms the question, "Who *really* runs your city?" Do the duly elected officials really run your city? The bankers? The clergy? The newspapers? Is it the politicians or a single boss *behind* the formal officeholders? Is it a small group of wealthy oldtimers who own half of the property and have been "calling the tune" on major community decisions as long as one can remember? Or is your city government of, by, and for all the people, as democratic theory would seem to suggest? The question has obvious ambiguities and is fraught with problems of definition and assumptions, but it is still sufficiently important that an increasing number of sociologists and political scientists have begun to focus their research interests on community power structure and decision making. Unfortunately much of this work is just beginning, but it should be helpful to examine briefly a few of the studies already completed.

Two separate studies have been made of the power structure of "Regional City" (Atlanta), a Southern city of about a half-million people. The first study, by Floyd Hunter, found a single pyramidal power structure with some thirty key decision makers running the community. These men, the top business leaders in the city, stayed in communication with each other in a variety of ways and were said to make the important decisions for the community and pass the word down to a few hundred persons making up the next lower level in the pyramid to be carried out.[6] The inner circle of decision makers did not include Negroes or labor leaders, although they were acknowledged to be growing in importance. The power of this "elite" was greatest at the city level of government and diminished progressively at higher levels. Many political scientists reacted violently to many aspects of Hunter's study, including the conspiracy theory which seems to be implied, his failure to consider many subtle limitations on the power of the elite, and a methodology which seemed to guarantee that decision makers would be found, whether they actually existed or not.[7]

A decision-making elite

A second study of Atlanta, by M. Kent Jennings, followed the Hunter study in point of time, but deviated from it significantly in the kind of power structure found.[8] After studying three kinds of participants in community

---

[6] Floyd Hunter, *Community Power Structure: A Study of Decision-makers* (University of North Carolina Press, Chapel Hill, 1953).

[7] *See,* for example, Herbert Kaufman and Victor Jones, "The Mystery of Power," *Public Administration Review,* XIV (Summer, 1954), pp. 205-212. Hunter's book is in the same vein as C. Wright Mills, *The Power Elite* (Oxford University Press, New York, 1956), although Mills denies that his is a conspiracy theory.

[8] M. Kent Jennings, *Political Statuses and Political Roles in Community Decision-Making* (Unpublished Ph.D. Dissertation, University of North Carolina, 1960).

decision making ("prescribed influentials," "attributed influentials," and "economic dominants"), Jennings concluded that the economic dominants, those occupying major economic posts, were least involved in community decision making and exercised relatively little political power. Concerning the various decision-making roles (initiation, priority-fixing, promotion, legitimation, and implementation), the formal political leaders of Atlanta made a much stronger showing of power and influence than Hunter's previous study indicated. Jennings concludes that the power structure is not monolithic, but that it lies midway between a monolithic and an amorphous typology.[9]

Atlanta re-visited

Studies of other cities have revealed a "polynucleated" or multi-centered power structure rather than a pyramidal form. Robert A. Dahl's rigorous study of "who governs" New Haven provides a rich body of new insights into urban community decision making.[10] He found many centers of power in New Haven, rather than a single pyramidal elite, with each group's power depending on their supply of such political resources as time, interest, ability, experience, friends, money, etc. A combination of resources used to achieve power in one situation will not necessarily assure power in a different situation. Dahl, while denying the concept of the single elite, suggests that the mayor's office comes the closest to being a single focal point for most community decision making.

Multi-centered power structure

Similarly, the study of New York City by Sayre and Kaufman found no single pyramid of decision makers, but rather a system of separate and numerous islands of power.[11] They describe the political process in New York as a contest for prizes with the contestants being party leaders, officials, bureaucrats, the electorate, and a whole host of nongovernmental groups.

A contest for prizes

They suggest that this "multi-centered" system of government is more favorable to the status quo than to innovations, but that over the past 60 years it has been surprisingly creative and adaptive.

There still is no easy answer to the question of who runs the city, but it is becoming increasingly clear that the single pyramidal conception is not a complete picture, at best, and is totally erroneous in many situations. Many economically powerful corporation executives refuse to "take sides" in many community issues for fear of hurting the company. Still other citizens may be highly influential but in practice take an interest in only one or two kinds of

---

[9] For a discussion of types of community power structures *see* Peter H. Rossi, "Power and Community Structure," *Midwest Journal of Political Science*, IV (November, 1960), pp. 390-401. He suggests four types of local political structure: pyramidal (highly centralized), caucus rule (the "cozy few"), polylith (separate power structures), and amorphous.

[10] Robert A. Dahl, *Who Governs?* (Yale University Press, New Haven, 1961).

[11] Wallace S. Sayre and Herbert Kaufman, *Governing New York City* (Russell Sage Foundation, New York, 1960.)

community decisions. Others appear to have unlimited power, but in reality have learned to recognize those times when it is safer not to try to cross certain lines. It does seem true, however, that the formal officials of city government are increasingly exercising power in their own right, rather than constituting mere "fronts" for invisible elite citizens hovering in the background. This should offer hope for the democratic ideal of popular control of the decision-making process in cities.[12]

MUNICIPAL ADMINISTRATION

The increase in scope and cost of municipal administration is the source of political and budgetary headaches in many of our cities, large and small. It accounts for much of the interest in the city-manager type of government, with its emphasis on efficiency and economy. The increase results from *Range and* the expansion of old functions and the rise of new functions for city *growth* governments to cope with. Law enforcement is an old function, but it becomes a greater task with the creation of more laws and ordinances to enforce and the devising of more ways for violating or evading them, often for profit. Mass transit and traffic regulation are old functions with new problems, including the seemingly unsolvable problem of adequate public and private parking. Fire fighting and prevention are old functions with new and expensive methods. Old and new steps are involved in dealing with juvenile delinquency, providing recreation facilities, regulating health and sanitary conditions, maintaining water supply, administering building and rental regulations, handling welfare cases, and carrying on other important activities. Many of the larger cities maintain airports beyond their corporate boundaries.

The wide functions of government and service bring the city into various financial and operational contacts with other units and agencies of goverance, whether county, regional, state, or national. Our expanding cities are continually in need of more funds and are increasingly looking to the state and federal governments for funds. These central governments have something to say in

---

[12] For more detailed discussion of community power structure, *see* Peter H. Rossi, "Power and Community Structure," *Midwest Journal of Political Science*, IV (November, 1960), pp. 390-401; Oliver P. Williams, "A Typology for Comparative Local Government," *Midwest Journal of Political Science*, V (May, 1961), pp. 150-164; Charles R. Adrian, ed., *Social Science and Community Action* (Michigan State University Continuing Education Service, East Lansing, 1961); E. W. Noland, "The Roles of Top Business Executives in Urban Development," *Research Previews*, VIII (February, 1961), pp. 1-8; and N. W. Polsby, "Power in Middletown: Fact and Value in Community Research," *Canadian Journal of Economics and Political Science*, XXVI (November, 1960), pp. 592-603.

326 connection with their furnishing aid to cities for public works, sewage systems, street improvements, and the like.

Adminis-trative organization

Every city of substantial size, whatever its type of government, has an organization of agencies or departments, which are more or less responsible to a central authority of mayor, manager, commission, or council. The heads of the different departments as well as the members of boards and agencies may be elected by the voters or by the council, or they may be appointed by the chief executive, according to state laws, city charter, and size of the city. Each department is organized from its head to its lowest rung of common labor and manned by personnel selected by political criteria or merit tests. While organization is complex for the larger cities, it is rather simple for villages and small cities and may consist of only two key administrative officers, sometimes known as "Mr. Inside" and "Mr. Outside." The "inside" man may be the director of finance, or simply the city clerk, but he will be responsible for much of the housekeeping work related to finance, personnel, purchasing, and the routine details of administration. The "outside" man is usually named director of public works and will handle such matters as street maintenance, parks, water supply, sewers, and planning.

A large city is likely to have a personnel office or board to recruit, examine, and certify applicants for appointment by the employing officers and also to perform duties with respect to position classification, promotion, salary scales, tenure, and other employee relations. Such a city must likewise have administrative officers to conduct financial affairs, including budgeting, purchasing, accounting, auditing, and general treasury management. It must have officials and facilities for handling tax matters, such as assessment and collection of property levies, issuing licenses of various kinds and receiving payments for them, and sometimes gathering in city sales and income taxes. The management of financial and personnel matters vitally affects the scope and effectiveness of all the agencies of a city administration, for no unit of government can function without men and money.

It is further recognized in city government, as in other government, that effective operation, or line work, requires general staff work at the center. The central staff organization of an increasing number of large and medium-sized cities includes a full-time officer or agency for research, study, and advice in the wide field of city planning. The recommendations of the planning authority, insofar as they are adopted, affect both the work of the operating agencies and the trend of city development. As in other levels of government, the planning establishment is likely to be closely linked to the chief executive authority. State planning assistance may be available to urban communities, especially the smaller ones.

Closely related to planning is the work or process of zoning through

laws or ordinances with administration by boards or officers. Zoning is really
enforced planning to designate or preserve areas for residential, commercial, industrial, or other purposes, with modifications and combina- *Land-use*
tions of these classifications. It affects both public and private enterprise, *planning*
and zoning authorities are often subjected to strong conflicting pressures. *and zoning*
Once a city takes the step of seeking to regulate land use and passes a comprehensive zoning ordinance, it then is faced with the never-ending task of "holding
the line" against creeping blight by "spot zoning" amendments and the granting
of variances and exceptions. Decisions or recommendations of planning agencies
are sometimes reversed by higher authority, such as a city council. It is common
for the tradition of "councilmanic courtesy" to exist in city councils, giving the
individual councilman virtually complete control over zone changes in his own
district.

The city as a concentrated center of society requires concentrated
attention to the problems of public safety. Urban police protection is covered
in the chapter on law enforcement. Fire protection is more completely a
local responsibility than is the maintenance of law and order. Fire and *Public*
police services are sometimes combined in one department, particularly in *safety; fire*
the smaller cities. But fighting fire is different from fighting crime, even *protection*
though a large fire creates problems for the police. Firemen, like policemen,
perform miscellaneous services besides their primary task; they may answer
calls for trapped persons or animals, flooded homes, storm damage, and the like.
Normally there is no attempt to corrupt fire departments and to limit their
effectiveness comparable to the kinds of pressure often brought to bear upon
police departments, and hence American urban fire service is generally efficient,
with competent men as well as modern mechanized equipment. But fire losses
in American municipalities far exceed the losses in European cities, largely
because of differences in the construction of buildings and in methods or habits
of fire prevention. Many American cities have antiquated building codes,
sometimes with inadequate inspection and enforcement to avoid fire hazards.
Political "pull" at times relaxes the administration of regulations. Preventing
fire, like preventing crime, is a large problem for urban America.

City governments are concerned with the construction, maintenance,
and use or operation of various types of public works and enterprise. It is often
the rule for original construction to be by private contractors, with
maintenance or operation becoming the responsibility of city authorities. *Public works*
Privately owned water systems were once rather common among American *and utilities*
cities, but municipal ownership prevails widely today. Many cities in
the Tennessee Valley have municipal authorities which operate under state
and federal laws in purchasing electricity from TVA and distributing it to
consumers. Similar municipal electric service is to be found in other river

328 regions with public power projects. Most of our cities, however, depend upon private enterprise to provide the utilities of heat, light, power, transportation, and communication. The private companies provide and sell the services under state or local franchises and regulations, which are supposed to safeguard the public interest and also permit a fair return for the utility operations. Private enterprise in housing has been supplemented by public provision of accommodations for low-income families in crowded cities, often on lands cleared of unsightly slums. Hundreds of municipal housing authorities and projects have been launched since 1937 under state and federal legislation and local sponsorship.

Cities have been centers of art and learning since the ancient days of Athens and Alexandria. As indicated in other portions of this text, American cities generally have their own school systems within a state framework

Education of financial support and standards. The city school board is locally elected or appointed, and the board generally chooses the superintendent. The school administration thus has a degree of technical separation from the routine politics and activities of municipal government. But through the purse and public interest the school system is linked to the fortunes of the whole urban community. It is by no means free from the influence of pressure groups, whether of teachers, parents, or local political powers. Much of the pressure is for achieving educational goals, with no little emphasis on professional standards and improvement of facilities. Sometimes, however, there are bitter battles over school issues, with victory not always on the side of progress. The politics of public education is discussed in more detail in Chapter 22.

Aside from public school systems, more than a dozen cities support or partly support municipal colleges or universities, notably New York, Cincinnati, Toledo, Louisville, and Omaha. Nearly every important city has a public library, which is customarily administered by a trained librarian responsible to a lay board. The library of a large city has a large staff and branches requiring additional personnel. The New York Public Library is one of the largest in the world, ranking next to the Library of Congress in size in the United States.

REGIONAL CITY

The life, work, and culture of Americans are geared to a multiplicity of cities more than to the 50 states. For us, "civilization," as Lewis Mumford has observed, "is citification." Every important city in the United States is the hub of a regional society, a regional economy, and a regional mixture of government. Politically the large city is the central member of a community of communities, in which no member is sole master of its civic destiny but each has autonomous ways of speeding up or messing up the order and progress of the urban whole. In the regional orbit no man, no family lives alone or in a single community, but each lives in a combination of concentric and overlapping communities. In this complex of civic units, a strong sense of community laissez faire and self-containment often prevails over and above any general concept of regional good. Intercommunity adjustment may be further hindered or complicated by the inertia or opposition of dominant private interests, which are sometimes subject to extra-regional and national control.[13] There is much here to provide the needs and makings of city states, if there were any constitutional practicability for such a step. Clearly the regionalizing of urban life has outstripped the regionalizing of governmental institutions. We have metropolitan communities without metropolitan government.

Reasons of ethics, esthetics, and maximum utility suggest the setting of limits to the laissez faire of urban communities, just as limits have been set to the laissez faire of urban individuals. Limits and standards for the purposes of regional synthesis and coordination may be applicable to landscape and skyscrape, to highways and alleyways, to the construction and services of home, shop, and office. The circumscriptions at the same time should allow leeway for local community diversity, incentive, and responsibility. It might be observed that no greater problem of government this side of the Iron Curtain confronts the American people than the balanced task of functionalizing and systematizing our metropolitan regions for decent and democratic living. The next chapter explores this unfinished business.

The prospect before us

SUPPLEMENTARY READINGS

Adrian, C. R., *Governing Urban America* (rev. ed.; McGraw-Hill Book Co., Inc., New York, 1961).

Allen, Robert S., ed., *Our Fair City* (Vanguard Press, New York, 1947).

Banfield, Edward C., ed., *Urban Government: A Reader in Administration and Politics* (Free Press of Glencoe, Inc., New York, 1961).

Bromage, A. W., *Introduction to Municipal Government and Administration* (Appleton-Century-Crofts, Inc., New York, 1950).

Childs, Richard S., *Civic Victories* (Harper and Row, Publishers, New York, 1952).

---

[13] This theme is discussed, with no tendency toward understatement, in *Our Fair City*, ed. Robert S. Allen (The Vanguard Press, New York, 1947). The nationally controlled city of Washington, D.C., is uniquely omitted from coverage by Allen's muckraking symposium.

330   Greer, Scott, *The Emerging City: Myth or Reality* (The Free Press of Glencoe, Inc., New York, 1962).

Kammerer, Gladys, Charles D. Farris, John M. DeGrove, and Alfred B. Clubok, *City Managers in Politics: An Analysis of Manager Tenure and Termination,* Social Science Monographs No. 13 (University of Florida Press, Gainesville, 1962).

Macdonald, A. F., *American City Government and Administration* (5th ed.; Thomas Y. Crowell Company, New York, 1951).

Mills, Warner E., Jr., and Harry R. Davis, *Small City Government; Seven Cases in Decision Making* (Random House, New York, 1962).

Mumford, Lewis, *The Culture of Cities* (Harcourt, Brace & World, Inc., New York, 1938).

Municipal Manpower Commission, *Governmental Manpower for Tomorrow's Cities* (McGraw-Hill Book Company, New York, 1963).

The Municipal Year Book (International City Managers' Association, Chicago, annually).

National Civic Review (National Municipal League, New York, monthly except August).

Peterson, E. R., ed., *Cities Are Abnormal* (University of Oklahoma Press, Norman, 1946).

Shaw, Frederick, *The History of the New York City Legislature* (Columbia University Press, New York, 1954).

Stone, Harold A., Don K. Price and Kathryn H. Stone, *City Manager Government in the United States* (Public Administration Service, Chicago, 1940).

Tunnard, Christopher, and H. H. Reed, *American Skyline* (Houghton Mifflin Company, Boston, 1955).

Williams, Oliver P., and Charles Press, *Democracy in Urban America: Readings on Government and Politics* (Rand McNally & Company, Chicago, 1961).

★ *18* ★

LOCAL GOVERNMENT:

METROPOLITICS

W_HEN_ C_HARLES_ E. M_ERRIAM_ made his frequently quoted statement that "the adequate organization of modern metropolitan areas is one of the great unsolved problems of modern politics,"[1] he might well have added that things would get worse before they would get better. In reporting the *Trends in* publication of Professor Robert C. Wood's book *1400 Governments*, which *metropolitics* gave a bleak picture of local government in the New York metropolitan region, the *New York Times* headlined its story as follows: "EXPERT PREDICTS REGIONAL CHAOS WITHIN 25 YEARS; More Urban Sprawl, Noise, Traffic, Air Pollution and Blight Foreseen; AREA DISUNITY BLAMED; Study Discounts Possibility of Accord Among 1,467 Local Governments."[2] While the New York region provides the outstanding example of the impact of the modern population explosion on traditional local governmental structure, it is by no means alone in its situation. The 1950 census report

---

[1] In Merriam's preface to Victor Jones, *Metropolitan Government* (University of Chicago Press, Chicago, 1942), ix.

[2] *New York Times*, July 17, 1961. Wood's volume, published by the Harvard University Press, is one of nine resulting from the New York Metropolitan Regional Study.

331

332   revealed that for the first time more than half the people of the United States live within the large urban centers designated "standard metropolitan areas," and by 1960 the metropolitan majority had risen to 63 per cent. (*See* Figure 18-1.) The government of these metropolitan areas is frequently described in such terms as "scambled eggs," "hopeless chaos," and "political disintegration," because each metropolis is governed by a strange proliferation of counties, cities, townships, and special districts.

    The outward push of the population from the central core city has been so strong that approximately one-half of all metropolitan area population is now located *outside* the corporate boundaries of the central cities. (*See* Figure 18-2.) Almost three times as many Bostonians live outside Boston's city limits as live inside (1,892,104 to 697,197). "Legal" Pittsburgh citizens are outnumbered by suburbanites in the same ratio as "legal" Bostonians, 1,801,103 to 604,332.

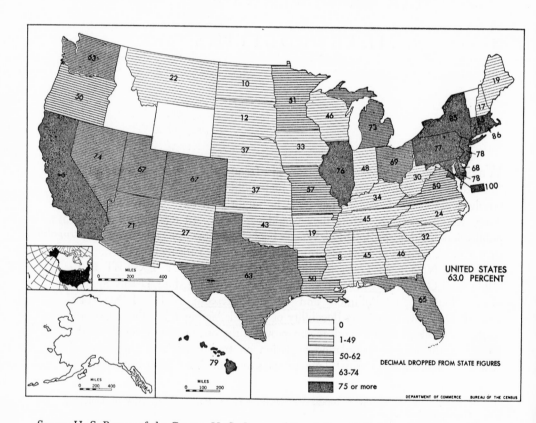

Source: U. S. Bureau of the Census, *U. S. Census of Population, 1960.*

Figure 18-1. *Per cent of population in standard metropolitan statistical areas; by states: 1960*

LOCAL GOVERNMENT: METROPOLITICS

Although St. Louis can rightfully claim more than 2,000,000 as the population of its metropolitan area, the incorporated city of St. Louis contains only 750,026. In even more striking contrast, the San Francisco-Oakland area numbers more than 2,750,000 in population, but San Francisco proper can claim only 740,316 as residents.

More and more the metropolis is being divided into one complex set of governments for the place of work of its citizens and another complex set of governments for their place of residence, with intricate overlapping and inter-twining of the two. Because the government of metropolitan areas constitutes a special problem distinct from city government as such, this chapter gives separate treatment to developments and trends in a field that might well be called "metropolitics."

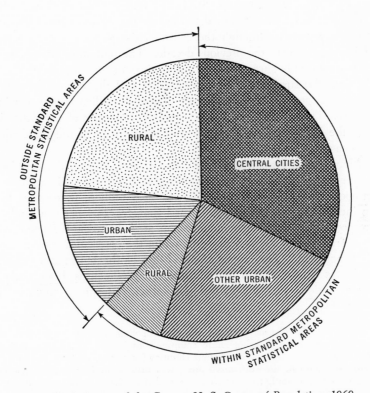

Source: U. S. Bureau of the Census, U. S. Census of Population, 1960.

Figure 18-2. Population by type of residence in metropolitan and nonmetropolitan areas: 1960

LOCAL GOVERNMENT: METROPOLITICS

334   The growth of metropolitan areas was reported in the censuses of 1920, 1930, and 1940 under the designation of "metropolitan districts," revealing a steady increase in the number of such districts, with 96 in 1930 and 140

Metropolitan   in 1940. The aggregate population of these districts in 1940 was about
growth   63,000,000 or 47.8 per cent of the national population. The number of metropolitan areas had risen to 168 by 1950, and to 212 by 1960, and contained almost 113 million persons. The terminology used for reporting metropolitan area population has changed from time to time, but a metropolitan area usually includes a core city of 50,000 or more, plus the surrounding county (or counties) which are designated as reasonably urbanized, contiguous, and interdependent with the core city.[3]

During the period from 1930 to 1940 the central cities as a whole increased in population only 4.7 per cent, while the suburbs increased 14.4 per cent. Several of the central cities actually declined in population, including Philadelphia, Cleveland, St. Louis, and Boston. Between 1940 and 1950 the suburban areas continued to outgain the central core cities, 35.6 per cent to 13.9 per cent, although the central cities showed a more respectable rate of increase than in the previous decade. The outlying parts of the metropolitan areas not only surpassed the central cities in rate of increase from 1940 to 1950, but also surpassed their central cities and the rest of the country in total numerical growth with an increase of over 9 million in the remainder of the country. Thus almost half of the population increase of the entire United States in the 1940's took place in the suburban fringe of the standard metropolitan areas.

Metropolitan growth was even more striking during the decade of the 1950's, in contrast to the slowdown in the rest of the country. The 1960 increase in metropolitan population over 1950 was 23.6 million, in contrast to a 4.4 million increase in the rest of the United States — 26.4 per cent and 7.1 per cent, respectively. Within the metropolitan areas between 1950 and 1960 the suburban fringe grew by 48.5 per cent while the core cities grew at a rate of only 10.8 per cent. (See Figure 18-3.) Nine of the ten largest cities in the United States lost population, according to the 1960 census, Los Angeles being the one exception. Houston gained population, but was a newcomer in the top ten in 1960.

[3] The Bureau of the Census replaced the "metropolitan district" with the "standard metropolitan area" in 1950, using entire counties containing a central city with at least 50,000 population, or groups of contiguous counties (or towns, in New England), as the basic unit. In addition, the "urbanized area" was utilized in its reporting first in 1950, excluding certain non-contiguous outlying area and not relying on the county as the basic unit. In 1960 the name of the "SMA" was changed to the "standard metropolitan statistical area" and slight modifications in definition were made. Still another category, the "standard consolidated area," was devised to fit the situations of New York and Chicago, where several contiguous SMSA's appear to have increasingly strong interrelationships.

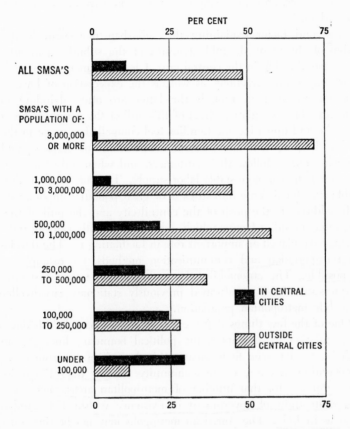

PER CENT

Source: U. S. Bureau of the Census, *U. S. Census of Population, 1960.*
Figure 18-3. *Per cent of change in population in and outside central cities by size of standard metropolitan statistical areas: 1950-1960*

What are the reasons for this tremendous movement to the fringe of every large city and the accompanying stagnation or slowdown in growth of the central city? The answer is threefold, involving first of all a vigorous outward push caused by the central city itself. Such conditions in the **Urban push** heart of the city as smoke, dirt, noise, and congestion join to induce the inhabitants to seek a more pleasant place of residence. The in-migration of minority groups to the core city has disturbed middle-class dwellers and contributed to their push out of the city. The relentless encroachment of business and industrial establishments on residential areas, the development of slums

336 ⸢and blighted areas, and the steady increase in property taxes also contribute to
⸤the outward push.

A second factor explaining the suburban movement is the pull or
magnetism of the many desirable features of the suburbs, particularly when
compared to life in the central city. Clean air, more room, and quietude

Suburban
pull
are important attractions, as well as the expectation of lower taxes and
better government, though the latter are often deluding motivating
forces. The cumulative effect of this pull of the periphery becomes clear
when middle and upper-income families feel compelled to move to the suburbs
in order "to keep up with the Joneses," when retail and service establishments
begin moving out to follow their customers, and when industries move to the
suburbs in search of a more stable labor supply. The role of the suburbs as less
vulnerable sites for defense industries is of great potential importance.

In addition to the push of the central city and the pull of the outlying
suburbs, there are other factors which, while not actually causing the suburban
movement, have played an important role in facilitating it. The development of
modern transportation and communication methods, for example, made the
exodus possible. The automobile, the various rapid transit systems, and the
wide expressways have transformed previously stationary city-dwellers into a
highly mobile metropolitan population.

One of the few things that seem forever stationary in this day of metropolitan population movements is the political boundary line. No metropolis
(or state) has seen fit to create a single unit of government capable of

Number of
local gov-
ernments
governing an entire urban community. Rather than 174 units of local
government for that number of metropolitan areas, there were 15,658
separate units of government in existence within 174 standard metropolitan areas in 1957. The American metropolis may not be the *best* governed
area imaginable, but it may well be the most governed, from a numerical standpoint. The distribution of governmental units in the metropolitan areas for
1957 is shown in Table 18-1.

TABLE 18-1

NUMBER OF LOCAL GOVERNMENTS IN METROPOLITAN AREAS: 1957

Counties	266
Municipalities	3,422
Townships	2,317
School Districts	6,473
Other Special Districts	3,180
TOTAL	15,658

Source: U. S. Bureau of the Census, *Local Government in Standard Metropolitan Areas*
(U. S. Government Printing Office, Washington, D. C., 1957), p. 1.

Table 18-2 indicates the local governments in the ten metropolitan areas with
the greatest number of units.

TABLE 18-2

LOCAL GOVERNMENTS IN THE TEN METROPOLITAN AREAS IN THE UNITED STATES
WITH THE LARGEST NUMBER OF UNITS: 1957

| Metropolitan Area | Number of Local Governments | | | | | |
	Counties	Townships	Municipalities	School Districts	Other Special Districts	Total
New York-Northeastern New Jersey	12	102	292	425	243	1,074
Chicago	6	108	198	355	287	954
Philadelphia	7	199	140	332	27	705
Pittsburgh	4	128	181	293	6	612
San Francisco-Oakland	5	...	53	156	200	414
St. Louis	4	46	153	110	87	400
Portland (Ore.)	4	...	30	143	160	337
Los Angeles-Long Beach	2	...	68	157	92	319
Detroit	3	54	72	107	14	250
Kansas City	4	15	47	138	32	236

Source: Adapted from U. S. Bureau of the Census, Local Government in Standard Metropolitan Areas, op. cit., pp. 9-47.

The New York-Northeastern New Jersey metropolitan area has over 1,000 separate local governments, and Chicago is not far behind with 954. Of all the metropolitan areas, 9 have more than 250 units of local government and 87 have more than 50 local governments. Only 17 metropolitan areas contain fewer than 10 governmental units, and 13 of these are in southern states where the systems of local government are generally far less complex. The trend is in the direction of even greater complexity and multiplication of units of government, particularly in the case of special districts and suburban cities. The high

338   "birth rate" for new suburban cities around Cleveland is shown in Figure 18-4
The single exception to the multiplication trend is the number of school
districts, which has dropped steadily in recent years through vigorous state action
promoting school consolidations.

PROBLEMS OF GOVERNING
METROPOLITAN AREAS

What have been the effects of the suburban movement upon government
of the metropolitan area? What happens when cities spread out like volcanic
lava, consuming the countryside and rendering their boundary lines
Governmen- unrealistic? Political problems of the first magnitude have resulted. Any
tal effects attempt to summarize the problems of government which have arisen
with the development of the metropolitan area runs the risk of oversimplification. However, a recent study of 112 metropolitan surveys conducted
since 1923 reveals striking similarity in the governmental consequences which
seem to occur almost universally in the wake of the metropolitan explosion.[4]
Summarized below are some of the more common — and more serious — problems of metropolitan government in the United States.

One of the most serious and visible results of the uncontrolled suburban
movement is the financial disadvantage suffered by the central city. While more
and more of the wealth of the city is moved outside the city limits and
Financial out of reach of the city tax collector, the cost of government for the central
inequalities city has shown no tendency either to decrease or remain stationary. On
the contrary, the suburbanites who escape city taxes continue to aggra-
vate the city's traffic and parking problems, use the city's streets and parks,
and frequently receive many other city services without charge, all of which
places an inequitable burden upon one group of metropolitan taxpayers. Bond
issues for various public works, voted and paid for by the central city dwellers,
are more often than not equally beneficial to suburban residents who enjoy all
privileges except the dubious one of sharing the costs. The blighted sections of
metropolitan areas, which, while paying few taxes, provide costly problems of
public health, crime control, fire protection, slum clearance, and the like, are
almost without exception located exclusively within the central city and never
in the wealthier suburbs most able to finance such services.

---

[4] See Daniel R. Grant, "General Metropolitan Surveys: A Summary," in *Metropolitan
Surveys: A Digest* (Government Affairs Foundation, New York, 1958), pp. 1-24.

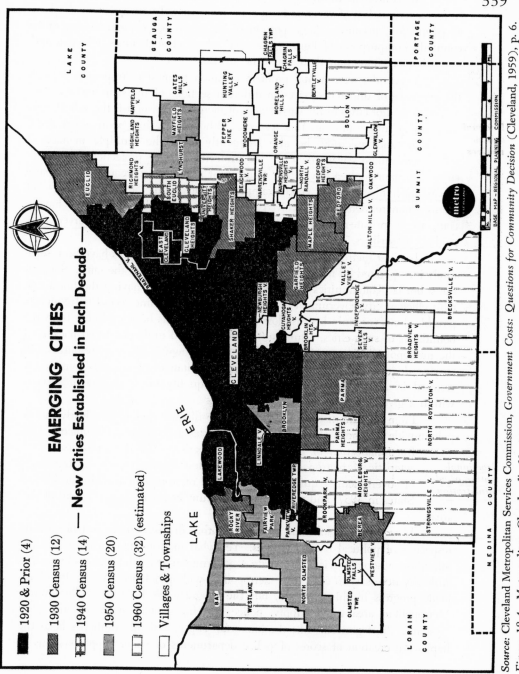

EMERGING CITIES

New Cities Established in Each Decade

- 1920 & Prior (4)
- 1930 Census (12)
- 1940 Census (14)
- 1950 Census (20)
- 1960 Census (32) (estimated)
- Villages & Townships

Source: Cleveland Metropolitan Services Commission, *Government Costs: Questions for Community Decision* (Cleveland, 1959), p. 6.

Figure 18-4. Metropolitan Cleveland's 62 cities

PROBLEMS OF GOVERNING METROPOLITAN AREAS

An additional thorn in the flesh of the central city is the fact that it suffers a serious loss of revenue from state taxes shared with cities on the basis of population, because a large portion of its "daytime" population cannot be counted. For purposes of figuring the city's share of such taxes, where a man sleeps is more important than where he works.

A second governmental problem common to most metropolitan areas is the existence of unequal services in different sections of the same metropolitan area. For cities in the early stages of metropolitanism it is the suburbanite who suffers most in this respect. Although he finds more room, fresh air, and quietude, he also frequently finds the multiple menace of inadequate sewage disposal, fire protection, police protection, and water supply, to name only a few. Prior to a recent metropolitan reorganization, suburban Nashville provided good examples — more than .150,000 of them — of metropolitan residents who received almost no municipal services, even having competitive, private-enterprise fire and police departments which served only paid-up subscribers.

Unequal urban services

In older metropolitan areas where suburban communities have been separately incorporated for many years, the over-all result is much the same. Some of the suburban communities may well pride themselves on having the finest and most efficient city government of the whole area. This fine record is frequently possible, however, only because low-value property has been excluded from the boundaries of such cities, resulting in unwanted and underprivileged pockets of the metropolitan community being left to their own inadequate resources. In varying degrees and in different forms, metropolitan dispersion has consistently resulted in an unhealthy difference in the quality of governmental services within a given metropolitan area.

From an administrative standpoint the illogical split-up of clearly metropolitan-wide functions of government constitutes a third serious problem. This fractionalization of administration is perhaps the most universal characteristic of metropolitanism, as indicated by the 15,658 separate units of government "required" to govern 174 metropolitan areas in the United States in 1957, and perhaps a larger number for the current total of 212 areas.

Fractionalization of administration

It requires no Solomon to point out that disease, crime, and fire are no respecters of political boundary lines. Yet what metropolitan area has had the minimum wisdom or vision to create a government with the metropolitan-wide authority necessary to cope with metropolitan-wide problems? A few cities have made progress in this direction, but the progress has been painfully limited. Metropolitan area water supply, police and fire protection, street, and park "systems," "just growed," like the immortal Topsy, and the result has been the haphazard creation of scores of police departments or water supply systems in a single urban area when one would be not only sufficient but also far more economical and effective. In the absence of a single, integrated, metropolitan government with authority to guide the progress of the whole urban region, unified policy formulation and execution is an impossibility.

In addition to the problem posed by dividing municipal administration into many illogical parts, there are troublesome and costly duplications inherent in the overlapping layers of local government. Even if large-scale annexation were to bring the metropolitan area within the boundaries of a single municipal corporation, there would still be one or more county governments and many special district governments overlying the city and duplicating many of its activities. Not even a baker's dozen of the standard metropolitan areas have tackled this problem by means of city-county consolidation or separation, so that most core cities in these areas are plagued with at least two tax assessors, tax collectors, law enforcement agencies, jails, health departments, and other agencies which operate in both city and county. This arrangement is bad at best, but is at its worst when the city and county are controlled by opposing political factions. *Many layers of government*

A final problem which arises from the dispersed condition of metropolitan government, and which is probably the most serious in the long run, is the inevitable weakening of citizen control over local government in the area. Which official or unit of government is to receive the credit or blame for over-all metropolitan goods or ills? Will the bewildered citizen blame the county, the central city, the suburban cities, or the many special districts, for sluggish commuter traffic? Who gets the blame for an ineffective attack on an epidemic, for "gangland" type crimes in various parts of the area, or for the low water pressure in the network of seventy-three different water supply systems? It should be fairly clear that citizens governed by such a maze of government as exists in metropolitan areas find it well nigh impossible to place the credit or blame for the respective deeds or misdeeds of their many governments. Democratic control by the people of the area as a whole has been dispersed and dissipated. *Weakening of democratic control*

PROPOSED REMEDIES

It may be said concerning remedies proposed for the various problems of governing metropolitan areas that "many are called but few are chosen." Political scientists have in recent years proposed many solutions to these problems and the more important of these proposals are summarized below, including the experience and prospects for each. *Alternative proposals*

Annexation of the surrounding urbanized territory to the central city is

342   the most commonly proposed, and perhaps the most obvious, remedy for the problem of suburbanitis. It was the method used by the nation's great

Annexation   cities to achieve their present size. The case for annexation is strong, both from the viewpoint of the suburbs and the central city: expensive public works, improvements, and services could be provided at lower cost than by the suburb alone; property values would rise; fire insurance rates would be lower; voting privileges in central city elections would be secured; the city's census standing would be higher; the base for financing municipal government would be broadened; and the city would bring about a suburban development consistent with its own development. For both city and suburban residents advantages result from functioning as one community, such as the capacity to make a unified attack on the metropolitan problems of disease, crime, slums and juvenile delinquency, as well as the efficiency and economy of larger scale operations.

In spite of the compelling logic of the arguments, it has been virtually impossible for the larger cities to keep pace by means of annexation with population growth on the margin of the city. Opposition to annexation is

Obstacles to   almost always strong in the suburbs, based upon several arguments: taxes
annexation   would be increased; the government of the central city is corrupt or incompetent; new services would be long delayed in arriving, if they arrive at all; and annexation is a nefarious scheme of the power-grabbing politicians and tax collectors in the city hall.

If the suburb to be annexed is already incorporated, the opposition may be exceedingly strong because of greater community spirit and unwillingness to lose its name, identity, and independence. Once a city is surrounded by separately incorporated satellite cities, the chances of annexation are slim. Boston, for example, has never been able to annex Brookline, Newton, and Milton. The suburban cities of Pasadena and Long Beach and even wholly surrounded Beverly Hills have been successful down through the years in resisting all efforts to incorporate them into the city of Los Angeles. More recent developments to metropolitan areas are equally discouraging to proponents of annexation except in cases where the metropolitan core cities are surrounded for the most part by unincorporated territory. Minneapolis became completely encircled by incorporated cities between 1940 and 1950, and ten new municipalities came into existence in the Chicago metropolitan area during the same period. Pittsburgh is surrounded by 181 municipalities, and Detroit by 72.

As long as each individual suburb remains the master of its fate concerning annexation, requiring a majority vote before coming under the jurisdiction

Liberalized   of the central city, annexation must be considered a thing of the past for
annexation   the older metropolitan areas. The procedure in some states, however,
procedures   makes it a great deal easier to accomplish annexation. Virginia statutes

provide for a special annexation court which judges the merits of each attempt, rather than allowing the voters of the city or suburbs to make the decision, and annexation has been a regularly recurring process in that state. Several Texas cities have been able to take advantage of home rule charters permitting them to annex by vote of the city council without a vote of the residents of either the city or the fringe area. In the past decade some of the largest annexations in the United States have taken place in Houston, Dallas, Fort Worth, and San Antonio. The Tennessee General Assembly in 1955 adopted a new annexation procedure which borrowed from both Texas and Virginia. Pushed through the legislature by the cities, the new procedure authorized annexation by a vote of the city council, subject to possible appeal to court for approval or disapproval according to standards of community welfare and progress.

Annexation activity in 1960 experienced a boom, both in terms of number of cities acting (712 cities with 5,000 population or more), and in terms of size of area annexed (1,083 square miles). It was the largest in 13 years. Kansas City, Missouri, and Oklahoma City annexed two of the largest areas in the history of American cities. Kansas City more than doubled its area by adding 187 square miles, to become effective at various times within a three-year period. Oklahoma City became the second largest city in area in the United States — next to Los Angeles — by annexing 149 square miles, making a total of 430 square miles. Mobile and Phoenix have also added large areas recently by the annexation route.[5]

In spite of successful annexations in these and other metropolitan areas, the fact remains that the central core cities of most of the larger metropolitan areas are finding it necessary to look to devices other than annexation to secure metropolitan political integration. The greatest opportunity for integration exists when the contiguous urban area is unincorporated and liberal annexation procedures are available. After the strait jacket of incorporated satellite cities has been wrapped around the core cities, they have been forced to turn from annexation to a variety of alternative proposals. *Limited value of annexation*

In the absence of annexation of the suburbs, a municipality is sometimes granted the right to exercise certain powers outside the city limits. Such extraterritorial powers have been sustained by the courts on the ground that they are essential to effective use of the intraterritorial powers granted to the city. The device takes such forms as the inspection of all sources of milk supply for a central city, even though the milkshed may extend many miles in all directions outside the city; the control of land platting outside *Extra-territorial powers*

[5] For details on recent annexations, see John C. Bollens, "Metropolitan and Fringe Area Developments in 1960," *The Municipal Year Book* (The International City Managers Association, Chicago, 1961), pp. 47-63.

the boundaries of the city; the control of contagious diseases for a certain number of miles beyond the corporate limits; the regulation of undesirable trades and the suppression of houses of prostitution within a certain distance of the city.

As a permanent device for furnishing integrated government to the whole metropolitan community extra-territorial power has important limitations. The problem of financing such activities in an equitable manner is perplexing. Furthermore, the exercise of governmental power over persons having no control over the government is not conducive to cooperation over the long run.

Probably the most widely used means of coordination in metropolitan areas is that of intergovernmental arrangements for municipal activities. The prevalence of contractual and informal agreements probably can be *Intergovern-* attributed to the fact that such arrangements seldom require fundamental *mental* change in the structure of government of the area and are least disturb- *cooperation* ing to political alignments. Local governments in California have made wide use of intergovernmental agreements, especially for county provision of service to cities. Los Angeles County, for example, had 887 contracts in 1959 calling for a wide range of services to cities. This procedure is sometimes called the "Lakewood Plan," because that city of 67,000 has contracted with Los Angeles to provide practically all of its governmental services. The ease with which cooperative agreements can be made is symptomatic of their major weakness, namely their inability to provide the fundamental changes necessary to achieve integrated metropolitan government. Intergovernmental cooperation includes such joint undertakings as the construction and maintenance of bridges, parkways and sewer systems, as well as a variety of lend, lease, or sale arrangements for such services to suburbs as water supply, fire protection, police protection, and health services. These and many other forms of cooperation find frequent use as an ad hoc approach to metropolitan problems, but voluntary cooperation is more difficult to secure when *regulation* and *control* are involved than in the case of primarily *service* functions.

Where annexation has been found politically infeasible or otherwise undesirable, some have proposed a type of metropolitan government which might be termed federal in that there would be a formal division of *The* powers between a central government and the constituent municipalities. *federated* Based upon a rough analogy to the relationship between the national *metropolis* government and the states, the larger unit of government would perform those functions which transcend municipal boundaries, while the component municipalities would continue to perform the purely local functions. The "federated metropolis" would cover the entire metropolitan area. In cases where the area coincides generally with the boundaries of a county, some plans provide for the county to become the central federated government. The federated government would be responsible for such activities as the operation of the water supply system, planning and zoning on a regional basis, police protection for unincorporated and rural areas, tax assessment and collection, sewage disposal, traffic control on arterial streets, and other functions beyond the capacity of any one municipality. Functions retained by the existing municipalities might include fire protection, police protection, garbage disposal, and similar activities more local in character, but the difficulty of defining "purely local" is quite obvious. In a day when it has become increasingly unrealistic to attempt a division between national and state functions, and between state and local functions, any further subdivision of local functions into those which are "area-wide" and those which are purely local would seem to be moving against the stream of governmental history.

For many years the city of London, having a two-tiered government consisting of a county council and several metropolitan boroughs, was the only metropolitan government which might properly be characterized as municipal federalism. But this characterization would be applicable only to the part of the city within London County rather than to the whole of Greater London. In 1953 the city of Toronto became the second metropolis to make use of the federal principle by uniting with its several suburbs in a federated city. New York City once approached the federal form, on paper at least, but the status of its boroughs is not so independent as might be required to conform to the federal pattern. It is even less an example of federalism under its latest charter. A federated plan of urban government was proposed as early as 1896 for Boston but without success, and a federated city-county government for Alameda County in California in 1922 was defeated by popular vote. A Pittsburgh plan in 1929 came closer to succeeding than any other and failed because it got the necessary two-thirds majority in only 58 of the 62 local units required.

Examples of municipal federalism

In spite of these and other failures to secure adoption, the idea of metropolitan federation is still very much alive, primarily because of the highly publicized Toronto experience and the more recent Miami "Metro" experience, which is federal in certain respects. The "Municipality of Metropolitan Toronto" was created by the provincial parliament in 1953 and given jurisdiction over several area-wide functions, both in the city of Toronto and in its 12 suburban "satellite" cities. The federation was actually a compromise between complete amalgamation (annexation), proposed by the city of Toronto, and complete independence as defended vehemently by the suburban cities. The result was to leave the 13 cities in charge of such activities as police, fire, health, library, and welfare services, while creating a new metropolitan level of government to handle water supply, sewage disposal, housing, education, arterial highways, metropolitan parks, and over-all planning.

The Toronto experience

346 In 1957 the 13 local police forces were taken over by the metropolitan government, causing some critics to say that metropolitan federation is merely "disguised annexation." Metropolitan Toronto has been widely publicized for an outstanding record of accomplishment in such activities as highways, rapid transit, water supply and sewerage, and regional planning. Although the Toronto plan has given new hope to metropolitan areas in the United States, it has not been without its own problems. Representation on the 25-member metropolitan council is ex officio and indirect, and equal representation for each suburb is far from equitable. Annual election of all but two of the council members is hardly consistent with the responsibility for long-range planning, and, in spite of its greatly expanded size, the metropolitan government still does not encompass the whole urbanized area.

The voters of Miami and Dade County in 1957 narrowly adopted (44,404 to 42,619) a two-tiered form of metropolitan government which incorporates, to a limited degree, the principle of federation. The heart of the Dade County "Metro" plan is the retention of the existing municipalities (Miami plus 27 suburban cities) for the performance of "purely local" activities, with the allocation of authority to Dade County for those governmental activities which are "essentially metropolitan" in nature. During its first five years of existence, while receiving nation-wide acclaim as a civic pacemaker, it was repeatedly fighting off the attacks of anti-Metro forces in the form of a multitude of lawsuits and three county-wide referendums which would have gutted the new structure. In addition to political battles it has had financial ones, stemming from the fact that it has many of the obligations of a city, but only the taxing power of a county. In technical terms, Dade County's Metro is more nearly a "municipalized county" than it is a federation of municipalities, since only cities with a population of 60,000 or more are allowed to elect a representative on the board of commissioners. But whatever the classification, this "great bold venture in modern government," as Metro Manager McNayr once called it, has offered a strong ray of hope to many other American metropolises.[6]

Partial federation in Dade County

Even before the adoption of the Miami proposal, in other counties in the United States political pressure from unserved suburban groups opposed to annexation and from reform groups discouraged in their annexation efforts has resulted in some cases in what might be called a "municipalized county." In spite of the county's legal position as an administrative district of the state, created to perform state functions, many states have

The municipalized county

---

[6] An increasing number of studies of the Miami experience are being published. *See,* for example, Edward Sofen, *The Miami Metropolitan Experiment,* Metropolitan Action Studies No. 2 (Indiana University Press, Bloomington, 1962), Reinhold P. Wolf, *Miami Metro: The Road to Urban Unity* (Bureau of Business and Economic Research, University of Miami, Coral Gables, 1960), and Gustave Serino, *Miami's Metropolitan Experiment* (Public Administration Clearing Service, University of Florida, Gainesville, 1958).

begun to grant counties authority to provide services traditionally considered municipal in type.[7] Probably the best known example of a county performing a multiplicity of municipal functions is Los Angeles County, as mentioned previously, with more functions than the city of Los Angeles and a budget exceeding that of the city. Among its many urban functions are street improvements, street lighting, sanitation, fire protection, police protection, library service, public parks, and regional planning.

Expansion of county functions evokes much less opposition than annexation or city-county consolidation. This fact doubtless explains the rapid advances in many states in the direction of transforming the urban county into a unit of metropolitan government. The one serious weakness of the movement to expand the county's functions is the fact that the county, as it is commonly organized, is still suited to the rural conditions of the horse-and-buggy era rather than to the task of administering muncipal functions. *Problem of county or-ganization* Its limited powers, numerous elective officials, serving almost as separate units of government, and cumbersome and impotent governing body are scarcely designed to facilitate effective and efficient performance of the heavy responsibilities of metropolitan government.[8] Many students of government feel, however, that it might be made suitable for local government in urban regions by drastic structural changes, such as the provision for a single county executive and the establishment of a county legislative body which is both representative and responsible.

One of the more popular piecemeal approaches to the problems of metropolitan government is the creation of special districts or authorities, distinct from other units of government and with boundary lines drawn to coincide with the boundaries of the problem or problems to be solved. *Special metropolitan districts* Special metropolitan districts are popular for a number of reasons. Experience with this device has demonstrated the ease with which seemingly insurmountable political boundary lines may be crossed. For example, the territorial jurisdiction of the Golden Gate Bridge and Highway District includes all of five San Francisco Bay area counties, all of another county, and part of a seventh. Districts meet relatively little resistance from politicians because they eliminate no jobs and usually do not disturb the organization's grip on the city government. So far as the suburban politicians are concerned, such ad hoc authorities are exceedingly popular because they lessen the pressure for annexation to the core city.

Special districts are frequently created for financial reasons, such as the

[7] *See* Mark B. Feldman and Everett L. Jassy, "The Urban County: A Study of New Approaches to Local Government in Metropolitan Areas," *Harvard Law Review,* January, 1960, pp. 526-582.

[8] *See* Chapter 16 for a discussion of problems of county structure.

348   need for equalizing the tax burden over an area wider than that of existing units or for enabling a unit of government to evade established tax or debt limits. In the latter case, existing units of government in a metropolitan area may already be up to their tax and debt limits, so that the only local means of providing additional revenue to finance a desired service is to establish a new unit of government.

      Among the better known special metropolitan authorities are the Chicago Sanitary District, organized in 1889, and the Massachusetts Metropolitan District Commission, dating back to 1889 for sewers, 1893 for parks, and

Examples of metropolitan districts

1895 for a water system. A more recent example is the Metropolitan Sewer District Commission created in the Louisville area in 1946. The growth of metropolitan areas across state boundary lines has led to the creation by means of interstate compacts of such districts as the Port of New York Authority and the more recent Bi-State Development Agency for the St. Louis area. The Port of New York Authority performs in a district of about 1,500 square miles with close to fifteen million residents.[9]

      There seems to be a growing willingness on the part of state legislatures to give special districts the power to exercise a number of functions, thus permitting multi-purpose special districts and making the title "ad hoc district" a misnomer. Some of its proponents hope that it might gradually evolve into a general area-wide government by the adding of functions as the failure of the smaller units of government becomes apparent. One such district was set up in 1958, the Municipality of Metropolitan Seattle, under a state law permitting cities and towns of Washington to act jointly in solving common problems. The only functions thus far are sewage disposal and water pollution, but the 14 component municipalities may give it such additional functions as transportation, water, parks, garbage disposal, and planning. A proposal to add transportation to the Seattle authority was rejected in a 1962 referendum. A multipurpose district was proposed for the St. Louis metropolitan area in 1959 but was defeated by popular vote.

      If the value of the special district is measured in terms of the limited objective of executing a specific project, special metropolitan districts have on the whole been effective in doing the job assigned. From the broader stand-

Districts as a mixed blessing

point of integrating metropolitan government, however, special districts not only weaken the bargaining power of those trying to sell annexation to the suburbs but also add to the confusion of the independent "thousand islands" of government making up the metropolis. Such districts confuse the

---

[9] For a discussion of the shortcomings of even the highly praised Port of New York Authority, when measured on other than "its own terms," *see* Edward T. Chase, "The Trouble with the New York Port Authority," in *Urban Government: A Reader in Administration and Politics,* Edward C. Banfield, ed. (Free Press of Glencoe, Inc., New York, 1961), pp. 75-82.

voters with additional layers of government and make it more difficult for the 349
citizenry to hold government accountable. In addition, special districts do not
improve the census rating of the central city — a matter of no small importance
as it relates both to promotion by the chamber of commerce and to receipts
from state-collected locally-shared taxes based upon population. In spite of these
long-run deficiencies, special districts continue to be very popular with metropolitan decision makers, though little known and little understood by the
metropolitan public at large.[10]

A few cities in the United States have resorted to city-county separation
in an effort to eliminate one of the layers of government under which the city
resident must live and pay taxes. This involves removal of the city's
territory from the jurisdiction of the county, consolidating city and county *City-county*
functions within the city limits and restricting the county government *separation*
to the residue of the former county. The four outstanding examples are
Baltimore, separated from its county in 1851, San Francisco in 1856, St. Louis
in 1875, and Denver in 1903. Judicial interpretations of the state constitutions
resulted in varying degrees of consolidation of city and county functions in each
case. In addition to these four cases, Virginia has a unique general scheme of
city-county separation for all first-class cities. When a city attains a population
of 10,000 it automatically becomes for governmental purposes almost entirely
separate from the county in which it is located. Second-class cities (over 5,000
population) are only partially separated governmentally from their counties,
continuing to make use on a pro rata basis of certain county officers and services.

City-county separation is always strongly resisted by the rural portions
of the county which are to become the "rump" county. The impoverished remains of the county may find it necessary to unite with surrounding counties in
the face of operating a suburban and rural government without sufficient tax
resources. On the other hand, city-county separation usually seriously complicates the future expansion of the city, because enlargement of the city-county's
boundaries is much more difficult than extension of the ordinary city's corporate
limits. The seriousness of the future annexation problem depends, of course,
on whether adequate annexations take place prior to separation of the city
from the county. Even though large annexations are carried out, however, it
is never very long before the city has grown beyond its legal boundaries. Both
San Francisco and St. Louis have been anxious for many years to reacquire
territory discarded earlier but have been unable to do so. Figure 18-5 depicts
this plight. Only in Virginia has city-county separation been coupled with a
practical plan for extending the city limits as the population spreads outside
the city.

---

[10] For a detailed analysis of the nature of special districts, *see* John C. Bollens, *Special District Governments in the United States* (University of California Press, Berkeley, 1957).

PROPOSED REMEDIES

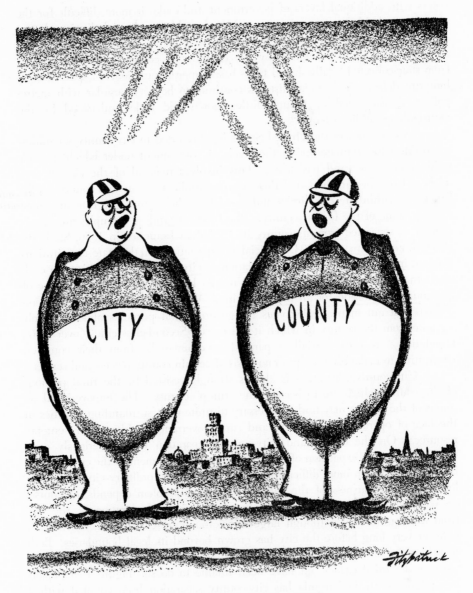

"MEET ME AT ST. LOOIE, LOOIE, —

Source: *St. Louis Post-Dispatch*, December 12, 1956. Reproduced by permission of the *St. Louis Post-Dispatch*.

Figure 18-5

LOCAL GOVERNMENT: METROPOLITICS

City-county consolidation constitutes a slightly different method of accomplishing substantially the same result as city-county separation. Under city-county consolidation the city limits are extended to coincide with the county boundaries and the two governments are consolidated, leaving no troublesome remnant county. The effects of the two methods are identical, so far as the territory under the new consolidated city-county is concerned, with the elimination of duplicate sets of officers for city and county functions and of overlapping jurisdiction between city and county. Philadelphia, New York, and Baton Rouge have adopted some form of consolidated city-county government, in addition to the cities mentioned previously as having achieved a similar result by means of city-county separation.

City-county consolidation

The advantages of consolidating county and city governments in metropolitan areas are fairly obvious, including such things as the taxpayers' benefit from eliminating one layer of government, the voters' benefit from the shorter ballot and more simplified structure of local government, and administrative improvements resulting from metropolitan-wide jurisdiction. This last benefit, governmental integration of the whole metropolitan area, cannot be claimed in all cases of city-county consolidation. The largest metropolitan areas in the United States spill over into more than one county as well as into neighboring states, so that consolidation with a single county would not encompass the whole urban area. Another difficulty of the consolidated city-county is the fact that future annexation to keep pace with the suburban movement necessitates detaching territory from adjacent counties, which would generally require jumping constitutional hurdles and working political miracles.

Pros and cons of city-county consolidation

Political scientists on several occasions have pronounced city-county consolidation to be a thing of the past, only to see it resurrected as a serious proposal in some major city. The merger of Baton Rouge and East Baton Rouge Parish in Louisiana in 1947 and more recent activity in Birmingham, Durham, Richmond, Nashville, and other cities indicate that city-county consolidation is still a live issue in metropolitan areas in the United States.

Voters of Nashville and Davidson County adopted a charter in June, 1962 consolidating the city and county governments into a single metropolitan government. Four years earlier a similar proposal had been rejected by the suburban and rural voters of the county but an ambitious annexation drive by the city of Nashville in 1960 caused many suburbanites to look at city-county consolidation in a more favorable light and the tide turned in favor of "Metro." The unique feature of the Nashville plan is an expandable "urban services district," beginning initially with the core city's boundaries but expanding with the urban growth and the extension of urban growth and the extension of urban services, and with a tax rate corresponding to the higher level of services. All persons are in the "general services district"

City-county consolidation in Nashville

352 and receive and pay for all area-wide services of the metropolitan government. All duplicate city and county departments, boards, executives, and legislative bodies, are merged into single, metropolitan counterparts. Architects of the plan contend that it has the benefits of unified government for the entire metropolitan area, without the inflexibilities of previous city-county mergers with respect to the problem of governing the developing suburban fringe and the more stable rural areas. Its constitutionality was upheld by the State Supreme Court in late 1962. Assuming that continued sympathetic treatment by the courts can be obtained, the Nashville plan can be expected to provide hope for many of the medium-sized and smaller metropolitan areas located entirely within single counties.[11]

Functional consolidation

Obstacles to city-county consolidation have caused many cities to resort to a more gradual approach, which takes the form of consolidating single functions common to both city and county governments without a complete political and territorial merger. Functional consolidation involves the performance by one unit of local government of an activity such as public health or sewage disposal, previously performed by two or more overlapping units, with no change in the general structural relations of these units. It may be brought about either by state action, permissive or mandatory, reallocating the functions of local government, or by some form of contractual arrangement between the local governmental jurisdictions. One of the better known examples of functional consolidation is the extensive plan for redistribution of functions between Atlanta and Fulton County which was approved in 1950. Although this device cannot be expected to solve the over-all metropolitan problem, it can provide a means of handling certain parts of the total problem without increasing the complexity of local government in the area. Functional consolidation is sometimes called the "Fabian" approach to eventual city-county consolidation, rather than the frontal attack, but it is also possible for a piecemeal solution to one or two of the more pressing problems to slow down or delay indefinitely city-county consolidation.

The future of metropolitan government

It is easy for advocates of integrated metropolitan government to become discouraged after running the gamut of the various proposed remedies for the ills of "metropolitanism." It seems that those "solutions" which are adequate are politically infeasible and those which are politically feasible are inadequate.[12]

---

[11] For an account of developments leading to the 1962 adoption of the Nashville plan, see Daniel R. Grant and Lee S. Greene, "Surveys, Dust, Action," *National Civic Review*, L (October, 1961), pp. 466-471, and Daniel R. Grant, "Urban and Suburban Nashville: A Case Study in Metropolitanism," *Journal of Politics*, XVII (February, 1955), pp. 82-99.

[12] For some reflective thinking on the relationship of American ideology to the difficulty of securing adoption of proposed metropolitan "solutions," see Luther H. Gulick, *The Metropolitan Problem and American Ideas* (Alfred A. Knopf, Inc., New York, 1962).

Two developments in the United States, however, may well hold the key to the future of metropolitan government. One of these is the increasingly interstate character of metropolitan areas which spill over state boundary lines and present a prima facie case for intervention by the federal government in some form. This is no small development, as evidenced by the fact that one out of four persons in the United States lives in a metropolitan area which either straddles or borders a state line. The U. S. Advisory Commission on Intergovernmental Relations has shown much greater concern for metropolitan areas and their governmental structures than any previous federal study group.[13]

The second development which concerns the future of metropolitan government is more recent than the interstate spillover, but conceivably more far-reaching. This is the use of the federal government's war powers in a wide sweep of activities affecting cities, providing almost unlimited opportunity to bring about either integration or disintegration of local government in metropolitan areas. An industrial dispersion policy of the federal government, even if carried out only half-heartedly, would magnify metropolitan problems by causing new industries to locate a considerable distance outside the central city's corporate boundaries. Other phases of the civil defense program point to the growing responsibility of the federal government to encourage the kind of metropolitan government which facilitates most effective use of resources in such fields as fire protection, police protection, and public health in case of enemy attack. It is improbable that the future of metropolitan government lies completely within the context of federal-municipal relations, but, as indicated in Chapter 3, there can be little doubt that the federal government will find itself more and more involved in the problems of governing these areas where almost two-thirds of the population dwells.[14]

SUPPLEMENTARY READINGS

Bollens, John C., ed., *Exploring the Metropolitan Community* (University of California Press, Berkeley, 1961).

Connery, Robert H., and Richard H. Leach, *The Federal Government and Metropolitan Areas* (Harvard University Press, Cambridge, 1960).

---

[13] *See*, for example, their study of *Factors Affecting Voter Reactions to Governmental Reorganization in Metropolitan Areas* (U. S. Advisory Commission on Intergovernmental Relations, Washington, D. C., May, 1962).

[14] *See* Daniel R. Grant, "Federal-Municipal Relationships and Metropolitan Integration," *Public Administration Review*, XIV (Autumn, 1954), pp. 259-267.

Council of State Governments, *The States and the Metropolitan Problem,* John C. Bollens, Director of Study (Council of State Governments, Chicago, 1956).

Editors of *Fortune, The Exploding Metropolis* (Doubleday & Company, Inc., Garden City, New York, 1958).

Fiser, Webb S., *Mastery of the Metropolis* (Prentice-Hall Spectrum Books, Prentice-Hall, Inc., Englewood Cliffs, 1962).

Government Affairs Foundation, Inc., *Metropolitan Surveys: A Digest* (Public Administration Service, Chicago, 1958).

Gulick, Luther H., *The Metropolitan Problem and American Ideas* (Alfred A. Knopf, Inc., New York, 1962).

Jones, Victor, *Metropolitan Government* (University of Chicago, 1942).

Martin, Roscoe C., *et al.,* *Decisions in Syracuse,* Metropolitan Action Studies No. 1 (Indiana University Press, Bloomington, 1962).

Mowitz, Robert J., and Deil S. Wright, *Profile of a Metropolis* (Wayne State University Press, Detroit, 1962).

Rush, J. A., *The City-County Consolidated* (Published by the author, Los Angeles, 1941).

Studenski, Paul, *The Government of Metropolitan Areas in the United States* (National Municipal League, New York, 1930).

Sweeney, Stephen B., and George S. Blair, eds., *Metropolitan Analysis: Important Elements of Study and Action* (University of Pennsylvania Press, Philadelphia, 1958).

U. S. Advisory Commission on Intergovernmental Relations, *Governmental Structure, Organization, and Planning in Metropolitan Areas* (U. S. Government Printing Office, Washington, 1961).

U. S. National Resources Committee, Research Committee on Urbanism, *Our Cities; Their Role in the National Economy* (U. S. Government Printing Office, Washington, 1937).

Wood, Robert C., with Vladimir V. Almendinger, *1400 Governments* (Harvard University Press, Cambridge, 1961).

Woodbury, Coleman, ed., *The Future of Cities and Urban Redevelopment* (University of Chicago Press, Chicago, 1953).

⋆ *19* ⋆

LAW ENFORCEMENT: PROTECTIVE

AND CORRECTIVE ACTIVITIES

GOVERNMENT, WHATEVER ITS FORM, is not government unless it maintains law and order. Liberty, as was emphasized in the fourth chapter, is always liberty under law. Thomas Jefferson, maximizing individual freedom and minimizing public control, left it clear that government should prevent citizens from injuring each other. Law enforcement is one of the oldest functions of government. Yet it is reported that serious crimes are increasing in the United States at a rate exceeding the population growth by four to one.[1]

Importance to government

Law enforcement is exemplified in the nearly universal American office of county sheriff, a functionary handed down from the shire-reeve of Saxon England as local keeper of the peace and enforcer of the law of the land. All units and most agencies of government are concerned directly or indirectly with the methods and effectiveness of law enforcement, of compelling obedience to legitimate authority and preventing disturbance of the public peace or safety. The realm of law enforcement is an important area of intergovernmental relations, involving cooperation and even competition or friction. The significant

---

[1] *See* A. F. Brandstatter, "Police Administration: Developments in 1960," *The Municipal Yearbook, 1961* (The International City Managers' Association, Chicago, 1961), pp. 392-395.

state units normally involved are the state government, the counties, and the cities or towns.

All officers of the "law" in a state, except those commissioned by the national government, are state officers, whatever may be their local functions, duties, and powers. County sheriffs and deputies, city policemen and detectives, and rural constables have the direct responsibility of enforcing state laws and apprehending violators of state laws within the territorial jurisdictions of their political subdivisions. Their own election or appointment is prescribed broadly or specifically by state statutes or constitutional provisions. Federal courts and federal legislation hold them responsible as agents of the state for respecting rights of persons guaranteed by the Fourteenth Amendment. The governor in many states has important powers of supervision, removal, and replacement over designated local officers in order to prevent neglect or laxity in matters of enforcement.

All officers are state officers

CENTRAL STATE FORCES

Every state has central agencies to facilitate or ensure the preservation of law and order in the commonwealth. The oldest of the state forces or potential forces is the "Militia," as designated by the federal Constitution, or "National Guard," as covered by later legislation by Congress. The states are forbidden to keep troops in time of peace except by the consent of Congress, and thus the national legislature has in various ways provided for the establishment and training of the state troops as well as for calling them into federal service with federal compensation when necessary.[2] Members of the National Guard pursue their regular civilian occupations in normal times, but are subject to call by state or national authorities. They may be ordered by the governor or his adjutant general to join their units in active duty to quell riots, to police communities visited by disaster, or to take over the whole law enforcement function in instances of complete breakdown of local administration. The Alabama state troops temporarily assumed complete administration of local government, for example, in Phenix City in the middle 1950's when the governor moved to put that gambler-ridden community under martial law. The use of the National Guard by governors to police strikes has at times provoked controversy on the political front, with charges of strikebreaking coming from organized labor. New Orleans authorities and citizens once complained that Governor Huey Long sent troops to patrol an open square in front of their city hall with little justification aside from factional politics.

The National Guard

---

[2] *See* James B. Deerin, "The National Guard," *The Book of the States, 1962-63.*

State and national authorities have met criticism at times for invoking martial law or using troops for purposes or pretexts of internal protection.[3] When members of the National Guard are largely or completely engaged in federal service, as in wartime, their intrastate role may be taken over by improvised home guards or state guards.

With the rise of state police systems, state governments in modern times have felt less need for utilizing troops to quell disorder. Centralized state police systems have developed throughout the country in one form or another since the organization of the Texas Rangers in 1835 to patrol frontier regions harassed by lawless elements. Massachusetts provided for state constables in 1865, and Pennsylvania created a regular state police system in 1905. *The rise of state police systems*

Several factors account for the growth and professional role of state agencies of public safety. Their routine performance stirs less curiosity or complaint than the sudden summoning of state troops. The universality of motor transportation on networks of superhighways requires enforcement of traffic regulations beyond the concern or capacity of local officers. State forces are likely to be best equipped to cope with intercity or intercounty operations of major criminals, not only for capturing them but also for procuring or testing clues and evidence through scientific methods. These central agencies may provide expert aid and service to local officers, and, if they are called upon by the latter, no issue of local pride or prerogative is likely to arise. They may strengthen the hand of the law consistently in sparsely populated regions and, at times, in areas or centers of commercialized crime where local authorities may be subject to the subsidy of influential bosses of vice.

Every state has a general police force or highway patrol or both. Three-fourths of the states have central police systems with full authority of law enforcement, and the others have state highway patrols which are concerned primarily or entirely with traffic violations, perhaps as units of the highway departments. State employees devoted to police protection range in number from a few dozen in Nevada or Alaska to more than 3,000 in California. There is no great degree of uniformity among the systems, but many states select the personnel of police or patrol on a merit basis and also provide for training of the members. Other factors affect the selection of the top officials, who are likely to have gubernatorial appointment and support. In a few states the head or superintendent of the force is chosen by a board, which may exercise substantial control over the activities of the agency. States *The state picture*

---

[3] It might be noted that martial law is not statutory or codified law or formal military government. It is a process of superseding municipal or political authority with military rule, applicable to civilians of the area or community, under circumstances of gross peril to life, law, and order.

with large or effective systems assign the men, on a more or less flexible basis, to routes or geographical sections for adequate territorial coverage. Some states also have a functional division, as between highway patrol service and other enforcement duties. The personnel is also likely to be organized in a military or semi-military manner, with companies, rank, and uniforms.

The states also have a miscellany of specialized officers or agencies for direct or indirect aid to security and law enforcement.[4] These include such functionaries as civil defense directors, fire marshals, game and fish wardens, liquor control officers, and different types of inspectors, who may be responsible to central regulatory agencies. There are state medical examiners to determine the cause of death in questionable or concealed circumstances. There are central offices or bureaus, with professional staffs, to make investigations with laboratory methods, including chemical and ballistic testing, to establish evidence of crime and identification of criminals. This service is of invaluable aid to prosecuting authorities throughout the state. Such testing sometimes establishes the innocence of suspects, since the methods are free from the bias or error of eye-witnesses.

COUNTY AUTHORITIES
AND ACTIVITIES

The American sheriff historically embodies the combination of a medieval factotum with a kingpin of the wild western frontier. The role of this officer has declined less in this country than in England, but our county sheriff

The sheriff   has yielded importance in many ways and in many regions to the state police and the city police, particularly as a keeper of the peace. He and his deputies are important enforcement and arresting officers in rural counties and in unincorporated fringes of many urban counties. The sheriff, with his subordinates, has two other regular responsibilities. He functions as an executive agent of state judicial courts in his jurisdiction, serving papers, subpoenas, processes, property attachments, and the like, in both criminal and civil matters. He guards prisoners in court and jail, administers or supervises jail quarters, provides food for prisoners, and arranges for escorting convicted persons to the penitentiary to serve sentence. He may, as in several states, have duties in connection with collecting delinquent taxes or disposing of property for non-

---

[4] See Earle W. Garrett, "Special Purpose Police Forces," *Annals of the American Academy of Political and Social Science*, CCXCI (January, 1954), pp. 31-38.

payment of taxes. "Sheriff's sale" has a folk meaning. Prior to the adoption of modern scientific methods of executing the death sentence and of the policy of administering this punishment in the central penitentiary in most of the states, many a sheriff, like Grover Cleveland when he was such an officer, had to fill the role of hangman, with the county jail or jail yard as the scene. Because of the availability of other enforcement forces, the sheriff today seldom exercises his traditional power to commandeer a *posse comitatus* of laymen to deal with excessive or riotous disorder.

The sheriff normally gets his position through political activity. He is chosen by the electorate in every state except Rhode Island, where selection is by the legislature. The term is likely to be for two or for four years, and many states forbid a sheriff to succeed himself. This restriction does not prevent a man from winning the office for alternate terms. There have been cases of two men teaming up to hold the restrictive office between themselves, with the "out" serving as the chief deputy for the "in" for a number of terms.

The sheriff's office; fees and politics

The attractiveness of the office is enhanced in many states and counties by the retention of the antiquated fee system, fees sometimes amounting to a fortune during one term in a large county. There may be a fee for every court order, process, or warrant served by the sheriff or a deputy for whatever purpose, with additional compensation for capturing or handling prisoners. Sheriffs have been known to make handsome profits in the business of lodging and feeding prisoners, sometimes supplementing the gains by providing outside luxuries for prisoners having ample funds. The office thus tends often to become a desirable entrepreneurial undertaking, and some have been known to reap further gain by peddling lucrative protection to criminal interests. The incumbent is often enmeshed in the unavoidable business aspects of the office, whether for selfish or for unselfish motives, and thus tends to function merely as an amateur in the sphere of law enforcement. In addition to his regular staff, he may commission deputies on a nominal or honorary basis for political purposes or for authorizing privately employed guards to act in an enforcement capacity for their employers.

More than in other fields of government is vigilance on the part of citizens essential for public effectiveness in the sheriff's office. Systematic or improvised merit systems for the selection of deputies offer one answer to the problem of county law enforcement under politically chosen officials. There have also been suggestions that the sheriff be restricted to the function of process-server as officer of the court and that his enforcement or public safety role be transferred to more expert agencies.

The constable is a sort of sheriff with duties inside the county. This officer is appointed in a few states but elected in most instances by the voters

360 of a town, township, or precinct. He generally has duties or responsibilities

within his electoral subdivision. As keeper of the peace, however, he

The con-stable has county-wide authority in some states and may act independently

of other enforcement officers. Constables have actually undertaken raids
on illegal establishments overlooked by urban police and sheriff. The constable
consistently acts as executive officer and process-server for minor courts or
justices of the peace, and this role has often become his sole or primary concern.
In certain states the constable may have duties with respect to delinquent taxes.
Like the sheriff, he finds compensation through fees. Like the justice of the
peace, he is only a part-time public functionary, and, like the J. P., he is tending
to disappear from the civic landscape.

The coroner is also a local lay official and is somewhat more outmoded than
the sheriff or constable. He is a popularly elected county officer in most states,

and it is his function to investigate the cause of death occurring in the

The coroner absence of witnesses and under circumstances indicating the possible use

of unlawful means. He may have the power of assembling a jury, usually
of six laymen, to conduct an inquest and render an official report on the testimony
and findings. The coroner has power to issue warrants for arrest, but neither
the coroner nor his jury may try a case for determining guilt or punishment. A
few states, with Massachusetts as pioneer, have replaced the coroner with a
local medical examiner, and the practice of choosing physicians for the office
or adding medical men to the coroner's staff has been adopted as an improvement.
Much of the work formerly performed by the local coroner is now handled by
central state agencies or bureaus of analysis, investigation, and identification, as
indicated earlier in this chapter.

The local prosecutor is an established and essential factor in state law
enforcement and criminal justice, and circumstances often combine to make him

a wielder of great power. His title varies among the states. He may be

The public prosecutor designated as prosecuting attorney, solicitor, attorney general, state's

attorney, district attorney, and the like. He usually serves a single county,

but several small rural counties sometimes may have a circuit-riding
prosecutor. He is selected by popular election in about nine-tenths of the states,
most commonly for a four-year term, although there are terms of two years and
of six years. He derives power from constitution, law, and custom, and is a
dominant force in criminal proceedings and trial court action from first clue to
conviction or acquittal. If strong and able, a lawyer in this position may inject
a civic spirit of energy and action into a complacent police department, sheriff's
staff, grand jury, and all investigators concerned with checking and detecting
crime. Populous counties or districts may have special investigators as well as
assistant attorneys attached to the chief prosecutor's office. There have been
examples of softness of prosecution toward commercialized crime, but some-

times a prosecuting attorney coordinates his own militant activity with an aroused public opinion in launching an attack upon vice or racketeering. Important public careers have been started or accelerated from the office of local prosecutor, as exemplified by the elder Robert M. La Follette, Hugo Black, and Thomas E. Dewey. The office of the public prosecutor is not on the decline.

Public prosecution is theoretically supposed at all times to serve the ends of objective justice, not partisan injustice, but a criminal case in court tends to become a game which the prosecuting attorney seeks to win on his own terms, leaving the defense to look out for itself or take the consequences. *The elusive* Wealthy or professional criminals are able to meet the prosecution with *goal of* equal or superior legal talent. But many accused may be handicapped in *"objective* this respect. The politics of harsh and lenient handling of criminal cases *justice"* was discussed in Chapter 15. The constitutional requirement that defense counsel be furnished in jury trials, at public expense if necessary, is often inadequate for the poor, since lawyers appointed by the court for this purpose are often unequal to the opposition in ability or experience and may at best put up a lame or nominal defense. To meet this dilemma, a number of individual counties or jurisdictions in different parts of the country have set up the office of public defender, putting this regular official on a par with the prosecuting *Public* attorney before the court. He has equal accessibility to public facilities *defender* for procuring or testing evidence. Connecticut and Rhode Island are the only states in which the system is used on a statewide basis.[5] The trial courts in more than three thousand counties continue to trust the assignment of counsel for the poor to the judge. Sometimes outside aid comes from such organizations as the American Civil Liberties Union, particularly in what seem to be conspicuous or flagrant cases of discrimination. Voluntary assistance may come from local sources, including legal aid clinics.[6]

URBAN POLICE

Urban police departments constitute the most important instruments of law enforcement and public safety in the United States today. City policemen outnumber all other state and local enforcement officers combined. One policeman or marshal may suffice for a small town, but New York City *General* requires a force of nearly 25,000, with many other cities using thousands. *importance*

---

[5] For a description of Connecticut's system *see* David Mars, "The Public Defender System in Connecticut," *State Government*, XXVII (February, 1954), pp. 29-30, 41.

[6] *See* Emery A. Brownell, "Availability of Low Cost Legal Services," *The Annals of the American Academy of Political and Social Science*, CCLXXXVII (May, 1953), pp. 120-126.

362   The urban police force has a large role for several reasons. The American population has become far more urban or metropolitan than rural, and cities provide the scene of a large amount of modern crime. Moreover, urban protective vigilance must function around the clock, for the city never sleeps, part of its population being always on the move for good or for ill. Aside from directly combatting crime and criminals, the city police must give constant attention to a moderate regimentation of the whole process of life, work, and play within its jurisdiction in order to prevent utter confusion. Multitudes of individuals leaving an auditorium or stadium, for example, require traffic direction, even if all the individuals should have the most saintly intentions. If fire damage leaves collapsible walls or buildings endangering life, the police must get on the job to protect the innocent and unsuspecting from self-jeopardy. Police specialists conduct searches and inquiries for missing persons, including minors and adults, whether crime is involved or not. The processes of urban civilization in the technological age make it necessary for the police to provide guidance and assistance for the obedient as well as force and compulsion for the disobedient.

American urban police administration has gone through a process of incomplete evolution from spoils practices to a merit-based professionalism with a wide application of scientific techniques. This evolution has come about

From spoils
to science
chiefly in the twentieth century, although progress occurred earlier in the wake of the reorganization of the London police in 1829 through reform action by Sir Robert Peel. The London "Peelers" or "Bobbies" wore copper buttons on their uniforms, from which the word "cop" was derived as a designation for an American policeman. In spite of improvement, however, many American city police departments still have far to go, and evidence of favoritism or corruption continues to appear in different parts of the country from time to time. There are a few state-controlled police departments, as in Boston, Baltimore, St. Louis, and Kansas City, Missouri, but most police forces are under local control. Hence their scientific or meritorious features tend to fluctuate with the ups and downs of local self-government. In comparison with Western Europe or Great Britain, American urban police systems have suffered through lack of attractiveness for the most competent career men. Ambitious young Americans too often have sought other outlets for their talents. Thought continues to be given by reform elements to the means whereby urban police service can be rendered an attractive career to the able, however, and some of the nation's more important cities are managing to recruit more able people for police work.[7]

---

[7] See Thomas M. Frost, "Selection Methods for Police Recruits," *The Journal of Criminal Law, Criminology and Police Science*, XLVI (1955-1956), pp. 135-145; O. W. Wilson, "Problems in Police Personnel Administration," *ibid.*, XLIII (1952-1953), pp. 840-847; and Charles F. Sloane, "Police Professionalization," *ibid.*, XLV (1954-1955), pp. 77-79.

The organization of police departments inevitably varies for different cities, particularly for cities of different size. The typical operating head, or chief of police, serves by local appointment in most cities but is chosen by state authorities for those few departments that are under state control. The municipal superior to whom the chief is responsible varies according to city charters and forms of government. This authority may be the mayor, city manager, police commissioner, or a local board. There are variations within the variations. A commissioner, for example, may be an appointee or may be an elected member of a city commission, and he may have jurisdiction over both police and fire departments. Police boards, where used, are not uniform and are not uniformly effective.[8] Theodore Roosevelt did a clean-up job as chairman of such a board in New York city in the 1890's.

Departmental organization

Modern police departments are organized and operated through functional divisions in order to make use of specialized training and experience for efficient service. Traffic regulation as an expanding function calls for the concentrated attention of one branch or bureau of the force. Another task is performed by regular police patrols, who move on foot or by motor to protect life and property and arrest lawbreakers. For every large or important city there is a separate unit or division of detectives working quietly and in plain clothes to run down crime and criminals. Every such city must also have a headquarters staff, including officers or employees for general records service, internal housekeeping, and other routine activity. A large department has a certain amount of police personnel administration. Police women are needed for special work among women criminals and prisoners. A city may have squads for special or temporary assignment, such as checking and investigating juvenile delinquency or raiding vice dens. A development of recent years is the auxiliary police for civil defense, which cooperates with other authorities in this functional area. The smaller cities, of course, cannot have the protection of police organization and mechanization on an elaborate scale except through central state or metropolitan arrangements.

Efforts, at least in scattered instances, have been taken in recent years to raise the standards of police personnel, to put more merit into the merit systems.[9] The Federal Bureau of Investigation conducts training courses for selected officers from state and local forces. Northwestern University and a few other insti-

---

[8] Thomas H. Reed and other authorities on municipal administration emphasize the disadvantages of board management of police departments. *See* J. E. Pate, *Local Government and Administration* (American Book Company, New York, 1954), p. 489.

[9] In this connection, *see* three articles in *The Journal of Criminal Law, Criminology and Police Science*: Charles F. Sloane, "State Academies for Police," XLV (1954-1955), pp. 729-735; George N. Beck, "Municipal Police Performance Rating," LI (January-February, 1961), pp. 567-574; and George E. Misner, "Recent Developments in Metropolitan Law Enforcement," L (January-February, 1960), pp. 497-508.

tutions of higher learning have offered courses for police training, while many others give short courses or institutes for policemen. Many urban police

Training and improvement; cooperative activities

departments sponsor or jointly sponsor training schools for the improvement of the service. The FBI and a number of state departments aid local police with fingerprint service and other mechanical facilities. Cooperation of law enforcement among the agencies and officers of overlapping units of government goes far to minimize friction and maximize enforcement. The urban police department is often at the center of this set of intergovernmental relations. A city police force or officer is likely at any time to round up a criminal for the authorities of another city or a county of any state or for the authorities of the United States.

PRISON ADMINISTRATION AND CORRECTIONAL ACTIVITIES

The 50 states, with their local units, have a wide variety of prisons and correctional systems, which are based upon several old or new theories of crime and punishment in relationship to the nature of man. These theories

Theories and purposes

are not mutually exclusive but overlap slightly with varied emphasis as applied to the multitudinous jurisdictions. Four of them should be noted. (1) There is the old, old theory that revenge should be visited by society upon the guilty person, holding him solely and individually responsible for his error and compelling him to pay his "debt" to society on the basis of an eye for an eye, a tooth for a tooth, a life for a life. (2) Closely related to the revenge theory is the general demand that punishment be sure, adequately severe, and sufficiently conspicuous to deter others from crime regardless of inclination. This idea calls for a calculated matching of crime and punishment, with large penalties to check large crimes and small penalties to check smaller violations. (3) There is the strong insistence that criminals be segregated behind walls in order to protect society from further violations by them until they learn their lesson. (4) There is a complex theory, with a modern socio-scientific bias, which assumes that society owes a debt of rehabilitation to lawbreakers, who are social defectives, partly or entirely, as victims of circumstances beyond their control. The circumstances may be physical, physiological, mental, economic, or social, with denial to the individual of the role of free agent. The theory of reform or rehabilitation has been particularly applied in recent times to juvenile offenders, but it is also taken seriously by many authorities and institutional officers in the treatment of adults.

The prisons having the least concern with problems of human restoration are normally the city and county jails, which serve primarily for the retention of accused persons pending trial and sentence or other disposition of their case. Such retention is not technical punishment, however unpleasant *Local jails* it may be, and is not to be associated with "hard labor." In many instances, however, short terms of punishment are served in such jails, sometimes by persons who serve time for lack of funds to pay fines.

There has been improvement in the living conditions and treatment of inmates in these local jails in the twentieth century. Many county jails are used jointly by the federal government for housing prisoners on a contract basis, and the federal government requires that certain standards be maintained and checked by inspection. Modern health regulations apply to jails and are sometimes enforced. For a few weeks in 1955 the city of Nashville, Tennessee, was without a municipal prison because of a condemnation decision by the local health department and had to rely entirely upon county law enforcement proceedings for purposes of public safety. Many a small city or county has antiquated jail facilities, and "jailbirds" in such places have an abundance of monotonous boredom.

Many cities and counties maintain work crews of prisoners whose terms of punishment are too short for transportation to state prisons. Much of this work is on streets or roads under the eyes of armed guards and in the view of all who pass by. The prisoners may return to jail for lodging, *Local prison* or may in some jurisdictions be quartered in camps or workhouses, al- *labor* though the title of chain gang hardly applies as in former days. Many states in the nineteenth century, especially in the South, allowed "convict-lease" systems for county prisoners to work in private industries, such as mining and lumbering. This policy has been reversed by legislative compulsion as a result of pressure by social reformers and organized labor. Normally local prison labor must be for public, not private, use.

The central state penitentiaries are often superior to local jails and workhouses in scientific management and treatment of prisoners, although many state systems are inferior to federal institutions in this respect. All have difficulty in providing useful and constructive employment for those who *State peni-* are serving sentence. Under various state and federal statutes prison *tentiaries* labor must not be used for the direct production of merchandise for the channels of commerce. It is often utilized for turning out items for state purposes, such as equipment and supplies for government offices or for state institutions. Penitentiary farms may provide food for the prisoners, who cultivate the crops and attend the livestock. This activity competes only indirectly with free labor, and it serves to keep the prisoners from idleness. Prisoners also have limited opportunities for vocational training, reading, recreation, and entertainment. Inmates may issue an institutional publication somewhat on the model of a school newspaper. One such journal is called *The Inside Story*. The best or largest of the penitentiaries are likely to have competent counselors, including chaplains, medical officers, and psychiatrists, as well as trained wardens. Serious cases of mental illness may be transferred to a special division of the state hospital for the insane.[10]

Yet it must be said that penal institutions have only a limited success in curing criminals of criminal tendencies, of checking the "rule" of once a convict, always a convict. A psychiatric expert, with clinical experience at New York's Sing Sing Prison, has urged that prisons as presently constituted should be abolished, since they destroy more disturbed personalities than they reclaim, with more than 60 per cent of the nation's federal and state convicts becoming repeaters. He points to the prison riots over the country as indicative of improper and unscientific treatment of the inmates.[11] According to his view, society is more concerned with keeping persons in prison than in keeping them out. Real treatment centers for the anti-social may be around the corner, but not an immediate corner. Most states lack adequate staffs and personnel for such expert assistance.[12]

The emphasis on the philosophy of correction rather than punishment has reached wider acceptance for the institutional treatment of juvenile offenders than for dealing with adult lawbreakers. For more than a century, leaders and organizations have urged sympathetic attention to delinquent children, matching the movement for more humane care of the mentally ill.

Juvenile delinquents

State reformatories for boys and girls often function under the name of "training school," "trade school," or "industrial school," and seek to measure up to the name. Their task is not easy, for many of the juvenile delinquents have mental limitations or emotional problems which cannot be overcome through institutional care. Furthermore, these institutions are not uniformly modern in methods and types of administrators. They sometimes have juvenile escapes. Private and public agencies give no little attention to methods of readjustment

---

[10] In California a prison advance has been scored in the establishment of the California Medical Facility filling the dual purpose of hospital and prison. *See* M. R. King, M. D., "Care of Handicapped Offenders at the California Medical Facility," *State Government,* XXIX (June, 1956), pp. 104-109, 116.

[11] Ralph S. Banay, "Should Prisons Be Abolished?" *New York Times Magazine,* January 30, 1955, p. 13. This article followed closely after a prison riot in the Massachusetts State Prison. The contagion of prison riots and mutinies worries other analysts also, who contend in consequence that we must re-examine administrative and professional standards in correctional work. *See,* for example, H. O. Teets and Walter Dunbar, "Standards for Prisons," *State Government,* XXVII (March, 1954), pp. 61-63.

[12] For a brief summary of three similar programs in Utah, New York, and New Jersey, highly structured for research in new correctional approaches, *see* Donald H. Goff, "State Correctional Systems," *The Book of the States, 1962-63,* pp. 418-423.

of problem children before the stage is reached for assignment to the reformatory.[13] Through the development and training of social workers, many city school systems have visiting teachers to deal personally and individually with pupils who are falling down in work, attendance, or behavior. These professional workers have ways of getting to the seat of the trouble, whether poverty, loneliness, broken home, or other difficulty, and of providing help before it is too late. Probation officers attached to local juvenile courts may also provide constructive assistance. Different service groups and clubs aid in the work of reducing or preventing juvenile delinquency.

SUPPLEMENTARY READINGS

American Prison Association, *Manual of Correctional Standards* (American Prison Association, New York, 1954).

Federal Bureau of Investigation, *Uniform Crime Reports* (United States Government Printing Office, Washington, D. C., semiannually).

International City Managers' Association, *Municipal Police Administration,* (5th ed.; Chicago, 1961).

Kefauver, Estes, *Crime in America* (Doubleday & Company, Inc., Garden City, 1951).

Korn, Richard R., and Lloyd W. McCorkle, *Criminology and Penology* (Holt, Rinehart & Winston, Inc., New York, 1959).

Northwestern University School of Law, *The Journal of Criminal Law, Criminology and Police Science.*

Penfield, Thomas, *Western Sheriffs and Marshals* (Grosset & Dunlap, Inc., New York, 1955).

Reckless, W. C., *The Crime Problem* (2d ed.; Appleton-Century-Crofts, Inc., New York, 1955).

Sellin, Thorsten, ed., "Prisons in Transformation," *The Annals of the American Academy of Political and Social Science,* CCXCIII (May, 1954).

Smith, Bruce, ed., "New Goals in Police Management," *The Annals of the American Academy of Political and Social Science,* CCXCI (January, 1954).

Smith, Bruce, *Police Systems in the United States* (2d rev. ed.; Harper and Row, Publishers, New York, 1960).

Vold, George B., "For Better Prisons the Need is Basic Research," *State Government,* XXVIII (February, 1955), pp. 37-39, 50-51.

Wilson, O. W., *Police Administration* (2d ed., McGraw-Hill Book Co., Inc., New York, 1962).

---

[13] For a state and local plan for delinquency control and some examples of state programs underway, *see* Bertram M. Beck, "State Programs to Combat Delinquency." *State Government,* XXVIII (June, 1955), pp. 128-130, 142-143.

★ *20* ★

PUBLIC POLICY TOWARD

PRIVATE ENTERPRISE

GOVERNMENT IS inevitably linked in one way or another with the economic and occupational life of its constituents. State and local units provide no exceptions to this rule. They have always manifested concern, wisely or unwisely, with problems of regulation, protection, and promotion of different types of private and professional enterprise within their borders. For these purposes they have increasingly made use of their public police power. The general constitutional aspects of this usage were explored in the fourth chapter; it seems appropriate here to take a closer look at the political, economic, and administrative ramifications of these problems and policies.

Scope and significance

It has already been noted that in many ways state regulation led the way for national regulation of corporate business, notably of railroads. Stiff treatment and regulation of railroads have characterized a number of important governorships, including those of William Larrabee of Iowa, in the 1880's, and of B. B. Comer of Alabama, Robert La Follette of Wisconsin, and Hiram Johnson of California, in the early years of the twentieth century. Charles E. Hughes became governor of New York after his success in 1905 as counsel for a committee investigation of insurance frauds in that state which resulted in drastic reform of the regulation of insurance companies in New York and other states.

Woodrow Wilson's gubernatorial term in New Jersey was characterized by the adoption of measures that lifted from that state the label "mother of trusts." Economic reform or regulation has featured movements in local government at times. An example is the establishment of the three-cent fare on city street-cars in Cleveland through the leadership of Mayor Tom L. Johnson, who was elected four times in the first decade of this century. It should not be forgotten that economic interests of diverse complexion rather constantly battle for the control of governmental policy at the state and local level, whether for protective labor legislation in New York, for lenient requirements as to corporate charters in Delaware, or for concessions to new industries in Mississippi.

The role of state and local government toward private operators and practitioners takes many forms within the American federal system. In its totality it embraces taxation, regulation, granting corporate charters or franchises, contractual relations for public works, issuance of licenses or permits   *A varied role* for the conduct of business and professions, inspectional procedures, offering aid or advice for the attraction of new enterprise, and various specialized or ad hoc arrangements. The role shows variations, as between an oil state like Texas and a mining state like West Virginia or between the older textile regions of New England and newer textile regions of the Southeast, particularly in the matter of retaining or attracting manufacturing establishments. The regulation of professional boxing or of the heating of multiple-apartment buildings in New York City is a different problem from what it is in Mississippi. The state government may have more responsibility with respect to horse racing in Kentucky than in the Dakotas. One may find differences in the economic policy of state and local governments between urbanized areas and rural regions, between coastal centers and hinterlands, and between desert counties and rain belts. There is wide variety as well as similarity in the regulatory action of the numerous jurisdictions.

REGULATION OF PUBLIC UTILITIES

Certain businesses, primarily in the fields of transportation, communication, and power, have come to enjoy special privileges granted by governments, but with these privileges have come various public regulations relating to rates charged and the quality and quantity of service provided. The definition of a public utility has never been very precise, but a modern list of businesses which have come to be known as public utilities would certainly include telephone, telegraph, and power transmission companies; water, gas, and electric service companies; and such transportation facilities as the railroads, airlines, and commercial truck and bus lines; and might possibly be extended to include public markets, toll bridges

370   and roads, airports, port facilities, and the like. Early state and local experience
with the public utility was related for the most part to transportation. Governments, ancient and modern, have manifested an interest in the routes
Historical   and facilities of transportation, an interest often transcending concern
background   merely for systems of highways. The Erie Canal represents early state
development of water transportation; airports in many cases reflect
modern joint action by states, municipalities, and even the federal government
in providing essential conditions for the speediest form of transportation.

Private transportation services have long been recognized in the common
law as "affected with a public interest," as pointed out by the Supreme Court
in *Munn* v. *Illinois*,[1] and a pattern of local, state, and federal regulation
has developed. The states pioneered in sponsoring the development of railroads through provisions for franchises, legal arrangements for securing rights
of way, and sometimes direct aid, frequently with further support by municipalities. There were examples of land-grant aid by the federal government
through the states as intermediaries. But the railroads of the nation got a
serious taste of state regulation as a result of the Granger movement, which
swept the country in the 1870's with a significant impact in the grain states.
Strong laws were passed, sometimes rigidly fixing freight rates, and state
railroad commissions were created to administer these laws. Legislation and
administration went through a process of moderation with the waning of the
Granger reform; farmers and shippers realized that they needed federal regulation of rates on interstate transportation; and the Interstate Commerce Commission was provided for by Congress in 1887. But the state railroad commissions remained in existence and took on new life in the next century, although
overshadowed in the transportation picture by the ICC.

It became necessary to regulate other forms of moving freight and passengers besides rail, and thus the railroad commissions were generally changed
in name and broadened in scope. They have frequently been named
Commission   "public service commission" and are likely to have intrastate regulatory
expansion   jurisdiction, not only over railways, but also over chartered bus lines,
motor-freight companies, electric power, telephone services, and similar
enterprises. State regulation of intrastate commerce may be prevented from
jeopardizing interstate commerce or the federal regulation of such commerce.
The ICC may intervene to prevent unjust discrimination against interstate
commerce by intrastate rates.[2]

---

[1] 94 U. S. 113 (1876). *See supra*, Chapter 4. On the subject of Granger legislation in the
states, *see* S. J. Buck, *The Granger Movement* (Harvard University Press, Cambridge,
1913).

[2] An important opinion affirming this point was delivered in the Shreveport rate case in
1914, *Houston, East and West Texas Railway Co.* v. *United States; Texas and Pacific
Railway Co.* v. *United States*, 234, U. S. 342.

Effective regulation of public utilities is not child's play, nor can it be done by well-meaning amateurs. The total investment in such utilities amounts to many billions of dollars, and the political power which can be brought to bear on a governor, a legislative body, or upon public opinion in a given policy controversy, is an awesome sight on occasion. The regulation of rates charged by the utilities is undoubtedly the most difficult of the jobs faced by the regulatory commission. The courts have long held that rates fixed by the commission must permit the utility to make a "fair rate of return" on a "fair value of the utility." Determining "fairness" in the first of these two respects is not a serious problem usually, with the courts accepting from five to eight per cent as reasonable. It is the second, determining the "fair value of the utility," which has come to be the universal headache for state regulatory commissions.

Problems of rate regulation

Why is it so difficult to determine the reasonable value of a public utility? A brief examination of the possible methods which might be used will give some insight into the frustrations of conscientious commissioners. (1) Why not apply the ordinary test of market value — what it could be sold for? It is obvious that this test is impractical because giant utilities simply are not sold from day to day, or year to year, like automobiles or houses. (2) Then why not use the market value of the utility stocks and bonds? It is true that a few shares may change hands from time to time, but their fluctuations in price make it impossible to use them as an accurate measure of the entire property's value. (3) Would it not be possible to examine the profits of the enterprise and determine a fair value in much the same way as is done for competitive businesses, that is, by "capitalization of earnings?" The problem here soon becomes apparent — the utility's profits are determined in the first place by an earlier rate-making decision of the commission, and capitalizing earnings would catch both the commission and the utility in a trap of circular reasoning, always justifying the status quo. (4) Another possibility is to determine value on the basis of original cost of constructing or acquiring the property, less depreciation. Yet either inflation or deflation has the effect of making original cost a poor measure of *present* value of a public utility, and owners complain bitterly about this method in time of inflation. (5) Then why not use the principle of "reproduction cost," whereby actual money invested is not the determinant, but rather the cost of re-creating the public utility plant and equipment at present prices? The practical effect of fixing rates by this method is to give the owners a handsome reward if prices are higher than when the property was acquired, and to hand them a severe loss if prices have dropped since acquisition of the property. (6) The "prudent investment theory" is still another method, being a modification of the original cost doctrine. Valuation for rate-making purposes begins with original cost, but subtracts costs

Competing theories of valuation

372   which would not have been made by a wise (prudent) businessman. This
method obviously complicates the regulatory commission's job even further,
but the philosophy is clear: a regulated monopoly should not be allowed to
include foolish or extravagant expenditures in its "fair value" which is the
basis for figuring rates charged the consuming public.

The foregoing list of possible methods of rate-making is by no means
exhaustive and is not given in an effort to qualify the reader as a specialist in
utility rates. It should merely give some indication of the magnitude,
Court shift
toward prag-
matism
complexity, and controversial character of this small segment of state
and local regulation of business. In the case of *Smyth* v. *Ames*,[3] before
the turn of the century, the Supreme Court held in effect that a formula
must be used in utility valuation, making use of a variety of factors rather than
relying on any one theory of valuation. More recently in the *Hope Natural
Gas* case the Supreme Court relaxed the rigidity of this formula requirement
to the extent of saying that "It is not the theory but the impact of the rate order
that counts. If the total effect of the rate order cannot be said to be unjust and
unreasonable, judicial inquiry is at an end."[4] This really offers the regulatory
commission no guiding rule for rate-making valuations, but it does permit
them a greater degree of pragmatic flexibility.

Many municipalities exercise regulatory functions with respect to local
transportation utilities. The Port of New York Authority is a bi-state metropolitan agency which operates or regulates important types of trans-
Local trans-
portation
utilities
portation facilities in several ports and municipalities. Several different
kinds of metropolitan area transit authorities have sprung up in recent
years, such as the San Francisco Bay Area Rapid Transit District, the
Chicago Transit Authority, and the National Capital Transportation Agency.
The latter agency looks toward an eventual interstate compact among Maryland, Virginia, and the District of Columbia to solve the mass transportation
problems of the Washington area.

Transportation service may be subject to other regulations outside the
jurisdiction of the expert commissions. Buses, for example, are required to obey
traffic regulations, and carriers of passengers must obey liquor and sanitation
laws in their restaurant service. States, in an increasing number, are requiring
that individual automobile owners carry liability insurance for the benefit of
accident victims. In the sphere of transportation, corporations and individuals
are amenable to a plurality of laws and authorities.

---

[3] 169 U. S. 466 (1898).

[4] *Federal Power Commission* v. *Hope Natural Gas Co.*, 320 U. S. 591 (1944).

The states undertake in varying ways and degrees to regulate private enterprise in the fields of banking, finance, and insurance. Despite the trend in recent
decades toward "national" banks and "federal" loan associations, many
banks, trust companies, investment houses, and lending firms continue *Scope*
to operate under state charter or license. Qualified state banks have *of state*
become members of the Federal Reserve System and have acquired *regulations*
protective connection with the Federal Deposit Insurance Corporation.

Financiers must comply with the requirements of the Securities and
Exchange Commission for reporting and registering security issues. Intentional
swindlers may receive federal punishment for fraudulent use of the mails.

The Supreme Court in 1944 reversed a long-standing position and
held that insurance is commerce and is subject to federal laws and regulations
if carried on across state lines.[5] Congress has used this new power with
discretion, however, partly by enacting legislation to be effective in instances
of state neglect of insurance regulation. In consequence, state insurance regulation has tended to expand rather than to decline, with more provision for the
protection of policyholders through reserves, factual information, licensed agents,
and examination of the business by official commissions or other authorities.

State governments and local authorities apply means and measures for
the financial protection of the little man or the uninformed, although the protection is not always adequate or effective. Starting in Kansas in 1911,
numerous "blue sky" laws have been passed to prohibit fraud and *Financial*
deception in the selling of securities. Ceilings on interest rates and *protection*
other restrictions have been aimed at abuses by "personal" finance *little man*
operators and loan sharks. Regulations for the prevention or exposure *for the*
of bogus charities in urban communities have come into vogue.

Non-governmental activities have supplemented the efforts of public
regulation in reducing these miscellaneous abuses. Legal aid clinics have been
helpful to low-income groups needing protection against the unscrupulous.
Education, publicity, and civic activities of business offer checks to frauds and
flimflams. But larceny by trick, like larceny by shoplifting, continues to strike,
much of it without detection.

The little man shares, of course, in the protection of enforced standards
of banking and insurance. His pocketbook is safeguarded through elimination
or clarification of fine-print clauses in sickness and accident policies. Supplanting
the common law doctrine and law suits for accident damage with automatic

---

[5] *United States* v. *South-Eastern Underwriters Association et al.,* 322 U. S. 533 (1944).

REGULATION OF PUBLIC UTILITIES

374 compensation to industrial workers constitutes an improvement of this picture among all the states.

Many of these protections are applied by automatic and administrative processes, as far as they go. Others depend upon the deterrent effect of apprehending and punishing individual culprits. This action in itself means nothing in the way of financial reimbursement to the victims of fraud, as in the story once reported from Memphis of a man who successfully cashed a phony check on The East Bank of the Mississippi.

CONSUMER RELATIONS

Range of regulation; health and safety

The police power is exercised in important ways by states and localities to regulate industrial, mercantile, and service establishments for safeguarding consumer and community interests. The regulation may have bearing on physical safety, health, pecuniary matters, moral habits, or general welfare and convenience, as well as the stability of the economic process that provides the goods and services. In the category of health and safety, shops and hotels must comply with measures to avoid fire hazards and elevator accidents; dining rooms and restaurants may be subject to test and inspection for sanitary standards of premises, equipment, and food, as well as the freedom from disease of employees; owners of apartment houses may have to meet specified requirements for the comfort of tenants; theaters and movie houses operate under precautionary regulations as to fire, overcrowding, and other hazards; drug stores have officially licensed pharmacists to fill prescriptions; dairies and milk distributors comply with standards of purity and cleanliness; and various other matters may be regulated. These procedures imply no exemption from compliance with federal food and drug regulations, although the latter may obviate the necessity for local inspection, as in the case of meat-packing for both interstate and intrastate commerce.

Economic practices

Public surveillance provides certain economic protections for customers and clients. Grocers have been called to task for adjusting scales to short-weight outgoing merchandise. Old laws of cotton states penalized ginners and farmers for "platting" high-grade fiber around poor cotton or extraneous matter in bales. State authority to regulate warehouse rates was established in the era of the Granger movement. Farmers often are exempt from state or municipal sales taxes and license fees in marketing produce from their farms. Certain states have sought to stabilize the prices of national brands and products by preventing price-cutting of such items. Consequent court battles brought about fair-price legislation by Congress in 1952 empowering manufacturers and retailers to set prices on trade-marked articles to be binding where state laws concur. This was in response to demands of conforming dealers rather than consumer pressure.

Government is pressured in its policy trends in contrary ways by big dealers and small ones, by chain systems and independents. The pressure may prompt taxation for purposes of policy, as in using license requirements to keep tab or limit on miscellaneous peddlers or increasing the business tax per unit on extensive systems of chain stores far above the levy upon operators of single establishments. The balancing of group pressures over revenue and regulation often determines the intrastate taxation of liquor stores and sales, with the competing interests involving consumers and non-consumers as well as dealers and producers.

The accessibility of goods and services to consumers is regulated in many ways under moral and social influences, with stimulus from religious teachings. This is notably true of business in alcoholic beverages, with variations, not only between states, but between communities or counties on a *Moral* local-option basis. In centers where sales are permitted, moral customs *factors* account for significant restrictions with respect to minors, closing hours, Sunday business, distance of taverns and saloons from schools or churches, sale of mixed drinks versus "package stores" only, and other observances. There are local restrictions on other types of Sunday sales and services, with variations across the nation, as in curfews for baseball. Not a few blue laws remain on the books without enforcement or observance.[6] Police censorship of newsstands and bookshops for indecent material is authorized and is attempted here and there, occasionally with court contests over the differentiation between legitimate matter and obscenity. A few places have undertaken to apply this censorship to movies. The operation of mechanical games of chance provides problems of definition and restriction for states and municipalities, with the federal government entering the field through the tax and interstate commerce powers. Further examples might be cited to show that the rights of entrepreneurs and patrons are not absolute.

TRADES AND PROFESSIONS

The states have an old but expanding function in licensing members of certain trades and professions and safeguarding the public against unlicensed

---

[6] *See* Chapter 4 for a discussion of recent Supreme Court decisions relating to "Sunday closing" laws.

376 practitioners. The licensing system also affords protection against unfair

Importance of the license system

competition to the qualified licensees, whose influence is a factor in making and maintaining the legal requirements. It is beneficial to both clients and practitioners to keep quacks out of the way. The system incidentally facilitates merit practices in the different units of government, which must employ persons of various qualifications. Furthermore, it facilitates the acquisition and publication of accurate information on American life by government agencies, including the Census Bureau, thanks to reports from registered members of licensed groups. It has stimulated training and education in significant ways, for license standards and professional school standards have moved upward together. Public licensing provides a certain amount of underpinning for group ethics, since a license may be revoked for unprofessional practice, not necessarily or technically connected with common crime. Aside from regulatory and protective aspects, the license policy tends to provide a stamp of recognition and professionalism for the initiated.

The states have developed a wide license coverage of occupations and professions, particularly in urban and industrial regions. For example, it might be noted that a recent New York *Legislative Manual* lists thirteen state

Wide license coverage

boards of examiners, exclusive of incidental functions by subdivisions of major administrative departments, such as education, labor, and agriculture. These central boards deal with the following professions and occupational groups: law, medicine, dentistry, pharmacy, veterinary medicine, nursing, accountancy, optometry, opthalmic dispensing, architecture, engineering and land surveying, certified shorthand reporting, and podiatry. To the occupational picture should be added sundry local permits to one-man taxi operators, plumbers, and the like. And state law provides for the recording and recognition of marriage ceremonies performed by ministers, priests, and rabbis ordained or licensed by religious authority.

Lawyers, along with doctors, make up the most consistently and continuously significant group of licensed professionals. It might be said, with a little waiving of exactness, that the states commission lawyers and lawyers

The legal profession

govern the states. Law being the essence of government, its craftsmen compose the judicial branch, predominate in the legislative branch, and hold strategic places in the executive branch. These learned craftsmen are also the architects of effective structures of private corporate government, although not seeking to change or challenge the common-law doctrine which bans corporate membership in learned professions. Theirs is primarily a masculine calling, with women constituting fewer than 10,000 members of the American bar, which numbers more than 200,000. Preparation for admission to the bar, under action or direction of the highest court of the state, can no longer be accomplished by perusing Blackstone or "reading law" as an apprentice. A combination of three successful years in an accredited law school and pre-law courses in college is coming to be the accepted approach to the examination for admission. As a result of stiff admission requirements, more than two-thirds of the lawyers of the country have attended law school, and most of these hold law degrees. Bar associations have constituted a factor in strengthening the prescribed standards, and about 20 states require that a practicing attorney be a member of at least one association.

Doctors have less occupational contact with government than lawyers. But the medical profession approximates that of law in antiquity of origin, growth, number of members, association influence, linkage with public interest, and improvement of standards of training and admission. It ***Medicine*** is a learned profession with a creed of service ethics derived from Hippocrates, the Greek "father of medicine," who was a contemporary of Herodotus, the "father of history." Yet the practice of medicine in America today is of the scale and nature of a public utility, although conducted largely as private enterprise.[7]

As in law, license requirements have been raised, partly through the impact of organizational pressure and solidarity. Modern medicine differs from modern law, however, in requiring longer and more expensive training for admission to practice, whatever the state and its license procedure. More human beings require individual medical service than require legal service, with consequent strain on training facilities rather than on the licensing process.

One effect of the comparative shortage of doctors and the private cost of medical care for families who are neither blessed with wealth nor burdened with poverty has been the creation of a many-sided controversy over public medical policy. The question has involved the federal government, state governments, medical organizations from the national to local units, and other public or semi-public groups. It has brought about legislative gains and defeats as well as litigation and a multiplicity of proposals or movements to improve policy in ways short of "socialized medicine."[8] The dispute is still unsettled. The issues affect not only doctors and their clients but also hospitals, medical schools, nurses, medical social service groups, and different interests concerned with providing financially for medical and hospital care through private, group, and public insurance or other cooperative arrangements.

The regulation of trades and professions is administered in a large and flexible context of intergovernmental comity, mutual obligations, and public relations. Although there is diversity of standards among the 50 states and the District of Columbia, a high degree of comparability and license acceptance

---

[7] J. H. Means, *Doctors, People, and Government* (Little, Brown & Co., Boston, 1953), p. 8.
[8] *Ibid.*, pp 167-197.

across state lines prevails. An architect, physician, or attorney, after proper examination and certification in one state, does not, as a rule, have to go

Reciprocity and public relations through the whole testing process upon change of residence to another state. Flexibility also applies to transitory activities by outsiders, as when a state or federal court in the South or West admits a New York lawyer to professional participation in a case. Dr. Paul White, the Boston specialist, did not have to get a Colorado or federal license when he flew to Denver to examine President Eisenhower's heart on federal premises. Professional men qualify for expert testimony before trial or investigative bodies, whether licensed by one state or another.

The context of relationships embraces certain rights of privacy for consultants and clients. Lawyers are immune from compulsory revelation of conversations with persons whom they represent in court. Inviolability also attaches to the privacy of the doctor-patient relationship, although silence is not compulsory and factual physical data may not be privileged. Professional advisers are not immune from prosecution for knowingly committing, causing, or compounding crime in their relations with clients. Court records indicate that, for gross and reckless negligence in preparing a financial statement, a certified public accountant may be held liable to damaged outsiders as well as to his client.[9]

LABOR RELATIONS

The states and many local jurisdictions have vital concern with labor relations and conditions in private business and industry, both because of and in spite of the important role of the national government in these

Common features matters. All the states have central administrative machinery, generally under a departmental head or commissioner, to carry on this work. All have legislation prohibiting or restricting and regulating child labor. All have provisions for employer liability or insurance for workers' compensation for accident. Local jurisdictions may enforce these measures by such means as requiring contractors to show certificate of adequate insurance coverage before issuing permits for private projects. All the states have systems of unemployment insurance in coordination and compliance with the federal Social Security provisions for financing these programs.

---

[9] Edmond Cahn, *The Moral Decision* (Indiana University Press, Bloomington, 1955), pp. 130 and 323, n. 3.

There are significant differences, in addition to similarities, among the **379**
states' labor policies and practices, and the differences are partly reflective of
regional backgrounds and outlooks. The states vary widely in licensing
or not licensing members of more than 50 skilled trades and occupations   *Diverse*
outside the learned professions. They show diversity in treatment of   *features*
unions. New York has a Labor Relations Board, with supporting legislation, to guarantee employees' organizational rights, to encourage collective
bargaining, and to conduct elections among workers to determine the bargaining union. Less than one-third of the states have labor relations acts of general
coverage. On another side of the picture, "right to work laws" prohibit or
restrict the "closed shop" and "union shop" in more than one-third of the
states, chiefly in the South and inland West. They usually provide that
obtaining and retaining employment may not be made to depend on either
membership or non-membership in a union.

An increasing number of states, now more than two-fifths, have commissions with mandatory power to prevent discrimination in employment on
account of race, creed, or national origin, among these being most of the
New England and Middle Atlantic states and the west coast states of California,
Oregon, and Washington. A smaller number of states have passed laws prohibiting employment discrimination against older workers, variously defined
as including persons over 40 or 45. New York and New Jersey, with the
consent of Congress, established a Waterfront Commission in 1953 to replace
the "shape-up" system in the port of New York by regularized and supervised
hiring of longshoremen.

Despite the multimillion membership of the unions, the states have less
even standards for labor relations than for the learned professions. Union pressure, however, moves for uniform standards through national action. Labor
enterprise, in the larger view, is enmeshed with interstate commerce, and
the federal government is not allowed to ignore this point. Labor economics,
like medical economics, is an unfinished story.

AGRICULTURE

Farming, as an ancient and widespread occupation, is seldom outside
the watchful concern of government, whether the concern be motivated by
farm statesmanship or the farm vote. Farm problems are problems of
nation, state, and locality. Farm pressure in politics continues to be   *Farming and*
important, with the decline in occupational numbers being offset by   *government*
growth or strengthening organizational activity. For traditional reasons,

380 farmers meet less avowed opposition in politics than do other groups; they are seldom denounced, even when their demands are denied or sidetracked. All states and most counties have agencies for safeguarding and serving the interests of agriculture, and this work has been expanded in many ways through federal aid and cooperation. It was not by chance that agriculture was included in the first systematic provision for federal aid to the states for applied higher education in the Morrill Land Grant Act of 1862, or that farmers in 1889 became the first occupational group to have functional representation in the president's cabinet. The governmental and organizational hookup for handling farm problems extends from Washington to the grass roots.

Every state has a central agency for agriculture, exclusively or in combination with related functions. The agency is likely to be a department, board, or commission, headed by a director, commissioner, or secretary. The establishment is prescribed in the constitution of several states, sometimes with requirement for popular election of the chief officer. It exercises the roles of promotion, dissemination of information, and regulation, as in enforcing measures for analysis of fertilizer, inspecting certain products or processes, and checking the spread of pests or disease among plants and animals. It maintains cooperative connections as one of four teams concerned with agriculture, the three others in the cooperative system being the federal Department of Agriculture, the agricultural college or division of the state's land grant college, and the farm agents of the counties of the state having agricultural interests.

Agencies and functions

The governmental programs for agriculture reach the farmers chiefly through these big-four powers operating separately or in conjunction. Among the programs are agricultural experimentation and demonstration, extension service, and crop controls and supports. In many activities non-agricultural agencies are involved, including those connected with labor, health, and conservation, not to mention education.

The scope of cooperative governmental functions in agricultural relations extends to many specialized and collateral activities, partly outside the scheme of immediate production or processing of commodities for market. Many states of broad acres have public sponsorship and regulation of agricultural aviation for applying insecticides and fertilizers, making surveys of soils or crops, spotting or checking forest fires, and other purposes. State and federal forest services dispense scientific information on the care and cultivation of farm woods. Soil-conservation districts are organized on a local basis under state laws with the use of federal funds and technical assistance in developing interest and understanding of conservation problems through meetings, informational literature, and demonstration farms. The TVA has developed fertilizer products and practices in cooperation with agricultural

Collateral activities

The work of public agencies on the agricultural front extends to various phases of rural life, including home and garden, pasture and fish-pond, and clubs for boys and girls. This diverse and dynamic front is not free from differences over purpose and policy among agricultural agencies and among agricultural organizations like the Farmers' Union and the American Farm Bureau Federation. Farm groups differ over relations with other interest groups in the realm of business and labor. The sharp issues of farm politics seem to be perennial.[10]

SUPPLEMENTARY READINGS

Becker, Joseph M., S. J., *Shared Government in Employment Security, A Study of Advisory Councils* (Columbia University Press, New York, 1959).

Commission on Intergovernmental Relations, *A Study Committee Report on Federal Aid to Agriculture* (U. S. Government Printing Office, Washington, 1955).

Commission on Intergovernmental Relations, *A Study Committee Report on Unemployment Compensation and Employment Service* (U. S. Government Printing Office, Washington, 1955).

Dimock, Marshall, *Business and Government* (rev. ed.; Holt, Rinehart & Winston, Inc., New York, 1953).

Fainsod, Merle, Lincoln Gordon, and Joseph C. Palamountain, Jr., *Government and the American Economy* (rev. ed.; W. W. Norton and Company, Inc., New York, 1959).

Fesler, J. W., *The Independence of State Regulatory Agencies* (Public Administration Service, Chicago, 1942).

Hanley, Dexter L., "Federal-State Jurisdiction in Labor's No-Man's Land: 1960," *Georgetown Law Journal*, XLVIII (Summer, 1960), pp. 709-735.

Hardin, C. M., *Freedom in Agricultural Education* (University of Chicago Press, Chicago, 1955).

Killingsworth, C. C., *State Labor Relations Acts* (University of Chicago Press, Chicago, 1948).

"Labor and Industrial Relations," continuing article in *The Book of the States* (Council of State Governments, Chicago).

McCune, Wesley, *The Farm Bloc* (Doubleday & Company, Garden City, 1943).

Means, J. H., *Doctors, People, and Government* (Little, Brown & Co., Boston, 1953).

Millis, H. A., and R. E. Montgomery, *Organized Labor*, Vol. III of *The Economics of Labor* (McGraw-Hill Book Co., Inc., New York, 1945).

"State Regulatory Activities," continuing article in *The Book of the States* (Council of State Governments, Chicago).

---

[10] *See C. M. Hardin*, "Farm Politics and American Democracy," *The Journal of Politics*, XVII (November, 1955), pp. 651-663, both for a point of view and for works cited.

★ *21* ★

HIGHWAYS, PUBLIC IMPROVEMENTS
AND NATURAL RESOURCES

Much of the energy of state and local government is devoted to the acquisition, development and preservation of routes and points of transportation; premises and facilities for the functions of education, recreation, and

Scope and
complexity

other public purposes; and such assets of nature as timber, water, wildlife, scenic beauty, and other resources. The role of government in this physical realm has come down from ancient times, but modern technology has provided both the means and the need for its extensive expansion.

Groups and interests, however, are far from being in accord as to just how any step of change or expansion should be taken. The location or relocation of a road or school can become a stirring issue with strong political, economic, and social overtones. Many a building program has been a source of spoils, whether in a metropolis or a sparsely settled county. Commercial exploiters and conservationists may differ sharply over public policies with respect to natural resources. Interests are frequently arrayed against interests over ways and means for financing these public undertakings. Issues of centralization versus decentralization of development or control frequently come to the front. Construction programs engage the attention of public officials from president to village alderman. Whatever the controversy, politicians

like to impress constituents by visible accomplishments in stone or concrete.
It is these governmental activities which provide some of the best examples of
politics at work in an intergovernmental setting.

HIGHWAYS AND RURAL ROADS

The American network of through highways, city streets, and rural
roads constitutes a veritable miscellany. It exhibits a combination of the
medieval and the modern in physical structure as well as in methods
of administration. Our thoroughfares vary widely in age, composition, *A miscellany*
width, and degree of curvature, not to mention in such factors as
strength of bridges, load capacity, and state of repair. The financial picture is
variegated, involving local, state, or federal support or combinations of these
sources, with a modern resurrection of toll systems for great turnpikes. There
were examples during the depression thirties of complete financing or construction by the federal government, sometimes in connection with special
projects. More than three-fourths of the rural mileage, which is in excess of
three million, is under local control, as are most urban streets. There are examples of interurban or interstate control of highway segments, as in metropolitan
areas or across river boundaries. The federal government controls a rather
extensive mileage on its own lands in the different states, including more
than 19,000 in California.

The coming of the automobile stimulated the movement for state systems
of highways with the support of federal aid. Associations were formed for this
purpose prior to World War I, and men were elected to Congress as
advocates of "good roads." The Federal Aid Road Act of 1916 launched *State systems*
a program of cooperative federalism for the financial sponsorship of a *with federal aid*
continental system of major highways, and the program was to undergo
subsequent expansion regardless of the political complexions of government in
states or nation. To share in federal funds on a matching basis, the states had
to establish central highway departments and adopt prescribed standards of
performance, and all states within a few years took steps for compliance.
Cooperation extended even to the uniform numbering of interstate routes,
such as "U. S. 90" or "U. S. 41." Federal legislation of 1941 provided for
coordinating trunk routes with connections through or around municipal areas,
thus making it possible to have "townless highways" and "highwayless towns,"
as Lewis Mumford would say.[1] Congress in 1944 overrode the technicality that

---

[1] For ideas of functional relationships between highway planning and community planning,

a street is not a road (something rural state legislatures had resisted doing), and provided aid to urban centers for their portions of through highways, basing the allocations on state populations. The states accepted or facilitated this new chapter in federal-state relations.

Regular federal aid amounted to 8.5 per cent of total revenues for all highway purposes in the period from 1921 through 1953. Table 21-1 gives total revenues for highway purposes by government for that period. Total highway construction expenditures for that period amounted to $44.1 billions, with regular federal aid amounting to 15.1 per cent of the total.

TABLE 21-1

TOTAL REVENUES BY GOVERNMENT FOR ALL HIGHWAY PURPOSES
1921-1953
(In millions of dollars)

	1921-31	1932-42	1943-53	Total
National Government:				
Regular Aid	$ 1,075	$ 2,254	$ 3,328	$ 6,657
Other	121	4,720	451	5,292
States	5,906	10,576	21,774	38,256
Urban places	6,403	3,847	5,269	15,519
Rural units	5,170	3,135	4,240	12,545
Total	18,675	24,532	35,062	78,269

Source: Commission on Intergovernmental Relations, A Study Committee Report on Federal Aid to Highways (U. S. Government Printing Office, Washington, 1955), p. 10.

These older programs and expenditure totals seem pale by comparison with the vast new program for 41,000 miles of interstate expressways now in progress. Initiated by the Federal-Aid Highway Act of 1956, the system to

The interstate expressway system be completed by 1972 is expected to carry 21 per cent of all highway traffic, even though it will comprise only slightly more than 1 per cent of all street and road mileage in the nation. The federal government's share of

see Lewis Mumford, *Technics and Civilization* (Harcourt, Brace & World, Inc., New York, 1934), p. 237, with citation from Benton MacKaye.

the cost of the interstate system is 90 per cent, far more generous than the traditional 50-50 basis for sharing with the states. The states determine how much, if any, of their 10 per cent must be borne by local governments. By 1962 more than 11,000 miles were already completed and in use, with an additional 5,000 miles under construction. Survey and planning or right-of-way acquisition had begun on another 10,000 miles. Total cost is estimated to be $41 billion, or an average of $1 million per mile, and the federal government's portion is about $37 billion. Actual cost per mile may rise far above the average as the expressways cut their way through congested metropolitan areas.

    While one is cruising smoothly down one of these four-lane expressways it may be easy to forget that this enormous public works project is simply another highly tangible result of the political process, with all of its pressures and influences, stops and starts, plans and counterplans. Decisions must be made concerning such politically volatile questions as location, how many "spokes" the major cities will have, type of construction, number and location of access points, method of financing, whether to reimburse utility companies for the cost of relocating their facilities, and whether to prohibit billboard advertising along the highways. To take billboard controls as an example, Congress has authorized a bonus of one-half of one per cent of the federal share to any state which will prohibit billboards for a distance of 660 feet on either side of the right-of-way. With only garden clubs and similar groups available to do battle with the billboard industry, securing passage in Congress was not easy, and only 16 states had adopted the ban by 1962. Some state highway officials contend that it would cost more to obtain the necessary easements from the landowners for the billboard ban than the federal bonus is worth, but authorization for a larger bonus was not passed.

Highways and the political process

    The other federal-aid highways, known as "the ABC system," consist of (a) the states' "primary highway system," (b) those city streets which are serving as federal-aid highways, and (c) the states' "secondary road system," consisting of feeder roads, rural free delivery mail routes, public school bus routes, and similar roads. The 800,000 miles of roads and streets in the ABC system account for 24 per cent of total mileage in the nation, but carry approximately half of all traffic. In spite of the current emphasis on the interstate expressways, these older programs continue to have strong political support at the local level and there seems to be little likelihood of diminished federal support.

    Highway administration shows various stages and types of modernization in the numerous local units of government among the 50 states. More than half of the states divide road authority between state and county, a few divide it between state and town or township, and several have a mixture of the three units of authority. North Carolina in 1931 became the first

Local administration

state to apply state management and maintenance to all roads outside cities. Delaware, Virginia, and West Virginia have also adopted state control of rural roads. Local autonomy may be restricted in other states, however, in definite ways, either by legislation or by regulation. Central aid may be accompanied by requirements for approval by state authority or the federal Bureau of Roads. Many large cities and wealthy counties utilize effective methods and mechanization for street or road maintenance, even if political factors sometimes affect the letting of contracts for new construction. Old-fashioned kickbacks are limited or prevented by modern legislation, including the Hatch Act in case of federal aid. Spoils politics may enter into the county or city purchase of expensive equipment, as has at times occurred in state highway practices. But, spoils or no spoils, motorized civilization must be served, and so engineers are found along with politicians in highway agencies up and down the line. It is also true that community side-roads and farm-to-market routes require more local understanding than normally can be achieved at highly centralized headquarters. Little roads, like little schools, are still with us along with the big ones, though increasingly dwarfed by comparison.

OTHER TRANSPORTATION IMPROVEMENTS

Highways are not the only transportation concern of states and localities. There was great public interest in the development of waterways prior to the railroad era, as was exemplified by the completion of the Erie Canal between Buffalo and Albany in 1825.

Waterways and railways

Later in the nineteenth century, states and municipalities became active in underwriting or subsidizing railway development, sometimes even acquiring rail lines. There are still examples of public ownership of rail properties. The state of Georgia, for example, owns a line running to Chattanooga from the heart of that state. The line is now under lease to an operating railway. Soon after the Civil War the city of Cincinnati built a rail connection to Chattanooga for the purpose of tapping the southern market. It eventually leased the road to the Southern Railway system. Other instances might be cited for the past century, including urban and interurban streetcar lines. New York City has a municipal transit system which includes over 200 miles of subway, along with a much greater bus-route mileage.

Boat, rail, and motor lines meet at the water front, and state port or dock facilities are to be found in such places as New York City, Mobile, and

New Orleans. There are municipal terminals to serve transportation on ocean fronts, inland waters, and rail sites. In 1954 New Orleans brought scattered railroads together by opening a municipal Union Passenger Terminal as a multi-million-dollar improvement project.

Airports vitally affect the public interest, since they require land tracts equal to plantations, and must be operated as union stations for multiple-line service, it being neither feasible nor possible for every single airline to have separate ground accommodations. Commercial aviation, further- *Airports* more, reached a stage of public encouragement and subsidy a century later than did railways and waterways. For defense and commerce air transport seems important to the nation and to the national government. The number of take-offs and landings at airports in the United States increased from 5 million in 1936 to 65 million in 1956, and a total of 115 million is forecast for 1975.[2]

For reasons of location and nature of service, airports are of most immediate concern to municipalities and urbanized counties; commercial airlines cannot conveniently make "whistle stops." This urban bias of aviation, when confronted by the rural bias of state legislatures, has meant that *Urban and* city airports have received even less sympathetic attention from state *rural interest* governments than city streets. The national government has turned a *in aviation* more sympathetic ear to urban airport promoters. Congress in 1940 appropriated funds for distribution to local governments for the development of strategic public airports deemed essential to national defense. Six years later Congress adopted broader provisions for aiding local units of government in the development of airports, authorizing the national government to deal directly with such units if not in conflict with state legislation. Many states promptly adopted cooperative legislation, some requiring that grants-in-aid and airport plans pass through state supervisory and coordinative authority. Federal, state, and local goverments are working in a certain degree of unison for the making of greater and better airports. The increased use of aircraft by farmers and ranchers, and the growing need for small rural landing fields may serve to stimulate greater state interest in both rural and urban airport needs. Agricultural aviation is a rapidly expanding industry involving about 5,000 aircraft specially designed for seeding or treating large land areas. Twenty airplanes, used in wiping out screw worm flies in Florida in 1959, covered 7,848,000 square miles, more than double the area of the United States.[3]

---

[2] See "Aviation Among the States," *The Book of the States, 1958-59*, p. 304 ff., and continuing article in later issues.

[3] *Ibid.*, 1962-63, p. 356.

General view
Government must build. It must provide housing for the direct activities of governance in capitol, courthouse, city hall, and administrative office. It must have buildings for schools, hospitals, and other institutional activities. It must have works and plants for such urban services as water supply, sewage disposal, and any other utilities not provided through private enterprise. Public parks are as much a part of urban living as are private groceries, and they require indoor as well as outdoor structures. The construction, maintenance, and administration of these various physical establishments and facilities require a constant flow of funds and the constant attention of boards or commissions and administrative directors. Much of the work in small counties may be under the direction of the regular governing body, perhaps with technical assistance from central agencies. Larger areas, including important cities, require the service of a full-time engineer or expert staff. The large city, like the state, may have a commissioner, director, or superintendent of public works. State and local planning agencies play important parts in various phases of developing or redevelopment. Policy-making in these affairs by legislatures and city councils should not be overlooked.

Special features
Special types of public works in different centers and regions are influenced by geography and cultural factors. Water systems supplied by lowland rivers are not the same as those connected with mountain springs. New Orleans, with streets below the level of the Mississippi, has elaborate drainage machinery of a kind not known in a city like Denver. Reclaiming or retaining land at the water's edge for public use may be important for particular coastal or lakeside centers, not for inland plains. Boston and New York are out of the ordinary in having airports on land dredged out of the sea. Climate, geography, and social trends account for distinctive municipal developments in such centers as Miami and Los Angeles. Some local governments give more attention than others to functions of municipal ownership and operation of central stadiums and auditoriums. Cleveland's Cain Park Theatre is the only municipally owned and operated dramatic project in the country. It is customary for cities served by TVA electric power to own and operate the local distribution systems. Some municipalities in other parts of the country operate gas or electric plants, occasionally under joint arrangements. Many are served by private corporations. On account of racial segregation, the South has had problems of duplicating physical facilities for education, recreation, and other public purposes. Shifting toward integration, in turn, entails interim problems of readjusting physical arrangements.

Both the nation and its cities became interested in the twin problems of 389
low-rent housing and slum clearance before President Hoover left the White
House; President Roosevelt declared that one-third of the Americans
were "ill housed" as well as "ill fed" and "ill clothed." The depression   *Housing*
of the Hoover-Roosevelt period brought constructive action, but only   *and slum*
with restriction and opposition lest public housing constitute a social-   *clearance*
istic interference with traditional free enterprise.

Among federal steps in the 1930's for improving housing conditions, two
measures should be noted which directly call for initiative by state or local
governments. Congress in 1932 authorized aid through the Reconstruction
Finance Corporation for self-liquidating projects to house low-income families
and for slum clearance under state or municipal auspices. But this program
did not get under way effectively until 1937. Federal legislation of that year
provided for federal loans and subsidies to local authorities for housing
projects for low-income families and for grants for clearing slums and blighted
areas. Local projects were subject to approval by federal authority and to authorization by state law. Many states and cities joined the program, and hundreds
of millions in funds had been channeled into the work by the beginning
of World War II.

The problems of housing increased after World War II, both for individuals and for communities. The needs were too great to be met entirely by
private arrangements. One answer was the sponsorship by the federal
government of credit for home ownership by veterans and others.   *Housing*
Another consisted of the expansion of public housing projects correla-   *since World*
tively with slum clearance or urban renewal.   *War II*

Legislation was adopted by Congress in 1949 providing for a six-year
housing program, a five-year slum-clearance program, and further support for
rural housing. The act pointed to the goal of 810,000 urban dwelling units.
It marked a change in the concept and practice of federal-municipal housing
relationships, with the states playing a helpful or permissive role. Most of the
states supported the program, providing for the establishment of local housing
authorities. A few of them extended further state aid for the purpose. Within
a few years about a thousand localities had public housing projects through
federal aid, embracing a total of nearly half a million dwelling units, primarily
for rental to low-income families. By 1962 the number had risen to 1,850
communities and almost 790,000 dwelling units.

Although Congress has continued to use the label "Federal Housing
Act," important changes have taken place in the character and scope of this
legislation since the original program for low-rent housing in 1937 and
the broader slum clearance and urban redevelopment assistance in the   *The shift*
1949 law. Subsequent housing acts have moved away from a narrow   *to urban*
renewal

public housing emphasis toward greater emphasis on comprehensive urban renewal efforts, with a more flexible array of tools for combatting urban blight than merely to replacing slums with institutional-type housing. The Housing Acts of 1954 and 1956 took note of the fact that new slums were developing at a faster rate than old ones were being cleared, and sought to encourage better planning, greater participation by private business in renewal projects, and rehabilitation and conservation of marginal property. The Housing Act of 1959 added still another dimension in local planning for urban renewal by authorizing grants for preparing a "community renewal program." The program is *city-wide* in scope, with emphasis on total community needs for urban renewal on a long-range basis. The federal government will pay up to two-thirds of the cost of preparing a community renewal program.

The attack on urban blight was broadened still further by the Federal Housing Act of 1961, with two new programs of special significance for the future: (1) federal grants to help local governments to acquire land to be used for permanent "open space," and (2) loans and grants for urban mass transportation planning and for "demonstration projects" which might help solve mass transit problems.[4] The urban planning assistance provided originally in the 1954 law, known as the "Section 701 program," was given a shot in the arm by the 1961 act, which increased the authorization for these grants from $20 million to $75 million, and changed the 50-50 matching basis to two-thirds federal, one-third local.

This legislative picture of steadily broadening assistance for rebuilding cities since the 1930's should not be permitted to obscure the fact that actual urban renewal accomplishments have been painfully modest, both in *Rebuilding* number of cities and scope of projects. Numerous obstacles contribute *cities at a* to the snail's pace: many persons in areas to be renewed oppose being *snail's pace* relocated; prolonged court contests by property owners are common; racial issues flare up with an occasional charge that "urban renewal projects" have really become "Negro removal projects"; the government housing aspect of the program is often fought by private real estate interests; the red tape of intergovernmental approval, supervision, and paper work, is a constant source of delay; and state governments have generally failed to assume active leadership in stimulating this work, with a few states still having no enabling legislation to permit urban renewal.[5]

It has become abundantly clear that there is more to the administration

---

[4] For details of federal and state legislation in the field, *see* the continuing article "The State in Housing and Urban Renewal," in *The Book of the States.*

[5] In this connection, *see* Peter H. Rossi and Robert A. Dentler, *The Politics of Urban Renewal: The Chicago Findings* (The Free Press of Glencoe, Inc., New York, 1961).

of public housing and urban renewal than merely solving problems of finance, engineering and maintenance, difficult as these may be. Administrators and lawmakers have to face or dodge problems of community relations and inter-ethnic adjustment for a diversity of clients or prospective clients. This set of dilemmas in public housing is set forth acutely on the basis of experience by Charles Abrams in *Forbidden Neighbors: A Study of Prejudice in Housing.*[6] Factors of this nature may also complicate decisions as to the location of housing projects as well as plans for the disposition of blighted areas. Nevertheless, urban renewal has begun to take root as both a basic and urgent function of government and may be expected to become a major concern of all levels of government in coming years.

CONSERVATION

The conservation of nature and nature's products is a many-sided task of national, state, and local units of government. It includes action through public regulation, education or propaganda, and outright government ownership of natural resources. It is by no means limited to farm and countryside. The city of New York has some two million trees on public premises. Communion with the visible forms of nature seems essential to wholesome urban living. The industrial pollution of streams poses a threat to the economy as well as to the blessings of nature for urban communities, at the same time making life unpleasant for ruralities.[7] Dwindling water supplies in and around the swelling metropolitan areas have caused cities to range many miles from home in their quest for additional sources.[8] The abuse or misuse of soil, subsoil wealth, and growing timber has resulted in "ghost towns" and "tobacco road" regions. But proposals to check or correct destructive practices may bring conflict between special interests and the general interest, between the short view and the long view.

A many-sided task

The concern for conservation became something of a national crusade with the disappearance of the American frontier and the rise of Theodore Roosevelt to popular leadership and to the presidency. He called the state governors into national conference in 1908 on the theme of conservation. His work was followed in the next two decades by federal

The national movement

---

[6] Harper & Row, Publishers, New York, 1955.

[7] *See* Chapter 18, "Who Killed the French Broad?" in Wilma Dykeman, *The French Broad* (Holt, Rinehart & Winston, Inc., New York, 1955).

[8] *See* Maynard M. Hufschmidt, "And Not a Drop to Drink: Water Resources Planning and Administration," *Public Administration Review,* XXI (Spring, 1961), pp. 81-89.

legislation for national-state cooperation in checking forest fires and carrying on reforestation. A later Roosevelt brought conservation nearer home to millions in the process of expending unprecedented funds for rural relief and rehabilitation. On this front the New Deal created or expanded land improvement practices for individual farmers, soil conservation districts and associations, reforestation belts, and flood control projects as notably exemplified by the multi-purpose TVA. It brought the federal government and the farmers into closer contact with county agents, land grant colleges, and state departments of conservation. The new patterns of relationships were to continue after the end of the depression that brought them forth. The system of federal aid or technical assistance was to remain, as were the problems of conservation, whether in regions of flood or dust bowl, whether in Democratic or Republican administrations.

Every state serves the cause of conservation through an administrative establishment with branches or through a plurality of agencies. Fish and game regulations, for example, are administered by a separate agency in some *State agencies and activities* states and by a division of the department of conservation in others. So are state parks. These departments and divisions have functions that are regulatory, educational, and promotional with respect to the resources of land, water, forests, farm woods, and wildlife. They may provide services in connection with preventing forest fires, distributing seedlings, stocking fish ponds, improving streams, and the like. They inevitably have cooperative or pressure contacts with clubs or associations of sportsmen, tourist-trade promoters, lumbermen, utility operators, and spokesmen of other interests, special or general. This variety of group interests sometimes renders difficult the balancing of policy between conservation and "development."

State conservation agencies may have working relations with other central or local authorities, including those concerned with agriculture, health, public works, planning, and law enforcement. They naturally have cooperative relations with federal agencies under the stimulus of federal aid and technical assistance, although state and national officers do not always see eye to eye on methods and measures of conservation.

One way for a government to conserve natural resources is to own and manage them. That has been distinctly recognized by the national government and even by a few local governments. Most of the states own wide *State ownership and management* tracts of land, partly as the result of federal aid or allocation in many instances. All but a few states have forest preserves, with an acreage usually ranging between a few thousand and a few hundred thousand. States topping a million acres in public forests are Idaho, Michigan, Minnesota, New York, and Pennsylvania. Public park lands are significant for many states, notably for California with more than half a million acres. It is hardly necessary to observe that trees growing in the wide spaces of state parks may constitute timber resources just as truly as if they were classified as forests. The states utilize their broad acres for scientific forestry, recreational resources, hunting preserves, wildlife sanctuaries, and other purposes. Some of the lands contain mineral deposits and oil reserves often for less conscious conservation.

World wars, world trends, and American politics have intensified the problems of conserving and controlling the petroleum and gas resources of the nation. The states have a large scope of discretion in determining what shall or shall not be done in this crucial industry, both on private and *Petroleum* state lands. As with other industrial resources, most of the oil states have *and natural* come lately to tasks of conservation, although this reserve is not limitless *gas* and not to be replenished. Under the spur of conservationist demands and an element of supporting opinion inside the industry, the states began to act, following the early lead of Pennsylvania and New York. Most of the states concerned have become parties to an interstate compact to prevent waste and to regulate petroleum production by applying quota systems in accord with demands for the output. Congress has restricted non-quota shipments in interstate commerce.

The states of Texas, Louisiana, and California have acquired strategic positions with respect to offshore petroleum resources under the Submerged Land Act of 1953. This measure disclaimed certain national rights or titles as set forth by the Supreme Court and undertook to "return" to the states the tidelands within their historic boundaries. Its passage fulfilled a political campaign promise of 1952, but many observers considered it a setback to national conservation. It has brought forward new points or old points of states' rights and states' responsibilities.[9]

The most recent trend in conservation emphasis has been a growing anxiety over fast-vanishing open space and the lost opportunities for outdoor recreational facilities as the metropolitan mowing-machines consume the countrysides for suburban housing, shopping centers, and industrial *Conservation* development.[10] The crowded metropolis is being forced to face, with *of recrea-* an ironic twist, the problem of open space in the "Space Age." President *tional* Kennedy took the cue in 1962 from a three-year study by the Outdoor *resources* Recreation Resources Review Commission and recommended to Congress a vast federal-state-local land-purchase program for park, recreation, and wildlife uses. There can be little doubt that our nation's population expansion, coupled with increases in worker productivity and leisure time, will provide increased

---

[9] For further discussion of this issue, in relation to states' rights, *see* Chapter 2.

[10] *See,* for example, *The Race for Open Space* (Regional Plan Association, New York, 1960).

394 political pressure for conservation, and perhaps reclamation, of recreational resources.

State planning

"Planning," as a recognized function of government, has received far more acceptance at the city level than at the state level of government. City planning and zoning involve a great deal of control over the use which private property owners may make of their land and the structures on it, but some of the strongest supporters of this function of urban government are business and real estate groups. Yet state planning, which has never involved much concern for "state zoning" or regulation of private property rights, has never received corresponding support or recognition as a function of state government. For a short period during the 1930's state planning organizations were created under the stimulus of federal grants-in-aid through the National Resources Planning Board. Much of their initial work involved coordinating of emergency public works projects aimed at the unemployment problem, but some progress was being made toward state land-use plans when the priorities of World War II intervened. During the post-war years state planning agencies in most states were lost in the shuffle of reorganizations which tended to downgrade any idea of comprehensive state-wide planning. Many of them were given new names and made primarily responsible for attracting tourists and new industries to the state, and approving local requests for federal aid. Only about one out of four of the states have what professional planners would recognize as real state planning agencies. The State of Hawaii gives cabinet status to its Department of Planning and Research and has developed a comprehensive state plan for 1960-80, which planners hope will serve as a prototype for other states.[11]

SUPPLEMENTARY READINGS

Banfield, Edward C. and Morton Grodzins, *Government and Housing in Metropolitan Areas* (McGraw-Hill Book Co., Inc., New York, 1958).

Abrams, Charles, *Forbidden Neighbors: A Study of Prejudice in Housing* (Harper & Row, Publishers, New York, 1955).

Commission on Intergovernmental Relations, *A Description of Twenty-five Federal Grant-in-Aid Programs* (U. S. Government Printing Office, Washington, 1955).

---

[11] See Harold V. Miller, "State Planning and Development," *The Book of the States, 1962-63,* pp. 451-455.

Commission on Intergovernmental Relations, *A Staff Report on Federal Aid to Airports* (U. S. Government Printing Office, Washington, 1955).

Commission on Intergovernmental Relations, *A Study Committee Report on Federal Aid to Highways* (U. S. Government Printing Office, Washington, 1955).

Commission on Intergovernmental Relations, *A Study Committee Report on Natural Resources and Conservation* (U. S. Government Printing Office, Washington, 1955).

Lilienthal, David, *TVA: Democracy on the March* (Harper & Row, Publishers, New York, 1944).

Maass, Arthur, *Muddy Waters* (Harvard University Press, Cambridge, 1951).

Moses, Robert, *Working for the People* (Harper & Row, Publishers, New York, 1956).

Nixon, H. C., *The Tennessee Valley: A Recreation Domain* (Vanderbilt University Press, Nashville, 1945).

Pinchot, Gifford, *Breaking New Ground* (Harcourt, Brace & World, Inc., New York, 1947).

U. S. Commission on Organization of the Executive Branch of the Government, 1953-1955, *Report on Water Resources and Power* (3 vols.; U. S. Government Printing Office, Washington, 1955).

Wengert, Norman, *Natural Resources and the Political Struggle* (Doubleday & Company, Inc., New York, 1955).

★ 22 ★

EDUCATION, HEALTH AND WELFARE

AMERICANS, IN their capacity to govern, channel billions of dollars annually into cultivating sound minds in sound bodies and reducing the toll of disease and poverty. In addition to direct expenditures, they extend various tax

General
importance

concessions and public privileges to privately endowed or supported institutions, organizations, and foundations that serve the interests of education, research, health, and charity on a non-profit basis. All regular levels of government are involved in one way or another in this great social process, which, with the passage of time and simple ways, has outgrown the governing power and autonomy of the local communities.

Cooperative aid from centralized sources has become the established and inevitable pattern for advancing this set of social services. This trend, in its national aspects, has been pointed up by messages to Congress in recent years by presidents from both political parties, calling for aid to states, localities, and institutions for meeting "human needs" in such fields as school construction, public housing, medical research, hospitalization, child welfare service, and problems of retarded children. The trend at the same time has been emphasized by calls within the states for centralized aid to cities and counties for similar purposes, such as one governor's request for three million dollars to aid cities in maintaining day care centers for children of working mothers, or another governor's recommendations to move his state up from the bottom of the list of 50 states in preventive and curative programs for mental health.

The states, counties, cities, and towns collectively require more funds and employ more men and women for these basic human services than for all their governmental activities in maintaining law and order and regulating private enterprise. They thus accentuate positive service, in comparison with negative restriction, in the affairs of men, although the accent may be inadequate for increasing needs.

EDUCATION

Half of all Americans between the ages of 5 and 34 are in school or college. More than four-fifths of these are enrolled in state or public systems and institutions, although two out of five college or university students find accommodations in private establishments. This conglomerate process of public education involves much more than an array of teachers and pupils. It functions under central and local boards, either elected or appointed. It requires a host of administrators, including superintendents, principals, presidents, deans, and supporting staffs of secretaries, divisional managers, and specialists. Decisions concerning education are now inextricably related to the birth rate, the flow of migration, urban and suburban blight and sprawl, unemployment trends, "cold war" problems of defense and prestige, tax structure, technological development, race relations, and a host of other things. There are complaints of too much administrative overhead in American education,[1] but reducing it is not easy. The public system of one of the major states might be described, in terms borrowed from interpreters of giant business, as a vertical and horizontal combination.

Scope, horizontal and vertical

State governments, through legislative and executive functions, have the key roles in public education, despite the importance of local initiative and the variation in school merit among the localities. The states have been the essential middlemen between federal aid and the schools ever since the adoption (prior to the Constitution) of the policy of donating a section per township of western lands to the new states for educational purposes. Most states made the shift in the nineteenth century from free schools for "poor" children to free schools for all, with provisions for centralized state-wide

State roles

---

[1] H. S. Commager, "The Problem Isn't Bricks—It's Brains," *New York Times Magazine*, January 29, 1956, p. 11.

standards for examining and certifying teachers. The states enacted compulsory school attendance laws, with Massachusetts taking the lead in 1852 and Mississippi making it universal in 1918. The states took steps to terminate many isolated one-room schools through consolidation, with larger districts and with bus transportation to and from the consolidated schools in rural regions. They have set up administrative procedures for the selection and adoption of textbooks, sometimes providing them for children without cost. As indicated in the chapter on finance, the states appropriate or earmark central funds for distribution to local school jurisdictions. By the middle of this century, these supplementary funds amounted to several billion dollars annually for all the states.[2] There are tangible reasons for referring to public schools as state systems.

Most tax-supported institutions of higher education are creations and wards of the states, and the few municipal colleges or universities are not immune from measures of state regulation and support. The state university or university system is a different entity for different states. It may embrace several campuses in different centers under one president, as in California or North Carolina; it may include the land-grant college of agriculture and mechanical arts as part of the central establishment, as in Illinois or Wisconsin; or it may separate the university in control and management from the land-grant college and other colleges of the state, as in Alabama or Texas. Some of the land-grant institutions have become universities in scope and name. Many states have separately controlled junior colleges and teachers colleges, and southern states have established separate colleges or universities for Negroes.

Higher education

Many states are without any over-all system or coordination for their several institutions of higher learning. But New York has a Board of Regents which exercises extensive policy-making and regulatory power over the state's entire educational system, including public schools, high schools, and higher institutions. These regents are elected by the legislature in joint session, one a year. Many states provide for the selection of university regents or trustees by gubernatorial appointment with senate confirmation under a staggered system, in an effort to prevent excessive control by any particular political administration. Undue political interference with the academic appointments or tenure of a university may bring unfavorable censure or non-recognition by associations of institutions and professional groups, as a few governors have discovered, with embittered alumni turning against them.[3] Federal aid to state institutions also carries certain safeguards against political manipulation of academic affairs.

The public schools below the college level are generally more dependent

---

[2] See Chapter 14, "Finance," for this and other aspects of financing education.

[3] Governor Eugene Talmadge of Georgia and Governor Theodore G. Bilbo of Mississippi encountered political difficulty in this way.

upon local financing than upon state and federal aid. They are points of direct contact with units of the Parent-Teacher Association and other pressure groups supporting school improvement and expansion. They are some- *The local* times centers of controversy over means and policy, as in the beginnings *hookup* of the school lunch program with food initially supplied from surplus products by the United States Department of Agriculture. In many centers they participate in undertakings to reduce juvenile delinquency, sometimes with the direct cooperation of visiting teachers and other social workers. They serve in different ways as units for applying public health protections, including inoculation processes. In many rural areas the public school provides the only facility for civic forums, farm meetings, and other community activities.

The far-flung educational systems are not free from problems, both local and central. One task is that of providing trained and competent teachers as well as adequate physical facilities for large and expanding enrollments. During the decade of the 1960's an estimated 1,600,000 new teachers *Problems:* will be needed to replace those leaving the profession, plus another *teacher* *recruitment* 400,000 needed because of enrollment increase. Yet the annual rate of training new teachers is supplying only half that number. The deficit is usually made up by temporary arrangements, often with substandard teachers. Sharp differences exist between states in salaries paid for teachers, with the average in 1960-61 varying from a low of $3,415 in Mississippi to a high of $6,700 in California.

The population pressure on our school system is greater than at any other period in our history. Public school enrollments in the decade of the 1950's jumped from less than 26 million to more than 37 million, but the problem is even more serious than national totals imply. The burden is *Population* badly out of balance in a few states, such as Florida and California, *pressures* where "crash programs" of school expansion have been demanded by phenomenal population growth. If a comparable increase continues in the 1960's, public school enrollment in the United States will have more than doubled within one generation. Overflow enrollments complicate already difficult problems of classroom space, teacher recruitment, and—basic to most problems—school finance. School authorities point to a variety of problems faced by local districts in seeking to accommodate the swelling student population: "(*a*) inadequate district size and tax base, (*b*) low debt ceilings, (*c*) delay in placing new properties on the tax duplicate, (*d*) delay in tax distribution, (*e*) inadequate knowledge of the future due to poor planning, and (*f*) inability to coordinate local governmental agencies and authorities."[4]

---

[4] Conrad Briner and William W. Wayson, "State Public School Systems," *The Book of the States, 1962-63*, p. 307.

One of the most dramatic reorganization movements in state and local
government of this century has been the increasingly successful drive to reduce,
by merger, the fantastic number of school districts in the United States.

*School
district
consolidation*   Although the total number of districts was cut sharply from more than
127,000 in 1932 to less than 37,000 in 1961, most school authorities still
consider this to be far too many for best educational and economical
results. The consolidations have come only after grueling political fights, with
opponents objecting to the impact of the larger consolidated schools on grass-
roots control of school policy, the loss of a rural community center, the "homog-
enizing" effects of an urbanized school on rural students, and the prospects of
large bond issues for the new consolidated schools. The public has generally
supported the views of the proponents of consolidation, who argue that the
nineteenth century districts were geared to the transportation of that period
and to the idea that few pupils would go further than the eighth grade, and
that consolidated schools provide greater educational opportunity for all. The
one-room school house (one-teacher elementary school), once almost a bio-
graphical prerequisite to elective office in some states, has been reduced to less
than 20,000 in number, in contrast to 143,000 such schools in 1932.

      School district organization involves not only urban-rural relationships;
it has recently become a difficult intra-metropolitan problem involving urban-
suburban relationships.[5] Wealthy suburbs with a low population density

*Metropolitan
school or-
ganization*   may fare ten times as well, educationally, as poorer suburbs with high
population density. Some suburban school districts may have "wind-
fall tax support" from a large industrial plant, while another suburb may
be blessed only with thousands of young working families with school-age
children. At the same time, large "core city" school systems are often arbitrarily
separated from suburban schools, taxable wealth, and—perhaps most important
—from its civic leadership, with a resultant fragmentation in educational planning and administration for the total community. This problem is closely related
to the discussion of "metropolitics" in Chapter 18.

      The problem of racial segregation in public schools was discussed as a
constitutional issue in Chapter 2, but it should be included in any listing of
the contemporary educational problems of state and local government.

*Racial
desegregation*   Since the desegregation decision of the Supreme Court in 1954,[6] reversing the long-standing "separate but equal" doctrine, school districts
in southern states have moved from crisis to crisis in a slow but steady
process of compliance with the law of the land. Integration statistics can be

---

[5] *See* Robert Havighurst, "Metropolitan Development and the Educational System," *The
School Review*, LXIX (Autumn, 1961), pp. 251-267.

[6] *Brown v. Topeka Board of Education* 347 U. S. 483 (1954).

deceiving in some respects, but the trend toward compliance is unmistakable. Of the 6,229 school districts in 17 southern and border states, 645 had desegregated by 1957 and 976 by early in 1963. Only 3,058 southern school districts have both Negro and white children residing within their boundaries. Over 300 state laws have been passed on the subject of desegregation, some to facilitate it, some to limit it to "token integration," some to oppose it with "massive resistance." Many opposition statutes have been invalidated by the courts and others remain to be tested. When South Carolina's Clemson College admitted Negro student Harvey Gantt early in 1963, no southern state remained which had not experienced some degree of school desegregation.

Segregation is not entirely a southern problem, particularly since the northern industrial centers now contain 48 per cent of the Negro population of the United States. Many of these school systems have a kind of *de facto* segregation paralleling segregated residential areas. New York **De facto** City has transferred pupils, both as a means of promoting integration and **segregation** relieving crowded schools. New Rochelle, New York, and Highland Park, Michigan, were ordered by the courts to integrate schools.

Religion must take its place by race as one of the knottiest of public school problems currently troubling governmental decision makers. It is sometimes a delicate matter to provide moral or spiritual instruction without running into complaints and court cases based on the constitutional **Religion** principle of separation of church and state. The issue is not simply **and public** whether individuals or groups can engage in prayer in the public schools, **schools** or even whether government officials can prescribe a particular prayer to be used in the public schools. In 1962 the Supreme Court answered the latter question in the negative in the New York Board of Regents case. Equally difficult and far-reaching is the question of tax support for parochial schools, either for specific programs such as pupil transportation, free textbooks, and free lunches, or for broad assistance for teachers' salaries or for school construction or maintenance. In coming years the judicial and political issues of separation of church and state will undoubtedly be closely interwoven as they relate to the public school system.

Still another unresolved question affecting the public schools is the role of the federal government. The educational and ideological case for federal aid is a persuasive one, based on the sharp differences between states in their financial resources and educational opportunity. The constitutional **Federal aid** question of federal aid to public schools is not really unresolved, for some of the oldest federal aid programs are really political, with the opponents consisting of (1) conservative taxpayers' organizations fearing a mass transfer of the school finance burden to the federal income tax; (2) some Catholic groups who oppose a federal aid bill which does not include aid to parochial schools;

EDUCATION

(3) states' rights groups fearing that federal aid will lead to undesirable federal controls, a fear voiced particularly by segregationists who see such aid as an additional wedge for racial integration; and (4) leaders from the wealthier states who oppose all strongly equalizing formulas as constituting too much of a "hand-out" to the poorer states. They tend to accept only very moderate equalization which either fails to provide much assistance for the weakest states or else becomes a very expensive program. Depending on the kind of bill being considered, the principal opposition forces might well be the opposite groups to the ones just cited, such as integrationist groups if segregation seems to be sanctioned, and protestant groups if aid to Catholic schools is included.[7]

Schools and politics

"Politics" is commonly looked upon as the enemy of "good public schools," and a commonly proposed solution to school problems is to "take the schools out of politics." The professional educator and PTA groups are often heard advocating the elective school board and the trained superintendent as means of keeping schools out of politics. Realism suggests that this is an impossibility. A writer observing the presidential primary in West Virginia in 1960 has described the character of elective school board politics in that state:

> Posts on local school boards are bitterly contested, from one end of the state to the other. 'Hell,' one local politician answered me, 'curriculum? They don't give a damn about curriculum, half of them don't know what the word 'curriculum' means. School board means jobs—it means teachers' jobs, janitors' jobs, bus-driver jobs. They'll pass the curriculum in five minutes and spend two hours arguing about who's gonna be bus driver on Peapot Route Number One. Bus driver means a hundred and sixty dollars a month for a part-time job.'[8]

The professional superintendent of schools is not really "out of politics," either. Like the professional city manager, he is inevitably a policy leader rather than a purely managerial follower, and this must be included in any definition of politics. One retired school superintendent explained his decision to run for the legislature in terms of his previous relation to politics:

> After I retired from the school business, I missed the public life and the chance to meet people and appear before the public that I had had as a superintendent. I did not think of politics before this, except that as a superintendent you're always in the political business. There's a lot of

---

[7] For a discussion of the history of federal aid to education since 1787, and the pros and cons, see Alice M. Rivlin, *The Role of the Federal Government in Financing Higher Education* (Brookings, Washington, D. C., 1961).

[8] Theodore H. White, *The Making of the President, 1960* (Atheneum Publishers, New York, 1961), p. 99. Reprinted by permission of the publishers.

The politics of public education is still an area largely untouched by the research of social scientists, but it is clear that much of the folklore about taking schools out of politics needs careful scrutiny. There is good reason to believe that the character of a school system may inevitably be a reflection of the total political system of the community and state. If this is true, school reformers would be wise to direct their efforts at shaping or controlling the total system, rather than at futile efforts to withdraw schools from the system of community and state politics.[10]

Aside from social issues and policies, special and routine problems of administration arise, such as mapping or rearranging school districts, adjusting or streamlining city and county activities, or improving methods of purchasing supplies. The organization of administrative housekeeping is as much a need and a problem in public education as in other phases of state and local government.

School administration

HEALTH AGENCIES AND HOSPITALS

The specific role of state and local governments in promoting the health of the American people, as distinguished from *private* responsibility for health, is not easy to define. Perhaps we can agree that if a do-it-yourself enthusiast hammers his thumb instead of the nail, his health is a private responsibility in this case. Similarly, we all agree that if the same man comes down with a highly communicable disease, state and local governments have a responsibility to prevent its spread to others in the community. But it is not enough to define public health solely in terms of prevention and private health solely in terms of curative measures. Private medical care is greatly concerned with the prevention of disease, and public health departments have well-established programs to treat tuberculosis patients, the mentally

What is public health?

---

[9] John C. Wahlke, *et al.*, *The Legislative System: Explorations in Legislative Behavior*, *op. cit.*, p. 87.

[10] For other examples of the politics of education, *see* the series of twelve paperbacks on *The Economics and Politics of Public Education*, published in 1962 and 1963 by Syracuse University Press; *see also* Alan Rosenthal, "The Special Case of Public Education," in *Cases in State and Local Government* ed. Richard T. Frost (Prentice-Hall, Inc., Englewood Cliffs, 1961), pp. 62-75; Vincent Ostrom, "The Politics of Education in a Democracy," in Joseph R. Fiszman, *The American Political Arena: Selected Reading* (Little, Brown and Co., Boston, 1962); and Thomas H. Eliot, "Toward an Understanding of Public School Politics," *American Political Science Review*, LIII (December, 1959), pp. 1032-1051.

ill, and the indigent sick, as well as various patients in experimental and pilot projects. Neither is the public health program concerned only with the indigent citizen, for many of its programs are directed at persons of all economic levels.

The distinction between the public and private sectors of medical care is essentially a political matter, determined pragmatically by an accumulation of decisions by boards of health, legislative bodies, and occasionally by popular votes, to give governmental agencies some degree of responsibility for health problems which the private sector seems ill-equipped or unwilling to handle. Thus, through the years the accepted functions of state and local health departments have come to include communicable disease control, mental health, sanitary engineering, maternal and child health services, dental health, public health nursing, industrial hygiene, radiological health, air pollution control, emergency health services, and such auxiliary functions as public health laboratories and vital statistics.

A pragmatic distinction

Public health administration has less personnel and less historical background than the educational systems of state and local government. But this type of public activity has acquired modern significance with the development of preventive medicine, vaccines, control of communicable disease, compulsory sanitation, and appreciation of popular scientific information on health problems. States, cities, and counties maintain health agencies or officers to perform regulatory and service functions, partly in cooperation with other authorities, including the United States Public Health Service. The work is not uniformly concentrated. Milk inspection, for example, may be directed by agricultural agencies, as in a few states, instead of being under the direction of health officers. The city of New York has a separate scientific Department of Air Pollution Control, and state conservation agencies may be charged with limiting stream polution.

Rise of public health work

Most of the states have central health boards or commissions, with memberships of three or more, for rather infrequent meetings, somewhat like a college or corporation board. The chief administrative officer of the health agency is likely to be called "commissioner," "director," "superintendent," or "officer." His department generally serves as a clearinghouse of technical asistance, information, advice, and regulatory instruction for local health boards or officers. It may perform or direct inspectional activities, dispense vaccines, and conduct laboratory tests to advance health service or control. The board or department in some states has broad powers to issue rules or orders for compliance by citizens, institutions, and even municipalities. There are miscellaneous other functions, with variations among the states.

State agencies and functions

Public health service or power reaches citizens primarily through local agencies, which may share in federal grants-in-aid as well as receive state assistance. Full-time staffs are found in most counties, sometimes with a local physician on part-time duty as director. Most important cities have agencies separate from the county, although a single or consolidated *Local admin-* health unit for city and county characterizes a considerable number of *istration* centers, including such metropolitan communities as Baltimore, Denver, Louisville, Memphis, Nashville, New Orleans, St. Louis, and San Francisco.

In addition to numerous services, the local health departments exercise powers of government with respect to matters of quarantine, compulsory vaccination, inspection of products and premises, elimination of unsanitary conditions, and closure or condemnation of establishments for non-compliance. If necessary, their legitimate orders are enforced through court action. By order of the health board the city of Nashville, as noted earlier, had to vacate its police jail for a period in 1955 and depend upon county imprisonment and prosecution. The social action programs of health authorities beget opposition and criticism as well as civic support.

Statistics on the number of hospitals operated by state and local governments are rather formidable, although demands are heard in many quarters for expansion and improvement. The figures run above 500 for states, 700 for counties, and 400 for cities or city-county combinations. These add *Hospital* up to a total smaller than that for all other types of hospitals in the *statistics* country, including church, private, and federal, but they represent a far greater number of beds — not far from a million. The state hospitals have an average capacity of more than 1,000 beds, a capacity which partly offsets the complete absence of public or private hospital facilities in hundreds of counties, not to mention inadequate facilities in many others. It is well to guard against relying too rigidly upon statistics, however, for private hospitals may serve public purposes under contractual arrangements with counties or cities for the care of indigent patients, and government hospitals may provide service for paying patients. Private hospitals are subject in many ways to state or local regulation.

Public hospitals frequently have their own boards of control and administrative officers. It is a prevailing state pattern to coordinate the central hospital facilities administratively and physically with the state university medical school for practical and scientific reasons. The states also *Hospital* provide general and special hospital services in central or district insti- *control and* tutions for the mentally ill, who have received increasing attention in *adminis-* contemporary times with the development of applied psychology and *tration* psychiatry. Special work in the field of mental derangement and its cure is also found in the larger regular hospitals and medical schools. Local public hospitals vary widely in management, size, and efficiency, with many inadequacies and difficulties of distance for inhabitants of rural areas. Local

hospitals, like local schools, may make gains through state and federal aid.
The public health interests are served in effective ways through non-governmental groups and movements, as notably exemplified in the popular fights against cancer, heart disease, and infantile paralysis. These

Foundations and associations activities tend to supplement and support the work of public health agencies and institutions, sometimes to blaze new trails in the field of preventive measures. An example of pioneering was the Rockefeller Foundation's successful sponsorship in the early years of this century of a scientific program for removing the hookworm handicap from poor people in the rural South. Movements of enlightenment with respect to mental disorders and venereal diseases have had inherent effects and have also stimulated legislative action, including federal aid.

Federal grants-in-aid to states and localities have exerted strong influence both on hospital construction and public health services. The Hospital Survey and Construction (Hill-Burton) Act of 1946 has stimulated con-

Federal aid: health and hospitals struction of new hospitals or additions to present buildings, with the annual appropriation rising from an initial $75 million to a total of $185 million for 1961. During the fifteen-year period following enactment of the program, $1.5 billion in federal aid was matched by $3.4 billion in state, local, and private funds, for 5,700 construction projects providing 239,000 new hospital beds. While urban and specialized hospitals have received assistance, the major emphasis has been upon rural and general hospitals. Official state hospital planning agencies reported in 1961 an additional need for close to 1.2 million beds.[11] Alternate approaches to financing medical care for the aged continue to be debated: grants-in-aid to the states for the indigent aged or a system of coverage through increasing the social security tax.

The major areas of federal aid for specific public health programs are cancer control, heart-disease control, mental health, turberculosis control, and venereal-disease control. In recent years a debate has developed over the

Block grants; pro and con idea of a general "block grant" in the field of health which would permit the states increased flexibility in its support for various programs.
Although this proposal has received general support from governors and other state officials, it is opposed by professional organizations interested in particular health categories (cancer, heart disease, etc.). Such groups are fearful that their particular program might be neglected. Federal officials have tended to side with the specialized grants as a means of obtaining the maximum stimulation of state and local health activity.[12]

---

[11] See "State Health Programs," *The Book of the States*, 1962-63, pp. 358-367.

[12] U. S. Advisory Commission on Intergovernmental Relations, *Modification of Federal Grants-in-Aid for Public Health Services*, (Washington, January, 1961), p. 11.

To promote the public, social, or general welfare is one of the great purposes of modern democratic government. In broad constitutional coverage, it would include public education and public health, which, however, have their own functional classifications in the state and local systems. *Meaning of* Hence welfare in more particular terms today connotes community or *the term* governmental action to relieve and prevent poverty, suffering, and human insecurity. Its modern meaning carries a more constructive psychological assumption and a stronger sense of social responsibility than the term suggested in the era of public reliance upon community almshouses and county homes for paupers, whose pathetic fate was summarized, in the phrase, "over the hill to the poor house." Through significant developments since the passing of the fabulous 1920's, the public welfare picture has been revolutionized in features and magnitude. For humanitarian and pragmatic reasons, it has acquired the twin supports of public philosophy and professional administration. It expresses the power of the purse of big government, little government, and middle government in a fashion strikingly symbolical of the new "cooperative federalism."

Temporary and permanent measures gave centralized momentum to welfare administration in the depression of the 1930's, when millions were unemployed and other millions could not pay debts or taxes. The burden of relief became too much for private or community charities, too much *Emergency* for local units of government, and too much for state governments. The *relief* federal government assumed the task in the first term of President Franklin D. Roosevelt, rapidly expanding activities and providing billions of dollars for employment of the jobless on numerous state and local projects. This Emergency Relief Administration became the Works Progress Administration, then the Works Projects Administration. Its various functions included, in addition to the regular farm recovery work, launching a rural rehabilitation program to aid stranded farmers and tenants such as those described by John Steinbeck in *The Grapes of Wrath*.[13] An incidental accomplishment of the WPA was the physical removal of malarial conditions in swampy regions of the South. Inside or outside the WPA there were federal agencies and funds to aid states and municipalities in highway improvement, slum clearance, park development, and other useful work that would offer employment without competing directly with private enterprise. This broad-guage action stimulated the states and localities to create or authorize agencies and projects of immediate and lasting importance.

---

[13] The Viking Press, Inc., New York, 1939.

The federal Social Security Act of 1935 has become a basic charter of cooperative welfare policy, as is attested by subsequent expansions by federal legislation and statutory implementation in all the states. It launched four broad programs of action. These are a strictly federal system of old-age and survivors insurance, federal-state systems of unemployment insurance, aid to the states for public assistance to needy persons of specified categories, and aid to the states for maternal and child welfare service. All but the first of these programs require state legislation and cooperation. The first, under federal administration, prevents a certain type of welfare problem from falling upon the states and local jurisdictions. In using federal insurance and welfare funds, state and local agencies must comply with certain standards, including merit requirements for their own personnel.

Social Security

The unemployment insurance systems of the states are somewhat varied, flexible, and complicated, since they are set up and administered by the states with the support of compulsory payroll taxes levied by federal legislation. The states orginally had little alternative but to take "voluntary" steps to use the compulsory levies within their borders. All states have unemployment systems, including Wisconsin which had adopted a plan prior to 1935.

Unemployment compensation

By federal requirement the unemployment insurance plan applies to commerce and industry, exclusive of the railroads, which had already been covered by a separate national system of labor security. In a roundabout process, a payroll tax is paid by each employer or establishment having four or more workers for parts of 20 weeks of the year, and the proceeds are segregated according to states. The maximum levy is 3 per cent of a worker's annual pay up to $3,000. This includes a flat three-tenths of 1 per cent to cover federal grants to the states for administering the program. The remaining 2.7 per cent is subject to reduction for a particular taxpayer according to his experience or merit rating as an employer under the state system. This portion of the tax goes into a federal trust account for use by the state concerned in making benefit payments to covered works for temporary periods of unemployment. State laws vary considerably in details, but essentially they determine the recipients, amounts, and conditions of unemployment compensation. The maximum benefit per week ranged among the states in 1961 from $28 to $55, and the maximum duration for benefits ranged from 20 to 39 weeks. A worker earns insurance credits when employed; upon becoming jobless, he files a claim for benefits with a public employment office and also registers with the office for reemployment. The Bureau of Employment Security of the United States Department of Labor administers the federal features of the process with a cooperative eye on state standards and practices. The amount of funds held in the federal treasury for state accounts extends into billions, and the number of workers receiving benefit payments in a year extends into millions.

Many persons are not protected from poverty or ill fortune by the systems of old-age and unemployment insurance. In recognition of this condition, the federal government aids the states in providing public assistance to four classes of needy persons: the aged, the blind, the permanently and totally disabled, and children without parental support. This help to more than seven million Americans is administered by state and local welfare offices and financed on a federal-state matching basis. Direct monetary assistance to other groups of needy persons is subject to state and local arrangements. *Welfare assistance and service*

One program inaugurated under the Social Security system affords service rather than financial payments to individuals. It is a matching program under federal requirements and with state or local administration for services in behalf of maternal health, child health, crippled children, and child welfare. The matched funds for these services are handled at the state level partly through health units and partly through welfare agencies. Federal responsibility rests with the Children's Bureau of the Department of Health, Education, and Welfare. Nongovernmental organizations and institutions also cooperate in carrying out relevant phases of the work, such as providing special training and opportunity for physically handicapped children. Red Cross teams move into relief action in case of sudden misfortune or disaster. Welfare policies and administrative practices are advanced by the professional influence of schools of social work and associations of social workers.

Social welfare for states and local units is also served by funds, activities, and agencies outside the technical scope of public welfare administration. Supervised parks and recreation facilities contribute to the well-being of the masses. Various agencies and jurisdictions of government take up relief tasks in case of a major flood in New England or California. Impoverished veterans of the armed services may avoid local relief rolls through public provisions for their care and benefit. Retirement pensions and job securities for teachers and other public employees contribute to the general welfare. So does public housing for low-income families. Mention should be made of fringe benefits for employees in many collective-bargain contracts. With labor union welfare funds mounting to significant proportions since the end of World War II. The proper administration of such funds is a matter of public concern, particularly in the industrial states. Economic and scientific progress ramifies the problems of public welfare and the methods of coping with them. *Collateral activities*

Ashmore, H. S., *The Negro and the Schools* (University of North Carolina Press, Chapel Hill, 1954).

Commission on Intergovernmental Relations, *A Study Committee Report on Federal Aid to Public Health* (U. S. Government Printing Office, Washington, 1955).

Commission on Intergovernmental Relations, *A Study Committee Report on Federal Aid to Welfare* (U. S. Government Printing Office, Washington, 1955).

Commission on Intergovernmental Relations, *A Study Committee Report on Federal Responsibility in the Field of Education* (U. S. Government Printing Office, Washington, 1955).

Commission on Intergovernmental Relations, *A Study Committee Report on Unemployment Compensation and Employment Service* (U. S. Government Printing Office, Washington, 1955).

Council of State Governments, *State Action in Mental Health* (Chicago, 1960).

Daland, R. T., *Government and Health: The Alabama Experience* (Bureau of Public Administration, University of Alabama, University, Ala., 1955).

DeVane, W. C., *The American University in the Twentieth Century* (Louisiana State University Press, Baton Rouge, 1957).

Drake, J. T., *The Aged in American Society* (The Ronald Press Company, New York, 1958).

"Education," continuing article in *The Book of the States* (Council of State Governments, Chicago).

Gardner, John W., "National Goals in Education," *Goals for Americans,* report of the President's Commission on National Goals (The American Assembly, Columbia University, 1960, reprinted Prentice-Hall, Inc., New York, 1960), pp. 81-100.

"Health and Welfare," continuing article in *The Book of the States* (Council of State Governments, Chicago).

McClure, William P., and Van Miller, *Government of Public Education for Adequate Policy Making* (University of Illinois Bureau of Educational Research, Urbana, 1960).

Means, J. H., *Doctors, People, and Government* (Little, Brown and Co., Boston, 1953).

National Conference of Social Work, *The Social Welfare Forum,* 1955 (Columbia University Press, New York, 1955).

White House Conference on Aging, *Aging in the States—A Report of Progress, Concern, Goals* (U. S. Government Printing Office, Washington, D. C., January, 1961).

Wyatt, L. R., *Intergovernmental Relations in Public Health* (University of Minnesota Press, Minneapolis, 1951).

Ylvisaker, Paul N., *The Battle of Blue Earth County* (rev. ed.; University of Alabama Press, University, Ala., 1955).

★ *23* ★

APPRAISAL AND PROSPECT

Alexander Hamilton, if he could view contemporary America, might observe that the states have become neither so powerful as he feared nor so subordinate as he hoped. John W. Burgess could not today find full confirmation of his prophecy of 1886 that the "meddlesome" and artificial states would come in the twentieth century to "occupy a much lower place in our political system" in comparison with gains of power by the "natural" communities of nation and municipalities.[1] Alexis de Tocqueville, looking over the modern scene, would hardly change the title of his *Democracy in America* (1835-1840) or find reason for drastic revision of his analysis of balance between the centralized national government and diverse local units. James Bryce might find more problems but less failure in our municipal government than he pointed out in *The American Commonwealth* (1883). All would be amazed at the urban revolution in American society and concerned about its accommodation to traditional patterns and ideas of government.[2]

Summoning the prophets

These analytical spokesmen of the past could today see substantial part-

---

[1] J. W. Burgess, "The American Commonwealth," *The Political Science Quarterly*, I (1886), pp. 34-35.

[2] The problems of relating traditional small-community political ideals to current metropolitan realities are discussed by Robert C. Wood in *Suburbia: Its People and Their Politics* (Houghton Mifflin Company, Boston, 1958).

411

412   nership as well as rivalry in our intergovernmental relationships. They could see cooperative and functional federalism in presidential utterances and the proceedings of a White House Conference on Education or a national Advisory Commission on Intergovernmental Relations. They could hear national labor leaders plead for more federal aid for state and local education and housing. They could meet mayors and other city officials in Washington seeking funds to supplement burdened municipal budgets. They might find politicians who campaigned as ardent states' rightists, once in office, clamoring for "bigger and better federal bounties."[3] Surveying the country as a whole, they might note sharper political cleavage between rural and urban, or even between urban and suburban, than between state and national elements.[4] They could find governmental virtues as well as faults, which, as De Tocqueville observed, are easier to detect. They could see both cooperation and conflict between economic interests and government at all levels, with business groups often influential in cities, farm groups frequently powerful in counties, and labor at times by-passing state and local government by taking its problems to the national government. They would find grounds for hope rather than either for despair or for complacency.

     The foregoing chapters have cataloged a multitude of reform movements aimed at progress in state and local government, as defined by substantial segments of society. Formidable and sundry obstacles stand in the way of

Obstacles to progress

such progress, no matter what the political entity or geographical section of the country. Constitutional barriers too often perpetuate the long ballot and prevent effective integration or streamlining of the executive branch of goverment at any level.

     Constitutions and systems of laws tend to deny adequate revenue power and facilities to local units, whether large or small. This condition is further complicated through the actual or partial pre-emption by the federal government of certain types or graduations of taxation. It is also intensified by anti-tax pressures of vested interests and the competition, or potential competition, of local jurisdictions for holding or acquiring private business and industry. Cities rely heavily upon the taxation of tangible property, a levy which does not touch hundreds of millions of dollars invested in state and federal government buildings located in the various municipalities. Many local property owners still assume that government is a necessary evil and meet their problems of assessment and tax payments with little appreciation of Justice Holmes' observation that taxes "buy civilization." In consequence, many a city with a Wall Street

---

[3] Robert S. Allen, ed., *Our Fair City* (Vanguard Press, New York, 1947).

[4] *See* G. E. Baker, *Rural Versus Urban Political Power* (Doubleday & Company, Inc., Garden City, 1955).

or a Main Street must get upwards of half of its total funds from shared collections, borrowing, and state or federal aid.

It may also be stated as an over-all generalization that state elections more than national elections, local elections more than state elections, are characterized by a high proportion of nonvoting, except in unusual circumstances. Americans manifest a philosophical or nonphilosophical apathy toward local civic matters, seemingly feeling that "what is everybody's business is nobody's business." Many citizens are too willing to "let George do it" without checking George's character or competence.

In many centers or regions social bias involving minority groups affects civic policy and effectiveness in housing, education, and other undertakings. Lumps in the meltingpot become lumps in government. The complex of prejudices and patterns brings discord, not only between citizens and government, but also between government and goverment. That complex may be an open or background factor in the relations between nation and states as well as between city and suburbs.[5] And such discords exemplify the truism that men of government are seldom free from the role of making a choice or compromising between new and old thought.

Clear gains in public administration have been registered in state and local government, upward, downward, and outward. Reasons of necessity, more than of righteousness, have brought about these changes in the last few decades, as has been indicated in previous chapters in passages *Points of* on administrative reorganization, budget and accounting systems, person- *progress,* nel management, city managerships, and various modernized practices. *trative* Many of these changes became necessary because of the expanding scope and cost of government. Changing standards of administrative performance, for example, came into being as the only way to tap federal or other central funds and as a more constructive basis for raising money locally from taxpayers and bond buyers. New standards accompanied the new work. Requirements of merit in personnel came down from the federal government through the state government to local units in the application of joint funds, and in some cases developed on the state level even before federal adoption of the merit requirement. The bringing of more engineers, scientific specialists, and other experts into the day-to-day administration of government inevitably modified or transcended the old-fashioned method of choosing jobholders at the dictation of political machines.

---

[5] Among the recent pertinent writings on this set of problems are Charles Abrams, *Forbidden Neighbors: A Study of Prejudice in Housing* (Harper & Row, Publishers, New York, 1955), H. S. Ashmore, *The Negro and the Schools* (University of North Carolina Press, Chapel Hill, 1954), and Walter White, *How Far the Promised Land?* (The Viking Press, Inc., New York, 1955).

APPRAISAL AND PROSPECT

Many students in colleges and universities prepare for government service through courses in government, particularly in public administration, sometimes with supplementary field work or internships. Distinctly professional careers in administrative service are now to be found in state and local as well as in national government. The sophisticated speak of the "science of administration" and of the "administrative process" as fundamentals of government in this technological age. Academic men and bureaucrats meet and mingle at learned sessions of the American Political Science Association and of the American Society for Public Administration. Since World War I different states and cities have recognized the value of analyzing their governments with the aid of staffs from research organizations located in New York, Chicago, or within their own borders. The resultant analyses have contributed to the reform movement in government management.

There is a linkage between advancement in administration and advancement in politics as found in our units of government. Merit systems and accounting systems reduce opportunity for certain types of political spoils. Inter-

Points of progress, political

governmental features and standards of social security and welfare administration reduce the dependence of the aged and the unfortunate upon urban political machines which was typical in the days of Boss Tweed of New Work. Somewhat in contrast to former eras, city reform regimes may last longer than one term or cast longer shadows into the future, as illustrated by the New York terms of Mayor Fiorello La Guardia between 1933 and 1945 and by the later tenure of Mayor deLesseps Morrison in New Orleans.[6] Federal prosecution for evasion of income taxes has contributed substantially to reducing secret graft in state and city politics, as is recognized in Louisiana and Missouri.[7] Economic pressure groups are stronger than in other days, but no Boss Quay or Boss Platt or Boss Pendergast dictates legislative or gubernatorial policy. There is a measure of hope and wholesomeness in the diversity of economic groups seeking to influence state legislation and city policy, sometimes with manifestations of countervailing power among groups, as between trucking interests and railway interests or between organized employers and organized employees.

In spite of reference and bill-drafting service, American legislatures today

---

[6] For an excellent analysis of the contemporary structure of big-city machines, factional alliances, and "nonpolitical elites," see James Q. Wilson, "Politics and Reform in American Cities," in *American Government Annual, 1962-1963*, ed. Ivan Hinderaker, (Holt, Rinehart and Winston, Inc., New York, 1962), pp. 37-52.

[7] See H. T. Kane, *Louisiana Hayride* (William Morrow & Co., Inc., New York, 1941), and M. M. Milligan, *The Inside Story of the Pendergast Machine* (Charles Scribner's Sons, New York, 1948).

are not free from the blight of mediocrity and venality.[8] Much of their work and policy-making is not glamorously spotlighted. Hence lobbyists and special interests may sometimes jeopardize the public interest at the state capital unless an able and alert governor asserts political leadership for the public good. The reapportionment impact of *Baker* v. *Carr* will be providing legislative news on the reform front for many years.

Strength in state government and strength in the governorship have developed together. In the second third of the twentieth century there has been less cause or movement than in the previous period for impeachment, recalling, or indicting governors. It should also be noted that the governor speaks for a state-wide constituency and is more responsible or responsive to urban voters than is the legislature. Georgia was exceptional in this regard until the elimination of its county unit rule for state nominations in 1962, for it had long ruralized the governorship in harmony with the composition of the lawmaking branch.

Much remains to be accomplished or to be adjusted in the broad field of intergovernmental relations, significantly so in most of the metropolitan areas, as was pointedly observed in the previous discussion of metropolitan problems. The growing importance and the continually debatable aspects of intergovernmental relations are expressed and implied in the language of at least three national commissions or committees on that subject in the last decade.[9] With varying emphases, these reports stress the joint responsibility and functional cooperation of the national, state, and local governments in such developments as agriculture, civil aviation, civil defense, education, employment security, highways, housing and urban renewal, natural disaster relief, public health, vocational rehabilitation, water resources, and welfare. Dissents and reservations on the part of individual members point up the dynamic and complex nature of the relationships, particularly as to striking the balance between centralization and decentralization as America faces the future.

Intergovernmental cooperation

The multipurpose development of far-flung river systems raises questions as to the roles of different units and levels of government as well as the part to be played by private enterprise. The Tennessee Valley Authority offers one example of this type of functional regionalism, interpreted by David Lilienthal as centralized authority with decentralized administration.[10] But no definite steps have been taken to repeat the TVA experiment in all of its fullness in

[8] See *Our Sovereign State,* ed. Robert S. Allen (The Vanguard Press, Inc., New York, 1949), particularly the introduction.
[9] See the reports of the Commission on Intergovernmental Relations, the Joint Federal-State Action Committee, and the Advisory Commission on Intergovernmental Relations.
[10] See *TVA: Democracy on the March* (Harper & Row, Publishers, New York, 1944).

other regions of the country. The TVA project resulted from national action and financial sponsorship, although it has been coordinated with the activities of many cooperative governments and groups in the Tennessee Valley. The commission report of 1955 on intergovernmental relations, however, favored, although without complete unanimity, greater initiative on the part of the states in water development projects. States have made regional arrangements among themselves, both through interstate compacts and through less formal processes. A well-known example of the former is the maintenance of the Port of New York Authority by the states of New York and New Jersey. Another is the Interstate Oil Compact by oil producing commonwealths to prevent or control the depletion of oil and natural gas. The states in different regions have undertaken regional approaches to higher education, following the lead of the South. In the field of planning, state-local developments have been stimulated by the incentive of federal funds for technical study and research.

Many organized groups of officials, experts, and citizens have become factors in the development of cooperative features of state and local government. One of the earlier organizations, which still has potential work ahead, *Leaders in governmental reform* is the National Conference of Commissioners on Uniform State Laws, dating from 1892. The Governors' Conference came into existence in 1908 under encouragement by President Theodore Roosevelt. This was followed by the organization of the American Legislators Association (1925) and later by the formation of other groups at the state level. The Council of State Governments has become a general clearinghouse for these several organizations. It issues biennially an almanac of information, *The Book of the States*, from 1313 East Sixtieth Street, Chicago. This address is also the location of many other establishments serving local units of government on an informational and organizational basis. The National Municipal League, with its office in New York City and a monthly publication, *The National Civic Review*, represents a cross-section of civic-minded officials, citizens, academicians, and reformers concerned with the improvement of state and local government. Its annual meetings, which are rotated from city to city throughout the nation, seek to stimulate a realistic approach to the issues and problems of the field. In important ways this work supplements or complements the work of the American Society for Public Administration at state and local levels. The American Political Science Association is an over-all academic group with a coverage of all fields and units of government.

Mention should also be made of regional associations concerned with the study and improvement of government and governmental processes nearer home than the national capital. Leagues of Municipalities in the different states and the American Municipal Association, their headquarters group, provide understanding and discussion of local problems, giving critics and officials opportunity to air their views. The National Association of County Officers provides a similar focus on the county. The International City Managers' Association keeps interest in its field alive, partly by publishing a comprehensive *Municipal Year Book* from its Chicago office. Bar associations supplement the work of the American Judicature Society in the exercise of active concern for the correction of shortcomings in judicial systems, making their weight count in matters of professional qualifications of judges. Leagues of Women Voters often exert an effective influence on civic life and action. Ad hoc reform groups make themselves heard on urgent occasions, sometimes with constructive results. An increasing amount of technical and statistical information on states, cities, counties, and intergovernmental relations flows from offices and agencies of the United States government.

Important tasks of unfinished business confront the champions of progress in state and local government. Among these tasks, which have received attention in previous pages of this study, are the problems of governing the exploding metropolis; of correcting the serious tendency toward ***Unfinished*** nonvoting and the apathy or cynicism which underlies nonvoting, par- ***business*** ticularly in local elections; of making legislatures more representative in accord with the words and meaning of the state constitutions; and of streamlining state constitutions, so as in many instances to rid them of what D. W. Brogan describes as "the botched, long-winded accumulations of petty legislation."[11] These points are interrelated, and they bear on other problems, such as those of adjusting the distribution of powers, burdens, and benefits equitably between city and country and between new and old constituencies; of facilitating executive-legislative teamship; of apportioning authority and responsibility constructively between central and local jurisdictions; and of attracting citizens of conscience and competence to public careers.

One might still ponder the comment of a foreign observer, which Woodrow Wilson quoted on the last page of *Congressional Government* in 1885, that tens of thousands of the best Americans "think it possible to enjoy the fruits of good government without working for them." In much the same vein, V. O. Key approaches the end of his *American State Politics* with emphasis on the need for better politicians "to strengthen states in the government process." To revert to certain points broached in the first chapter of this book, it is essential that states and local units be preserved as political communities in the larger context of American democracy.

(For supplementary readings see titles mentioned in the text and footnotes of this chapter.)

---

[11] D. W. Brogan, *Politics in America* (Harper & Row, Publishers, New York, 1954), p. 31.

APPRAISAL AND PROSPECT

★ INDEX ★

A

Abrams, Charles, 391, 413
Absentee voting, 120–121
Adams, John, 138
Adams, Samuel, 154
Adams, Sherman, 234
Adler et al. v. *Board of Education of the City of New York,* 79
Administrative organization, 238–245
  problems, 251–254
Administrative reform, 413–414
Admission of new states, 34
Adrian, Charles R., 140, 320, 325
Advisory Commission on Intergovernmental Relations, 174, 272, 353, 406, 415
  creation of, 45
Agriculture, 379–381
Agriculture, U.S. Department of, 399
Airports, 61, 63–64, 387
Alabama, 398
  area, 21
  constitution, 90
  elected department heads, 229
  governor, 219
  legislative apportionment, 204
  legislative pay, 174
  legislative volume, 186
  legislature, 172
  population, 21

urban-rural cleavage, 205
voter registration, 118
voting qualifications, 113, 116
Alameda County, 345
Alaska, 266
  area, 21
  boroughs, 295
  constitution, 90, 91, 99–100, 105
  governor's reorganization powers, 242
  legislature, 172
  population, 21
  short ballot, 228–229
  voter registration, 118
  voting qualifications, 113
Albuquerque, degree of nonpartisanship, 140
Alcoholic beverage control, 270
Allen, Robert S., 207, 412, 415
Allentown-Bethlehem-Easton metropolitan area, population, 66
Altgeld, John P., 32
Amendments, constitutional, 97, 101–105
American Academy of Political and Social Science, 291
American Bar Association, 291
American Civil Liberties Union, 361
American Farm Bureau Federation, 381
American Judicature Society, 291, 417
American Legion, 150
American Legislators Association, 416
American Medical Association, 150

419

424

N

O

435

T

elected department heads, 229
highways, 386
legislature, 173
population, 22
voter registration, 119
West Virginia State Board of Education
v. *Barnette*, 80
Wheare, K. C., 27
Wheeling metropolitan area, population, 66
White, David M., 18
White, Dr. Paul, 378
White, Theodore H., 402
White, Walter, 413
White primary, 141–142
Wichita, degree of nonpartisanship, 140
Williams, G. Mennen, 213
Williams, Oliver P., 325
Wilmington metropolitan area, population, 66
Wilson, James Q., 140, 414
Wilson, O. W., 362
Wilson, Woodrow, 156, 212, 225, 417
Wisconsin, 247, 266, 398, 408
area, 22
direct primary, 139
governor, 9
legislative apportionment, 202

Legislative Reference Bureau, 176
legislature, 173, 194
lobbying, 201
open primary, 142
population, 22
voter registration, 119
Wolf, Reinhold P., 346
Wood, Robert C., 14, 15, 313, 411
Wooley, Edward A., 292
Works Progress Administration, 54–55, 407
Works Projects Administration, 407
World War II, federal-city relationships, 55
Wyoming, 266
area, 22
legislature, 173
population, 22
voter registration, 119

Z

Zeller, Belle, 146, 168, 169, 194
Zimmermann, Frederick L., 48
Zorach v. *Clauson*, 79